The Matica and Beyond

National Cultivation of Culture

Edited by

Joep Leerssen (*University of Amsterdam*)

Editorial Board

John Breuilly (*The London School of Economics and Political Science*)
Katharine Ellis (*University of Cambridge*)
Ina Ferris (*University of Ottawa*)
Patrick J. Geary (*Institute for Advanced Study, Princeton*)
Tom Shippey (*Saint Louis University*)
Anne-Marie Thiesse (*CNRS, National Center for Scientific Research*)

VOLUME 21

The titles published in this series are listed at *brill.com/ncc*

The Matica and Beyond

Cultural Associations and Nationalism in Europe

Edited by

Krisztina Lajosi
Andreas Stynen

BRILL

LEIDEN | BOSTON

This book is part 4 of the NISE proceedings.

Cover illustration: *Job Lot Cheap* by William Michael Harnett, 1878. From the Reynolda House Museum of American Art. Wikimedia Commons.

Library of Congress Cataloging-in-Publication Data

Names: Lajosi, Krisztina, editor. | Stynen, Andreas, editor.
Title: The matica and beyond : cultural associations and nationalism in Europe / edited by Krisztina Lajosi, Andreas Stynen.
Description: Leiden ; Boston : Brill, [2020] | Series: National cultivation of culture, 1876-5645 ; vol.21 | Includes bibliographical references and index.
Identifiers: LCCN 2020007967 (print) | LCCN 2020007968 (ebook) | ISBN 9789004423749 (hardback) | ISBN 9789004425385 (ebook)
Subjects: LCSH: Matica srpska (Novi Sad, Serbia)--History. | Learned institutions and societies--Europe--History. | Nationalism--Europe--History.
Classification: LCC AS345.3.N68 M37 2020 (print) | LCC AS345.3.N68 (ebook) | DDC 306.094--dc23
LC record available at https://lccn.loc.gov/2020007967
LC ebook record available at https://lccn.loc.gov/2020007968

Typeface for the Latin, Greek, and Cyrillic scripts: "Brill." See and download: brill.com/brill-typeface.

ISSN 1876-5645
ISBN 978-90-04-42374-9 (hardback)
ISBN 978-90-04-42538-5 (e-book)

Copyright 2020 by Koninklijke Brill NV, Leiden, The Netherlands.
Koninklijke Brill NV incorporates the imprints Brill, Brill Hes & De Graaf, Brill Nijhoff, Brill Rodopi, Brill Sense, Hotei Publishing, mentis Verlag, Verlag Ferdinand Schöningh and Wilhelm Fink Verlag.
All rights reserved. No part of this publication may be reproduced, translated, stored in a retrieval system, or transmitted in any form or by any means, electronic, mechanical, photocopying, recording or otherwise, without prior written permission from the publisher.
Authorization to photocopy items for internal or personal use is granted by Koninklijke Brill NV provided that the appropriate fees are paid directly to The Copyright Clearance Center, 222 Rosewood Drive, Suite 910, Danvers, MA 01923, USA. Fees are subject to change.

This book is printed on acid-free paper and produced in a sustainable manner.

In memory of John Neubauer (1933–2015)

Contents

Acknowledgements IX
List of Figures X
Notes on Contributors XI

Introduction 1
   Joep Leerssen

1   The Buda University Press and National Awakenings in Habsburg Austria 11
     Zsuzsanna Varga

2   The Matice Česká 30
     Magdaléna Pokorná

3   The Slovak Matica, Its Precursors and Its Legacy 48
     Benjamin Bossaert and Dagmar Kročanová

4   The Matica in an Ethnic-Regional Context: Sorbian Lusatia and Czech Silesia in Comparison 75
     Miloš Řezník

5   The Slovenian Matica: The 'Foundation-Stone' 97
     Marijan Dović

6   Framing a Regional Matica, from Dalmatian to Croatian 118
     Daniel Baric

7   Macedonian Societies in the Balkan Context 138
     Liljana Gushevska

8   Language, Cultural Associations, and the Origins of Galician Nationalism, 1840–1918 162
     Xosé M. Núñez Seixas and Alfonso Iglesias Amorín

9   Félibrige, or the Impossible Occitan Nation 181
     Philippe Martel

10 Educational, Scholarly, and Literary Societies in Dutch-speaking
    Regions, 1766–1886   204
      Jan Rock

11 A Century of Change: The Eisteddfod and Welsh Cultural
    Nationalism   233
      Marion Löffler

12 "Racy of the Soil": Young Ireland and the Cultural Production of
    Nationhood   255
      Roisín Higgins

13 Competing National Movements: School Associations and Cultural
    Nationalism in the Baltic Region   271
      Jörg Hackmann

14 The Galician-Ruthenian Matica (1848–1939)   292
      Iryna Orlevych

15 Tatar Cultural and Educational Organizations and Charities: Muslim
    Self-Organization in the Russian Empire   325
      Diliara M. Usmanova

    Afterword: The Maticas in a World of Empires   357
      Alexei Miller

    Index   363

Acknowledgements

This book has been in the making for a long time. The foundations of *The Matica and Beyond* were laid in February 2011, when scholars gathered in Budapest for a two-day comparative workshop on cultural institutions in Europe and their role in nation building. This joint initiative of the Central European University (then Budapest), NISE (Antwerp), and SPIN (Amsterdam) was a success thanks to the inspiration of Miroslav Hroch and an enthusiastic international collaboration in terms of theoretical as well as practical matters. In the first editorial stage, the critical minds of Alexei Miller, John Neubauer (†) and Louis Vos were essential in shaping the individual papers into a coherent whole. With its series on 'National Cultivation of Culture,' Brill was the ideal environment for publishing a historical survey of this kind. We owe a great deal to Gerda Danielsson Coe, Gene Moore, Wendel Scholma, Pieter van Roon, and the two anonymous reviewers for their help in turning the workshop into a book that will hopefully inspire future scholars to venture into the field of cultural nationalism studies.

More than eight years separate this volume's conception in a stylish Hungarian salon from our now being able to hold it and turn the pages. The editors are very grateful to all those who have contributed (and/or remained patient) along the way.

Figures

5.1 The quantitative growth of Slovenian-language newspapers (in copies printed) from the late eighteenth to the mid-twentieth century   100

5.2 The growing number of subscribers to the annual book collection of the St. Hermagoras Society (1860–1939)   101

5.3 Peter Kozler, "Map of the Slovenian land and provinces." Supplement of the first annual Slovenian Matica collection (1865). ZRC SAZU Institute of Slovenian Literature and Literary Studies   107

5.4 Janez Trdina, book cover of *History of the Slovenian Nation* (1866). ZRC SAZU Institute of Slovenian Literature and Literary Studies   110

5.5 The main façade of the Slovenian Matica building in central Ljubljana (on Congress Square) today. The Slovenian Matica Archive   113

Notes on Contributors

Daniel Baric
studied history and philology (Slavic, German and Hungarian) in Paris, Berlin, and Budapest. He was assistant professor at the Department of German Studies in Tours before joining the Department of Slavic Studies of the Sorbonne Université in 2018. His teaching and research focus mainly on the cultural history of South Slavs, especially on cultural transfers from the early nineteenth century to the present, exploring various sources ranging from texts and persons to institutions (such as libraries). He published *Langue allemande, identité croate: Au fondement d'un particularisme culturel,* Paris, 2013 (also available in Croatian: Zagreb, 2015).

Benjamin Bossaert
studied Eastern European Languages and Cultures (Russian, Czech and Slovak) at the University of Ghent and at the University of Ss. Cyril and Methodius in Trnava (Slovakia). He is currently working as a lecturer in Dutch language and culture in the Department of German, Scandinavian, and Dutch studies at the Comenius University in Bratislava. He is also involved in a Ph.D. study programme at Palacký University Olomouc (Czech Republic) under the supervision of Prof. Dr. Wilken Engelbrecht, where he does comparative research on the Flemish and Slovak national movements. He engages in theory of literature, literary translations from Slovak, Dutch language acquisition, and (cultural) history.

Marijan Dović
is Associate Professor and Senior Research Fellow at the ZRC SAZU Institute of the Slovenian Literature and Literary Studies (Ljubljana). He also lectures at the Faculty of Arts (University of Ljubljana) and the School of Humanities (University of Nova Gorica). His books include *Sistemske in empirične obravnave literature* (Systemic and Empirical Approaches to Literature, 2004), *Slovenski pisatelj* (The Slovenian Writer, 2007), *Mož z bombami* (The Man with the Bombs, 2009), *Prešeren po Prešernu* (Prešeren after Prešeren, 2017), and *National Poets, Cultural Saints: Canonization and Commemorative Cults of Writers in Europe* (with J.K. Helgason, 2017). He has co-edited thematic volumes on literature and censorship, publishing, book history, the spatial turn in literary studies, and literature and music. His major publications in English address Romanticism, European cultural nationalism, national poets and 'cultural saints', the literary canon, systems theory, the interwar avant-garde in the Balkans, and

the theory of authorship. He is Editor-in-Chief of the comparative literature journal *Primerjalna književnost* (2016–).

Liljana Gushevska

is a professor in the Department of History of the Balkans and Macedonia (1800–1914) at the Institute of National History in Skopje, Republic of Macedonia. Her research interests are history of the Macedonian language and Macedonian literature, as well as the history of the Macedonian national movement in the nineteenth and at the beginning of the twentieth century. She is also a part-time professor at the Department of Macedonian Language and Literature at the University of Tetovo.

Jörg Hackmann

is Alfred Döblin Professor of East European History at the Department of History and International Relations, University of Szczecin, Poland, and is also associated with the University of Greifswald, Germany. He holds a Ph.D. from the Free University Berlin and has been a visiting scholar at many universities in the Baltic Sea region, among others in Riga, Stockholm, Tartu, und Turku, as well as in Chicago. His research interests focus on the entangled history of East Central Europe, on memory cultures and history politics, and on the history of civil society in North Eastern Europe.

Roisín Higgins

is a Reader in Modern History at Teesside University. She completed her Ph.D. at the University of St Andrews and has lectured at universities in Ireland, England, and Scotland. Her research focuses on social and cultural history, with particular interest in the politics of historical memory. Her book *Transforming 1916: Meaning, Memory and the Fiftieth Anniversary of the Easter Rising* (2012) was awarded the ACIS James S. Donnelly Sr Prize for the best book in History and Social Science. In 2016 she was involved in many aspects of the Centenary of the Easter Rising, invited to deliver keynote lectures in Australia, America and Europe, and to give public lectures in Ireland and Britain. She is also the leader of a public history project exploring the lives of women and widows after the First World War. She was one of the curators for National Treasures, a public history project run in association with RTÉ, the National Museum of Ireland, and the Irish Broadcasting Authority.

Alfonso Iglesias Amorín

is a postdoctoral fellow in the History Department of the University of Santiago de Compostela and member of the research group HISPONA (Political

History and Nationalisms), where he received his Ph.D. in 2014. His main lines of research are Spanish colonial conflicts in modern times, collective memory, and nationalism. He has published several monographs and articles in scientific journals, and has been a guest researcher at Trinity College Dublin and at the University of Porto.

Dagmar Kročanová
graduated from Comenius University in Bratislava in Slovak, Russian and English linguistics and literatures, and completed her Ph.D. at the same university in 1997 on the theory and history of Slovak literature. She has also studied at University College London and at Indiana State University in Bloomington, Indiana, USA. From 2006 to 2012 she taught Slovak at Bologna University in Forlì, Italy. She is an Associate Professor (Reader) at the Faculty of Arts, Comenius University in Bratislava (Slovakia), where she currently heads the Department of Slovak Literature and Literary Studies. She teaches and researches twentieth-century Slovak prose and drama. She has edited several books by early twentieth-century Slovak writers. Her monograph on Slovak drama and theatre between 1945 and 1949, entitled *Nerozrezaná dráma* (*Uncut Drama*), was published in 2007. She publishes in Slovak and English, and occasionally translates from English.

Joep Leerssen
is Professor of European Studies at the University of Amsterdam, where he leads the Study Platform on Interlocking Nationalisms (SPIN). A comparatist by training, his research deals with the intellectual and cultural history of national movements in Europe, the history and theory of cultural and national (self-)stereotyping, and the history of the humanities. Among the books he has authored or (co-)edited are *Imagology* (with Manfred Beller, 2007), *National Thought in Europe* (3rd ed. 2018), *Commemorating Writers in Nineteenth-Century Europe* (with Ann Rigney, 2014), *The Rhine: Romantic Visions, National Tensions* (with Manfred Beller, 2017), and the *Encyclopedia of Romantic Nationalism in Europe* (Amsterdam University Press, 2018, online at ernie.uva.nl).

Marion Löffler
completed her Ph.D. at the Humboldt University in Berlin and was appointed a Research Fellow at the University of Wales Centre for Advanced Welsh and Celtic Studies in Aberystwyth in 1994. She regularly appears on Welsh radio and television, and is Assistant Editor of the *Dictionary of Welsh Biography*. She is currently a Reader at Cardiff University whose research focuses on the cultural and economic entanglements of nineteenth-century Wales with Europe,

Empire, and the world. Her published works include *The Literary and Historical Legacy of Iolo Morganwg, 1826–1926* (2007) and *Political Pamphlets and Sermons from Wales, 1790–1806* (2014).

Philippe Martel
completed his Ph.D. in History in 1993 with a study of *Les félibres et leur temps, 1850–1914*. From 1983 to 2009 he was an investigator at the Centre National de Recherche Scientifique, and from 2009 to 2015 Professor in the Occitan Department at the Université Paul-Valéry in Montpellier. His specialty is the cultural history of Southern France, more precisely the history of the Occitan renaissance in the nineteenth and twentieth centuries. His major works include *Les Cathares et l'histoire* (Toulouse: Privat, 2002); *Les félibres et leur temps, 1850–1914* (Bordeaux: Presses universitaires de Bordeaux, 2010); *L'école française et l'occitan: le sourd et le bègue* (Montpellier: PULM, 2007); *Études de langue et d'histoire occitanes* (Limoges: Lambert-Lucas, 2016); and *Vidas, des hommes et une langue* (Limoges: Lambert-Lucas, 2018).

Alexei Miller
is Professor and Director of the Center for Studies in Cultural Memory and Symbolic Politics at the European University at Saint Petersburg. He has published many books and edited volumes on comparative history of Empires, nationalism, history of ideas and concepts, memory politics.

Xosé M. Núñez Seixas
completed his Ph.D. at EUI Florence, and is Full Professor of Modern History at the University of Santiago de Compostela. He has published widely on the comparative history of nationalist movements and national and regional identities, as well as on overseas migration from Spain and Galicia to Latin America, and on the cultural history of war in the twentieth century. Among his most recent books are *Suspiros de España: El nacionalismo español, 1808–2018* (Barcelona, 2018) and (coedited with E. Storm) *Regionalism and Modern Europe: Identity Constructions and Movements from 1890 to the Present Day* (London, 2018).

Iryna Orlevych
is currently Head of the Department of New History of Ukraine at the I. Kryp'yakevych Institute of Ukrainian Studies, National Academy of Sciences of Ukraine (Lviv), and a researcher at the Lviv Museum of the History of Religion. She graduated from the History Department of the Ivan Franko National University of Lviv, and from 1995 to 1998 she was a graduate student at the I.

Kryp'yakevych Institute of Ukrainian Studies, National Academy of Sciences of Ukraine. In 2000 she completed her Ph.D. thesis on "The activities of the Stauropegion Institute of Lviv from the late eighteenth to the mid-nineteenth century", which has been published as a monograph. She explores the ideology and institutional development of the Ukrainian national movement in Eastern Galicia from the late eighteenth to the twentieth centuries, and the question of the origin and evolution of the Russophile movement in the nineteenth and twentieth centuries.

Magdaléna Pokorná

lectures on history at the Faculty of Arts (Department of Czech History) at the Charles University in Prague and works as a historian in the Institute of History of the Czech Academy of Sciences. She focuses on the development of historical consciousness in Czech literature and journalism in the nineteenth century, on the history and development of Czech scientific institutions, and on the early years of Franz Joseph's reign (to 1859). She explores problems of censorship and collaborates on the editions of correspondence of important Czech personalities such as Božena Němcová and Karel Havlíček.

Miloš Řezník

is a historian and Director of the German Historical Institute at Warsaw (since 2014). He completed his Ph.D. in history at the Charles University in Prague (1989–1994) with a thesis on territorial patriotism in Polish Prussia in the eighteenth century (2001). Habilitation at the University of Olomouc in 2007. In 1995–96 he was a specialist advisor for Poland at the Ministry of Foreign Affairs of the Czech Republic; from 1998–2001 at the Charles University in Prague; in 2001–02 researcher at the Research Centre for History and Culture of East-Central Europe (GWZO) in Leipzig; from 2002–2008 junior professor; and since 2009 Professor of European Regional History at the University of Chemnitz and since 2009 Co-Chair of the Czech-German Historians' Commission. His fields of research include Polish history, the Habsburg monarchy, nation-building, collective identities, historical memory, elites; and history from the late eighteenth to the early twentieth century.

Jan Rock

is Assistant Professor of modern Dutch literature and culture at the University of Amsterdam. He is assistant editor of the *Encyclopedia of Romantic Nationalism in Europe*, edited by Joep Leerssen. He has published on cultural nationalism and the history of vernacular philology in the Low Countries, in *Science in*

Context, Variants, Spiegel der Letteren, The Making of the Humanities III (eds. Rens Bod, Jaap Maat, and Thijs Weststeijn), and elsewhere.

Diliara M. Usmanova

is a professor of Russian history at the Kazan Federal University (Russia). She was a visiting fellow at SFB-640 at Humboldt University in Berlin (Germany, 2009–11), and a foreign visiting professorial fellow at the SRC at Hokkaido University (Japan, 2014). Her research interests include the modern political history of Imperial Russia, the history of Muslims in Russia, the socio-cultural history of Tatars, and visual history of Russia in the late Imperial period. Diliara Usmanova has participated in the international joint projects *Muslim Culture in Russia and Central Asia* (1996–98) and *Islamic Education in the USSR and its Successor States* (2002–05), whose results were published in several volumes. Along with many articles and chapters in collective monographs and international volumes, she has authored (in Russian) the books *Muslim Representatives in the Russian Parliament, 1906–1916* (Kazan, 2005), *Deputies from Kazan Province in the State Duma of Russia, 1906–1917* (Kazan, 2006), and *Muslim Sects in Imperial Russia: The Vaisov Holy Regiment of Muslim Old Believers* (Kazan, 2009).

Zsuzsanna Varga

studied English, Hungarian, and Portuguese language and literature at Eötvös Loránd University, Budapest, and completed her Ph.D. in nineteenth-century English literature at Edinburgh University. Since 2008 she has taught Hungarian Studies at Glasgow University, and she is also in charge of the Hungarian library collection at the University of Oxford. Her research interests include nineteenth-century women's writing, travel writing, and translation history. Her recent publications include *Worlds of Hungarian Writing* (with András Kiséry and Zsolt Komáromy, 2016), *Popular Cinemas in East Central Europe* (with Dorota Ostrowska and Francesco Pitassio, 2017), and *Antal Szerb: Reflections in the Library: Selected Literary Essays 1926–1944* (2017).

Introduction

Joep Leerssen

Since Benedict Anderson's *Imagined Communities*, it has become a truism to link the rise of nineteenth-century national identities to the modern reading market. Reading a shared reservoir of texts in common circulation, Anderson argues, welded individual readers together into reading communities. It bolstered that process traced by Jürgen Habermas where the physical sociability of coffee houses, theaters and benevolent societies would, thanks to the growing role of the press, become a more disembodied, mediatized ambience for opinion-making: the 'public sphere.' Anderson described this nation-building role of the printed media as 'print capitalism': an entrepreneurially driven print production aiming for maximum circulation and in the process drawing the masses into its ambit rather than merely the lettered elite. The rise of active literacy in the European vernaculars, rather than in the high languages of learning, church, and state, was boosted by print capitalism and in turn boosted the imagined community's political sentience.

There is no doubt that Anderson's model is in its main outlines robust; but without wanting to derogate from its fundamental soundness there seems room to tease out the details, and in some cases the complexities, involved. One factor lies in the changing technology of print and book production. The industrial revolution did not leave book production unaffected. Prior to 1790 books were made from loose-letters settings printed individually, sheet by sheet, on manually operated printing presses. In the following decades, paper production began to involve the use of wood pulp, making paper much cheaper to produce (and, as historians know, undermining its long-term durability). Steam-operated presses emerged around 1813. Between 1800 and 1820, the number of possible prints per minute increased fivefold, roughly from eight to forty. The movable, loose-letter page sets, which would be pressed out of kilter by repeated imprints were, in the stereotyped printing process perfected by c. 1830, cast into metal full-page clichés which could be printed many time more often, facilitating much larger print runs. This scale enlargement received another impetus in 1843 with the invention of the rotary printing press (Bolza 1967). In short, the decades between 1800 and 1840 witnessed a second Gutenberg revolution, with books and periodicals becoming much cheaper and much more numerous.

The fact that most historians see a tipping point in the emergence of nationalism in precisely these decades must surely be correlated with this paradigm shift in communication technology.[1] Not only the contents of the nineteenth century's reading materials mattered to the self-articulation of Europe's national communities, but also the media infrastructure. Nationalism history, in other words, needs to be cross-calibrated with book history as much as with literary history. If, for example, the Belgian Romantic novelist and Flemish cultural activist Henrik Conscience is habitually celebrated as 'the man who taught his nation to read', then what matters is not only the content and national rhetoric of his tales (Conscience is usually seen as a Walter Scott adept) but also the way in which his writings penetrated into far-flung rustic and often semi-literate communities, which were indeed stimulated into increased literacy by his alluring writings. How did those books reach his emergent readership? What booksellers and lending libraries were there? How could Conscience play into a vestigial infrastructure of almanacs, newspapers and devout religious material (cf. Leerssen 2017)?

Book history must necessarily go beyond the aspects of production (which is what a phrase like 'print capitalism' would gravitate towards), and look, then, at the means of diffusion and the modalities of reading as well as the means of production. Path-breaking studies in this field were Rolf Engelsing's *Der Bürger als Leser* (1974), Roger Chartier and Guglielmo Cavallo's *History of Reading in the West* (1999), William St. Clair's *The Reading Nation in the Romantic Period* and Steven Roger Fischer's *History of Reading* (both 2004). Literary historians are themselves becoming more concerned with the reception of literature: no longer seeing the text merely as the end-product, they study the social lives of texts in the trajectory through the reading market, and the 'afterlives' of authors beyond the writing-moments.

How would such a diffusion- and reception-oriented book history complete and deepen Anderson's notion of print capitalism and national consciousness? To understand that question means that we have to trace the mechanism of the book trade in nineteenth-century Europe and contextualize it in the emergence of national consciousness. Some episodes are already known, almost mythically so: e.g. the clandestine trade in Lithuanian books smuggled into Russian-dominated Lithuanian lands across the Prussian border following the interdict on non-Cyrillic print by Alexander III. The politics of scholarly book reviewing by the likes of Jacob Grimm is known, as is the function of almanacs in rural low-literacy areas (like the Baltics) for spreading vernacular

---

[1] For most of the information collected in the following pages, I am indebted to, without specifically referring to, the various contributions to this volume, as well as the *Encyclopedia of Romantic Nationalism in Europe* (ERNiE 2018).

reading material. In the social history of reading, the role of the lending libraries and the rise of the roman-feuillleton have been studied intensively.

One aspect ties the history of book diffusion directly into the rise of national movements, and it is linked to a social structure that has been studied better by the likes of Miroslav Hroch and Dieter Langewiesche than by Anderson: the ongoing presence of sociability and city- or town-based civil society in the rise of nationalism. Alongside the 'imagined' communities, there still remained, and forcefully so, 'embodied' communities, notably in the form of cultural sociability and associations.

An earlier volume in this series has looked at the importance of choral societies in bringing people together for cultural leisure activities with a national and nation-building function.[2] One might think of sports and athletics clubs as fulfilling a similar role. But the role of sociability and associational life for the purpose of book production and book diffusion is a particularly relevant topic, and it forms the theme of the present volume.

Nowadays we tend to think of reading as a uniquely private act; the solitary, silent individual's intimate engagement with the printed page transports his or her mind away from the here and now, and establishes an almost telepathic link to a textual cloud-world, where other readers, distant in space and time, may also dwell, but unbeknownst to each other. But that Romantic mind-travel was not always the default. Reading often meant reading aloud, in company (cf. Williams 2017); or reading in the ambience of a library or reading room which itself was a forum for social intercourse. "Forum": indeed many titles of nineteenth-century reading materials, especially periodicals, evoke social concourse and interaction: Athenaeum, Forum, Museum, *Bibliothèque* (referring not only to a book collection but also to the institution where such a collection was housed). As such titles recall, reading was a thing that was often done in public rather than a private setting. The second half of the eighteenth century saw the emergence of a great number of reading societies (*Lesegesellschaften* and *leesgezelschappen*) in Germany and Holland, mainly among the upper and middle classes of the towns and cities; after 1800, special venues were established in some cities (*Leeskabinetten* and *Leesmusea*) (generally Buijnsters 1984, Dann 1981, Millstein 1972, Prüsener 1973). These were the forerunners both of the public libraries and of the still-popular reading clubs or readers' circles, meeting regularly over a common programme of book reading and discussions, either privately or in the framework of a public library (Rehberg Sedo 2011). Such circles had overlaps with learned societies as well as convivial clubs;

---

2 See Krisztina Lajosi and Andreas Stynen, eds., *Choral Societies and Nationalism in Europe* (Leiden and Boston: Brill, 2015).

they also influenced the book trade. Book publishing was done increasingly by subscription, and many of the subscribers were, in fact, reading circles and libraries. In turn, they formed an important amplification platform for the public outreach of book publications.

It appears that the role of reading circles dwindled as large-volume printing and an increasingly well-established network of public libraries took shape, i.e. after the mid-century; but that is a trend that affected, specifically, middle-class North-West Europe; and it is on that social and geographical core area, and on the period from 1700 to c. 1850, that most existing research is focused, as part of the study of bourgeois modernity. However, the wider European literary system, including its social and geographical peripheries, maintained a sociability of organized readerships well beyond 1850, which continued throughout the long nineteenth century to play an important role in the spread of literature and *belles lettres*, the spread of literacy, and nation-formation. These cultural and literary associations are the topic of the present volume.

The prototypical organization, in many ways, emerged in Budapest, which in the early nineteenth century was taking over from Venice as a publishing center for the Serbian language.[3] Local notables and wealthy citizens established a Serbian book-printing society in Pest in 1826 in order to provide financial resources for a periodical, the *Letopis* ("Chronicle"), which had been started in at the Novi Sad *Gymnasium* in 1824. The venture recalled to some extent the relationship between the Prague National Museum of 1818 and its periodicals (in both Czech and German, as of 1827). In the Pest/Serbian case, the association was meant to provide a solid financial basis for publication initiatives beyond the precarious income from subscriptions. While that format was also employed by learned societies and city academies (using associations for the financing and distribution of publications to a core membership), it also presents the gestating format of a book club with paying members. Such book clubs were, in fact, emerging in various places in Europe, often for specialized antiquarian or bibliophile editions. Examples from North-Western Europe, from the same period, include the Roxburghe Club, founded in 1812; its Scottish counterpart the Bannatyne Club (founded by Walter Scott in 1823), the Camden Society (1838) and the Percy Society (1840); in Flanders, there was the Maetschappij der Vlaemsche Bibliophilen (1839). Such book clubs were antiquarian in nature and gravitated towards philological editions of ancient MSS or ballads, whereas the purpose of the Serbian venture was more popular and contemporary in nature. The association called itself the "Serbian beehive" (*Matica srpska*)—a richly-layered metaphorical name. It suggested, not only

---

[3] On the role and outreach of Buda's university press, see Varga's contribution in this volume.

the well-known symbolism of bees as selfless labourers providing sweetness (honey, delectation) and light (wax, candles, instruction), but also a concourse where roaming workers might meet and share their resources, and where cross-pollination could take place. It also symbolized the fixed institutionality of the organization as established in its actual location, and the far-ranging outreach of its swarming associates: both the embodied and the imagined community. The authorities were less than enthusiastic about the venture, which was formed during the early years of Pan-Slavism (marked by the writings of Jan Kollár and Pavel Josef Šafarík, one of the Novi Sad-based editors of the *Letopis*). The Matica's logo, accordingly, placed the beehive between two Slavic linden trees, suggesting a cross-pollinating mediation between the various Slavic lands.

The inspirational value of the *Matica srpska* for other Slavic communities was immediately obvious and is demonstrated by the great ramification of the matica format. Its earliest offshoots were established in the two main Slavic crownlands of the Habsburg Empire: Bohemia and Croatia. A Czech matica was established in Prague in 1831;[4] an Illyrian matica in Zagreb in 1842 (soon renamed the "Croatian matica"), with a Dalmatian matica briefly following suit in 1849. To the North, a Czech-inspired Sorbian matica was established in Bautzen in 1845.[5] The leading members were all well-regarded actors in different cultural fields: Palacký in Prague, Gaj in Zagreb, Zejler and Smoler in Bautzen. They were all of them involved also in the Slavic Congress of 1848, in which year a Galician/Ruthenian matica with overtly political roots was also founded in Lemberg/L'viv.[6]

The échec of 1848 briefly stopped the spread of the associational club format. Even so, the matice, withdrawing into educational and civic roles, maintained a certain presence in the years that followed. Catholic matica-style book clubs (above suspicion in the post-1848 climate) were founded for Moravian and Slovenian readers in 1853, in Brünn/Brno and Čelovic/Klagenfurt respectively. In 1854 The *Matica srpska* played a brokering role in the "Vienna declaration," which established the unity and standard of Serbo-Croatian for official purposes and prepared the translation of the Habsburg law codes into the Empire's Slavic languages.

A second matica wave followed in the 1860s as the Habsburg Empire, challenged by Russian-oriented Slavophilia, gave freer rein to its minority cultures (culminating in the 1867 *Ausgleich*). In 1864 the Serbian matica, eyed less than

---

4   See Pokorná's contribution in this volume.
5   See Řezník's contribution in this volume.
6   See Orlevych's contribution in this volume.

favorably by the Hungarian authorities, relocated from its original domicile, Budapest, to its intellectual and cultural moorings in Novi Sad, in the Vojvodina. In 1863 a Slovenian matica was founded in Ljubljana, as well as a Slovak one whose founding committee members were domiciled in Budapest;[7] In 1877 a Silesian matica was founded in Opava and a Dalmatian one in Zadar.[8] In Lemberg/L'viv, the earlier Galician-Ruthenian matica (which harbored both Ukrainian and Russian sympathizers) was confronted by two rivaling organizations. A very active Polish matica was established on the initiative of the celebrated novelist József Ignacy Kraszewski in 1882; and in 1870, a scholarly society for Ruthenia, the *Prosvita* (founded in 1867) had changed its remit towards popular education, including book publishing. The situation here is comparable to that in the Baltic regions, where educational activities were caught up in the growing rift between culturally distinct social layers, elite and vernacular.[9]

By 1870, the matica model of cheap book publishing was complemented by another institutional type: that of the reading room. The prototype here was the Bulgarian *čitalište*. Often financed by private philanthropists, they had been established first in 1856 in Shumen, Lom, and Svishtov. By the 1880s, there were about one hundred thirty of them. The 'reading room' format was applied in Trieste for the local Slovenian readership in 1861; it was copied for Croatian readers in Istrian towns in the later 1860s.[10] Within the Bulgarian cultural community, the *čitalište* was complemented by a *Bǎlgarska matica*, founded originally in Istanbul in 1909 but with some twenty branches by 1911 (Žecev 1992). Obviously, the concept was not only reticulating and replicating itself from city to city and from one Slavic cultural community to another; it was also broadening its remit and overlapping with more general pedagogical programmes for popular and cultural literacy. Significantly in its second wave, the spreading matica format was flanked by the rapid proliferation of Slavic gymnastic and athletic societies, the so-called Sokol clubs,[11] whose public events were more in the line of mobilization and manifestation than the reading activities sponsored by the matica.[12]

---

7   See Dović's and Bossaert/Kročanová's contributions in this volume.
8   See Řezník's and Baric's contributions in this volume.
9   See Hackmann's contribution in the present volume.
10   See Barić, in this volume, and the sources there.
11   Conceived as a Slavic response to the German *Turnverein*, the original Sokol club was founded in Prague in 1862, soon copied in the Habsburg Cisleithanian (Slovenian, Croatian, Polish) lands.
12   As Gushevska's contribution to the present volume shows, Macedonian developments were more excentrically driven, with Serbian cultural support under a vigilant Ottoman government. Macedonian cultural associations, when they did spring up (in the 1890s),

INTRODUCTION   7

Not only did the matica provide, in the absence of autonomous governance institutions, the closest institutional equivalent to a separate public sphere; it was also pan-Slavic, and that in a double sense. First, the reticulation of the concept and name across various Slavic-language communities created a practical sense of that *Wechselseitigkeit* or 'Slavic reciprocity' which had already been at the core of Jan Kollár's writings. Secondly, the matice, which fostered literacy not only by sponsoring original writing but also by translating foreign authors, seem to have shown, in their translation lists, a preference for authors from other Slavic communities. And while pan-Slavism, like other macronationalistic movements, failed in its stated aim to create a unifying cause for all Slavic nations, it provided each separate Slavic community with a morale-boosting amplification platform for its own specific ambitions by providing a sense of greater solidarity networks beyond its own frontiers. Pan-Slavism made all the separate nation-building movements benefit individually from the others' cultural and ideological proximity. In this sense, the matice replicated at a higher level of aggregation what book clubs and reading rooms did for each reader individually: to de-individualize the act of reading, and hence to make it a potentially political activity.

The same function can also be observed in other literacy associations and initiatives in other parts of Europe. Much as individuals would merge into a choir, or sports team, and as these choirs or teams would then meet in festivals, associations and federations, manifesting both the individual support base and the trans-individual and trans-local outreach of the national community, so too did literary-cultural associations have a nationalizing function. Flemish book clubs like the Catholic *Davidsfonds* and the Liberal *Willemsfonds* established a Flemish (indeed, an avowedly, deliberately and assertively Flemish) reading community even at times and in places where these were economically non-viable through the means of commercial publisher-bookshop distribution;[13] they could rely on the well-established postal service in a country with advanced modernization, like Belgium. At the same time we also see how here, as well as in in some Slavic lands, these organizations both reflect and transcend denominational differences within society.

Transnational phenomena can be translational or situational; they may be the result of direct transfers and communicative influences—the reticulative spread of the matica model in the Slavic lands is a case in point—or else result from parallel responses to similar circumstances. One of the greatest challenges

---

emerged in extraterritorially located metropolitan centers: Belgrade, St. Petersburg, and Sofia.

13   See Rock's contribution in this volume.

of the comparative method in history is to gauge, from case to case, the relative weight of translational communication or situational parallel. Historians will need to resist a habitual focus that explains cultural practices from ambient socio-economic or political infrastructures. To explain everything from generic conditions like modernity, the non-dominant status of a given ethnic group, or the self-serving strategies of 'elites' (however defined) reduces all transnational phenomena to a mere situational parallel; this magnifies a shared ambience into a determining motivation, and reduces communicative acts to mere secondary enablers of a general historical inevitability. The selection of studies in the present volume presents an interesting array of samples from which to address this vexed calibration between the translational and the situational. The matice were obvious replications and reticulations of a single prototype; the various 'Tatar' Muslim communities of the Russian Empire likewise developed their activities in a shared communicative ambience (an *umma*, or 'community' in the Islamic sense of that word) within a single state.[14] But it would be problematic, or at last a challenge, to see whether direct lines of communication or inspiration existed between those two; or whether the Latvian and Estonian initiatives emerged solely within an emancipatory dynamics vis-à-vis Baltic-German elites, or with models from Finland or the Russian-Galician borderlands playing an inspirational role there.

Conversely, however, different social and political conditions will give different inflections to transnational phenomena like cultural and literary sociability. The asymmetrically repressive regimes between the Habsburg, Romanov, and Ottoman Empires (or, within the Habsburg Empire, between its Cis- and Transleithenian parts after 1867) confronted their ethnic minorities with different possibilities and restrictions in their associational life. Belgium, a tolerant state with an advanced modern infrastructure, nevertheless saw its rural and urban lower-middle classes in Flanders disadvantaged not only socially, but also culturally. In this respect it showed some parallels to Spanish Galicia, and to post-Famine Ireland, which would suggest a typological/situational rather than a translational comparison between these three West-European cases.[15] In Wales and the French Midi, where the non-dominant languages had a high cultural prestige and were cultivated with upper-middle-class patronage, the situation differed, yet at the same time Wales and Ireland were linked, as Löffler points out in her contribution, by some pan-Celtic cross-currents.[16] Here, as in the case of the minority Romance-language communities, a sense

---

14 On which, see Usmanova's contribution in this volume.
15 See the contributions by Núñez/Iglesias and Higgins.
16 On which, see Löffler's and Martel's contributions in this volume.

of linguistic kinship is shot through by considerable political discontinuities, whether across the Irish Sea or the Pyrenees.[17] What, across the European landscape, did translational and situational elements mean for the literary and cultural sociability in non-dominant vernaculars? And how did each individual case fit into this context of the national cultivation of culture in Europe's long nineteenth century? These are questions for the reader to ponder on the basis of the rich palette of cases assembled here.

Bibliography

Anderson, Benedict. *Imagined Communities: Reflections on the Origin and Spread of Nationalism*. London: Verso, 1983.

Bolza, Hans. "Friedrich Koenig und die Erfindung der Druckmaschine," *Technikgeschichte* 34:1 (1967), 79–89.

Buijnsters, P.J. "Nederlandse leesgezelschappen uit de 18e eeuw," in Buijnsters, *Nederlandse literatuur van de achttiende eeuw: Veertien verkenningen*. Utrecht: n.p., 1984, 183–98; cf. also his contribution to Dann, 1981.

Chartier, Roger and Guglielmo Cavallo, eds. *A History of Reading in the West*. Oxford: Polity Press, 1999.

Dann, Otto, ed. *Lesegesellschaften und bürgerliche Emanzipation: Ein europäischer Vergleich*. München: Beck, 1981.

Engelsing, Rolf. *Der Bürger als Leser: Lesegeschichte in Deutschland, 1500–1800*. Stuttgart: Metzler, 1974.

ERNiE. *Encyclopedia of Romantic Nationalism in Europe*, ed. J. Leerssen with A.H. van Baal and J. Rock. 2 vols. Amsterdam: Amsterdam University Press, 2018; online at https://ernie.uva.nl.

Fischer, Steven Roger. *A History of Reading*. London: Reaktion, 2004.

Genequand, Christiane. *Sociétés et cabinets de lecture entre lumières et romantisme*. Actes du colloque organisé à Genève par la Société de Lecture le 20 novembre 1993. Genève: Société de Lecture, 1995.

Hroch, Miroslav. *Social Preconditions of National Revival in Europe: A Comparative Analysis of the Social Composition of Patriotic Groups among the Smaller European Nations*. New York: Columbia University Press, 2000.

Lajosi, Krisztina, and Andreas Stynen, eds. *Choral Societies and Nationalism in Europe*. National Cultivation of Culture 9. Leiden: Brill, 2015.

---

17 For an Occitan-Catalan comparison, cf. Zantedeschi 2019.

Langewiesche, Dieter. *Zur Freizeit des Arbeiters: Bildungsbestrebungen und Freizeitgestaltung österreichischer Arbeiter im Kaiserreich und in der Ersten Republik.* Stuttgart: Klett-Cotta, 1980.

Leerssen, Joep. "Conscience onder de analfabeten," in Kris Humbeeck *et al.*, eds., *De Grote Onleesbare: Hendrik Conscience herdacht.* Gent: Academia Press, 2016, 369–90.

Manguel, Alberto. *A History of Reading.* London: HarperCollins, 1996.

Milstein, Barney M. *Eight Eighteenth-Century Reading Societies.* Bern/Frankfurt: Lang, 1972.

Prüsener, Marlies. "Lesegesellschaften im achtzehnten Jahrhundert," *Archiv für Geschichte des Buchwesens* 13 (1973), 370–595.

Rehberg Sedo, DeNel, ed. *Reading Communities from Salons to Cyberspace.* Basingstoke: Palgrave Macmillan, 2011.

St. Clair, William. *The Reading Nation in the Romantic Period.* Cambridge: Cambridge University Press, 2004.

Williams, Abigail. *The Social Life of Books: Reading Together in the Eighteenth-Century Home.* New Haven: Yale University Press, 2017.

Zantedeschi, Francesca. *The Antiquarians of the Nation: Monuments and Language in Nineteenth-Century Roussillon.* Leiden: Brill, 2019.

Žecev, Nikolaj. "Bălgarska Matica v Carigrad," *Makedonski Pregled* 15:1 (1992), 33–66.

CHAPTER 1

The Buda University Press and National Awakenings in Habsburg Austria

Zsuzsanna Varga

While the term 'matica' is commonly associated with the Slavonic cultural organizations that emerged in Habsburg Austria during the nineteenth century, these cultural organizations did not work in isolation from the general culture of literary publishing within the region. The maticas were literary and scholarly societies or 'intermediary structures,' that served the reading public's education in matters of national language and national history. They accomplished this aim by publishing treatises concerning national philology and historical tracts that uncovered details of the nation's past, often in the form of yearbooks and other serial publications which also contained nationally-minded poetry and foreign translations. Much of the maticas' activity was preceded and assisted by the publications of the Buda University Press (1777–), the best equipped printing press east of Vienna, which held exclusive legal entitlement to print in the Cyrillic alphabet before 1825 and was in charge of publishing some of the foundational texts of the Romanian, Serbian, and Slovak national awakenings.

This chapter will therefore not argue for the existence of a Hungarian 'matica' or a similar cultural organization; instead it will examine the role of the Buda University Press in the support of national awakening, the rise of national historiographies, and the struggle for a unique or unified modern language. Language was a particularly sensitive point: in order to establish modern literacy, each language had to separate itself from a dominant other language: for Romanians, the prevalence of Church Slavonic and Greek had to be confronted, along with the fundamental issue of the Cyrillic vs. Latin alphabet; Church Slavonic was also a problem for Serbs; whilst for the Slovaks, the Czech influence had to be diminished. This task was bound up with elementary education, and was closely linked to the reform and unification of orthography, which had been completed in Germany by the end of the eighteenth century, but for most of Habsburg Austria did not start until 1800, and consensus was achieved only after 1840.[1] The Press was instrumental in fostering the writing of dictionaries, grammars, and national histories and mythologies, often in the new literary languages but just as frequently in 'languages of international circulation' such as Latin and German. My first section examines the early history of the Press and the legislation that necessitated and enabled its work as a publisher of fundamental treatises contributing to national awakening; the subsequent sections discuss Romanian, Serbian, and Slovak publications, and the coda offers references to the afterlife of this multi-ethnic enterprise.

1 The Buda University Press: History, Legislation, Structure

By the early 1800s the Buda University Press had a long and distinguished history in publishing. First established in 1577 in Nagyszombat (Trnava) by Miklós Telegdi, the Catholic bishop of Pécs and chief administrator to the Archbishop of Esztergom (1582–86), the Press was set up to counter the spread of the Reformation by printing religious tracts and liturgical texts in the service of the Catholics. The establishment of the Jesuit Academy of Nagyszombat (Trnava) in 1635 by Péter Pázmány, the Catholic archbishop of Hungary and the moving force behind the re-Catholicization of the country, endowed the Press with particular significance, and in 1644 it became affiliated with the Academy.[2] The close connection between the Press—at that time the only Catholic printing press in Hungary—and the Academy resulted in the emergence of a very powerful institution to serve the Catholic Counter-reformation, but the Press itself had already been a successful enterprise for decades. Its seven hundred ten books printed before 1711 included not only works of theology, rituals, prayers and catechisms, but also books on history, law, and natural science.[3] In the period 1711–73 at least two thousand books and several thousand pamphlets were published in Hungarian, Latin, German, French, Slovak, and Croatian, enriching the repertoire with other branches of science and literature.[4] Several government publications were also published, such as the *Corpus Iuris Hungarici*.

The centralizing and unifying efforts of the eighteenth-century Habsburg emperors, and especially Empress Maria Theresa's enlightened absolutism, gave a unique role to the Press in the Empire. The rulers' decrees reflected the

---

[1] Király, 71.
[2] Iványi and Gárdonyi, 13–17.
[3] Ibid., 57.
[4] Ibid., 89.

desire that their subjects should become proud and conscious of belonging to the Empire, and that this sense should be developed through literacy. In 1777 the Press moved to Pest-Buda, which was gradually coming to replace Pozsony (Bratislava) as the seat for the central governmental bodies of Hungary such as the Diet, the Chamber of Finance, and the Governor's Local Council (the *helytartótanács*, the central administrative body in charge of Hungarian affairs). The dissolution of the Jesuit order by Pope Clement XIV in 1773 transformed the Jesuit Academy into a secular state university, and when it moved to Buda, it also acquired the secular faculties of law and medicine.[5] The move coincided with the introduction of new, enlightened measures concerning elementary and secondary education. The *Ratio Educationis* (1777) introduced a unified system of secular elementary and secondary schools in Hungary, Croatia, and Slavonia, and also stipulated that elementary education (reading, writing, arithmetic, and agriculture) should be conducted in the language(s) spoken by the people in the individual villages.[6] To this end, schoolbooks were commissioned in the languages of the country, and in 1779 the Press received the exclusive right to publish these books.[7] The governance of the monarchy further promoted the publication of scholarly work (dictionaries and grammars) that would provide a basis for education.[8]

The privileges of the Press were expanded in 1795, and the equipment required for printing in Cyrillic was purchased from the Novaković printing press of Vienna. It came with the exclusive right to print in the oriental languages for the whole of Austria, including the crown estates, and also for Hungary (with the exception of Transylvania), including the Cyrillic, Greek, and Hebrew alphabets.[9] Cyrillic for education was necessitated by the *Ratio Educationis*, but the printing of religious books was also motivated by the fear that Russia would use the provision of liturgical texts for the Orthodox Church to increase its political influence. The University Press retained the right to print in the Cyrillic alphabet until 1835, but between 1825 and 1835 this right was limited to liturgical texts. Widespread printing using the oriental alphabets began only in

---

5   The move to Buda was itself a complex enterprise organized by a committee: its equipment was transported to Szered, on the river Vág, and was moved down the Danube by boat. Although some of the press remained behind until it was finally closed down in 1797, it was still a major industrial enterprise by contemporary standards. The press was accompanied by nine employees, including printers and compositors.
6   Király, 22.
7   Ibid., 6; Iványi and Gárdonyi, 106. The Royal patent was dated 5 November 1779.
8   Király, 8; the State Council met from 9–23 November 1793.
9   From 1770 to 1792 "Illyrian and Oriental printing" was in the care of Joseph Lorenz von Kurzböck at the Vienna University Press, which printed about fifteen hundred books in Serbian.

1803.[10] The combination of these two sets of rights meant that the Press held the exclusive right to schoolbooks and (broadly understood) educational materials in all languages, and also general printing in the non-Latin alphabets.

Under the Enlightenment rulers of the late eighteenth century, the University Press gradually acquired a broad range of functions. The University represented the main national authority for state education, and was governed directly by the Governor's Local Council through the agency of the Committee of Studies, making the Press effectively into a state-financed publishing house. It also worked on a commercial basis on commission by those authors who could cover their expenses. Censorship concerned both religious-moral and political content, with particular regard to works threatening the stability of the state: the former was under the jurisdiction of religious censorship, while the ultimate authority on the latter was the Governor's Local Council. The newly added languages made it necessary to employ new censors for both religious and secular publications; after 1795, Serbian and Romanian censors were employed, often men of the cloth who were in charge of censored content and also served as language editors.[11] Concerns about the lack of unified spelling and the low levels of literacy was expressed in a memorandum of the Governor's Local Council in 1806 clearly requesting the Serbian and Romanian school authorities to unify their spelling.[12]

The Press also had a highly developed distribution system to support the sale of the books. One system was a chain of stockists working on commission in more than seventy cities across the land. Quarterly fairs in Pest-Buda also played a particularly important role in marketing printed publications, not only from an economic but also from a social and cultural perspective: merchants from Serbia and elsewhere gathered regularly for the fairs, and they regularly transported books back home. The publishing schedule of the Press followed the patterns of the fairs, and the Serbian matica also scheduled its annual meetings to coincide with the fair.[13]

2 Public and Print Culture in Pest-Buda

The cultural and economic character of Pest-Buda is noteworthy: in 1800, with its main languages of Hungarian and German, the joint population of the twin

---

10   Iványi and Gárdonyi, 112.
11   Király, 57–59.
12   Iványi and Gárdonyi, 136.
13   Sziklay, *Pest-Buda*, 53.

cities numbered around fifty thousand, making it the largest city in the region between Vienna and Constantinople.[14] The twin cities increasingly assumed the role of the capital, not only for the presence of governmental organizations, but also for the appearance of what could be called, in today's terminology, 'knowledge institutions.' Already in the eighteenth century, several private libraries were established with significant collections, and by 1790 the University Library itself boasted some twenty thousand volumes. Count Ferenc Széchényi's donation of his own collection established the National Museum and Library in 1802, and in 1825 his son Count István Széchenyi's generous offer of his own funds led to the foundation of the Hungarian Scholarly Society (*Magyar Tudós Társaság*, later the Hungarian Academy of Sciences), whose primary function was the promotion of language renewal and modernization. The first permanent Hungarian-language theater was established in Pest in 1837, largely with donations from the general public. Simultaneously with these unique national landmarks, Pest-Buda witnessed a flourishing publishing industry: by the 1830s, another three established publishing houses were issuing regular publications, and book series and scholarly and popular periodicals were also coming out in predictable patterns.[15]

The institutions of Pest-Buda offered opportunities befitting a cultural center (secondary education, the university and the university press, public service) and by the end of the eighteenth century, they also offered financial and career opportunities for middle-class professionals. The University conferred status on the twin cities; it offered financial stability and a vibrant intellectual milieu, and also reflected the multi-ethnic nature of the Empire. As Sziklay argues, the University was less specifically national in character than, for instance, the universities of Vienna or Paris, and "this was not just because in the country, 'Hungarus patriotism' [i.e., the notion of being a subject of the Hungarian crown rather than of having a particular nationality] was the connecting element between the inhabitants of the multi-ethnic country, but also because it had many foreign professors appointed from above (i.e., by the court in Vienna)."[16] The language of instruction for a long time was Latin, and the use of the national languages was only gradually introduced, with concomitant frictions.[17] The Press and the University hosted a community of scholars working together, and often provided education and experience for scholars such as

---

14   Maxwell, 45.
15   Gécs, 85–95.
16   Sziklay, *Pest-Buda*, 66.
17   Sziklay, *Helikon*, 505.

the subsequent founders of the Belgrade-based Serbian Association for Literature and Science (*Društvo Srpske Slovesnosti*, 1841).[18]

3 Romanian Publications: The Daco-Romanian Continuity

For the Romanian enlightened and nationally-minded literati, the Buda University Press also provided the opportunity to publish on secular subjects. Romanian literacy outside Habsburg Austria was scarce: although there had been publishing in the Principalities since 1640, the publishing houses mostly printed liturgical and administrative texts, increasingly in Romanian rather than in Slavonic or in Greek, but exclusively using the Cyrillic alphabet.[19] In the period 1780–1830 Bucharest produced 318 titles, Iași 272 titles, and Nagyszeben (Sibiu) 187 titles, whilst the Buda University Press brought out 200 Romanian titles, which made it the third largest publisher.[20] Here, the Cyrillic and the Latin fonts were used simultaneously; Latin became the alphabet for Romanian only in 1860.

In the spirit of the *Ratio Educationis*, it fell to the Press to supply the Transylvanian Greek Catholic primary schools with schoolbooks, and the career opportunities offered were quickly grasped by those Transylvanian-Romanian intellectuals who became known as the 'Transylvanian trio' ('Erdélyi Triász'). The members of the trio—Samuil Micu-Klein (1745–1806), Gheorghe Șincai (1754–1816), and Petru Maior (1761–1821)—were all employed by the University Press as censors and language editors. They were all Greek Catholic (or Uniate) priests of Transylvanian origin, and thus belonged to the group which, according to Miskolczi, provided "the most dynamic element of Romanian life."[21] They had studied theology in Rome and Vienna, and remained committed to service even after leaving the order. They made their political claims clear by their contributions to the *Supplex libellum valachorum* in 1791, a petition demanding the same legal position (proportional representation in administrative positions) for the Romanians of Transylvania as for its other inhabitants.[22] As censors, they were in charge of the editorial process for schoolbooks and books for national education. By elaborating a theory of the origins of the Romanians and the Latin origins of the Romanian language, they contributed to

---

18   Póth, 236.
19   Drace-Francis, 54–57.
20   Miskolczi, 105; see also Domokos and Veress, 8.
21   Miskolczi, 95.
22   Drace-Francis, 62; Miskolczy, 98–99.

the development of a sense of national identity rooted in history, and established the cultural parameters of Romanian modernization.

The eldest member of the trio, Samuil Micu-Klein (1745–1806), worked as a censor from 1804 to 1806.[23] Already in Vienna, he and Șincai wrote the first descriptive grammar of Romanian (in Latin, 1780), recommending the use of the Latin alphabet in order to emphasize the relationship between the two languages.[24] He published the first ever book in Romanian printed with the Latin alphabet: his *Carte de rogacioni* (Book of Prayers) came out in 1779 in Vienna.[25] In 1806 the Press in Buda published his *Istoria, lucrurile și întîmplarile românilor pe scurt* (A Short History of the Romanians and Their Historical Events), in four parts. The first part covered the occupation of Dacia by the Romans, who, according to his theory, became the ancestors of the Romanians, while the remaining parts covered the Middle Ages, the principalities, and Transylvania. Central to his argument was the claim that the Romanians were of pure Roman origin, without mixing with other peoples.[26] His notion of unmixed purity also influenced his understanding of the character of the Romanian language. Klein published very little in his lifetime, but in 1804 he began compiling a four-language dictionary (Hungarian-Latin-Romanian-German) which Maior would later finish.

The Enlightenment historian and linguist Gheorghe Șincai worked in Vienna with Micu-Klein on the grammar after completing his theological studies in Rome.[27] As a government administrator in charge of Romanian schools in Transylvania, he set up more than three hundred schools between 1780 and 1795.[28] He moved to Buda in 1803, was appointed censor in 1807, and took employment with the aristocratic Wass family in Transylvania after his resignation in 1809. His embeddedness in the cultural elite of Habsburg Austria is shown by his receiving a commission to contribute the Romanian chapter (1805) to *Onomasticon*, a multilingual volume to honor the Palatine. His most scholarly achievement was an outline of the Daco-Roman theory in his *Elementa lingua daco romanae sive valachiace* (Buda, 1805). He insisted on the sameness of the Romanian language both inside and outside of Habsburg Austria, asserted its similarity to other Romance languages, championed the use of

---

23 For the trio, see also Käfer, 136–38.
24 Miskolczi suggests that this was the first Romanian grammar (95); Drace-Francis states that there was an earlier Romanian grammar from 1757, although it was not published (58).
25 Domokos, 23–24.
26 Ibid., 23.
27 Ibid., 24–25.
28 Ibid., 10.

the Latin alphabet, and was probably the first scholar to introduce the term 'Daco-Romanian.'[29] Whilst much of his work uses his earlier grammar of 1780, there is a notable difference in that his spelling proposal reflects contemporary common pronunciation rather than Latin etymology.[30] His other important work, *Hronicul romanilor* (The Chronicle of the Romanians and Other Peoples), was published only partially in the popular annual series *Calendarul de la Buda* (1808, 1809), used several sources, and discussed the history of the peoples in the Balkans. A man of the Enlightenment committed to educating the general public, he was also the compiler of an agricultural manual, *Povățuire către economia de câmp* (Advice on Agriculture, 1806), which also came to be used in Romanian schools as a schoolbook.

Petru Maior (1761–1821) was a native of Marosvásárhely (Târgu Mureş), Micu-Klein's student in Transylvania, and Şincai's fellow student in Rome.[31] An Enlightenment scholar and a historian, he was the Romanian censor at the Press between 1809 and his death in 1821. He wrote his most important works in Buda, and his long career enabled him to bring out several works left unfinished by his predecessors. His main work, *Istorie pentru începutul Românilor în Dachia* (A History of the Origins of the Romanians in Dacia; Buda, 1812) includes his *Dissertation on the Beginnings of the Romanian Language* and *Dissertation on the Old Literature of Romania*. The history argues for the Romanians' direct descent from the Romans and therefore for their early presence in Transylvania. The chapter dealing with language argued that Romanian was not corrupted Latin (the standpoint represented by Şincai and Micu-Klein) but had originated from the Latin vernacular spoken by the people; hence there was no need to adjust its orthography to the Latin.[32] This theory became the basis of Romanian diachronic linguistics. In his last work, *Dialogu pentru începutul limbei româna* (A Dialogue on the Origins of the Romanian Language; Buda, 1819) he suggested the removal of non-Latin words from Romanian in order to purify it and make it closer to Latin.[33]

The crowning achievement of the trio was the multi-volume *Lexicon Budense* dictionary (*Dictionarul de la Buda*, Romanian-Latin-Hungarian-German, Buda, 1825) started by Micu-Klein and brought to fruition by Petru Maior. This lexicon is the first Romanian etymological dictionary and also an encyclopaedia of language history, describing Romanian orthography and the

---

29   Király, 475 and 534; Domokos, 24–25.
30   Domokos, ibid.
31   Ibid., 25–26.
32   Käfer, 138.
33   Domokos, 25–26.

history of the Romanian language. The *Lexicon* was arguably the largest and most important single enterprise of the University Press.

In their efforts to adapt Romanian for modern purposes, the members of the trio put forward powerful arguments for the Roman origins of the people and their language, disagreeing only about its distance from classical Latin. But modernizing efforts were also carried out by intellectuals from the principalities who also used the Press for the diffusion of enlightened ideas.[34] The Moldovan Alexandru Beldiman (1760–1826) published a translation of Voltaire's *Orestes*, while the Wallachian boyar Constantin Golescu (1777–1830) published his travel book *Insemnare* (1826), a travelogue about western Europe and social progress.

4 Serbian Publications: Pest-Buda as the Center of Serbian Literary Culture

The condition of Serbian publishing in the early nineteenth century was similar to the Romanian situation: though some publishing activity existed outside the territory of Hungary, these initiatives were small and served contemporary literary and scholarly purposes. Modernization in the case of Serbian required gaining autonomy from Church Slavonic, which was the only language used for writing until the early nineteenth century. While the Romanians of Hungary lived predominantly in Transylvania and were mostly peasants, the Serbian presence was more scattered and also more stratified socially. Serbian settlers first moved to Hungary after 1690 at the invitation of the Habsburg Emperor Leopold I, when Patriarch Arsenije Crnojević of Ipek (Peć) himself helped to settle about thirty thousand Serbs.[35] The privileges received from the Emperor brought about the emergence of a rich Serbian merchant class which was to stand behind cultural modernization.[36]

In the spirit of the *Ratio Educationis* and as a result of the purchase of the Kurzbeck-Novaković press in 1795, the University Press also became responsible for supplying educational and liturgical texts for the Serbs of the Empire. The publication of Serbian books represented the largest contribution of the Buda University Press to the Central European language renewal; of the publications in languages other than Hungarian, German, and Latin, the number of

---

34   Drace-Francis, 61.
35   Kimball, 12.
36   Ćurčić, 155.

Serbian texts was the highest.[37] Between 1777 and 1800, one hundred eighteen books were published in Serbian, and the catalogues of Serbian publications published after 1796 show that between 1795 and 1800, at least seventy-six titles were printed for the Serbian readership. From about 1800, the annual output was between ten and twenty volumes.[38] Some five hundred Serbian books were printed between 1795 and 1830, and the total number of titles was over six hundred by 1848.[39]

The contribution of the Buda University Press to Serbian national and linguistic renewal needs to be measured against the condition of Serbian culture both outside of Habsburg Austria and within it. Serbs lived in four geopolitical units: many under Ottoman rule, a small number in the independent duchy of Montenegro, and most of them either in the increasingly independent Serbia or in Habsburg Austria, where their numbers were roughly identical. In the first three geographical units Serbian cultural institutions were scarce if extant at all. But in several towns and cities of Habsburg Austria, there were aspirations to renew Serbian secular literacy and culture: the first Serbian newspaper, Jernej Kopitar's *Srpske Novine*, was published in Vienna between 1813 and 1822, and the rich merchant towns along the Danube (Sremski Karlovci, Novi Sad, and Szentendre) had Serbian secondary schools and churches. The first *gymnasium* was established in Sremski Karlovci in the 1790s. But the critical mass of intellectual life took place in Pest-Buda in the early nineteenth century; it was the most populous Serbian settlement, and, until the opening of a press in Belgrade in 1832, Buda was the only center of Serbian book production.[40]

The Serbian books printed by Buda University Press before 1825 reflected enlightened intentions to spread practical, medical, agricultural and other kinds of knowledge for the good of the general readership, but some of the titles also reflected notions about the communality of South Slavs. The first book printed there was by Ferenc Schraud, a medical professor, whose *Kratkoe pouchenie* was a two-page pamphlet about the methods for protection from pestilence (1795). In 1797 a series of readers (*Bukvar*) was launched for schools, in a language that was predominantly Slaveno-Serb (i.e., Church Slavonic mixed with Russian and Serbian elements).[41] Beginning in 1796, catalogues of Slavo-Serbian books appeared regularly in Serbian and German (*Verzeichnis*

---

37   Käfer, 116.
38   Ibid., 134.
39   Póth, 230.
40   Sziklay, *Pest-Buda*, 48.
41   Király, 232.

der Slawo-Serbischen und Walachischen Bücher), using both Church Slavonic and Gothic fonts. Books were also published on domestic economy, and for religious instruction, such as the catechism (1797) of Jovan Rajić (1726–1801), whose *Svetnik* (1802) contained translations of Latin and Greek writers into Church Slavonic via German. Its significance consisted in its justification for the use of Church Slavonic: his preface argued that this was a language that all Slavs understood. The Press also published his later work, including his *Istorija raznih slovenskih narodov* (History of Various Slavic Peoples, 1823–24), which offered the first systematic history of the South Slavs. Other important books by the Enlightenment thinker Dositej Obradović (1739–1811) were also published: his *Basne* (1800) contained parables about animals, but it was also a politically important text because it was here that the concept 'Slaveno-Serbs' was first used, denoting not only the people of Serbia but also those of Bosnia and Dalmatia.[42] His *Soveti zdravago razuma*, published first in Leipzig and then in 1806 in Buda, put forward the idea of South Slavonic unity: Obradović argued that the peoples of Dalmatia, Croatia, and Slavonia belonged to one nation and one language and that therefore they should belong to one country.[43]

A new era in the history of Serb literacy started with *Letopis,* the Serbian annual, which predated the Czech *Časopis* (1827) and the Polish *Czasopism Naukowych* of the Ossolineum (1828). After an initial year in Újvidék (Novi Sad) in 1824–25, *Letopis* moved to Buda in the hope of securing the financial support of the city's wealthy Serbian community, and indeed Pest-Buda remained the home of *Letopis* until 1864.[44] The annual, whose first editor was the writer and historian Georgije Magarasević (1793–1830), was launched with an all-Slav mission: it intended to cover everything that concerned all Slavs from the Baltic to the Black Sea, with particular emphasis on the Serbs, including history, biography, literature, and translations.[45] Its institutional framework was provided by the *Matica srpska*, established in Buda in 1826 by six wealthy Serbian merchants and the young lawyer Jovan Hadzić (1799–1869), who set out to run an organization designed to spread knowledge for the public good of all Serbs.[46] From 1832, the young lawyer Teodor Pavlović (1804–54) edited the periodical in Pest, somewhat narrowing its geographical range by focusing only on the Southern Slavs from Pest to Crna Gora, but he expanded the range of its genres.

42   Ibid., 239.
43   Ibid., 240.
44   Ćurčić, 164.
45   Vujicsics, *Szerbek Pest-Budán*, 37.
46   Vujicsics, *Magyarok és szerbek*, 97.

The periodical generated a strong sense of Serbdom and love for the pre-Ottoman past.[47]

Letopis and the University Press played a rather equivocal role in the renewal of the Serbian language. By 1826 two different versions of a new, modern Serbian literary language had emerged as replacements for Church Slavonic. Dositej Obradović represented the majority view by basing it on the language of the Serbian middle class living in Habsburg Austria, while Vuk Karadžić, whose work was published in Vienna, argued for the renewal of the Serbian language on the basis of the language of the people expressed in folk songs and folk poetry. The Buda University Press generally favored the views of Obradović, but made one minor exception by publishing one of the early works that had influenced Karadžić—*Salo debeloga jera*, by Sava Mrkalj (1810)—which proposed a reform of Serbian.[48] The lack of agreement about Serbian orthography became increasingly disconcerting towards the 1840s. At the request of the *Matica srpska*, both Karadžić and the conservative Sava Tekelija (1761–1842) were asked to submit their proposals, which were published in *Serbski narodni list*.[49] Karadžić argued for the use of an orthography reflecting Serbian and for a decision about which dialect should serve as the basis of the literary language; Tekelija argued for a unified Slaveno-Serb spelling. The turning-point in the debate was represented by Djura Daničić's (1825–82) *Rat za srpski jezik i pravopis* (The Battle for Serbian Language and Orthography; Buda, 1847), which espoused the pro-Karadžić position. Finally an agreement was reached about a unified Serbo-Croatian based on the *što*-dialect of the South-West. Though *Letopis* was no platform for modernizers, it nonetheless rendered an important service to the people of Serbia by acting as a platform for Serbian literature and Slavonic linguistics.

The intellectual ferment of the city of Pest-Buda, with its concentration of Serbs and of economic and intellectual power, also provided inspiration for the establishment of institutions. The Hungarian Scholarly Society (*Magyar Tudós Társaság*) was an acknowledged model for the founding of the *Matica Srpska* in 1826. The Arad landowner Sava Tekelija, whose plan was to transform the *Matica* into a scholarly academy, set up the *Tekelianum* in 1838 for the education of poor Serbian students in Budapest, and it became an important base for generations of Serbian intellectuals (at least four hundred students in the humanities, medical sciences, engineering, and arts) from Serbia and Habsburg

---

47   See Kovaček.
48   Milisavac, 510.
49   Király, 309.

Austria.[50] The foundation used different competitions to inspire Serbian intellectual life with poems, grammar, historical works, historical epic poetry, and studies promoting the development of Serbian education.[51] Teodor Pavlović, the secretary of the *Matica*, wanted to develop it into a secular cultural institution of modernization, leading to the foundation of the Library and the Museum.[52] The library opened in 1838 with seven hundred eighty-seven volumes, and the addition of a substantial bequest in 1839 made it the largest Serbian library in the world at that time.[53]

Other inspirational forces included Hungarian-language journals and the national theater.[54] Serbian serial publications appeared again in Pest-Buda in 1835, when Teodor Pavlović launched the *Serbski Narodni List*, followed by the *Serbske Narodne Novine* (1838–48).[55] The *List* focused on literature and significant cultural events, and often published patriotic poetry to inspire national sentiment. The *Novine* was meant to serve explicitly political ends, and in the 1840s also published articles concerning social reforms and technological advancement. Among literary almanachs, Sima Milutinović Sarajlija's *Zorica* (Dawn) stands out, which was modelled on the Hungarian *Aurora* and represented the harbinger of national romanticism. The beginnings of Serbian-language theater are also related to Pest-Buda: the first act was the staging of István Balogh's *György Cserny* (i.e., Karadjordje) in the Buda Rondella in 1812, with Róza Széppataki Déry, the most famous Hungarian actress, singing a song in Serbian, which was probably the first instance of Serbian words spoken from the stage. This was soon followed by a full-length play, August von Kotzebue's *The Parrot* (1792), translated into Serbian and performed with the help of Serbian-speaking Hungarian actors. This staging soon went on tour in smaller towns with Serbian populations in Hungary, and the play was also taken to Kragujevac, the capital of Serbia until 1841.[56]

5 Slovak in the University Press

Unlike the Romanians and Serbs, the Slovaks had no territory outside Habsburg Austria in the early nineteenth century. Pest-Buda therefore emerged without

---

50 Vujicsics, *Szerbek*, 45–47.
51 Ferdinandy and Gogolák, 36.
52 Vujicsics, *Szerbek*, 39; Milisavac, 511.
53 Póth, 235.
54 Ćurčić, 165.
55 Póth, 232.
56 Ibid., 233–34.

rival as the center for Slovak literary life.[57] The settlement of Slovaks, mostly unskilled laborers from the northernmost counties, first started in the twin cities between 1725 and 1750, but towards the end of the eighteenth century professional migration to Pest-Buda became significant. The intellectual and professional opportunities offered by government administration, the Royal Chamber, and the University were rather attractive: Anton Ottmayer's position as dean of the Law Faculty (1832–33) was matched by Martin Hamuljak's career in government administration.[58] By the 1820s a Slovak-speaking literary center also emerged, following the example of the Serbs and also with close personal connections between the two groups.

The significance of Pest-Buda as a venue and hotbed for the Slovak national revival can best be seen in its relations to the formation of a unified, modernized national language suited to secular purposes. The late eighteenth and early nineteenth centuries saw the development of two alternatives for a modern language: the Slovakized Czech language (*bibličtina*) was cultivated by the Protestants well into the nineteenth century, whilst around Nagyszombat (Trnava) a literary language emerged that was based on Western Slovak elements and was mostly cultivated by the Catholics. Printing in Slovak in Pest-Buda started in 1780 with the provision of elementary schoolbooks translated from the German. Books spreading knowledge for the masses about scientific, agricultural and medical matters were also published regularly from 1780s onwards,[59] but a unified language did not emerge until the middle of the nineteenth century.[60]

The University Press played a significant role in the Slovak national language renewal by publishing in the Western Slovak language, primarily the works of the Catholic priest Anton Bernolák. Bernolák believed in the separateness of Slovak from Czech, and wanted to base his language on the phonetics of the Slovak pronunciation of the educated classes. His works were primarily linguistic in nature: *Slowakische Grammatik* came out in 1817, and sought to provide a normative basis for Slovak primarily for learners of the language. His five-language lexicon *Slowar* (Czech, Latin, German, Hungarian, and Slovak; Buda, 1825–27) was also meant to serve as a codification of the Western Slovak language, and it appeared at the same time as the *Lexicon*

---

57 As Käfer explains, the tradition to publish in Slovak had already started in Nagyszombat, and 105 Slovak-language texts were published in the quarter-century after 1777 (116).
58 Fried, 35–37.
59 Király, 124.
60 Ibid., 118; see also Szarka, 20. The Lutheran custom of using *bibličtina* as a literary language came to an end in 1842 when Štur's language reform was introduced.

Budense. Bernolák's main purpose and achievement were the systematization of Slovak literary language and ortography.

Whilst Bernolák argued for particularity, Ján Herkel's (1786–1865) *Elementa Universalis Linguae Slavicae* (1826) pursued the universal: he was attempting to create a common Slavic language, and can arguably be credited with the creation of the term 'Pan-Slavism.'[61] Herkel's grammar was a testimony to the nation, emphasizing the brotherly love connecting the sixty million Slavs and the unity of Slavs in literature. Nation-building in the form of creating foundational national myths was also promoted by the University Press. The Catholic priest Ján Hollý (1795–1849) was a follower of Bernolák in his commitment to Western Slovak. His poem *Cirillo-Metodiada* (Buda, 1835) chronicles the lives of Cyril and Methodius and the religious belief system and heroic past of the pagan Slovaks.

The *bibličtina* tradition and the attempt to root the Slovak literary language in Czech were most vocally represented by Ján Kollár (1793–1852) and Pavel Jozef Šafárik (1795–1861). Kollár was the Lutheran minister of the Pest Slovak community and a promoter of Slavonic unity. His poem *Slávy Dcera* ("The Daughter of the Slavs" or "The Daughter of Glory," 1824) and his reader *Čitanka* (1825) were brought out by the University Press. The poem—now an anthology piece—appealed to Slavonic consciousness by emphasizing the unity of the Slavs, and was very influential amongst the Czechs, Moravians, Slovenes, Croats, Galician Ukrainians, and Russians. The Press also brought out his two-volume collection of Slovak folk songs (1834–35). Šafárik, who had previously worked as the headmaster of the Serbian Orthodox secondary school in Ujvidék (Novi Sad) and had immersed himself in the similarities between the Southern and Western Slavic languages, published two German works in Buda: his *Geschichte der slawischen Sprache und Literatur nach allen Mundarten* (1826) attempted to provide a linguistic account of all the Slavonic languages. In *Über die Abkunft der Slawen nach Lorenz Surowiecki* (1828), Šafárik argued for the ancient presence of Slavs in Europe and assumed that Czechs were identical with Slovaks.

The University Press and the surrounding literary culture of Pest-Buda played a particularly important role in the rapprochement between the two camps, and both the Czechists and the Slovakists had their works printed by the Press. Hamulják was instrumental in holding these two trends together; as a government administrator, he organized the printing of Bernolák's dictionary. He also established the *Spolok Milovníkow* (Society of the Friends of Slovak Language and Literature) where he succeeded in bringing the two camps

---

61   Király, 144.

together: the Society was presided over by Kollár but also published Hollý's poems. Hamuljak was also instrumental in setting up the *Zora* almanac, which, like the Serbian *Danica*, was modelled on the Hungarian periodical *Aurora*, and published both Catholic and Lutheran authors.[62]

6   Epilogue

The Buda University Press played an important role in the publishing of the first wave of dictionaries, scholarly grammars, and national histories for the Serbs, Romanians, and Slovaks. This was enabled by the legally codified duties of the University Press, but the multi-ethnic milieu of the twin cities, their vibrant intellectual life and cultural infrastructure also contributed to the role of the Press as an incubator for ideas of a modern national identity articulated through the modern use of language. The fact that no rival publishing opportunities existed outside Habsburg Austria only enhanced its role as an ethnocultural center. The atmosphere of intellectual tolerance is also evidenced by the fact that neither the Press nor the censors objected to the publication of works that argued for the long-standing presence and continuity of Romanians in Transylvania, or to works emphasizing the reciprocity and sameness of Slavs north and south of the Hungarian-populated territories. This tolerance vis-à-vis different national endeavors could probably also be justified by the fact that debates about the origins and languages of the various peoples were felt to be scholarly in nature rather than the intellectual foundations of nationally assertive political movements. That this was the case is evident from the history of the Serbian scholarly society: although a Serbia-based Serb scholarly association (*Društvo Srpske Slovesnosti*) had been formed already in 1841, the Pest-based *Matica Srpska* continued to assert its separateness by refusing to merge with the other institution in the South.[63]

After 1848 Pest-Buda rapidly lost its significance as a center for the Serbs. Eventually, inspired by young, aspiring generations of Serbs, in 1864 the *Matica Srpska* relocated to Újvidék (Novi Sad).[64] Yet despite this departure, Pest-Buda continued to provide a home for its Serbian inhabitants: the Naum Bodza foundation was set up in 1870 to support the early careers of merchants, medical students and other professionals. Another Serbian foundation was the

---

62   Käfer, 179.
63   Vujicsics, *Magyarok*, 99.
64   Érdújhelyi, 184; see also Milisavac, 511.

Saint Angelina Orthodox Women's Foundation (1898), which provided homes for young Serbian women who had moved to Budapest to pursue secondary and vocational education.[65]

The Hungarian attitude was distinctly more hostile towards Slovak efforts to achieve cultural autonomy. The *Matica Slovenska* was finally authorized by Emperor Franz Joseph in 1862 to act as a national association in the service of literary and moral education, with the support of individual donations for its establishment and maintenance.[66] The *Matica Slovenska* was launched in 1863 in the small town of Turócszentmárton (Martin) in one of the ethnically purest Slovak counties; but in 1875 it was closed down for its perceived anti-Hungarian tendencies and for transgressing its original cultural function by supporting the Pan-Slav political cause.[67] An assessment of such accusations is beyond the scope of this essay, since it would require an analysis of the political debates among Hungarian politicians and also among Slovak patriots, several of whom continued to argue for a multi-ethic homeland with due measures to secure cultural autonomy.[68] But it is fair to say that the articulation of national identity in the greater taxonomy of languages and nations was in any case vastly enabled by the scholarly publications of the Buda University Press.

Bibliography

Ćurčić, Lazar. "A pesti egyetem nyomdája és a szerb könyvnyomtatás" [The Printing Press of the University of Pest and Serbian Book Printing]. In Sztoján Vujicsics, ed., *Szomszédság és közösség: délszláv-magyar irodalmi kapcsolatok* [Neighborhood and Mutuality: Literary Contacts between South Slavs and Hungarians]. Budapest: Akadémiai, 1972. 153–66.

Domokos, Sámuel, and Endre Veress. *A Budai Egyetemi Nyomda román kiadványainak dokumentumai 1780–1848* [Documents of the Buda University Press, 1780–1848]. Budapest: Akadémiai, 1982.

Domokos, Sámuel. *Magyar-román irodalmi kapcsolatok* [Hungarian-Romanian Literary Contacts]. Budapest: Gondolat, 1985.

Drace-Francis, Alex. *The Making of Modern Romanian Culture: Literacy and the Development of National Identity*. London: Tauris, 2012.

---

65 Vujicsics, *Szerbek*, 47–50.
66 Szarka, 20.
67 Ibid., 21.
68 Maxwell, 51–52.

Érdújhelyi, Menyhért. "A szláv maticák" [The Slavonic Maticas]. *Századok* (1895), 183–86 and 282–85.
Ferdinandy, Mihály, and Lajos Gogolák. *Magyarok és délszlávok* [Hungarians and South Slavs]. Budapest: Officina, 1940.
Fried, István. *A névadás lehetségessége* [The Possibility of Naming]. Pozsony: Madách-Possonium, 2004.
Gécs, Béla. "Pest-Buda nyomdái 1723–1895" [The Printing Presses of Pest-Buda 1723–1895]. *Magyar Grafika* 3 (2004), 85–95.
Iványi, Béla, and Albert Gárdonyi. *A Királyi Magyar Egyetemi Nyomda története 1577–1927* [The History of the Royal Hungarian University Press, 1577–1927], ed. Albert-Czakó Elemér. Budapest: Királyi Magyar Egyetemi Nyomda, 1927.
Käfer, István. *Az Egyetemi Nyomda négyszáz éve 1577–1977* [Four Centuries of the University Press, 1577–1977]. Budapest: Magyar Helikon, 1977.
Kimball, Stanley. *The Austro-Slav Revival: A Study of Nineteenth-Century Literary Foundations.* Philadelphia: American Philosophical Society, 1973.
Király, Péter. *A kelet-közép-európai helyesírások és irodalmi nyelvek kialakulása: a Budai Egyetemi Nyomda kiadványainak tanulságai, 1777–1848* [The Formation of East-Central European Orthographies and Literary Languages as Reflected in the Publications of the Buda University Press, 1777–1848]. Nyíregyháza: Imprint Kft, 2003.
Kovaček, Božidar. *A szerb matica* [The Serbian Matica]. Budapest: Szerb Önkormányzat, 2001.
Maxwell, Alexander. "Budapest and Thessaloniki as Slavic Cities (1800–1914): Urban Infrastructures, National Organisations and Ethnic Territories." *Ethnologia Balkanica* 9 (2005), 43–64.
Milisavac, Živan. "A szerb matica pesti korszaka 1826–1864" [The Serbian Matica: The Pest Period 1826–1864]. *Helikon* 4 (1979), 509–12.
Miskolczi, Ambrus. *Románok a történeti Magyarországon* [Romanians in Historical Hungary]. Budapest: Lucidus, 2005.
Póth, István. "Pest-Buda: az egyetemes szerbség kultúrközpontja" [Pest-Buda: The Universal Serbian Cultural Center]. *A Budapesti Történeti Múzeum évkönyve: Tanulmányok Budapest múltjából XII* [Yearbook of the Museum of the History of Budapest, vol. 12]. Budapest: Budapesti Történeti Múzeum, 1988. 225–38.
Szarka, László. "A szlovák Matica" [The Slovak Matica], *Historia* 2 (1993), 20–21.
Sziklay, László. "Pest-Buda többnemzetiségű irodalmi élete a XIX. század első felében" [The Literary Life of Multi-ethnic Pest-Buda in the First Half of the 19th Century]. *Helikon* 4 (1979), 504–08.
Sziklay, László. *Pest-Buda szellemi élete a 18–19. század fordulóján* [The Intellectual Life of Pest-Buda at the Turn of the 18th and 19th Centuries]. Budapest: MTA-Argumentum, 1991.

Vujicsics, Sztoján. *Szerbek Pest-Budán* [The Serbs of Pest-Buda]. Budapest: Városháza, 1997.

Vujicsics, Sztoján. *Magyarok és szerbek* [Hungarians and Serbs]. Újvidék: Fórum, 1997.

CHAPTER 2

The Matice Česká

Magdaléna Pokorná

The history of the Czech nation and the history of Czech literature are closely linked, and Czech literature has played a vital role in the formation of modern Czech society. The writing of Czech books kept the Czech language alive; despite a temporary decline in both the spoken and written language, Czech literature maintained its link with the period of exceptional cultural blossoming at the end of the sixteenth and the beginning of the seventeenth centuries. In addition, such a high esteem for the status of books continued the earlier traditions according to which the salvation of one's soul depended on the reading of good or bad books.

It is therefore not surprising that the very real and important role of literature was simultaneously mythologized: books were ascribed a principal role in the national revival, and sometimes they were even seen as the only influence in this process; the public viewed writers as prophets who could forecast the future and change the present through their use of words. It was not enough merely to write; it was equally important to take care that a readership should be found for these books. For this reason, all patriotic writers also became amateur booksellers, offering and distributing their own books and those of their friends. For this reason, patriots promoted each and every library and embraced the reading public, and consequently the Matice Česká became one of the principal national institutions. The Matice Česká was established under the protection of the Museum of the Czech Kingdom (nowadays the National Museum) for the purpose of publishing Czech scientific literature, and later literary works (belles-lettres) in Czech. Its tasks were educational, cultural, organizational, and representative.

1 The Matice Česká in the Context of Contemporary Publishing Houses

The foundation of the Matice Česká in 1831 was inspired by the establishment of the Serbian Matica (*Matica srpska*), but it was not the first publishing house in the Czech environment based on voluntary donations from individual members. As early as 1669 the Jesuit Matěj Šteyer established the Legacy of

St. Wenceslas (*Dědictví svatováclavské*), an institution which published Catholic religious literature and disseminated it amongst the public either free of charge or at low cost. In 1831, thanks to Father A. Hanikýř, the Legacy of St. John (*Dědictví svatojánské*) was established, whose aim was to publish cheap and high-quality educational books in the Czech language. In Moravia, in 1850, the local Catholic clergy founded the Legacy of Saints Cyril and Methodius (*Dědictví sv. Cyrila a Metoděje*) to ensure the education of the peasantry based on the Catholic faith. Several similar institutions emerged in the following years: the Little Ones' Legacy (*Dědictví maličkých*) in Hradec Králové in 1859; the Legacy of St. Prokop (*Dědictví sv. Prokopa*) in 1860; and the Legacy of St. Ludmila (*Dědictví sv. Ludmily*) in 1863. Along with such institutions, there also existed a number of publishing houses in the Czech environment; yet the greatest role in the Czech National Revival was doubtless played by the Prague firm of Václav Matěj Kramerius. He published very popular newspapers and operated his Czech Expedition (*Česká expedice*), which combined book publishing with distribution, as early as 1790. Czech Expedition became the leading center for the patriotic intelligentsia and for the entire national movement in Prague, and Kramerius also succeeded in attracting and gathering other national activists in the countryside around his activities.

2 The Matice Česká: Its Foundation, Nature, and Organization

In 1831, the aristocracy resident in the Czech Kingdom established the Patriotic Museum, an important scientific and educational institution which, however, operated at first on the principle of patriotism defined in terms of land. Czech patriotic society wanted the Museum to reflect its national needs more effectively, and gradually succeeded in implementing this goal (as reflected in the change of the museum's name from Patriotic Museum to National Museum). Patriotic activities were also aimed at the establishment of an independent foundation for the publication of high-quality books in Czech. The Committee for the Scientific Improvement of Czech Language and Literature was established in 1830 in order to take care of the standardization, improvement, and refinement of the written language and to prepare a Czech encyclopaedia. The Committee and the management of the National Museum decided to set up a special treasury from voluntary contributions donated by the broadest sections of the nation in order to secure funding for this project. Once it was set up, this treasury was given the name *Matice česká*. It introduced itself to the public in a Proclamation dated 1 January 1831 signed by Josef Jungmann, Jan Svatopluk Presl, František Palacký, and Rudolf, Prince Kinský, declaring its aim as "to promote and even to assist the publication of good-quality Czech books, either those beneficial or even scientific and literary (belles-lettres)."

The Matice Česká was a part of the Society of the Museum of the Czech Kingdom. It was responsible to the Society for the results of its economic activities and its management. The Matice Česká was originally managed by a three-man committee, but the number of members increased over the course of time and came to include many important personalities. This committee was headed by the so-called curator, i.e., the representative of the Society of the Museum, who was to be responsible for checking the economic activities. All accounts were presented to the Society of the Museum of the Czech Kingdom for control.

3 The Matice Česká and Its Membership in the Initial Period of Its Existence

Those who deposited a certain sum of money (fifty Austrian gulden) became members of the Matice Česká and were thus entitled to receive published books. There were also other types of membership; for example, an association of corresponding members was established in 1863 whose primary task was to promote the Matice Česká.

Information about donors and how much was donated to benefit the Matice Česká was published in the *Journal of the Czech Museum* (*Časopis českého musea*). The publication of membership data not only pursued practical, or one might say monitoring aims, but also created bonds between the center and the provinces and principally represented a clear declaration of the members' patriotic attitudes.

Miroslav Hroch has researched the lists of contributors for the years 1831 to 1848, and we owe him gratitude for his detailed analysis of the membership base of the Matice. The largest professional group among the contributors until the mid-1840s was the clergy, especially chaplains and priests; the Catholic hierarchy appeared only exceptionally. Overall, the share of the clergy decreased, from approximately 45% in the 1830s to 28–30% in the 1840s.

The second largest group amongst the patriots around the Matice Česká gradually came to be students; in the second half of the 1840s their share even exceeded that of the clergy. The social standing of students was mixed, but a higher education obviously provided theoretical opportunities for moving up the social ladder, even to those who were currently struggling in poverty.

The share of civil servants fluctuated between 10–15% in the 1830s, and after 1841 it reached 20%. Members of the upper state bureaucracy were rare amongst the patriotic civil servants; however, there were many civil servants from the patrimonial administration. Throughout the 1840s the number of contributors from the ranks of white-collar workers in private companies and state or municipal councils increased. Contrary to the commonly widespread view, the share of teachers amongst the contributors to the Matice Česká was relatively low. Not merely poor teachers, but also relatively well-off grammar school professors represented a modest share, forming approximately 5–8% of contributors.

Thanks to Hroch's research, the Matice contributors for the period 1831–48 can be distinguished in terms of their places of permanent residence, or the places where they worked. More than 30% of the Matice contributors lived and worked in Prague; another 31% were in towns with more than two thousand inhabitants; and 28% were in small towns and villages with fewer than one thousand inhabitants. The remaining 11% consisted of the inhabitants of towns and small towns with fewer than two thousand inhabitants. The superiority of the town element is thus obvious.

Membership of the Matice Česká between 1838–1849

Year	1838	1839	1840	1841	1842
Membership	125	74	49	76	231

The decline in the membership of the Matice Česká at the end of the 1830s and the beginning of the 1840s was influenced by the publication of rather costly scientific projects. Yet following a change of direction in its publishing strategy, and editorial decisions to publish literature more accessible to a wider public (as formulated in the Manifesto of the Matice Česká dated 15 December 1841), membership numbers again increased rapidly:

Year	1843	1844	1845	1846	1847	1848
Membership	381	517	917	1157	1443	1135

SOURCE: KAREL TIEFTRUNK, *A HISTORY OF THE MATICE ČESKÁ* [*DĚJINY MATICE ČESKÉ*], PRAGUE 1881

4 The Matice Česká: A Public Matter

Immediately after its foundation, the Matice Česká became a public matter in patriotic society; its activities and importance were certainly discussed during personal meetings when new members were also recruited. Evidence of the nature of these discussions can be found in contemporary periodicals (with particular attention to the observations of the journalist Karel Havlíček), correspondence, and memoirs. The medical doctor, writer, and translator Josef Bojislav Pichl, for example, recalled how Josef Jungmann and some of his students persuaded many other individuals to become members of the Matice Česká, and even the library of their grammar school became an institutional member and one of the founders of the Matice Česká.

Membership in the Matice Česká could, in a way, serve as a test of the sincerity of such patriotic attitudes. This was the view of Božena Němcová, who in a letter to her husband dated 14 March 1858 refused to send him her copy of František Palacký's seminal work *Dějiny národu českého v Čechách a na Moravě* (History of the Czech Nation in Bohemia and Moravia) to lend to his colleagues, saying that if people wanted to declare how Czech they were, they should become members of the Matice, and if not, "it is rather a shame.—They want to be called Czechs, let them support the cause, otherwise they can go to blazes with their flag-waving patriotism ..." (from Robert Adam *et al.*, eds., *Božena Němcová: Korespondence* IV, Praha 2007).

The activities of the Matice Česká were influenced not only by the outstandingly creative personalities who have already been mentioned, but also by those who disseminated an awareness of its existence amongst the public, not merely in the center but in the provinces as well. One of these was a priest, Josef Šmidinger (1801–52), who joined the Matice Česká as early as 1832 and became one of its most enthusiastic members. He distributed its books throughout the Czech countryside and recruited new members for the Matice Česká with a passion bordering on fanaticism. He lent money for deposits to potential members and would then demand repayment from them, using unscrupulous methods as well. In the fifteen years of his involvement, as noted by Lubomír Sršeň, he recruited more than four hundred new members for the Matice Česká and collected over twenty thousand (Austrian) gulden, amounting to one-fifth of its contemporary principal fund. He was very persuasive; for example, in his place of work, in the South Bohemian town of Strakonice, he even managed to convince twenty-six burghers to subscribe to Czech books although they neither read nor even spoke Czech! One of his 'missionary' trips for the Matice Česká became fateful: after a long walk under unfavorable winter conditions he fell ill and died. His life story provided inspiration for the Czech historical novelist Alois Jirásek (1851–1930), in whose novel *F.L. Věk* the character of the priest Matyáš Vrba was based on Father Šmidinger.

Czech patriots also showed their faith and trust in the Matice Česká by donating considerable sums of money or endowing it with bequests from their estates. Czech society was still poor, and such decisions cannot be judged only with regard to the actual amounts of the gifts, but also on a symbolic level as an act with long-term impact and one worthy of emulation. Josef Jungmann's friend, the well-known priest Antonín Marek, established an endowment for poor students by making a lump-sum gift of one thousand gulden. In 1846, Vojtěch Melan, a technical engineer, made a bequest in his will of one hundred gulden to the Matice Česká, with no strings attached. On the other hand, in the initial period of its existence the Matice Česká received an offer of five hundred gulden that was conditional on their setting up an independently run restricted fund to cover the publication of 'folktales,' i.e., traditional narratives. The Matice Česká could not accept the conditions thus imposed and the gift was declined.

During the Revolution of 1848 the important representatives of the Matice Česká, like many other representatives in Czech public life, were swept into the whirlpool of political events. The publication of the *Journal of the National Museum* came to a halt and the publication of other works was also postponed. The building in the center of Prague to which the National Museum had recently moved became the center of the political events that were happening on the streets of Prague. Later on, from 1891 onwards, the Matice Česká also found its seat in the newly constructed Neo-Renaissance building of the National Museum in the very heart of Prague, on Wenceslas Square.

5   The Matice Česká versus the State

Despite its modest beginnings, the Matice Česká lived up to its promise. In the pre-March period it grew to become probably one of the most important institutions that was unambiguously national in its nature. A keen self-interest in the existence of the Austrian co-state, as well as an effort to gain support from the highest circles as a sort of defense against the suspicions of the national authorities, led to the publication of a collection of poems entitled *Hlasy vlastenců ke dni 1.měsíce března 1832 na památku čtyřidcetiletého slavného panování J.M. císaře a krále Františka I* (Patriots' Voices on the First Day of March 1832 to Commemorate the Forty Years of the Glorious Rule of H.M. Emperor and King Francis I). Fifteen Czech poets submitted their contributions to this truly magnificent typographic artwork. The representatives of the Matice Česká graciously accepted the thanks of the Ruling House; they perceived them as bright rays of hope that Czech literary efforts would be truly appreciated. Yet, at the very time when the Matice Česká was paying tribute to Emperor Franz Joseph I. and was to receive official thanks for it, the Matice Česká was also facing the open mistrust of the official authorities. Even the very title of the institution had to be changed (to the Finance Foundation or the Treasury of the Czech Museum for the Publication of Czech Books).

Three years later, another such work, *Hlasy vlastenců při radostném vítání císařských královských majestátů Ferdinanda I a Marie Anny* (Patriots' Voices on the Occasion of a Joyful Welcome to his Imperial and Royal Majesty Ferdinand I and her Imperial Majesty Empress Maria Anna) was published on the occasion of their visit to Prague in 1835. In 1854 the Matice Česká honored the occasion of yet another imperial visit to Prague, this time by Emperor Franz Joseph I and his new bride Elisabeth, with the publication of an almanac, *Perla česká* (The Czech Pearl).

The state's antagonistic attitude towards the Matice Česká came to a head as a result of the Revolution of 1848–49. The activities of the Matice Česká were subject to an ostentatious display of police supervision; its key personalities were ousted, especially František Palacký, who continued to promote the publication of a Czech encyclopaedia, thus continuing his original project from the early 1830s. After the Revolution of 1848–49 he remained keen on this fundamental academic and social endeavor and saw it as an opportunity to offer academic work to those who could not find self-realization due to the changed and oppressive social circumstances. However, it is not certain whether the Czech academic community would have been able to undertake such a task in the early 1850s. However, their preparatory work was not wasted; it was used ten years later by the enterprising publisher Ignác Leopold Kober, who purchased this material and, in cooperation with the politician František Ladislav Rieger, realized this project between 1860–74 as *Riegrův slovník naučný* (The Rieger Educational Encyclopaedia).

The activity of the Matice Česká was also paralysed by the refusal of the authorities for several years to approve its Code of Rules, a document fundamental for the normal functioning of any institution. In this connection the authorities created complications for the Matice Česká; they hindered its activities and impacted adversely on its public appeal. At this time, the historian Václav Vladivoj Tomek, who acted as Secretary of the Matice Česká from 1854, proved to be a very influential figure. The position of the Matice Česká stabilized at the beginning of the 1860s. The Code of Rules, finally approved in 1862, enabled its normal functioning and also specified its relationship with the Museum.

The *Památník na oslavu stých narozenin Františka Palackého* (Album Celebrating the Hundredth Anniversary of the Birth of František Palacký), published in 1898, was in effect a manifesto. It was issued in cooperation with the Czech Academy of Sciences and Art and the Royal Czech Society of Sciences.

After the foundation of the independent Czechoslovak Republic in 1918 the Matice Česká also began to have access to state grants. When celebrating the hundredth anniversary of its foundation (1931), President T.G. Masaryk recognized its significant achievements by attending a festive assembly in the Pantheon, the heart of the historical building of the National Museum. A wide range of institutions from both home and abroad and many important personalities from political and cultural life took this occasion to convey their congratulations as well.

6 The Matice Česká and Its Main Publishing Projects

In the hundred years of its existence the Matice published one hundred ninety-four titles from all the scientific disciplines and popular manuals as well. It launched its publishing activities with very ambitious projects, and published seminal works of contemporary Czech science, such as Josef Jungmann's *Slovník česko-německý* (Czech-German Dictionary, 1835–39), and Pavel Josef Šafařík's *Slovanské starožitnosti* (Slavonic Antiquities, 1837). It gradually published in the Czech language the fundamental work of modern Czech historiography, František Palacký's *Dějiny národu českého v Čechách a v Moravě* (The History of the Czech Nation in Bohemia and Moravia, 1848–76).

The Matice Česká also contributed to the process of solving academic and scientific problems which continue to be topical and under consideration to the present day: for example, is it possible to promote literary creativity by running competitions? Karel Havlíček, the most respected journalist of his time, called attention to contemporary problems in Czech fiction through his critique of Josef Kajetán Tyl's work *Poslední Čech* (The Last Czech), which was well regarded and was awarded a prize in a Matice Česká competition in 1844. The Matice Česká also discussed the need for scientific criticism of the highest quality, both in terms of the proces of writing reviews and literary criticism in general. František Palacký and Pavel Josef Šafařík also joined this discussion as early as the mid-1840s. It became clear even then that no competition, no appeal to reviewers to discharge their duties properly, and even no amounts of honoraria for reviews could guarantee the emergence of high-quality work. Such work had to be written, as is still the case, from one's own convictions, which needed time to mature.

Following a re-assessment of financially costly projects dating to the first years of its existence, which came to be reflected in the diminishing public interest in paid membership, the Matice Česká decided to accommodate the reading tastes of its membership and establish specialized editorial series.

Following a decision in 1841, four such series were to be established, yet not all of them were fully realized. The *Novočeská bibliotéka* (New-Czech Library, 1841–1937, 52 vols.), designed for the publication of scientific literature and fiction, lasted the longest. The *Staročeská bibliotéka* (Old-Czech Library, 1841–80, 5 vols.) published literary documents from before the seventeenth century. The *Bibliotheca of Classics Old and New* in Czech translation did not materialize to any great extent; translations were published, but without mentioning the name of the planned series. The *Home Bibliotheca* was originally destined for the popular sciences and moral educational works, but it was converted into the *Malá encyklopedie nauk* (Little Encyclopaedia of Science, 1842–53, 11 vols.) and also served educational purposes, with maps also published within its scope. Translations of William Shakespeare's works within the framework of the *Dramatická díla Williama Shakespeara* (The Dramatic Works of William Shakespeare, 1856–72, 36 vols.) formed an independent series. Some time later, there emerged a library of *Památky staré literatury české* (Literary Documents of the Old Czech Literature, 1876–90, 10 vols.) in which works of Czech literature prior to the eighteenth century were published.

The Matice Česká also published literary works from its very beginnings, yet apart from certain exceptions, such as František Ladislav Čelakovský's *Spisů básnických knihy šestery* (A Collection of Poems in Six Volumes, 1847), no contemporary novels or poems were published. However, the Matice contributed greatly to literary historical research through a range of synoptic works, starting with Jungmann's *Slovesnost* (Verbal Art, second expanded edition, 1845) and including *Výbor z literatury české* (An Anthology of Czech Literature; 1868, etc.), edited by Karel Jaromír Erben. The Matice Česká also published (especially in its early years) a number of practical handbooks that were much in demand by readers, for example, Jindřich Felix Paulický's *Domácí lékař aneb Kniha o šetření zdraví* (House Doctor, or the Book on Staying Healthy, 1833), or František Pixa's *Klíč štěpařský* (Keys to Plant Grafting, 1848).

For a number of years the *Malá encyklopedie nauk* (Little Encyclopaedia of Science) published by the Matice Česká came to stand in for the as yet unrealized project of a Czech encyclopaedia. Works which embodied the contemporary state of scientific research in various disciplines were published within its framework: for example, V.V. Tomek's *Krátký všeobecný dějepis* (A Brief General History, 1842); *Děje země české* (Events in the Czech Lands, 1843); *Děje mocnářství rakouského* (Events in the Austrian Empire, 1845); Václav Staněk, *Přírodopis prostonárodní* (A Simple National Natural History, 1854); Karel Ferdinand Hyna, *Dušesloví zkušebné* (Soul Testing—or in current terminology, Psychology, 1844); Karel Vladivoj Zap, *Všeobecný zeměpis* I–IV (General Geography I–IV, 1846–51); František Matouš Klácel, *Dobrověda* (The Science of Good Deeds, 1847); or Filip Stanislav Kodym, *Naučení o živlech* (Lessons on the Elements,

THE MATICE ČESKÁ

Matice, maps were also published: *Zeměpisný atlas* 1849), etc. Thanks to the *pramenův a pomůcek* (A Geographical Atlas of the Most Recent podle nejnov*ějších* rces and Tools, 1842) and *Malý příruční atlas všech částí země* cent W*ajo*ncise Atlas of All Parts of the Land, comprising 27 sheets, 1846).

(A s*im*ly the Matice Česká also published scientific works within the framework of its other editorial series at the beginning of its activities, for example the works of Josef Smetana, *Silozpyt čili fysika* (Silozpyt, or Physics, 1842); or Antonín Marek's *Základní filosofie: Logika: Metafysika* (Fundamental Philosophy: Logics: Metaphysics, 1844); or Josef Svatopluk Presl, *Počátkové rostlinosloví* (Initial Plant Terminology, 1848), which appeared in the New Czech Bibliotheca.

In the following period the Matice Česká presented fundamental surveys of progressively developing scientific disciplines (chemistry, geology, technology, etc.). Between the years 1855–1901, Vladivoj Tomek's twelve-volume *Dějepis města Prahy* (History of the City of Prague) was published. The Matice Česká promoted the development and popularization of Czech science as the years went by; after the founding of the Czech University (1882), it also focused editorially on scientific literature which was accessible both in terms of language and style.

7 The Matice Česká: Guardian of the Language

The Matice Česká pledged from its very beginnings to promote the quality of the written language and to develop it organically. In this sense, the Matice could consider the *Slovník česko-německý* (Czech-German Dictionary, 1835–39) as the central pillar of all its activities. This work was published under the direction of Josef Jungmann and was the crowning result of an entire generation of long-term research in the language. However, it was not possible to implement a conversational Czech dictionary as envisaged by František Palacký and František Ladislav Čelakovský, as this was seen as a rather too forceful expression of Czechness. Thanks to the Matice Česká, another theoretical and comparative linguistic work appeared, namely František Ladislav Čelakovský's *Čtení o srovnávací mluvnici slovanské na universitě Pražské* (Readings on a Comparative Slavonic Grammar at Prague University, 1853). Based on Jungmann's proposal, long-term pre-publication work on *Brus jazyka českého* (The Purification of the Czech Language, 1877) was also undertaken.

In the early 1840s the Matice Česká was even involved in complicated discussions on Czech spelling. Ever since the earliest days of its existence the Matice Česká was confronted with the dogmatic suggestions of the language 'purists.' According to these zealous defenders of the language, the Matice Česká should assume the role of an arbiter of proper linguistic standards not only in its own publications, but to supervise, according to their demands, the standard of the language in which other journals were to be published.

In its work *Hlasové o potřebě jednoty spisovného jazyka* (Voices for the Unity of Literary Language), the Matice Česká also responded to later developments in Slovakia, i.e., to the split of the Slovak language away from the commonly used language that was initiated by the circle of Ludovít Štúr. At that time (from February to May 1845) the Matice Česká rapidly prepared a publication funded by one of the founding members, Prince Kinsky, which contained thirty-three statements by Czech, Moravian, and Slovak writers on the Czech language and the close literary links between Czechs and Slovaks. This publication (five thousand copies) was to be distributed primarily in Slovakia. However, its reception and especially its impact were not conclusive.

Through the publication of many academic works (on natural science, philosophy, physics, etc.) the Matice Česká played an important role in the process of establishing relevant terminologies for these individual disciplines. Although these works might not by themselves have become a foundation or served as turning-points in scientific research, they summarized contemporary developments and also documented the current degree of Czech language development. They gave witness to the 'encroachment' into areas where the Czech language could gradually come into its own.

By 1832 the Matice Česká wholeheartedly embraced the idea of promoting a greater use of the Czech language in public life, especially in schools. They published a memorandum whose authors (František Palacký, Josef Jungmann, and Karel Vinařický) also attempted to advocate a wider use of Czech in schools by arguing for the need to improve instruction in the German language, since in their view, pupils who did not achieve competence in their mother tongue faced difficulties in mastering other languages, and the whole process led in its consequences to intellectual and moral decline. The authors of this Memorandum also formulated demands and justifications for why the Czech language should be taught at secondary schools, namely at grammar schools in German regions (referring here to positive experiences in the town of Cheb). However, the response of the authorities to the Memorandum was slow in the years to come—and the proposal ultimately failed. Discussions on the use of Czech in higher education were held from 1845 onwards. Even the future Minister of Culture and Education, Count Leo Thun, supported these efforts.

At the time of the revolutionary changes in 1848–49 the Matice Česká also attempted to introduce Czech as a civic and municipal language. As many legislative changes were taking place, the need to improve the quality of legal terminology was felt acutely, and members of the Matice Česká (namely Pavel Josef Šafařík, Karel Jaromír Erben, Václav Vladivoj Tomek, Josef Jireček, etc.) participated in this revision and expansion of its scope. A similar involvement was expected with regard to personnel appointments to a potentially relevant commission for the preparation of specialist terminology for secondary schools, should this be required. The Matice Česká assisted secondary schools in other ways as well, for example, by offering them a cash discount when purchasing relevant Matice publications for school use during the revolutionary changes of 1848–49.

8   The Matice Česká as a Mediator between Past and Present

The Matice Česká mediated the legacy of the past to the present (and future) in several ways. The publication of an Old-Czech literary document, the legal work of Viktorin Kornel of Všehrdy (1841) was an important milestone which aroused interest not only in Old-Czech law but also in Old-Czech legal terminology. The Matice Česká, in close cooperation with the Museum, played an important role in collecting and preserving valuable manuscripts for future generations. Where it was not possible to obtain an actual manuscript, the Matice Česká strove to lay its hands on a good-quality copy. As early as 1844 a physician, Josef Podlipský, transcribed a manuscript from the Viennese Library which included a biography of Charles IV; another physician, Josef Čejka, arranged for the transcription of Rahses' rare book on early medicine. The Matice Česká also acquired the manuscripts of the Czech medieval philosopher Tomáš Štítný, for example; and thanks to Václav Hanka, a librarian, the Library of the National Museum purchased a very valuable medieval Czech bible. The Matice Česká also published ancient literary documents; in addition to Kornel's work, it also made accessible many other primary sources and Old-Czech documents in the following decades (despite problems with the censorship of J.A. Komenský's work, for example). The Matice Česká, in cooperation with other institutions, published or co-published useful bibliographical handbooks.

In addition, the Matice Česká became a very important center which mediated access to Old Slavonic relics. In December 1851, at the request of Pavel Josef Šafařík it purchased a typeset of Glagolitic letters which were unavailable in a similar quality anywhere else in Europe. As a result, the Matice was able to publish a unique work, *Památky hlaholského písemnictví* (Literary Documents of Glagolitic Literature, 1853). Still, František Palacký's *Dějiny národu českého v Čechách a v Moravě* (The History of the Czech Nation in Bohemia and Moravia) became its seminal historiographical undertaking. This work became not only the pillar of modern Czech historiography but also a contemporary inspiration for works in all genres, including belles-lettres.

9 The Matice Česká as a Mediator of Cultural Values

The Matice Česká mediated and interpreted contemporary knowledge by publishing scientific works and also the *Journal of the National Museum*, thè earliest Czech scientific journal, which appeared in Czech and German from 1827. Thanks to its being published by the Matice Česká from 1832, its continued existence was preserved despite economic problems. The *Journal* became the mouthpiece of contemporary Czech science not only for its subscribers but also for a wider circle of people who could borrow copies. Evidence of this practice can be found in many comments in contemporary correspondence. In addition to this *Journal*, from 1853 the Matice Česká published a natural history journal *Živa* (Alive) thanks to Jan Evangelista Purkyně's initiative, and from 1855 *Památky archeologické a místopisné* (Memorials Archeological and Topographical), edited by Karel Vladislav Zap. The publication of scientific journals in the 1850s—which was rather difficult for the Matice Česká economically—also became a topic of discussions on the very importance of journals for the scientific community between the historian Václav Vladivoj Tomek in Prague and the literary historian and civil servant Josef Jireček and his brother Hermenegild, also a civil servant and legal historian. In a letter dated 13 November 1860, Tomek rejected the proposal by the Jireček brothers that the Matice Česká should give up its journals, arguing that a private publisher could never adequately sponsor a narrowly specialized scientific work, not to mention the amount of remuneration offered. In his appeal he emphasized that a scientific journal caring for successive generations should be published under one 'umbrella' so that it might be readily and reliably accessible to the interested parties, and so that the results of research should not be scattered in years to come amongst a number of individual titles dependent on current economic opportunities and the strategies of private firms. He concluded his apology with the following words: "I am of the opinion that the Museum journals should continue as before, as long as this remains possible. How long it might be, only the future will show …" (Magdaléna Pokorná et al., eds. *Spoléhámť se docela na zkušené přátelství Vaše…: Vzájemná korespondence Josefa Jirečka a Václava Vladivoje Tomka z let 1858–1862*, translation by author).

Apart from the above-mentioned periodicals, a narrowly specialized *Sborník vědecký Muzea království českého* (Scientific Proceedings of the Museum of the Czech Kingdom) was founded in 1868. It appeared in two series:

one philosophical-philological-historical (from 1868) and the other natural-scientific (which took over the role of the journal *Živa*).

Scientific institutions would traditionally donate gifts and exchange publications in the course of their activities, and the Matice Česká was no exception. As early as 1844 its protocols mention a shipment of books to a Czech regiment in Mainz. The Matice donated its books to the library of the Imperial Hospital in Vienna in 1846, and afterwards to the library of the Military Hospital in Prague and to the Evangelical Theological Institute in Vienna. It was a matter of course that the Matice should send its publications to other institutions in Vienna and Prague.

In addition to these donations, the Matice Česká was actively involved in the exchange of publications. Thanks to this, on the one hand the Matice made itself known to its partners, while on the other hand it received additional books for the Museum Library. The first official discussions on the exchange of publications with the Munich Royal Academy took place in 1846 upon Palacký's initiative. In 1848 exchanges started with the Matica of the Lusatian Serbs/Sorbs, the University of Moscow, and the Illyrian Matica in Zagreb (1851). Further exchanges took place with other institutions: with the Matica in Kiev and the Archeological Association in St. Petersburg, alongside domestic institutions, for example from Brno (1850). In 1851 exchange links were forged with the USA (Washington) and with Denmark (Copenhagen). Thus, the Matice Česká succeeded, through its efforts, in becoming a considered and respected cultural partner abroad, which was vitally important for a nation without its own nation-state.

The Matice Česká also played an exceptional role in the history of Czech translation. In 1843 it published John Milton's *Paradise Lost* for a second time, this time in Josef Jungmann's translation. It also published translations of the works of antiquity (Aeschylus, Aristophanes, Aristotle, Plato, Sophocles, Terence, Virgil, and Homer's *Odyssey*). In 1847, with reference to the wording of its Code of Rules, the Matice declined a proposal submitted by the Union for the Promotion of Industry in the Czech Lands (*Jednoty pro povzbuzení průmyslu v Čechách*) to publish translations from German on economic themes. František Palacký's suggestion that the Matice Česká should publish translations of important historical works did not materialize either, but his proposal for the translation of foreign travel journals succeeded. At first, only French travel journals were under consideration, yet Josef Jungmann expanded the Palacký proposal by recommending the publication of early Czech travelogues (and the work of Kryštof Harant of Polžice was published).

However, it was pivotal for Czech literature and culture that the Matice Česká began to publish William Shakespeare's works from the 1840s thanks to the efforts of Ladislav Čelakovský, Josef Čejka, František Doucha, Josef Jiří Kolár, and particularly Jakub Malý.

10 The Matice Česká after the 1860s

From the 1860s onward, a period of gradual political relaxation and of the undoubted economic and social rise of the Czech nation, the Matice Česká had to learn to live with powerful competition, including that of independent publishers. It continued the publication of the *Museum Journal*, one of the most crucial periodicals for Czech science. On the occasion of its fiftieth anniversary in 1881, the Matice Česká published its own biography from the pen of Karel Tieftrunk. From 1897 onwards, the Matice made its name also through its cooperation with another prestigious institution, the Czech Academy of Arts and Sciences, which involved, for example, the principal works of an important historian, Zikmund Winter: *O životě a vysokých školách pražských, knihy dvoje* (On Life and Schools of Higher Learning in Prague, in Two Books, 1899); *Kulturní obraz XV. a XVI. Století* (A Cultural Image of the 15th and 16th Centuries, 1899); *Život a učení na partikulárních školách v Čechách v XV. a XVI. století* (Life and Teaching at Particular Schools in the Czech Lands in the 15th and the 16th Centuries, 1901); *Kulturně historický obraz* (A Cultural Historical Picture, 1901); *Dějiny řemesel a obchodu v Čechách ve XIV. a XV. Století* (The History of Crafts and Trade in the Czech Lands in the 14th and 15th Centuries, 1906); and *Český průmysl a obchod v XVI. Věku* (Czech Industry and Trade in the 16th Century, 1913). This Jubilee also provided an opportunity for the Matice Česká to commission Jaroslav Prokeš to research and assess its activities since the 1848 Revolution. At that time Antonín Grund also published a list of works published by the Matice: *Sto let Matice české* (One Hundred Years of the Matice Česká, 1931).

Since that time the relationship between the Matice Česká and the Hapsburg monarchy remained unchanged until the birth of the new Czechoslovak state on 28 October 1918.

11 The Matice Česká during the Second World War and under Socialism

The Nazi occupation paralysed the activities of the Matice Česká, which shared the fate of other scientific and enlightenment institutions. Its state subsidy was withdrawn, and a ban on the publication of the *Museum Journal* was instituted (from 1941 onwards). To a certain extent the Matice was able to implement its revived publishing intentions after the liberation of the Republic in 1945, yet not until 1949 were two new Bibliothecas established—*Naše minulost* (Our Past) and *Příroda a věda* (Nature and Science)—and the Bibliotheca *Památky staré literatury české* (Literary Documents of the Old Czech Literature) was restored.

The activity of the Matice Česká following the communist coup d'état in February 1948 was influenced by property rights relations concerning the National Museum. The National Museum was nationalized on 1 January 1949. The Society of the Friends of the National Museum (of which the Matice Česká was a part) was deprived of the support of this institution, which it had held since the very beginning and thanks to which it had managed for one hundred twenty-even years. The Society of the Friends of the National Museum continued to exist, but it was only tolerated and was forced to collaborate in accordance with the political and ideological priorities of the management of the National Museum. In 1949, due to new legislation, the Matice Česká lost its publishing rights; it was henceforth only allowed to hold lectures. In this way, at least it could strive to remain an intermediary between the National Museum and the public.

A short-term resumption of its activities in 1968, when the members of the Matice Česká included Václav Havel, Ladislav Hejdánek, etc., was soon frozen by the beginning of the new political order following the occupation of Czechoslovakia by the armies of the Warsaw Pact countries (1968). The Matice Česká was able to survive as a mere Division of the Society of the Friends of the National Museum and through its close cooperation with the Library of the National Museum. At that time it focused its activities on the organization of lectures on literary-scientific topics and librarianship.

The activities of the Matice Česká were not influenced by the division of Czechoslovakia into the Czech and the Slovak Republics in 1993. In Slovakia there was an independent Slovak institution (the *Matica slovenská*), but its activities and its role in society were quite different.

12   The Matice Česká Today

The activities of the Matice Česká were restored once again in 1990, this time as a Division of the Society of the National Museum. A lack of financial means limited its *Magdaléna* publishing projects, and the publication of books was only resumed in 2005: Josef Pekař's *František Palacký* (2005); Věra Brožová's *Karafiátovi Broučci v české kultuře* (Karafiat's Fireflies in Czech Culture, 2011); and the most recent book, Lumobír Sršeň's remarkable *Nevšední příběhy portrétů* (Tales of Unique Personalities, 2011). Another project of the Matice Česká currently under way is *Čeští spisovatelé v regionech České republiky* (Czech Writers in the Regions of the Czech Republic).

Bibliography

Adam, Robert, Jaroslava Janáčková, Magdaléna Pokorná, Lucie Saicová Římalová, and Stanislav Wimmer (eds.). *Božena Němcová: Korespondence* IV. Prague: Nakladatelství Lidové noviny, 2007.

Grund, Antonín. *Sto let Matice české*. Prague: Matice česká, 1931.

Hanuš, Josef. *Národní muzeum a naše obrození I.–II.* Prague: Nákl. Národního musea, 1921, 1923.

Hlaváčková, Ludmila. "K účasti lékařů v našem národním obrození (Lékaři v České Matici v letech 1831–1849)," *Farmakoterapeutické zprávy* 3:15 (1969), 227–29.

Hroch, Miroslav. *Die Vorkämpfer der nationalen Bewegung bei den kleinen völkern Europas: eine vergleichende Analyse zur gesellschaftlichen Schichtung der patriotischen Gruppen*. Acta Universitatis Carolinae Philosophica et Historica, 24. Prague: Universita Karlova, 1968.

Hroch, Miroslav. *Na prahu národní existence: Touha a skutečnost*. Prague: Mladá fronta, 1999.

Hroch, Miroslav. *Social Preconditions of National Revival in Europe: A Comparative Analysis of Patriotic Groups among the Smaller European Nations*. Cambridge: Cambridge University Press, 1985.

Kořalka, Jiří. *František Palacký (1798–1876): Der Historiker der Tschechen im österreichischen Vielvölkerstaat*. Wien: Verlag der österreichischen Akademie der Wissenschaften, 2007.

[Kusáková, Lenka]. "Matice česká." In Vladimír Forst, ed., *Lexikon české literatury: Osobnosti, díla, instituce*, 3/I M–O. Prague: Academia, 2000. 165–169.

Muchka, Pavel, Ivana Mudrová, Jiří Kořalka, Richard Šípek, Eva Ryšavá, Josef Johanides, Magdaléna Pokorná, and Martin Kučera. *Informační panely v regionech České republiky*. In: *Sborník Národního muzea v Praze*. Řada C—Literární historie. Praha: Národní muzeum 54, č. 1–4 (2009), 50–56.

Pokorná, Magdaléna, et al., eds. *Spoléhámť se docela na zkušené přátelství Vaše…: Vzájemná korespondence Josefa Jirečka a Václava Vladivoje Tomka z let 1858–1862*. Prague: Academia, 2008.

Prokeš, Jaroslav. *Z těžké doby Matice české, 1850–1860 (K stoletému výročí založení Matice české)*. Prague: Časopis Národního musea 105, 1931.

Sklenář, Karel. *Obraz vlasti: Příběh Národního muzea*. Prague: Paseka, 2001.

Sršeň, Lubomír. "Voják a kněz: dvě tváře Josefa Šmidingra: Dějiny a současnost," *Kulturně historická revue* 32:5 (2010), 12.

Svejkovský, František. "Palackého a Šafaříkův projev z roku 1845 k otázkám kritiky na zasedání Matice české," *Sborník Národního muzea v Praze*, Series C, No. 5 (1963), 225–31.

Tieftrunk, Karel. *Dějiny Matice české*. Prague: V Komissí u Františka Řivnáče, 1881.

CHAPTER 3

The Slovak Matica, Its Precursors and Its Legacy

Benjamin Bossaert and Dagmar Kročanová

The idea of establishing a Slovak *matica* first appeared in the 1820s, soon after the Serbian Matica was founded, and was revived in the 1830s, with the rise of the Czech Matica.[1] It was Pavol Jozef Šafárik who mentioned the possibility of establishing a Slovak *matica* in a letter to Ján Kollár and Martin Hattala in 1827; while working in Novi Sad, he had noticed that a Serbian Matica was founded there and functioned well. A decade later, in the periodical *Hronka*, Karol Kuzmány described how the institution could be organized. In 1838, Alexander Boleslavín Vrchovský wrote about the need for a Slovak *matica* in a letter to the association promoting the (Czecho)slovak language.[2] However, no practical steps were taken in this period. In the 1830s and 1840s, Slovaks needed first to resolve religious differences and reach a collaboration between Catholics and Protestants,[3] to resolve the issue of whether to use Czech or vernacular Slovak as a literary language,[4] and to gain political experience through negotiating with the authorities in Vienna and Pest for the acknowledgment of Slovaks as a separate nation.[5] This dynamic was closely related to the creation of a Slovak

---

1 The co-authors of this chapter divided the work as follows: the Introduction was written jointly, Part 1 is by Benjamin Bossaert, and Part 2 is by Dagmar Kročanová.
2 Winkler, Eliáš, *et al.*, 32–33.
3 This agreement was officially reached in 1847.
4 A Catholic priest, Anton Bernolák, had prepared a Slovak grammar (in Latin) already in the 1780s, but only a handful of the Catholic intelligentsia used it. Bernolák's norm for Standard Slovak was based on Western Slovak dialects and was therefore quite close to the Czech language, which was traditionally used as a literary language, especially among Slovak Protestants. In 1843, Ľudovít Štúr (himself a Protestant) introduced a new norm for the Slovak language that was based on Central Slovak dialects, and thus quite different from Czech. This innovation was perceived as a dangerous 'schism.' The opponents of Štúr's Slovak, led by Ján Kollár (also a Protestant), responded to Štúr's Slovak by introducing 'Old Slovak' (*staroslovenčina*), basically Czech with some regional varieties spoken in Slovakia. The language issue remained unresolved until 1852, when Martin Hattala (a Catholic) wrote a grammar based on Štúr's Slovak, with some minor alterations.
5 In 1848, the 'Requests of the Slovak Nation' (*Žiadosti slovenského národa*) were compiled and presented to the Hungarian diet. The 'Requests' included fourteen points concerning, among other things, Slovak autonomy, recognition of the Slovaks as an equal and independent nation, parliamentary seats for Slovaks, Slovak as an official language, Slovak flag and guards, freedom of the press, a general franchise, and liberation from the lieges.

identity, a long and often disturbed process which Peter Káša characterized as follows:

> The image of 'Slovakness' encompasses a codified signification of 'reciprocities' that determine and define the steps of national identification from within and without. One could thus say that the whole Slovak national movement consisted of tactical maneuvering by certain intellectuals, and the search for an optimal strategy in this labyrinth of reciprocities. This 'game of the nation,' which had not only a political but also an existential character, can be compared with a simultaneous chess party on five boards: the Pan-Slavonic, Czecho-Slovak, Slovak-Hungarian, Slovak-Austrian, and Slovak-Slovak (Protestants versus Catholics, moderates versus radicals/ revolutionaries).[6]

Outlining the context of the Slovak national movement requires us to focus on the geographical and sociological characteristics of the various movements. Research has shown a continuous interaction with the Habsburg and Hungarian authorities and with intellectuals situated in the bigger cities: in Vienna, Pest, Prešporok (the old name for Bratislava, the crowning city of the Hungarian kings and seat of the Hungarian parliament), and to a lesser extent in (Turčiansky Svätý) Martin. Sociologically speaking, there was a small base of intellectuals who considered themselves ethnic Slovaks; this consciousness gradually developed during the nineteenth century by creating greater and broader support for the idea of Slovak nationalism.

Language was a frequent issue in thoughts about how to develop a nation, a process that can be traced back to the eighteenth century. According to Stanislav J. Kirschbaum, the increasing use of the Slovak vernacular was enhanced by two important developments that gave impetus and substance to the Slovak national awakening: the *Patent of Tolerance* (1781) and other Josephinian reforms, and the spirit of the French Revolution.[7] Education in the vernacular was encouraged by the Emperor Joseph II, which meant that the spread of literacy was also an urgent issue; otherwise the spread of his ideas would be irrelevant.

Overviews of research on literary societies in the Slovak national movements can be found in the works of Libuša Franková (2000) and Elena Mannová (2006). Recent research on Ľudovít Štúr reveals that there was also another burgher initiative for national awakening in the form of the Hungarian

---

6   Cited in Vojtech, 83.
7   Kirschbaum, 89.

Casino movement.[8] In what follows, we try to situate these movements, societies, literary initiatives, and nation-building cultural activities within a broader context before turning towards the actual Slovak Matica.

By including its precursor institutions in our analysis, we can achieve an overview of notions of cultural nationalism throughout the nineteenth century. Framing the Slovak national movement shows that the conditions provided by the Habsburg authorities were unfavorable to the Slovak community's quest to develop fully a popular sense of the nation. In the course of events that eventually led to the foundation of the *Matica slovenská*, several precursor institutes, societies, reading clubs, and communities existed on Slovak soil, but they proved unsuccessful. However, they cannot be ignored altogether, since in hard times, during revolutionary years or years of hard oppression by the imperial or Hungarian authorities, they provided fertile conditions and initiated lobbying efforts which the *Matica* could later develop further.

1 The Precursors of the Slovak Matica

The first among these forerunners was the *Slovenské učené tovarišstvo* (Slovak Learned Society) founded in 1792 by the Catholic priest Anton Bernolák, together with other nation-developing initiatives and features of nationwide Catholic groupings. This society elicited a reaction from the Protestant intelligentsia, to be found within the Bratislava Protestant Lyceum, where Professor Juraj Palkovič founded the so-called *Česko-Slovanský ústav* (Czecho-Slavic Institute). A generation of promising Slovak students felt the urge to spread national thought throughout Slovakia. Their actions generated tensions among the Protestant intellectuals over the question of what was more likely to succeed: a policy of cultural and mutual Slavonic awareness, or building a more Slovak identity within the Hungarian framework? The former policy found an ardent supporter in the protestant pastor Ján Kollár, while the latter approach was supported by the followers of Ľudovít Štúr.

The academic background for all these discussions was provided by the Bratislava *Ústav reči a literatúry Česko-Slovenskej* (Institute for Czecho-Slovak Language and Literature, in the environment of the Protestant Lyceum from 1803 onwards). The most promising student was the later journalist, teacher, activist, politician, philologist, and revolutionary leader Ľudovít Štúr, who deserves special attention since he educated some of his students to found other

---

8 See Kowalská.

learning societies in other parts of Slovakia. He was also a founding member of *Tatrín* (Son of the Tatras, 1844), the first such cultural society to receive nationwide support. There was also the *Spolok milovníkov reci a literatúry Slovenskej* (Association of Lovers of Slovak Language and Literature), a society that functioned in Pest from 1834 onwards. These societies differed in their social stratifications, funding, activities, and organizational structures, but they influenced one another.

1.1 The Slovak Learned Society

At the instigation of Joseph II, a Catholic seminary was opened in 1784, and students there founded the *Societas excolendae linguae slavicae* (Society for the Cultivation of the Slavic Language), whose primary aim was to translate the Bible into the vernacular. For this purpose Anton Bernolák, a Catholic priest at this seminary, codified the Slovak language according to Western Slovak. This was the subject of his *Dissertatio philological-critica de litteris slavorum* (A Philologico-Critical Dissertation on the Letters of the Slavs) and a *Grammatica Slavica*. The Bratislava seminary closed in 1790, but Bernolák and his followers founded the *Slovenské učené tovarišstvo* (Slovak Learned Society), which was needed to help them spread the new codification of their Slovak language. This led to reactions from some Protestant intellectuals in Bratislava.[9]

The *Slovenské učené tovarišstvo* wanted to spread the new codified language by printing books. The organization had two kinds of memberships: one for authors and one for subscribers. The first head of the society was Bernolák; Juraj Fándly was the comptroller or secretary, and the treasurer was Václav Jelínek. The collectors of contributions for the publication of the society's books worked as intermediaries in the organizational structure. This society was different from others because it had branches all over Slovakia: in Nitra, Velké Rovne, Banská Bystrica, Solivar, Jágr, and Rožňava. The seat was in Trnava, which was often considered the cultural capital of the Roman Catholic Slovaks, especially when the archbishop of Esztergom fled there to avoid the dangerous Turkish sieges. In Bernolák's time, the episcopal seat was already back in Esztergom, but Trnava remained an important cultural center.

According to a document from 1792, the society was supposed to print five hundred copies of each book, one hundred of which would be for the authors instead of an honorarium. In its nine years of existence, the *Slovenské učené tovarišstvo* published eleven books in twenty volumes: eleven treated a religious theme, five addressed economic issues, and one was a work of history.

---

9   Kirschbaum, 89; Franková, 24–26.

They were all by five Slovak authors and translators. Juraj Fándly, for example, wrote works about beekeeping and a history of Slovakia, the former meant to educate the farmers and the lower classes, and the latter aimed at the educated classes. An article from 1795 mentions that the society intended to broaden its goals. Although the goal was to spread Bernolák's codified language, five of the volumes were still published in Latin. This happened, of course, because the society's main public consisted of Catholic scholars.

Analysis of the membership of the *Slovenské učené tovarišstvo* shows the dominance of the Catholic clergy: out of five hundred eighty members, more than half were Catholic priests, and 16% were theologians. One-fifth of the membership had a civil profession: about fifty of them were tradesmen and craftsmen, twenty-three were local authority clerks, and others were professors, teachers, doctors, notaries, technical clerks, and six squires. Only one member of this overwhelmingly Catholic society was a Protestant pastor.[10] The branches in Trnava and Velké Rovne counted the most secular members. Two persons were of paramount significance: Alexander Cardinal Rudnay, the Slovak-born and Slovak-speaking archbishop of Ostrihom (in Hungarian: Esztergom) provided financial support for the publication of Bernolák's dictionary; and another priest and professor of theology, Canon Jur or Juraj Palkovič, gave financial support to the promising priest and poet Ján Hollý (his former student at the seminary in Bratislava) to publish his poems. Thus Hollý, the first Slovak poet, was raised within the cradle of the *Slovenské učené tovarišstvo*, using Bernolák's language for literature.

Like other societies, the Slovak Learned Society faced the pressure of censorship. All its editing and publishing activities were under the supervision of the Hungarian press censorship. Within the society, Anton Bernolák himself fulfilled the role of the censor.

Despite the best efforts of the Society, Bernolák and his fellow supporters of Slovak codification were unsuccessful. The Society's work was hampered by Slovakia's geography, and a significant part of the intelligentsia, namely the Protestant clergy, wished to continue writing in Biblical Czech.[11] The Slovak intelligentsia remained linguistically divided, and this issue needed first to be resolved. The Society ceased to exist shortly after Bernolák's death, but a second generation of Catholic intellectuals sought a compromise with the Protestants, who were gaining importance within the national movement.

---

10   Mannová, 78.
11   Mannová, 75–81; Kirschbaum, 93–94.

1.2 *The Protestants and Their Societies in the Early Nineteenth Century*
The activities of Bernolák's supporters, especially their efforts to revive and strengthen the Slovaks culturally, were also supported by several Protestant scholars, such as Štefan Leška and Ján Vyskydenský, who showed a lively sympathy for the domestic vernacular. However, the Protestant intellectuals were always more closely linked to their Czech counterparts, in keeping with a tradition that started with the coming of the Czech Brethren to the Slovak-Hungarian lands. In their liturgy, they continued to use the Czech language taken from the *Králická biblie*, a kind of Bible Czech enriched with Slovakisms.

By the end of the eighteenth century the Protestants had failed to develop a center of organization. As early as 1783, Juray Ribay tried to set up together with superintendent Martin Hamaliar a *Spoločnosť slovensko-česká* (Slovak-Czech Society) with a library and a publishing and printing house, but without success. Ribay had already designed an organizational structure for the society and aimed to spread the use of Czech in Slovakia to promote historical studies and to collect books, manuscripts, archive materials, and other sources of Slovak history. It was, however, the Protestant professor Juraj Palkovič (not to be confused with his Catholic namesake) and Bohuslav Tablic who worked out these ideas by creating an *Ústav reči a literatúry česko-slovenskej* (Institute for Czecho-Slovak Language and Literature) together with two other institutions: the *Slovenská učená spoločnosť* (Slovak Learning Society) and a *Katedra reči a literatúry česko-slovenskej* (Department of Czecho-Slovak Language and Literature) in Bratislava. By 1803, only the *Katedra* had been founded, with Palkovič as chairholder.[12]

The Protestant activity of spreading literature was not limited to the capital; in 1810, Bohuslav Tablic founded his *Učená spoločnosť banského okolia* (Learning Society of the Mining Region) in Banská Štiavnica, and between 1810 and 1832 Jan Fejes managed the *Učená spoločnosť Malohontská* (Malohont Learning Society) in Nižný Skalnik. The Banská Štiavnica society was able to support a chair of Biblical Czech in the mining town, whereas the Malohont society was able to publish the *Solennia Bibliothecae Kishontanae* (Yearbook of the Kishont Regional Library), a general-interest publication that welcomed contributions in Latin, Hungarian, Czech, and German.

In Bratislava, the Protestant intellectuals provided a useful debating culture within an academic environment. It was here that the young Ján Kollár studied and met the Czech intellectual František Palacký. Later on, Kollár developed further his ideas about a Czech-Slovak and even a Slavonic reciprocity, a theory

---

12   Kirschbaum, 95; Franková, 25.

about the mutual and beneficial interaction of libraries, books, knowledge, and cultural exchange among the Slavonic nations. The ideas of Kollár proved to be very influential when he moved to Pest to work as a pastor for the Slovak community between 1819 and 1849.[13]

The second half of the 1820s witnessed an increasing number of joint initiatives from Protestants and Catholics in spreading literature and publishing books. Martin Hamuljak for example, a young Catholic supporter of the Bernolák movement, initiated a correspondence with the president of the *Učená spoločnosť banského okolia* in Banská Štiavnica and with Bohuslav Tablic; he also began to donate books to them. In Pest Hamuljak generated an impetus to unite the two confessional sides.

1.3 A Compromise Group in Pest: the Spolok milovníkov reči a literatúry Slovenskej

In the summer of 1826 in Pest, nation-uniting activities were launched with Martin Hamuljak's suggestion to start a *Slovanský čitateľský spolok* (Slovak Reading Club), and in 1829 also to establish in Pest or in Buda a *Slovanská knižnica* (Slavonic Library), but without success. Five years later, again on the initiative of Hamuljak, the *Spolok milovníkov reči a literatúry Slovenskej* (Association of Lovers of Slovak Language and Literature) was founded on 1 August 1834. Their aim was in the first place to 'promote the Slovak tongue and literature.' For member Anton Ottmayer, a Catholic, two goals were paramount: (1) to give the more educated people nourishment in their own language; and (2) to show the Hungarian public the capacities of the Slovaks. No political or social remarks appeared in the foundational by-laws of the Slovak society; however, there was a failed attempt in 1843 to change the original aims of the Society, which mentioned that they would focus more on improving people's lives in spiritual-confessional and economic ways.

The Society focused on publishing and editing. It produced four editions of an almanach called *Zora* (five hundred copies were printed of the first two editions) along with a volume of Ján Hollý's poems. The members debated about publishing a folk calendar and a journal of its own (1839), but these plans were never realized. There were also lively discussions in the Society about the language issue and literature. Contributions were anonymously peer-reviewed within the Society.

The organizational structure of the Society was based on a contract: each of the Society's ten divisions was expected to contribute a basic budget for

---

13   Kirschbaum, 95–96; Franková, 25–26.

publishing the yearbooks. The by-laws were formulated on the basis of this contract. The oldest member, Ján Kollár, had to become the President. Martin Hamuljak became secretary, and Martin Suchaň, whose house became the seat of the Society, was the treasurer. Each member had one vote, and in the case of economic or financial issues, voting rights were distributed according to the numbers of shares.

The membership of the *Spolok milovníkov reči a literatúry Slovenskej* was remarkably smaller than the *tovarišstvo*. Kollár and Suchaň, both Protestants, were supposed to symbolize the compromise character of the *Spolok*, but they left it after the first year, so that the *Spolok* consisted thereafter only of Catholic members. In 1840 there were twenty members, among them three university professors, nine clerks, and six lower and two higher clergymen.

Since the Catholics had the larger share in the Society, the higher Catholic clergy supported their ideas and contributed financially. A large part of the Esztergom Catholic hierarchy was of Slovak origin, and the Society provided them with publications in return for their support. The Society had at its disposition about 300–450 gulden.[14]

Unsurprisingly, the Slovak intelligentsia began to work together on Slovak soil as well; here the Protestant societies and the student clubs, consisting of groups of young educated Slovak intellectuals, played an important role.

1.4 *The Nation United on Slovak Territory: Protestant Initiatives*

From the second half of the 1830s, the Slovaks began to unite on the language issues, looking more and more for a compromise that would serve as a unifying factor in the national movement. The Bernolák movement and the Catholics supported the ideas of a younger generation of Protestants, who had first believed in a Czech-Slovak unity but then began to develop different views. Four centers of activity emerged. The most important was the Bratislava Lyceum, where at the *Katedra reči a literatúry česko-slovenskej* (Department of Czecho-Slovak Language and Literature) Professor Palkovič was succeeded by the younger Ľudovít Štúr. A *Spoločnosť česko-slovanská* (Czech-Slavonic Society) functioned from 1829 until 1837; and when the Hungarian authorities forbade all student organizations, they continued as the secret societies *Vzájomnosť* (Reciprocity, 1837–40) and the *Ústav slovanský* (Slavonic Institute, 1837–45). In Levoča, a student youth movement, the *Jednota mládeže slovenskej* (Union of Slavonic Youth) existed from 1845 on; furthermore students discussed language and literature issues at the Protestant lycea in Banská Štiavnica and Kežmarok.

---

14   Mannová, 75–83; Franková, 27.

The young Protestants did not formulate any political or economic programs but mainly studied literature and the issue of a unified language for the Slovaks. They sought cooperation with the Catholic seminary students in Trnava, Esztergom, and Spišské podhradie, as well as with intellectuals such as Hamuljak, of the Bernolák movement.[15]

In 1843, Ľudovít Štúr codified the language based on Central-Slovak dialects, but Ján Kollár, who still believed in a Czechoslovak language, heavily opposed it at that time; the Catholic wing, however, was able to find a compromise with Štúr. Eventually, the foundation of the literary society *Tatrín* put an end to the language issue and unified the Slovak intelligentsia for the first time.

1.5 The Founding of Tatrín

Tatrín (Son of the Tatras) was founded in 1844 in Liptovský Svätý Mikuláš. The first publication in Štúr's Slovak grammar was the almanach *Nitra* (1844), a collection of poems roughly based on traditional folk songs. The genre became very popular when Kollár and the members of the Pest society began collecting Central-Slovak folk songs.[16]

Tatrín considered itself as a *jednota milovníkov národa a života slovenského*, a unity of lovers of Slovak life and a Slovak nation, without regard for differences in class or religion. In the revised by-laws of 1846, Tatrín defined itself as a literary society designed to help the literary and industrial scholarship of the Slovak people in Hungary. This was the first time a literary society had formulated other than literary and educational aims in its by-laws.

The activities of Tatrín were mainly in publishing, but its members also had the task of sponsoring and educating. Five books were published in four years, along with five thousand copies of the *Žiadosti slovenského národa* (The Demands of the Slovak People), a political charter for the revolution of 1848. There were also projects for publishing manuals, textbooks, encyclopedias, and methods for Slovak schools, but these never materialized. Tatrín also sponsored students with scholarships and anti-alcohol societies, and it invested money in Sunday schools, libraries, and more.

The organization met regularly for general meetings, and meanwhile the Executive Board and the President carried on its business. Regional officials gathered the member contributions from collectors. New members had to be recommended by existing members. The President's vote was decisive, but his authoritarian power was limited in the adjusted by-laws of 1846.

---

15   Franková, 27–29.
16   Žigo, 133.

In its by-laws Tatrín proudly boasted of the interest of some six hunderd members, but by the time of its second meeting only seventy-seven were registered, together with one hundred twelve supporters. Most of them were Protestants, some were teachers, others were freelancers, and some were women. In 1845, two out of the nine members in the Executive Board were Catholic, but it was not until the meeting of Tatrín in Čachtice in 1847 that the Catholics showed a greater interest in joining Tatrín. The use of the Štúr-codification often made them reluctant to cooperate, and they were also dependent on their patrons, who disliked that the Society had no by-laws approved by the authorities. Each of the regular members paid five gulden every year; together with the supporters, Tatrín managed to collect yearly between five hundred and eight hundred gulden.

The Society had lots of problems with the Hungarian authorities. Tatrín's original by-laws were turned down after a report of the general censor's office, the directors in Košice and Prešporok, and the general inspector of the Protestant church. Slight changes in the by-laws, such as omitting the adjective 'Slovak' in 'supporting Slovak students,' or omitting the publication of methodologies, were rejected on the grounds that supporting or strengthening the Slavonic nation in Hungary and such attempts in the mother country were not in accord with the Constitution.[17]

Tatrín ceased to exist during the years of the Hungarian revolution of 1848–49. Several attempts to revive the Society failed after the revolution. Some intellectuals discussed the question of whether a new compromise, a society that would provide literary, publishing, literacy and educating facilities to the Slovaks, should be named *Matica* or *Tatrín*. Ctiboh Zoch, a supporter of Štúr, opined that it should be *Matica*, because this would remind members of having a mother in Slovak. After the revolutionary years the Slovak nation needed the feeling of belonging to a family, not to a mountain range of stones and dead material.[18] The first successful new Society would be the Slovak Matica (1863).

1.6   *Conclusions*

Comparing the main precursors of the Slovak Matica, we can conclude that the language issue, together with the confessional divide, strongly hampered the foundation of a nationally supported society that would be able to develop national thought, as was already the case among Serbs and Czechs. However, there was a lively network of correspondence among all the Slovak intellectuals.

---

17   Mannová, 75–81. More about the by-laws of Tatrín can be found in Polla, 9–33.
18   Polla, 41.

The initiative of forming a literary society was taken first by the Catholics, then by the Protestants, and sometimes they worked together. Some of them believed in support from the Czechs, while others favoured activities in Pest or within a Hungarian framework. The Hungarian authorities were reluctant to accept the foundation of several Slovak societies, which became more obvious with the arrival of the revolutionary years of 1848–49. As in the case of Tatrín, the societies generated more political demands as the revolutionary years drew nearer.

There are indications that the scope should be extended even beyond literary circles, taking the Casino movement into account. As Eva Kowalská's recent research has shown, the reports of the Slovak Casino in Modra, founded after the example of the big Casino in Prešporok, indicated some remarkable political activity. Whether this was only a coincidence needs further investigation. At first sight, it appears that the innocent meetings of the higher burgher classes also discussed cultural and political issues, which suggests that the Slovak community was growing more and more sensitive and open to the idea of building a whole nation.

2   The Slovak Matica (*Matica slovenská*) 1863–75

The Slovak Matica was founded fifteen years after the defeat of the Hungarian revolution, and four years before the Austro-Hungarian *Ausgleich*. It existed for twelve years.

Based on their experiences in the first half of the century, in June 1851 the Protestants Ján Kollár, Karol Kuzmány, Matej Štefko, Jonáš Záborský, and Daniel Lichard asked the authorities in Vienna for permission to advertise the Slovak Matica in the newspapers, and in November 1851 they submitted its preliminary by-laws.[19] However, their request was turned down in March 1852. Five years later, Ján Palárik, a Catholic living in Pest, took over the initiative of

---

19   They belonged to the 'Old Slovaks,' adherents of Czech as a literary language. The 'New Slovaks,' adherents of the new Standard Slovak, wished to revive their association *Tatrín* (1844–48). They argued that the *matica* should focus on Slavic reciprocity, whereas *Tatrín* should promote the economic and cultural development of Slovakia. The 'New Slovaks' ironically called the institution under discussion a 'Czech' *matica*, and emphasized that the Slovaks needed enlightenment and public education more than a scientific institution.

establishing a Slovak *matica*.[20] Unfortunately, the by-laws compiled at a meeting in Bratislava in 1857 have not been preserved. By the 1860s, the Austrian government was more amenable to the claims of various nations and ethnic groups within the monarchy, and the Slovak nationalists overcame the religious and language issues. At a national assembly in Turčiansky Svätý Martin held on 6–7 June 1861, a document known as the *Memorandum of the Slovak Nation* was adopted.[21] The *Memorandum* requested, among other claims,[22] that an association promoting Slovak cultural life—the Slovak Matica—be established.[23] To facilitate the process of setting up a Slovak *matica*, an Interim Committee was created with four members—two Protestants (Ján Francisci and Viliam Paulíny-Tóth) and two Catholics (Ján Gotčár and Ján Palárik)—all of them living at that time either in Pest or Buda. The committee prepared the first version of the by-laws, and Francisci submitted it to the Hungarian council in Buda on 1 August 1861. In October, the Hungarian council required that some paragraphs in the by-laws be amended.[24] In December, the Austrian Emperor Franz Joseph I received a Slovak delegation led by bishop Štefan Moyses.[25] The Emperor eventually approved the Slovak Matica on 21 August 1862. In October,

---

20 Others did not want to support a foundation of the Matica in Pest, since this was the heart of the Hungarian nationalist movement.

21 The minutes of this meeting were signed by 193 participants, which gives one an idea of the emerging nation. The Slovak population at this time was about three million, or at least this number was cited in a speech delivered by the first Vice-Chairman of the Slovak Matica at an assembly in 1868.

22 These claims included: recognizing Slovaks as a nation equal to other nations in Hungary; recognizing the Slovak language as a separate language equal to the other languages spoken in Hungary; recognizing Slovak territorial autonomy; introducing more Slovaks into the state administration, courts of law, and schools; and establishing a Slovak law academy, a department of Slovak language at the University of Pest, and state support for Slovak literary and cultural associations (yet to be founded).

23 At the same time, Catholics and Protestants tried to obtain permission for their respective religious associations: for *Spolok sv. Vojtecha* (the Association of St. Adalbert, established in 1870) and for *Spolok Komenského* (the Comenius Association, established in 1898).

24 For example, the word 'national' could not be used; instead of the 'Slovak National House,' the expression 'House of the Slovak Matica' was to be used in all documents.

25 The delegation submitted to the Emperor a document known as a *Prosbopis* (Plea), which was, in fact, very similar to the *Memorandum*. The Emperor promised to deal with the requests of Slovaks. This was considered an achievement, and Moyses was praised for his diplomatic success. Bishop Štefan Moyses had worked previously as a censor in Zagreb, and was one of the founders of the Illyrian Matica.

the Council in Buda required that additional changes be introduced into the by-laws,[26] but the document was finally approved on 23 October 1862.[27]

2.1   The Ambitions of the Slovak Matica

As Karol Rosenbaum writes, the Slovak Matica "was *that* which parliaments, governments, ministries, large prosperous organizations, and political parties were for other nations. Such an institution could only originate in a freedomless nation."[28] The Slovak Matica was designed as "a unity of lovers of the Slovak nation and life, and its goal is to awaken, spread, and strengthen the moral virtue and intellect of the members of the Slovak nation, to perform and promote Slovak literature and the arts, and in this way also to help enhance the material wealth of the Slovak nation."[29] It was not supposed to deal with political or religious agendas. Its activities centered around four areas: (1) publishing and distributing Slovak books and works of art; (2) discussing and researching literature and the arts, as well as moral and educational issues; (3) collecting

---

26   The period of service for Chairmen and Vice-Chairmen had to be altered, no regional branches were supposed to be established, and a state supervisor with the right to inspect all of the *matica*'s agenda was appointed. Yet another problem was the seat of the new *matica*. In the original proposal it was to be located in the town of Brezno, but some members of the Brezno municipality questioned the mayor's decision and eventually rejected it in a second round of voting. The negotiations in Brezno lasted from August 1862 until April 1863, and only when it was obvious that Brezno was not viable did the members of the Interim Committee of the Slovak Matica contact other towns. The municipality of Turčiansky Svätý Martin was in favor of hosting the *matica*, and this change was introduced into the by-laws. The problem with the *matica*'s seat reflects sociological facts: the Slovak intelligentsia was not only sparse but also mostly of rural background. In this sense, the rising Slovak nation was 'plebeian' and 'peasant': at this time, none of the larger towns and very few burghers would consider themselves 'Slovak.'

27   The entire text of the by-laws (all 36 paragraphs) dated 5 February 1862 can be found in Botto's *Dejiny Matice slovenskej (1863–1875)*. The approval of the Slovak Matica was announced in *Pešťbudínske vedomosti*. Very little is known about how this news was received among other Slavic nations. Winkler (47) mentions that the Czech paper *Hlas* (Voice) welcomed the Slovak Matica, whereas *Národní listy* (National Letters) criticized the Slovak submissiveness and loyalty to Vienna. A cordial response came from Serbia.

28   Rosenbaum, 15: " … *bola tým, čím pre iné národy boli snemy, vlády, ministerstvá, veľké prosperujúce organizácie a politické strany. Taká inštitúcia sa mohla zrodiť iba v neslobodnom národe.*" The emphasis on the word 'that' is mine.

29   "*Matica slovenská je jednota milovníkov národa a života slovenského a jej cieľ: v členoch slovenského národa mravnú a umnú vzdelanosť budiť, rozširovať a utvrdzovať, slovenskú literatúru a krásne umenia pestovať a podporovať, a tým i hmotný dobrobyt slovenského národa napomáhať a na jeho zveľadení pracovať*" (Winkler, 47); translation mine. Rosenbaum (17) notes that the *matica* was a unity of lovers of the Slovak *nation*, whereas previous associations, such as the *Spolok milovníkov reči a literatúry slovenskej* established in 1834, had united lovers of Slovak *language and literature*.

various artefacts (books, works of art, antiques, as well as objects related to natural sciences); and (4) supporting Slovak artists and scientists. The by-laws stated that the Matica would have a separate building, the Slovak National House, which would serve as an administrative center, library, and museum exposition as well as a facility for meetings.

The Slovak Matica was supposed to have a patron—a *mecene* (Maecenas)—but this position remained vacant since there were no suitable candidates.[30] There were four categories of membership: founders, regular members, supporters, and honorary members.[31] The administration consisted of the Chairman, two Vice-Chairmen, a Secretary, an Accountant, Legal Workers, and Curators of Collections. The committee included the Chairman, the Vice-Chairmen, the Secretary, and thirty members.[32] The Matica's capital (to be accumulated before any activity would start) was supposed to remain untouched; only the current account and interest could be used to cover operating costs. Founding and regular members were supposed to receive one copy of every Matica publication.

The period before the first assembly was dedicated to raising money for the Matica, recruiting members, and dealing with other administrative issues.[33] Ján Francisci acted as the Chair of the Interim Committee, Jozef Viktorin as the main treasurer, and Michal Chrástek as secretary, while others coordinated regional activities. Appeals in the newspapers, personal letters, and direct collections during visits to towns and villages were used to raise money. The list of contributors was regularly published in *Pešťbudínske vedomosti*. By the time

---

[30] The Slovaks lacked a nationally-oriented nobility or clergy. One of the possible candidates for the post of patron, Bishop Štefan Moyses, was appointed the first Chairman of the Slovak Matica.

[31] A founding member had to pay one hundred gulden, or twelve gulden every year for nine years. A regular member had to pay fifty gulden, or six gulden every year for ten years. Regular membership cost three gulden annually, with no further obligations. A supporter of the Slovak Matica either had to pay fifty kreuzer or to donate books, collections, etc. Someone who had made a significant contribution to Slovak national life could be approved as an honorary member at the Matica's annual meetings.

[32] Fifteen of them were founding members and fifteen were regular members. They were elected for three years. Every year, one-third of the founding members and one-third of the regular members were expected to resign, and these vacancies were to be filled by new members of the committee.

[33] Some money came from donations. For example, a Protestant Minister Natan Juraj Petian donated nine thousand gulden. Some financial support came from abroad. For example, Josip Juraj Strossmayer, a Croatian bishop from Dakovo who also supported the *maticas* of other Slavic nations, sent one thousand gulden. On the occasion of Matica's first assembly, the Emperor donated one thousand gulden and bishop Moyses two thousand gulden towards the Matica's activities.

the first assembly met in August 1863, about ninety-four thousand gulden had been collected.[34]

The first assembly of the Slovak Matica took place in 1863 in Turčiansky Svätý Martin, in honor of the millenial anniversary of the mission of Saints Cyril and Methodius.[35] Between four and five thousand people arrived in the town.[36] On 4 August, following a Catholic mass and a Protestant church service, the assembly began. It was presided over by Bishop Moyses, led by Francisci, and the minutes were written by Chrástek. Francisci described the steps that preceded the assembly. He also presented the by-laws and explained the modifications that had to be made. In his speech, Francisci compared the Matica's by-laws variously to a "golden bull," an "abolition decree," a "citizenship diploma," and a "testament to national unity" giving Slovaks the chance to experience freedom and equality.[37] Afterwards, he revealed the current numbers of the Matica's members and introduced the candidates for the committee.[38]

In August 1863, the Slovak Matica had 441 regular founding members, 431 regular permanent members, 112 regular annual members, and 1,318

---

34 Winkler (56) mentions that membership fees were around seventy-two thousand gulden, the value of shares was about nine thousand gulden, contributions to support the activity were about three thousand gulden, and the interest from shares was about ten thousand gulden. Out of this amount, about thirty thousand gulden were available in cash.

35 At this period, Turčiansky Svätý Martin was a small town of approximately two thousand inhabitants. The mayor of the town, Andrej Švehla, was a member of the Matica's committee. The town supported the Slovak Matica and also promoted contacts with other Slavs. In 1863, it gave honorary citizenship to five representatives of other Slavic nations, among them the Ruthenian politician Adolf Dobriansky and the Serbian politician Svetozar Miletić.

36 A wooden shelter was built just for this occasion next to the Catholic church. It was decorated by flowers, wreaths and the stemma of the Slovak Matica. A bust of the Emperor and state (Austrian) flags were placed inside the shelter. The 'protocol' of the assembly emphasized the collaboration between the Protestants and Catholics.

37 Francisci's entire speech, along with other speeches made during the first Matica assembly, can be found in Botto's *Dejiny Matice slovenskej (1863–1875)*.

38 Moyses was elected the Chairman, Kuzmány the Vice-Chairman, Ján Országh the second Vice-Chairman, Pavol Mudroň and Michal Chrástek secretaries, Tomáš Červeň treasurer, and Fraňo Fila and Jozef Škultéty accountants. These choices respected religious parity and the fact that Banská Bystrica, mostly thanks to Moyses, could become another center of Slovak cultural life. The assembly decided to send a delegation led by Moyses to the Emperor to express the gratitude of Slovaks for his support. It was agreed that this delegation would not bring up other *Memorandum* requests. The audience at the Emperor's court took place on 10 September 1863, and the delegation also met the Hungarian Chancellor Anton Forgach (Forgáč).

supporters.[39] An additional 1,250 persons donated smaller amounts of money. The minutes of the assembly were signed by 534 members.[40] In the first year of its existence, the Matica recruited about one hundred new members and its capital increased by twenty-four thousand gulden. Around fifty-two thousand gulden were deposited with private and bank entities, at an interest rate of 5–6 %. The museum collections of the Matica also increased thanks to donations.[41] The negative aspect was that, out of approximately one thousand regular members, only about two hundred paid the membership fee.

The second assembly of the Slovak Matica took place in August 1864 and was attended by about four hundred members. This assembly took an important step towards unifying the nation by supporting Martin Hattala's version (1852) of Štúr's Slovak grammar. It also issued honorary memberships to foreigners and awarded scholarships to students of secondary schools and universities. Around 1864, the Matica also began editorial and publishing activities.[42] On 6 April 1864 the corner-stone was laid for the new municipal house that was also supposed to house the Matica.[43] In August 1865, an assembly of the Slovak Matica and a theater performance took place in the building even though it was not yet finished. At first, the Matica only rented several rooms in the new municipal house. In 1869, it bought the whole building for twenty-one thousand gulden, and in 1870 it opened the first Slovak museum there.

By 1863 the Matica had 984 regular members (and 1,318 supporters), and membership remained steady in the following years: 1,111 members in 1864, 1,112 in 1867, 1,052 in 1870, and 1,191 in 1874. Along with the collective members

---

39 Winkler (55) mentions that the association *Tatrín* (1844–48) had twenty-three founding members, and in the four years of its activity the membership rose only to one hundred.
40 Winkler, 55–56.
41 For example, Jozef Ľudovít Holuby (a Protestant minister and polymath interested in many scientific fields) donated two thousand fossils and a herbarium with six thousand plants.
42 Among the first books published were *Rozhovory o Matici slovenskej* (Talks about the Slovak Matica) by Daniel Lichard, the second volume of *Mluvnica slovenská* (Slovak Grammar) by Martin Hattala, *Myšlienky o záhradníctve* (Thoughts on Gardening) by Štefan Moyses, the second volume of *Slovenská čítanka* (A Slovak Reader) by Emil Černý, *Národný kalendár 1866* (National Calendar), and other publications. This incomplete list shows the variety of publications that were aimed at both peasants and educated readers.
43 The corner-stone carried an inscription stating that the Slovak Matica was a national *svetlica* (the word means a 'room' but also connotes 'light' or 'illumination'). Silver coins and a ring with the engraved word 'Memorandum' were laid together with the corner-stone. The building was designed by the architect Karol Hörer from Nitra. Ján Bobula from Turčiansky Sv. Martin adapted the project and supervised the construction. The project was financed with funds the municipality had received for selling a forest and from public collections, as well as with money lent to the town by the Slovak Matica.

(towns and associations), the membership consisted mostly of priests (356), merchants and craftsmen (302), teachers (123), clerks (93), medical doctors, lawyers, and engineers (45), landlords (8), peasants (14), and soldiers (3). Fifty-two members did not state a profession, and twenty-five of them were women. The members were from various counties, the highest number from Turiec, Zvolen, and Nitra. Since the Slovak Matica was not allowed to have local branches, it introduced the office of collaborators who mediated communication between the members and the headquarters. In 1867, the number of collaborators was seventeen; by 1870 it rose to sixty, and by 1874 to sixty-nine. The Slovak Matica also had representatives in Pest, Vienna, Prague, Brno, and Zagreb, as well as in Russia. It maintained contact with forty-five members and institutions abroad.[44]

Viliam Paulíny-Tóth, the only Slovak member of the Hungarian Parliament, became the Matica's first Vice-Chairman in 1866, when Kuzmány died. In 1867, he wrote *Príhlas Matice slovenskej k národu slovenskému a milovníkom jeho* (An Address by the Slovak Matica to the Slovak Nation and Its Lovers), in which he described the role of the Slovak Matica and encouraged Slovaks to support it morally and financially.[45] This address reflected a stagnation in membership (which had increased only by two hundred in four years), as well as Slovak fears resulting from the *Ausgleich*. After 1867, Slovak nationalists faced a dilemma similar to that following the revolution of 1848, namely, whether to negotiate with Vienna or with Budapest. There were also different factions within the Matica itself: some members wanted it to be a scientific institution, while others favored mass education or entrepreneurial activities.[46]

2.2 Finances and Activities

The Slovak Matica organized three major national campaigns to raise money: the first was launched before the Matica officially began its activity (1863–64); the next was organized in order to buy the municipal house in Turčiansky Sv. Martin (1869–70, 1870–71); and the last was held in 1872 under the slogan 'In Response to Our Accusers' and was meant to defend the Matica.

The Slovak Matica had an annual budget of four thousand gulden. This amount covered the salaries of three administrative staff members and

---

44   Winkler, 71–73.
45   This document was also published among the supplements to Botto's *Dejiny Matice slovenskej (1863–1875)*.
46   For example, Jozef Hložanský sent an open letter to the sixth assembly of the Slovak Matica in 1868 recommending that the Matica should reduce its cultural activities and scholarhips and should focus instead on enterpreneurial activities and on cultivating the Slovak intelligentsia.

scholarships (1,500–2,000), as well as publishing activities (2,000–2,500). In the area of publishing, the Slovak Matica had to cover many genres ranging from manuals for farmers and national calendars through literary works to scientific volumes. It also issued the *Letopis Matice slovenskej*, a chronicle that made available documents and practical information as well as articles and essays.[47] In twelve years (1863–75) the Slovak Matica published twenty volumes of *Letopis*, twenty popular and scientific books, and about forty smaller prints, such as brochures and occasional eulogies.[48] All the publications consistently used Hattala's version of Štúr's Slovak grammar.

In spite of the scarcity of authors, the Matica refused to publish works by living poets and fiction writers, and it was also very cautious about publishing political and historical treatises. Some projects were stopped when the political atmosphere became more tense. For example, a map of Upper Hungary by Dionýz Štúr containing those counties that the *Memorandum* considered Slovak territory was not published after the Austro-Hungarian *Ausgleich*. Complete documents from the *Memorandum* prepared by Andrej Sládkovič or Jonáš Záborský's treatise on history were also refused publication. Even though one of the Matica's main goals was to increase the general education of peasants by publishing works of popular science, in particular those dealing with national history, it was impossible to find suitable texts. In 1873, a Section for Folk Writing (*Odbor spisov pre ľud*) was established, and a public competition was announced with a prize of four hundred gulden to be awarded the winner. However, none of the seven works submitted was recommended for publication. The report by the head of the Section to the Matica's committee in January 1874 stated that the problem of popular writing needs to be addressed, together with the Matica's scientific profile.

In order to promote scientific research, scientific committees (boards) were proposed for the Matica's organization. The various proposals recommended different divisions among the scientific fields (the number of proposed boards ranged from two to six).[49] The last proposal in 1873 stated that

---

47   These represent about half of the approximately 190 contributions by 32 authors. All the articles were evaluated before publishing. Hence *Letopis* was among the first Slovak scientific periodicals and facilitated the rise of professional reviews.
48   Winkler, 29, 79.
49   The first proposal in December 1864 suggested that five scientific boards be created. Another in August 1865 talked about three boards, and the one from 1868 about six boards. This last proposal was discussed at an annual assembly in August 1868, but the state commissar present at the meeting objected to it since, in his opinion, it represented an unapproved alteration of the Matica's original by-laws. The Hungarian Home Ministry eventually decided in December 1868 that including scientific boards in the Matica's structure

only two boards should be established (for the humanities and natural sciences), that research should be financed from the Matica's own resources instead of outside sources, that two volumes of the *Letopis* should be published annually, and that each member of the board should submit one work every two years and participate in other scientific activities such as discussions and evaluations. A final, polished version of this document on scientific boards was in preparation when the Matica was closed down in 1875.

The Matica's by-laws also stated that it should maintain close contacts with similar institutions in other Slavic nations. The Matica's membership was open to people with nationalities other than Slovak,[50] and some representatives of other Slavic nations were offered honorary memberships.[51]

As the Slovak Matica was unable to establish itself as a scientific institution, the core of its international activity was the exchange of literature. It was very cautious about other forms of international contact, especially with Russia, because it was afraid to be accused of Pan-Slavism. The Slovak Matica sent only three official delegations abroad. In 1867, two Matica members travelled to Zagreb to celebrate the tercentenary of the death of Nikola Subić Zrinski.[52] In 1873 a small delegation was sent to Prague to celebrate the hundredth anniversary of Josef Jungmann's birth, and in 1874 another group went to Zagreb to celebrate the opening of the university. However, the toast that F.V. Sasinek pronounced on this occasion, *Date nobis ex oleo vestro, quia lampades nostrae*

---

would not violate its original by-laws. However, the organization of the scientific boards changed again in 1869 and in 1870.

50   Among these were Adolf Dobriansky (a Ruthenian), J.J. Strossmayer and Metel Ožegovic (Croats), and V. Il. Lamanskij, M.T. Rajevskij, and A. Budilovic (Russians). Conversely, some Slovaks were members of other national *maticas*: the poet, linguist and historian Pavol Jozef Šafárik (Pavel Josef Šafařík in Czech) was a member of both the Serbian and Czech Maticas (founded in 1826 and 1831), since he had worked as headmaster of a grammar school in Novy Sad in Serbia (1819–33) and as a professor in Prague (1833–61). The Catholic bishop Štefan Moyses had worked as a censor in Zagreb and was one of the cofounders of the Illyrian Matica in 1842. Ján Kollár and Ľudovít Štúr supported the idea of the Matica of the Lusatian Serbs/Sorbs founded in Bautzen in 1847, whereas Bohuslav Šulek supported the rise of the Dalmatian Matica founded in Zadar in 1861 (Winkler, 28).

51   Among the honorary members of the Matica were the Ruthenian bishop Jozef Gaganec, the Serbian bishop Nikanor Gruić, the Croatian county administrator Ivan Kukulievć Sakcinski, the Slovenian scholars Fran Miklošič (Franz Miklosich) and Jan Bleiweis, and the Czech scholars František Palacký and Anton Beck.

52   Zrinski's death was commemorated in Turčiansky Sv. Martin on 11 September 1866 with two religious services and a theater performance about Zrinski. A volume of proceedings was published.

exstinguuntur ('Give us some of your oil, since our lamps are dying') was considered a provocation.[53]

Since the Slovaks did not have a museum or a national library of their own, collecting objects and books was also among the activities of the Matica. The first acquisitions and donations were stored at a bishop's residence in Banská Bystrica. The first initiatives to establish a permanent public exposition were between 1867 and 1869. In 1870 the collections were transferred to Turčiansky Sv. Martin and exhibited in two rooms of the municipal house. The library section contained about ten thousand books and three hundred manuscripts. Other collections included approximately twelve thousand coins, one hundred archaeological objects, two thousand drawings, twenty paintings, and one hundred eighty statues. The collections of plants, herbs, and fossils ranked among the largest ones. Unfortunately, a part of the numismatic collection was stolen in 1874. The annual budget for museum activities was, however, only about three to four hundred gulden. In 1875, the estimated value of the museum collection was 5,773 gulden.

2.3 Tensions and Closure

After the 1867 *Ausgleich*, the existence of the Slovak Matica was no longer in accordance with governmental policy. In March 1869 Hungarian soldiers were garrisoned in the municipal house without the permission of the Matica or the town. This was perceived as an unjust attack. From the 1870s onwards, tensions and attacks between Hungarians and Slovaks became more fierce and more frequent. The Matica was often labelled as pan-Slavic and anti-Hungarian, and accused of being involved in politics.[54] In response to these voices, the Matica's committee prepared a document entitled *Pro Memoria Matice Slovenskej* and submitted it to the Hungarian Prime Minister József Szlávy on 15 January 1873.[55] This document refuted the accusations of Pan-Slavism by comparing Germans, Italians, and Slavs. Whereas Germans and Italians in the past had had strong states and shared a common history, the Slavs had never had a common state, language, or religion. Slavs shared only a common origin and similar languages. In fact, the safest strategy against Pan-Slavism would be to enable the various Slavic nations to develop.

---

53 Winkler, 94.
54 These articles were published in the Hungarian periodicals *Reform* and *Hon*. Obviously, Záborský's and Sasinek's interpretations of history, as presented in their contributions to the Matica's chronicle, were incompatible with Hungarian historiography.
55 This document, along with Szlávy's response, was also published among the supplements to Botto's *Dejiny Matice slovenskej (1863–1875)*.

On 29 December 1874 the chief of police in Pest visited the Slovak Matica and officially launched an investigation. On 6 April 1875 the Hungarian Home Minister suspended the Matica's activities on the grounds that it did not promote culture but was actually involved in politics and used its budget contrary to its by-laws. On 13 and 14 April the Matica's capital (about ninety-five thousand gulden), together with its building, museum collections, and documents, were seized by the state authorities.[56] On 12 November 1874 the Hungarian Home Ministry decreed the closure of the Slovak Matica, which was confirmed by the Emperor twelve days later.

Some pro-governmental Slovak periodicals, such as *Svornosť* (Unity) from Banská Bystrica, welcomed this decision. *Svornosť* wrote that the Matica was a Slovak shame, a kind of Pan-Slavic 'Sodom and Gomorrah.'[57] The Matica's Chair, Viliam Pauliny-Tóth, tried to refute the accusations in an article in *Národné noviny* (the National Newspaper). On 3 December 1875, Svetozar Miletić, a Serbian member of the Hungarian Parliament, interrogated the Hungarian Home Minister about the Slovak Matica and its property, referring to paragraph 34 of the original by-laws, which stated that the Matica's property should be returned to the Slovak nation if it ceased to be active. The Minister responded that there was no problem with the property since, as far as he knew, there was no Slovak nation to which the property could be returned. This denial of the nation's existence by Hungarians entered into the standard rhetoric of Slovak martyrdom. In 1876, the leaders of the Slovak Matica submitted two 'defenses' of the Matica to the Home Ministry, but to no avail.

2.4 *After 1875: The Aftermath and the Nation's Struggle to Survive*

In 1885, when the Home Ministry decided to donate the Matica's property to FEMKE (the Hungarian education association for the Slovak region), the Matica's former leaders compiled a *Pamätný* (known also as *Prestolný prosbopis*, a Memorial or Court Plea) and submitted it to the Emperor. Another claim to return the Matica's property was raised in 1896 following a congress of the non-Slavic nations of Hungary.

The lawyer Franko Kabina (1844–1931), who aspired to become a member of the Hungarian parliament, carried on a lawsuit between 1903 and 1905 in which he demanded that the Slovak Matica should either be allowed to continue its activities or that his membership fees since 1874 should be returned to him with interest. In 1910 Kabina asked the Hungarian Prime Minister to reopen the

---

56   The Matica's collections were first stored in a barn in Turčiansky Sv. Martin. In 1902, they were transferred to Nitra. Some objects were later moved to Budapest. The collections were given back to the Slovak Matica in 1923 and 1942–43.
57   Winkler, 96.

Slovak Matica as well as the Slovak grammar schools closed in 1874. Kabina's initiative led to a series of articles on the Slovak Matica in the Hungarian paper *Világ* and to an article by Pavel Mudroň entitled "A tót Matica" published in the *Národné noviny* (nos. 49–50, 1910).

In 1910 Mudroň, a leader of the Slovak National Party, submitted to the Hungarian government a *Pamätný spis* (Memorial File) with requests similar to those raised by Kabina, but the legal and administrative issues regarding the Slovak Matica remained unresolved until 1919, when the Czechoslovak Republic was established. Winkler mentions that about three hundred documents comprising approximately fourteen hundred pages from the period between 1876 and 1919 were preserved at the Hungarian Home Ministry.[58]

In the last third of the nineteenth century, many Slovaks emigrated to the USA and established numerous associations there. The first attempts to unite them date back to the 1890s. On 26 September 1893 the 'Slovak Matica in America' was founded in Chicago with about twelve hundred members, but it gradually split and finally closed down in 1897.

2.5 The Slovak Matica in the Twentieth Century

In terms of territorial claims, the Slovaks never had a political state throughout their entire history (or not since Great Moravia in the ninth century). In 1848 and 1861 they requested from the Austrian and Hungarian authorities some kind of territorial boundaries, as well as autonomy and parliamentary seats for Slovaks. In the twentieth century the (Czecho-)Slovak territory and state(s) were eventually recognized by international agreements.

The emergence of the Slovak political nation from the *natio hungarica* and from the Czechoslovak 'tribe'[59] occurred in a complex historical framework of rising and declining empires. The Matica's institutional discontinuity reflected a larger historical and political discontinuity, and it remained most active in those historical periods when Slovak national identity and statehood were evolving.[60] One could analyze the Matica's position and role in discussions of the new rules of Slovak orthography in 1931–32, the Czecho-Slovak federation in the 1960s, or the Czecho-Slovak split in the 1990s,[61] and also consider its

---

58 Winkler, 100.
59 See especially the work of Ján Kollár (1793–1852), a leading personality of the Czech and Slovak national movements, a poet, linguist, politician, an influential figure in creating a common Czechoslovak national ideology based on the existence of a Czechoslovak 'tribe,' one of several Slavic 'tribes.'
60 Obviously, in the twentieth century the Slovak idea was contrasted primarily with the Czechoslovak (or Czech) concept rather than with Austro-Hungarian or Hungarian claims, though the Slovak-Hungarian relationship remained a delicate issue.
61 See the so-called 'National Program' (*Národný program*) of the Matica since 1992.

solid membership base and popularity in the nationally mixed regions of southern Slovakia. From 1959 onwards, one could also research the activities of the Slovak Matica Abroad (*Zahraničná Matica slovenská*).

The Slovak Matica was re-established (or 'resurrected') in 1919, and its new ('second') building was constructed in Martin in 1926.[62] In the interwar period, the Matica focused on research and editing activities, and its local branches promoted cultural life in the Slovak regions. Among the most successful Matica volumes were the literary monthly *Slovenské pohľady* (Slovak Views, founded in the 1840s) and the popular children's periodical *Slniečko* (Sun). In the early 1940s, the Slovak National Library, the printing house Neografia, and a radio broadcasting station were established within the Matica. From the 1930s onward, many Slovak intellectuals who opposed the idea of one (Czechoslovak) nation, or adhered to the idea of Slovak autonomy, worked in the Slovak Matica in Martin; some of them (for example, Jozef Cíger-Hronský, Stanislav Mečiar, Ján Okáľ, and Štefan Polakovič) emigrated in 1945, mostly to Argentina or the USA.

Once the Communist regime had been installed, the Matica's by-laws were changed and by 1950–51 its membership base ceased to exist. Since the Slovak Academy of Sciences and Arts (founded in 1946 and reorganized in 1953) was supposed to carry out research, the Matica became the Slovak National Library (*Slovenská národná knižnica*) in 1954. In 1963 the corner-stone of a new Matica building was laid in Martin, and in 1975 a new facility was opened. In 1968 a new law was adopted and membership in the Matica again became possible. However, this lasted only until 1973–74. From the 1960s onwards, bibliographical services, museum studies, and contacts with Slovaks abroad were the major Matica activities. From roughly 1920 until 2010 it published about 4,500 books and periodicals.[63]

After the fall of Communism, new laws were enacted in 1990 and 1991 defining the new role of the Slovak Matica as a "national and scientific institution whose societal mission is to act nationally and patriotically both on Slovak territory and beyond it."[64] Its organizational structure included a central institutional hub with local branches and associations. Between 1990 and 1993 (i.e., before the Czechoslovak split), the Matica organized numerous 'roundtable discussions of national consensus,' arranged meetings in the southern

---

62   The motto "Resurrected, I welcome a resurrected nation!" (*Vzkriesená vítam vzkriesený národ!*) was inscribed on the Matica's building in 1919.
63   Winkler, 29.
64   Ibid., 14: "*Zákon z roku 1991 charakterizuje Maticu slovenskú ako národnú a vedeckú ustanovizeň, ktorej spoločenským poslaním je národne a vlastenecky pôsobiť na území Slovenskej republiky i mimo jej územia.*"

regions of Slovakia, promoted Slovak sovereignty, argued for the drafting of a Slovak Constitution, and proposed its own version of the language law.[65] It also wished to be involved in preparing school syllabi and textbooks, especially in the humanities. In 1992 and 1998, it organized the *Matica World Festival of Slovak Youth*. Among other initiatives, one should mention the *World Year of Slovaks* (!) set for the period between July 1997 and September 1998. In the early 1990s, the Matica also became involved in privatization and started its own investment fund. In 1993 it launched a call for donations towards a National Treasury. In 1994 it acquired shares in the printing house Neografia, and started a transformation from a state institution to a public one. Law No. 68 in 1997 defined it as a public cultural institution whose activities are partially financed from the state budget. Its main goals were stated rather generally: to promote Slovak culture and statehood, to spread moral values, and to address national and environmental issues.

Within the past twenty-five years (and especially since 1998, when Vladimír Mečiar's government ended) the Slovak Matica has been struggling to find its place in Slovak society. A supplement to the 1997 law, No. 183 of 2000 on libraries, separated the Slovak National Library and the Memorial of National Culture (*Pamätník národnej kultúry*) from the Slovak Matica. The Slovak government's decision to limit the Matica's role and property, along with a radical cut to its budget, led its leaders to engage in numerous pathetic and passionate protests, including a series of *Pro Memoria*. The Slovak Matica has its historical legacy in representing Slovak national interests, but claiming exclusivity and emphasizing martyrdom are counter-productive.[66] The Matica was established as a cultural institution, not as a political organization. It generally observed this line, though its intrusion into the political scene, especially in the 1930s, the 1990s, and also during Communism, needs to be researched more thoroughly.

3 Conclusions

Building the Slovak nation in the nineteenth century involved processes of denial and separation as well as of identification and unification which

---

65 Slovak was first approved as an official language in the Slovak Republic, which the Matica criticized. On 15 November 1995 the Parliament passed a law making Slovak the state language.

66 In his essay on the Slovenian Matica, Marijan Dović has noted that this institution is 'self-referential.' In the case of the Slovak Matica, most of the studies of its history (especially monographs and books) were indeed written by its employees and published by the Matica itself.

continued throughout the twentieth century. These processes manifested themselves as linguistic and cultural nationalisms, as claims of territorial autonomy and, eventually, as political separatism.

Between roughly 1790 and 1860, the established literary languages of Latin, Hungarian, German, and Czech were gradually abandoned in favor of a vernacular standard Slovak with a generally accepted norm. Parting with the tradition of writing in Latin, Hungarian, and German was not particularly painful, but separating from the Czech language meant a 'schism' (felt as such especially by Protestants) and a 'split' within an allegedly homogenous Czechoslovak 'tribe.'[67] The Slovak Matica, by supporting Hattala's elaboration of Štúr's codification, helped to ease the conflicts over the language issue. Agreeing on a language norm became very important in the following decades, when Hungarian policy towards non-Hungarian nations became tougher.

The 'infrastructure' of Slovak culture was still quite weak when the Slovak Matica originated. There was a tradition of periodicals in Slovak, and there had been some Slovak associations before the Slovak Matica, but these usually had very few members and represented only a fraction of Slovak (professional or religious) viewpoints. As mentioned, there were no Slovak institutions of higher education, nor was there a national academy, a Slovak museum, or a theater group with a repertoire in Slovak. Literature written in Štúr's Slovak had a tradition of about twenty (!) years when the Slovak Matica was established, and most of the literary production was still Romantic.

The Slovak Matica was a lay organization and was able to represent the whole nation, regardless of the religion or social status of its members. Slovak nation-building coincided with the shift from feudalism towards capitalism in Hungary, and this shift was reflected in the national consciousness of the nobility, the rising bourgeoisie, and the peasants within the country. The Matica's members, however, were mostly clergymen and craftsmen. Some of the Matica's activities show that it sought to bridge the gulf between the Slovak cultural elite and the peasants.

Even though the Slovak Matica managed to reconcile some differences, equivocal ideas about its role and aims persisted throughout the entire period of its activity. It is also clear that it attempted to perform too many tasks but managed to deal only with a few. It functioned only for twelve years, and its

---

67 Up to the 1930s it was not uncommon to claim that Slovak was very suitable for literature but not for political representation and state administration. This opinion was clearly an attempt to mediate the Slovak language 'split' and the theory of a single Czechoslovak nation that was inevitable for the survival of a new state in 1918. However, even during the Communist regime, many Slovak politicians in the central Communist Party organs spoke Czech.

activity was abruptly curtailed. It was also underfinanced: in his *History of the Slovak Matica*, Július Botto mentions that the Matica would have needed a capital of three hundred thousand gulden to cover all its activities.[68]

Among the numerous activities that the Slovak Matica carried out between 1863 and 1875, the most successful were editing/publishing and book/museum collections. Its administrative and entrepreneurial activities were equally important, as was the experience from negotiations with authorities. The Matica's foreign contacts in the latter half of the nineteenth century favoured Zagreb and Prague, but the idea of a Slavic 'reciprocity' and brotherhood outside Hungary was very much present. Though the Matica wished to be a scientific and research institution, it lacked the background necessary for this task.

Bibliography

Botto, Július. *Dejiny Matice Slovenskej (1863–1875)* (A History of the Slovak Matica [1863–1875]). Turčiansky Sv. Martin: Matica Slovenská, 1923.

Franková, Libuša. *Slovenské národné obrodenie, 1780–1848: Ideové podnety, ciele, špecifiká, periodizácia, národnoobrodenecké snahy* (The Slovak National Awakening, 1780–1948: Ideological Impetuses, Goals, Specific Aspects, Periodization, Attempts at National Revival). Prešov: Metodické centrum Prešov, 2000.

Ivantyšynová, Tatiana, ed. *Ján Kollár a slovanská vzájomnosť: Genéza nacionalizmu v strednej Európe* (Ján Kollár and Slavic Reciprocity: The Origins of Nationalism in Central Europa). Bratislava: Spoločnosť pre dejiny a kultúry strednej a východnej Európy a Historický ústav SAV, 2006.

Kirschbaum, Stanislav J. *A History of Slovakia: The Struggle for Survival.* London: Macmillan Press, 1995.

Kowalská, Eva. "Prvé meštianske kasíno—neznáma kapitola z novších dejín Modry a procesu národného prebúdzania" (The First Town Casino—An Unknown Chapter in Modra's Modern History and the Process of National Awakening). In Beata Mihalkovičová, ed., *Nové kontexty života a diela Ľudovíta Štúra* (New Contexts in the Life and Works of Ľudovít Štúr). Modra: Modranská muzeálna spoločnosť, 2012.

Mannová, Elena, "Spolky a národná emancipácia Slovákov" (Associations and the National Emancipation of the Slovaks). In Tatiana Ivantyšynová, ed., *Ján Kollár a slovanská vzájomnosť: Genéza nacionalizmu v strednej Európe* (Ján Kollár and Slavic Reciprocity: The Origins of Nationalism in Central Europe). Bratislava: Spoločnosť pre dejiny a kultúry strednej a vychodnej Európy a Historický ústav SAV, 2006.

---

68   Botto, 104.

Mihalkovičová, Beata, ed. *Nové kontexty života a diela Ľudovíta Štúra* (New Contexts in the Life and Works of Ľudovít Štúr). Modra: Modranská muzeálna spoločnosť, 2012.

Polla, Belo. *Matica Slovenská a národnostná otázka* (The Slovak Matica and the National Question). Martin: Matica Slovenská, 1997.

Rosenbaum, Karol. "Matica slovenská v dejinách nášho národa" (The Slovak Matica in the History of Our Nation). In Augustín Maťovčík, ed., *Biografické štúdie 16* (*Biographical Studies 16*). Martin: Matica slovenská, 1990. 15–24.

Vojtech, Miloslav. *Literatúra, literárna história a medziliterárnosť* (Literature, Literary History and Interliterary Relations). Bratislava: Filozofická fakulta Univerzity Komenského, 2004.

Winkler, Tomáš, Michal Eliáš, et al. *Matica slovenská: Dejiny a prítomnosť* (The Slovak Matica: History and Presence). Martin-Bratislava: Matica slovenská, 2003.

Žigo, Pavol, et al. *Slovacicum: Kapitoly z dejín slovenskej kultúry* (Slovacicum: Chapters from the History of Slovak Culture). Bratislava: Studia Academica Slovaca, 2004.

CHAPTER 4

The Matica in an Ethnic-Regional Context: Sorbian Lusatia and Czech Silesia in Comparison

Miloš Řezník

All national movements in the nineteenth century faced problems of regional diversity, sometimes in very different and ambiguous ways, ranging from a need for national integration and unification by smoothing away regional, dialectal, and cultural differences, to pointing out regional differences as evidence of cultural richness. In some cases, the specificities of certain regions could even be declared to be treasures of unspoiled national culture, traditions, and speech (e.g., Karelia in the Finnish or Samogitia in the Lithuanian national movements). As centrality and regionality represented two sides of the same coin, the national interests could be pursued at the same time by eliminating regional specificities as well as by emphasizing them even on an organizational level.[1] Probably we can risk the thesis that the more an entity claims the ability to act as an autochthonous *and* autonomous *and* subsistent coherent unity, the more this entity tends to establish and develop differentiated internal structures. For nations, this is true not only for the social complexity of a group according to the stage of its historical development, but also for territorial discourses and structures. Against this background, the following contribution will discuss the mutual connections between the ambiguity of national unity and regional plurality on the one hand, and the development of the institutional form of the *Matica* on the other. Even though the perspective of cultural transfer among the Slavic national movements is taken into account, the main accent will lie on a comparative approach.

The institutional form of the Matica was typical for advanced stages of ethnic-national movements in the nineteenth century in their "phase B" (Miroslav Hroch), i.e., during the period of national agitation represented by a group of intellectuals who aimed to propagate national identity within their non-dominant ethnic group.[2] Thus, the spread of Maticas—both as a form and as

---

[1] On nationality and regionality in Central and East-Central Europe in the context of modern nation-building, see: Ther *et al.*; Haslinger (2000); Schattkowsky and Müller; Müller and Petri.
[2] Hroch, 22–24.

the name of the institution—can be considered as a sign that national movements had reached their agitation phase and that their speakers referred to ideas of Slavic solidarity or mutuality, since the Maticas remained reserved to the non-dominant South- and West-Slavic groups. It is symptomatic that, firstly, this name was not used among the Poles—who can still be regarded as the dominant or (semi-)dominant ethnic group in the Polish countries even during the period of partitions—until the foundation of the School Maticas (*Macierz Szkolna*); and that, secondly, the only other (East-Slavic) group using the marking of Matica were the Ruthenes (Ukrainians) in Polish-dominated Galicia, i.e., within the Habsburg monarchy, where they could use their contacts with other Slavic national movements.

The main purposes of the Maticas were on the one hand to support the development, codification, and conservation as well as the "nobilitation" of national languages and literatures, and on the other to obtain funding for literary and scientific publications. Further, in some Maticas school instructions *in* and *about* the national language, or even financing and organizing a national school system, became the central fields of action. Corresponding to the further development of national patriotism towards a mass ethnic movement as well as its functional, political, and regional differentiation, different specialized Maticas followed the pattern of the original 'central' maticas founded between the 1830s and 1860s (Serbian, Czech, Illyrian, Sorbian, Ruthenian, and Slovak). A period of setting up various 'partial' Maticas came in the 1870s. These were specialized functionally, territorially, or even politically. Some Maticas concentrated their activity on the field of school instruction, raising money, organizing schools or courses, and issuing school books in the national language, and some acted also as foundations granting fellowships to poor children or students. The Czech *Matice školská* or the Polish *Macierz Szkolna*, mentioned above, were such cases: both organized public or private schools, printed textbooks, etc. At the beginning of the twentieth century, even a *Kashubian Matica*, oficially called *Macierz Kaszubska Verlags- und Sortimentbuchhandlung GmbH*, was established at Sopot near Gdańsk in the German province of West Prussia.[3]

In the Czech case, several local school *Matices* were established in the 1870s in Bohemian and Moravian cities, e.g., in České Budějovice (Budweis) or Olomouc. The *Central School Matice* (*Ústřední Matice školská*) was formed in 1880 in Prague with the leading political authority of the Czech movement, František Ladislav Rieger (1818–1903) as its chair. This came about as a result of the new

---

3 *Statut spółki Macierz Kaszubska Verlags und Sortimentsbuchhandlung Eingetragene Genossenschaft mit Beschränkter Haftpflicht w Sopotach* (Gdańsk, 1911).

language policy in Austria since the government cabinet under Count Eduard Taaffe (1833–1895) liberalized the linguistic agenda (the so-called Stremayr's language regulations). As a counterpart to the German *Schulvereine*, established since May 1880, the Central School Matice aimed at supporting, establishing and financing Czech schools and kindergartens in the linguistically mixed or predominantly non-Czech regions of Bohemia, Moravia, and Austrian Silesia, but also in Vienna. In this context, the support of the so-called 'inner Czech minorities' in the field of education was the main purpose of this institution—national centrality combined with a regional agenda.

Thus, the differentiation of partial Maticas during the last third of the nineteenth century proceeded not only in a functional, but also in a regional context. The Polish *School Matica* (*Macierz Szkolna*) exemplifies such a differentiation in both contexts at the same time because several such Maticas were founded in different parts of the Polish countries: the first one was the *Macierz Polska* (or *Macierz Szkolna*) in Lemberg/Lwów/Lviv, the capital of Austrian Galicia, founded in May 1882 to support Polish education and initiated by the wrtiter and author of popular historical novels József Ignacy Kraszewski (1812–1887).[4] Three years later, the Protestant priest Paweł Stalmach (1824–1891) set up the regional *School Matica in the Teschen Duchy* (*Macierz Szkolna dla Księstwa Cieszyńskiego*), the Austrian part of Silesia inhabited by Poles, Germans, Czechs and Jews, a territory that was increasingly involved in both the Polish and the Czech national movements and would soon become a site of Czech-Polish tensions. The *Macierz Szkolna* at Teschen (Cieszyn in Polish, Těšín in Czech) closely followed the model of the Czech *Central School Matice* and the Czech-Silesian *Matice Opavská*. Finally, after Polish instruction in private schools was allowed by the Russian authorities in Poland during the revolution of 1905, a *Polish School Matica* (*Polska Macierz Szkolna*) was established in Warsaw the following year;[5] the famous writer Henryk Sienkiewicz (1846–1916) became its honorary chair. With its 116,000 members, 800 schools, and 63,000 pupils, the *Polska Macierz Szkolna* became a genuine mass organization of the Polish national movement. It was abolished by the Russian government in 1907 as soon as the revolutionary crisis had passed, so that the *Polska Macierz Szkolna* acted in secret until it was allowed again by the German occupation administration in the spring of 1916.[6]

---

4 Stemler; *Macierz Polska*; Amborski.
5 *Ustawa Towarzystwa Polskiej Macierzy Szkolnej* (Statutes of the Society of the Polska Macierz Szkolna; n.p., 1906).
6 *Ustawa Towarzystwa Polskiej Macierzy Szkolnej* (*zatwierdzona przez Generał-Gubernatora Warszawskiego d. 26 kwietnia 1916 r.*) (Statutes of the Society of the Polska Macierz Szkolna [confirmed by the General Governor of Warsaw on the 26 April 1916]; Warszawa, 1916).

The *Comenius-Matice* (*Matice Komenského*) was constituted in the Czech Lands at the beginning of the 1870s, named after the seventeenth-century Evangelic Moravian philosopher and educationalist John Amos Comenius (Jan Amos Komenský, 1592–1670), who holds a prominent place in the memory of the Czech mass national movement.[7] Like the Czech and Polish school Maticas, its actions were oriented towards education and pedagogy, but concentrated—unlike the school Maticas—rather on the publishing and dissemination of educational, didactic, or pedagogical works, i.e. methodological writings addressed to teachers, as well as on the publication of the works of Comenius.

This *Matice* is not to be confused with another Czech institution: the *Comenius Evangelical Matice*, also called the 'Comenium,' which was established following the model of other Maticas in 1890 as a foundation for humanities and literature, but was defined at the same confessionally by the tradition of the Bohemian Brethren. Its main forms of activity were publishing Protestant literature and organizing public readings and reading circles and a library, as well as popularizing literature and the humanities. According to its main areas of activity, the 'Comenium' consisted of sections which themselves were called 'Matice': the Evangelical Science Matice (*Evangelická Matice vědecká*) took care of publishing writings on theology and history, whereas the People's Evangelical Matice (*Evangelická Matice lidu*) concentrated on popularization. The 'Comenium' also published the writings of Comenius, John Hus (c. 1370–1415), Petr Chelčický (c. 1390–c. 1460), and others. The *Evangelic Matice "Comenium"* combined a clear confessional (Evangelical) character with a national agenda in the—predominantly Catholic—Czech context, but without regional accents. However, the 'Comenium' was a rather special case in which the constituting role was played by a minority confession. Thus we can see that the brand of the 'Matice' underwent a kind of inflation in Czech culture during the second half of the nineteenth century; the notion could be used as a synonym for foundations, or as a generic name for reading clubs or book series (such as the *Matice lidu* or People's Matice from 1867 in Prague).[8]

Both the functional field of action (mostly in education) and the territory seem to have been the most important defining principles of partial, specialized, and non-central Maticas during the second half of the nineteenth century. In some cases, new partial Maticas, founded on a territorial principle,

---

7 Řezníková *et al.*
8 A short overview of Matice-institutions around 1900 from the Czech perspective can be found in the *Ottův slovník naučný* (Otto's Encyclopedic Dictionary, vol. 16; Praha, 1900), 981–91.

developed specific regional agendas, which was in most cases defined in terms of a realization of national interests under specific regional or territorial circumstances. Perhaps the first example of such was the Moravian Matice (*Matice Moravská*) in Brno from the 1850s. In this way, the various regional Maticas competed not only with their counterparts representing other national movements (e.g. the Czech *Central School Matice* vs. the German *Schulvereine* since 1880, or the Czech vs. the Polish *Matica*-organizations in Austrian Silesia), but occasionally also with other Maticas or similar organizations in their own national context. The regional Maticas dealt with the tensions and conjunctions between ethnic-national and territorial-regional identities; they represented both of them in the whole broad spectrum of the roles regionalism could play within the national discourse. Both the ambivalence and the engagement between nationality (ethnicity) and territoriality (regionality) can be considered as characteristic of the role of regions as a mediatory 'foil' of nationality and vice versa.[9] Finally, it was this mediation that made the incorporation of abstract national categories into the social and cultural discourse of regional or local communities possible.

In the following parts, two specific but different cases of such a position between regionality and nationality will be discussed and compared: the example of the Sorbian Maticas in Lusatia on the one hand, and the Czech Opavian Matice (*Matice Opavská*) in Austrian Silesia on the other. Despite the concentration of these ethnic-territorial societies in Opava and Bautzen (and in Cottbus as well), we will also make some remarks and comparisons regarding the Moravian Matice (*Matice Moravská*) in Brno and, to limited extent, the Czech Matice (*Matice Česká*) in Prague. However, these comparative considerations will only serve to elaborate the regional aspects of the associations mentioned above.

1   The Sorbs in Lusatia and the Czechs in Austrian Silesia

At first sight, both cases appear quite different in their institutional character, and the time of their formation was marked by different phases of ethnic movements in Central Europe. The Sorbian Matica (*Maćica Serbska*) was established from 1845 to 1847 in Bautzen (Budyšin), the cultural center of the Sorbian movement and of the Saxon part of Upper Lusatia.[10] In this sense its

---

9   Rettalack; Applegate.
10   For a summary of basic information about this *Maćica*, see Musiat. See further Völkel, Jermakova, the contributions in the theme issue of the review *Rozhlad* dedicated to its

formation is comparable to that of the central national Maticas among the Slavic ethnic groups, especially given the fact that the Sorbian movement entered its phase of national agitation in this decade. Further, the *Maćica* in Lusatia was not 'derived' from another, central Matica-organization in its own ethnic context, but was inspired from abroad, above all by the *Czech Matice* in Prague. The most important initiator of the Sorbian *Maćica*, Jan Arnošt Smoler (1816–1884), referred to the Czech model already in his early projects during the 1840s, i.e., soon after the foundation of the institution in the Bohemian capital; but this reference remained concealed from the Saxon authorities during the official registration.[11] Its predecessor organizations, which represented only a personal continuity with the *Maćica Serbska* and its ideal background, were rather the Lusatian students' patriotic groups in Bautzen and at universities outside of Lusatia, in Breslau (Wrocław), Prague, and Leipzig. Especially Prague, with its national-patriotic institutions, as well as Breslau with its enormous significance in the 1840s for the connections among West-Slavic national movements (Polish, Czech, Slovak, Sorbian and Kashubian), developed patterns for the new organizational forms and functioned as focal points of mutual cultural transfer.[12] But it was especially the Bautzen Slavic Society (*Societas Slavica Budissinensis*, 1839)[13] and the Sorbian Reading Society (*Leserverein*) in Bautzen (1841) which created a direct organizational base of the Sorbian movement in the last decade before the *Maćica*'s formation.[14] Accordingly, the organizers and first members of the *Maćica* were priests, intellectuals, and teachers. Another common feature with the 'central' Maticas was the fact that the Sorbian one was established und represented by a large part of the leading group of the Sorbian national agitation. Its action was oriented—at least programmatically—towards the whole of Sorbian culture and territory, in spite of the political limitations imposed by the division of Lusatia between Saxony and Prussia and by the restrictive language policy of the Prussian government. The main purpose of the *Maćica Serbska* lay in coordinating, supporting, and financing various activities in education, literature, research, popularization, and patriotic agitation, including the organization of further institutions like the museum or 'Wendish House' in Bautzen.

150th anniversary, and Šołta and Kunze. On the foundation of the *Maćica*, see e.g. Šołta *et al.*; Jenč, 256–262; Sergeevič Myľnikov; and, with some new interpretations, Kunze (1995), 95–104.

11   Kunze (1995), 98.
12   Achremowicz and Żabski.
13   Musiat, 46–52.
14   Kunze (1995), 96–97.

The central areas of activity developed by the *Matice Opavská* (Opavian Matice) since the 1870s were similar. Like the *Maćica Serbska*, it was oriented primarily towards the activation of a national movement in various directions: research (publication and popularization more than original scientific investigation), the organization of a museum, an educational agenda, literature, the documentation and propagation of folk culture, etc. The *Matice Opavská* was established in 1877 as a cultural and educational institution of the Czech national movement in Austrian Silesia with its head office in Opava (Troppau in German), the country capital. In contrast to the *Maćica Serbska*, the Opavian *Matice* was a typical example of the functionally and/or regionally specialized Maticas of the 'second generation' established in the second half of the nineteenth century.

At the same time, it could borrow the models and continue the traditions of other national and regional Maticas. It was influenced in its formation and organization not only by the *Czech Matice* at Prague, but also by the *Moravian Matice* at Brno and even the Slovak Matica (*Matica Slovenská*). Its specialization lay in representing Czech national interests in Austrian Silesia by taking into account the specific conditions of the country. Thus, the *Opavian Matice* was anything but an institution representing the nation or ethnic group as a whole. On the contrary, particularity within an ethnic national collective was the principle of its construction from the very beginning. The group which stood behind its foundation was composed of the leaders of the national movement in the region. As in the *Maćica Serbska*, priests—Catholic in Silesia, both Catholic and Lutheran in Lusatia—played a very important role, followed by intellectuals, teachers, and state and municipal officials, as well as (in the Czech-Silesian case) peasants.[15] However, the leadership depended not on the Czech movement in general, but on the local cultural elite of the national action. In addition, whereas the Czech movement in Bohemia reached its mass phase in 1848 and again at the beginning of the 1860s, it developed advanced forms of national agitation (phase B) only in the Silesian context. This fact represents the central point of Silesian specificity within the Czech movement—and provided a base for the corresponding regionality.

2   Regionality and Regionalism

In spite of the fact that the *Maćica Serbska* in Bautzen represented, as stated above, the rather 'central' type of the *Maticas* of the 'first generation,' both the

---

15   See note 36.

Maćica Serbska and the *Matice Opavská* expressed differing forms of regionality. To be sure, the *Maćica Serbska* addressed its activities to the entire Sorbian ethnic group, but this could be regarded as an expression of regional patriotism from the Saxon (or Prussian and German) point of view because of the fact that following its further political and juridical integration into the Kingdom of Saxony in the first half of the nineteenth century, the Saxon part of Upper Lusatia lost its partly specific character as a political unit inherited from the period of its formal allegiance to the Czech Crown.[16] With regard to the domination of the German language and German-speaking elites, Lusatia offered possibilities for the formulation and articulation of 'German'-Lusatian regional patriotism and 'German'-Lusatian regional identity. Theoretically, the ethnic culture and speech of the Sorbs could be regarded as an element of regional specificities and used by German-speaking intellectual and patriotic elites (together with history, monuments, 'antiquities,' landscape, etc.) to imagine their own Lusatian regional or local 'home country' or 'little' fatherland (*Heimat*). Thus, even the representatives of the *Maćica Serbska* took this potentiality into account and hoped for a collaboration with the German-speaking patriots. Such a patriotic 'marriage' would have followed the pattern of the coalition between the Czech national agitators and the political and territorial, predominantly German-speaking Bohemian aristocratic patriots; yet with the significant difference that the Bohemian territorial patriots cooperating with the Czechs were representatives of the Bohemian estates (until 1848) or of the conservative nobility, and identified with the political unit of the Kingdom of Bohemia as a point of reference.[17] However, a similar constellation was not available to the Sorbian activists. Moreover, the possibilities for winning German-speaking patriots for common activities turned out to be limited. Consequently, the German-speaking regional or local patriots used Sorbian culture as a not very important symbol of their *Heimat*. Worse yet, due to the nationalist awareness of the German-Slavic conflict in Central Europe, quite new after the revolutions of 1848–49, the representatives of the Sorbian movement faced increasing suspicions of pan-Slavism from the German nationalists at least since the 1840s. Their intensive cooperation with the Czech movement and contacts with Polish patriots, as well as the role played by ideas of Slavic mutuality, only nourished such accusations.

---

16 For Lusatia in the nineteenth century, see Belzyt and Rautenberg. For literature in English on the Sorbs and Sorbian culture and history, Stone is still useful (for the *Maćica Serbska*, see pp. 28–29).

17 See Krueger.

On the other hand, some kind of regionality resulted from the political circumstances confronting the *Maćica Serbska*. The most important seems to have been the more liberal language policy of Saxony in comparison with Prussia, since the Sorbian territories extended into both countries. After the correction of the Saxon-Prussian border in favor of Prussia at the Congress of Vienna, not only the whole of Lower Lusatia, but also a large part of hitherto Saxon Upper Lusatia including Görlitz (Zhorjelc in Sorbian) was annexed by the Hohenzollern monarchy, in addition to the western part of its province of Silesia (Provinz Schlesien) administrated from Liegnitz (Legnica in Polish). Only the western, central, and southern parts of Upper Lusatia remained Saxon, with Bautzen as the most important center; 80% of altogether 250,000 Sorbs were Prussian subjects after 1815.[18] The middle of Saxon Upper Lusatia was also the region with the highest density of Sorbian-speaking population, with the other 'core territory' around Lower Lusatian and the Prussian city of Cottbus. The major center, Bautzen, developed into the focal point of Sorbian agitation in the first half of the nineteenth century, but the main activities of the *Maćica* remained limited to this part of Lusatia and found little echo in Prussia. This is especially true for Lower Lusatia.

These limitations were not only a result of Prussian restrictions and difficulties in communication. Other problems were caused by linguistic, traditional, and confessional differences between the regions, especially between Upper and Lower Lusatia. A large majority (some 87%) of the Sorbs were Protestants, but most of the Catholics lived in Upper Lusatia. Lower Lusatia was predominantly Protestant, with transitional regions in the northern part of Upper Lusatia. The population of the Saxon part of Upper Lusatia and the surroundings of the Prussian Hoyerswerda (Wojerecy) and Görlitz were mixed Catholic and Protestant, and only in the Kamenz (Kamjenc) district in the west of Saxon Lusatia were Catholics in the majority.[19] Catholic religiosity remained an important constituent of Sorbian culture in this region, which resulted in the role played by the Catholic clergy in the Sorbian patriotic movement. Since the early modern period, the Catholic Sorbs had been a regional and confessional exception in orthodox-Lutheran Saxony,[20] a circumstance

---

18 For the evolution and structure of the Sorbian population, see Tschernik.
19 Tschernik, 34–35.
20 By the beginning of the seventeenth century, orthodox Lutheranism had prevailed over other forms of Reformation to become the only legal confession; in consequence, Saxony developed a restrictively intolerant religious policy until the eighteenth century. Catholicism was prohibited, as were Calvinism, Lutheran Philippism (defamed as Crypto-Calvinism), and later Pietism. The exception of the Sorbian Catholics was due to the fact that Lusatia devolved to the reign of Saxon electors during the Thirty Years' War but

which defined the confessional form of Sorbian otherness but also divided the Sorbian ethnic group into two different parts. Another problem represented (and still represents) the dialectal variety which has not yet been overcome by the adoption of a common language. This disunity was marked not only by differences between the Upper Sorbian (Upper Lusatian) dialect, which is closer to Czech, and the Lower Sorbian (Lower Lusatian) one, which is much closer to Polish, but also by regional forms of speech, which contributed to a certain limitation of communication, especially with the regions using the dialect preferred by the *Maćica*. Even within the Upper Sorbian dialect, two forms of orthography developed: a 'Protestant' one and a 'Catholic' one, the latter again influenced more by Czech because the Catholic priests had studied at the 'Lusatian Seminar' in Prague and were in closer contact with the Czech national movement.

The *Maćica Serbska* manifested its aspiration to act as a central institution integrating all Sorbs on the basis of a common culture and identity, and made intensive attempts to overcome inner differences. As for confessionality, the *Maćica* succeeded by urging the cooperation of both Protestant and Catholic members of the association from the very beginning, even if efforts were necessary to preserve the relationship.[21] Concerning the dialectal problems, the results remained limited, but the elaboration of a new, common Upper-Sorbian 'analogous' orthography to replace the hitherto Catholic and Protestant versions was one of the first goals of the *Maćica* and was realized in the first phase of its existence. On the other hand, its concentration on Upper Sorbian—hardly any 'Catholic' books in Lower Sorbian were published by the *Maćica* in the first decades of its existence—led to a very limited influence in Lower Lusatia.[22]

The differences in the political conditions for the Sorbian movement did not disappear after Germany's unification and the beginning of the *Kulturkampf*, even as Saxony's policy towards non-German minorities and immigrants

---

remained a Czech (Bohemian) fiefdom, so that the thorough legal integration of Lusatia into Saxony remained impossible before the first half of the nineteenth century. The Lutheran Reformation having been declared on the ideal and spiritual basis of Germanness, the confessional otherness of the Sorbs obtained a new significance in the latter half of the nineteenth century. As for Saxony, the partly Catholic court constituted a new exception to orthodox-Lutheran domination following the conversion of Friedrich August I (in the context of his election to become the King of Poland) at the end of the seventeenth century; another exception was due to the settlement of the so-called Moravian Brethren in Upper Lusatia some two decades later.

21 Kunze (1995), 101–103.
22 Musiat, 190.

became more restrictive. Prussia's anti-Slavic (i.e., primarily anti-Polish) policy in the so-called 'eastern provinces' posed similar problems for the Polish movement, especially in Poznania (Greater Poland, the Province of Posen) and for the Sorbian patriots in Prussian Lusatia. Despite confessional differences between the Poznanian Poles, whose national discourse was influenced by the growing role of Catholicism, and the Lower Lusatian Protestant Sorbs, a rapprochement between the Polish and the Lower Sorbian activists occurred against a background of Prussian restrictions.

The collaboration was based on a form of political alliance, on increasing Polish interest in other Slavic groups in Prussia, and also on the inspiration of the Sorbian activists by the Polish political, social, and cultural methods of so-called 'organic work' (*praca organiczna*) in Greater Poland. All these political, historical, dialectal, and strategical preconditions led to further developing a distinct Lower Sorbian movement without breaking the common Sorbian ethnic-national unity. Several Polish 'experts' tried to establish intense connections with Lower Lusatia and support the Sorbian movement there. The most prominent initiator was the young Polish lawyer from Kalisz (in the Russian part of Poland) Alfons Parczewski (1849–1933), a supporter of the Lusatian-Sorbian movement and a member of the *Maćica Serbska* from 1875, who promoted the idea of a new society in Lower Lusatia. He not only formulated its agenda but also contributed financially.[23] In 1880, a separate Lower Sorbian Matica, the *Mašica Serbska*, was founded in the Lower Lusatian capital of Cottbus (Chóśebuz in Lower Sorbian), formally as a subsidiary of the *Maćica Serbska* in Bautzen, but with its own structures and agenda.[24] Some of the founders of the Cottbus *Mašica* had been active members of the Bautzen *Maćica* for years, and they understood this organizational decision as a step toward developing the actions of the *Maćica* in Lower Lusatia. However, the *Mašica* in Cottbus never attained the significance of its 'mother' institution in Saxony and never laid claim to a central function in Sorbian culture, whereas the *Maćica* in Bautzen remained a leading authority of the Sorbian movement from the 1840s until the first quater of the twentieth century.[25] Cottbus developed activities in areas similar to those in Bautzen, but took efforts to anchor them in their own region, using and taking into account both their knowledge of regional specificities and the political situation in Prussia. Consequently the *Mašica* (Cottbus) did not center its program on scientific activities but concentrated rather on identity policy, popularization, the preservation of speech in its regional

---

23   See Konarski.
24   For detailed information on the *Mašica* in overview, see Musiat, 188–93.
25   Musiat, 73.

forms, and the organization of social and cultural actions that would represent and internalize Sorbian identity both within and outside the reference group. By 1895 the *Mašica* had published some sixty books and organized its own library in Cottbus, and from the 1890s it regularly organized the Lower Sorbian choral festivals (*Gesangfeste*).[26]

Along with personal connections, goals, and to some extent methods, another common feature of both societies was the central role of priests as initiators: in Cottbus, too, most of the founders and the most important supporters were priests and teachers, such as the first chair Jan Bjedrich Tešnař (1892–1898), the promoter of Lower Sorbian worship Jan Bjarnat Kruświca (1845–1919), and several representatives of the later 'Young Sorbian Movement' in Lower Lusatia.[27] Before limitations were imposed on the *Mašica*'s activity in the Nazi era, all the chairs and three of five vice-chairmen were priests in the Lower Lusatian country.[28] At the same time, a large part of the membership consisted of peasants and handcraftsmen, a fact which makes the *Mašica* in Cottbus different from the *Maćica* in Bautzen and, as we shall see, quite similar to the regional *Matice Opavská* in Austrian Silesia. Nevertheless, this multiple diversity caused a form of *de facto* regionalization of the institutions with central aspirations in the Lusatian case, despite the fact that the Cottbus *Mašica* saw itself as a kind of subsidiary of the Bautzen society.

In Czech Silesia, both the regional specificity and the regionality of the *Matice Opavská* were constituted in a different way. Despite the consciousness of the regional and cultural variety of the ethnic groups to be included in Czech nation-building, the Czech regions of Austrian Silesia remained rather marginal in the territorial and national discourse of the national activists in Bohemia until late in the nineteenth century, and Silesia appeared rather marginally as a subject for national action.[29]

The first impulses to develop a *Matica*-like agenda in Silesia came from Moravia. In April 1849, the Moravian National Unity of Saints Cyril and Methodius (*Národní jednota moravská sv. Cyrila a Metoděje*) was established in the Moravian capital Brno with the important participation of Czech national activists from Prague (the liberal journalist Karel Havlíček, the historian František Palacký, the physiologist Jan Evangelista Purkyně) but with an explicit regional agenda that included both Moravia and Silesia. Accordingly, an important role was expected from the Moravian and Silesian members.[30] The main purposes

26 Noack and Schurmann, 16.
27 Ibid., 23–27.
28 Musiat, 188.
29 See also Haslinger (2010), 99.
30 Chocholáč; see also Traub and Jan. The considerations on the *Moravian Matice* are based on these contributions.

of the association were publishing books, journals, and literary works, and organizing libraries, reading circles, and nature or art collections, as well as providing financial support for Czech instruction in elementary schools.[31] Already in the early 1850s, the Unity faced a crisis caused by conflicts among the members between laymen and clergymen, and by the political situation under neo-absolutism, so that unification with the Czech Matice (*Matice Česká*) was up for discussion. Finally, a separate Czech-national and Moravian-regional Moravian Matice (*Matice Moravská*) was established in 1853/54 in order to "support Czech literature, with special reference to Moravian needs by publishing good writings or by contributing to this purpose."[32] Periodic cycles of development and stagnation followed in the nineteenth and twentieth centuries. One characteristic specific to the Moravian Matice was the role played by Moravian aristocrats: Count Egbert Belcredi acted as chair of the *Matice* for almost three decades (1868–1894), and Count Friedrich Sylva-Taroucca (1816–1881) supported the association with generous donations. This engagement was possible through the connection between both Czech cultural and Moravian territorial patriotism. But the activities of the *Moravian Matice* were oriented predominantly towards scientific research and popularization, above all in Moravian history (the press organ *Časopis Matice Moravské* has appeared since 1868), and remained limited to Moravian subjects. Silesia stood apart from the interests of the *Matice*.

Meanwhile, the Czech movement began to develop in Silesia, especially after the constitutionalization of Austrian political life in the 1860s. Whereas this movement reached the stage of mass support (Hroch's "phase C") in Bohemia and Moravia at the latest just after 1860, Czech patriotism in Silesia was characterized by the fact that it reached only the stage of national agitation. It would be worth special research to address the question of whether the Silesian case could confirm the thesis that national conflicts in the ethnically mixed regions were caused not by inner tensions but were imported from the centers of national movements.[33] At the same time as Czech, German, and Polish national movements were able to mobilize masses of population in their 'core countries' in the Habsburg monarchy, in Austrian Silesia, hitherto on the margins of the nationalist territorial discourses, national competitions began to arise during the 1860s and 1870s. In spite of the political domination of German liberals and nationalists in the country's capital, Czech associations, institutions and newspapers began to emerge, so that Opava (Troppau) became the

---

31   Chocholáč, 3–4; Řepa, 99–101.
32   Quoted in Chocholáč, 4–5 and 28.
33   See Müller and Petri.

center of the Czech movement in Silesia. Simultaneously, a Polish movement developed rapidly in Silesia, especially in its eastern parts (Teschen Duchy). The tensions among Czech, German, and Polish nationalisms intensified during the following decades up to the First World War und even further.[34] The growing influence of Czech national activities alarmed the German national representatives in the city and country, one expression of which was the rise of German nationalism and the foundation of the so-called *Nordmark* in May 1894. Its leading slogan "In Silesia keep German what is German" (*In Schlesien deutsch erhalten was deutsch ist*) reflected the mixture of offensive and defensive national feelings caused by the growing influence of non-German nationalisms.[35]

In this situation, the Czech movement needed institutional forms for disseminating national 'cultural goods' among the Slavic inhabitants, for the propagation and activation of national consciousness as well as for the organization of Czech school instruction. So when the *Matice Opavská* (Opavian Matice) was founded in 1877,[36] unlike its Moravian affiliated organisation it concentrated not only on scientific research and editions, but especially on the promulgation of common books in Czech, organizing reading circles, and, above all, founding Czech schools and kindergartens, based on the model of the Czech 'school Matices' which aimed to support Czech schools in predominantly German-speaking regions of Bohemia and Moravia (the Opavian society was directly inspired, among others, by local school Matices, e.g., at Olomouc). The *Matice Opavská* succeeded relatively quickly in founding a number of kindergartens and schools. In cooperation with the Central School Matice (*Ústřední matice školská*), the *Matice Opavská* was even able to establish a Czech gymnasium in Opava—one of only two Czech gymnasiums founded by the Central School Matice before the First World War (the other was in Uherské Hradiště in Moravia), with the Czech historian of Silesia and the later chair of the *Matice Opavská*, Vincenc Prasek (1843–1912), as its first director. This Czech-Silesian model was then followed by the Polish-Silesian School Macierz of the Duchy of Teschen (*Macierz Szkolna Księstwa Cieszyńskiego*) mentioned above: its foundation was inspired by the establishment of the Czech gymnasium at Opava, but its Polish counterpart, the gymnasium at Teschen, could

---

34　After the First World War, Troppau was declared the capital of the Province of Sudetenland and as such became a part of German-Austria (Deutsch-Österreich), and after the war a part of Czechoslovakia (Gawrecki *et al.* (2003), 296–305).

35　For the situation in Opava see Myška; Gawrecki (2006), 234–270. For Silesia and the Czech, German, and Polish movements see Gawrecki *et al.* (2003), 235–46; Grobelný.

36　Jakubíková; Knapíková, 9–23. Unless otherwise stated, most of the information here on the *Opavian Matice* is based on the monograph by Knapíková.

only be opened in 1895. In addition, the Czech Matice of People's Education in Teschen Silesia (*Matice osvěty lidové pro Těšínské Slezsko*) was founded in 1897 with the aim to establish Czech schools in this easternmost part of Austrian Silesia, as a regional form of school *Matice*, again inspired by the Czech-Silesian and local Polish models.[37]

One feature specific to the Opavian Matice, in comparison with the Czech Matice in Prague and partly the Moravian Matice in Brno, was the important continuing role of Catholic priests as leading representatives and activists, along with the active participation of peasants. Several clergymen played a central role already at the beginning of the *Matice Opavská*; of the eleven chairmen until 1918, two were parish priests in Silesia and two were peasants. The other chairmen between 1877 and 1918 came from the local *Bildungsbürgertum*; there were three teachers (a director and a teacher of the Czech gymnasium and a director of the Matica school in Opava), a physician, a journalist, and two lawyers.[38] In the first years after the formation of the *Matice* a third of its members were Catholic priests, but a large part consisted of peasants and even workers. Numerically smaller parts of the whole membership were represented by teachers, lawyers, tradespeople, and students.[39]

Both the leadership and the membership of the *Matice Opavská* originated from the region, mostly from the nearby surroundings of Opava, but rather seldom from the city itself due to the German numerical and political domination in the Silesian capital. A small part of the membership lived in Moravia, Bohemia, Vienna, or even Prussian Silesia, among them several leading authorities of the Czech movement. The number of members from the city of Opava, from more distant parts of Austrian Silesia as well as from Moravia and Bohemia grew in the 1880s and 1890s, but generally the regional character of the membership with its focus on the Opavian countryside did not change.[40] The regional agenda remained oriented towards Austrian Silesia, but the main purpose—support of Czech culture, identity and national movement in the country—was realized on several levels. Besides the concentration on education and on an 'identity policy' for that part of population which should be involved in the Czech nation as conscious members, the competition with the German and Polish movements in the region grew into one of the dominant points on the *Matice*'s agenda. Czech-German tensions in the Silesian capital,

---

37 For the Czech *Matice of People's Education*—however rather for the inter-war period— see Habrmanová.
38 Knapíková, 208.
39 The social composition of the membership has been analysed by Myška (1989), 45–56.
40 Myška (1989); Knapíková, 21–26.

where German officials tried to counteract the *Matice*'s activities, culminated in rioting in the streets, especially in the first two decades of the twentieth century (for example, on the occasion of the 'Matice Day' in 1914).[41]

However, the regionality of the *Matice Opavská* was evident from its concentration on Austrian Silesia and its efforts to deal with the specific conditions there. Occasionally, its Silesian 'identity' was manifested even in active interest in other, Prussian parts of Upper Silesia. Attention for the situation of the so-called Moravians (an ethnic Slavic-speaking group considered as Czechs from the Czech part) in the neighboring Prussian territories around Ratibor (Ratiboř in Czech, Racibórz in Polish) was awakened by the anti-Slavic policy of the Prussian authorities, especially at the beginning of the twentieth century, which coincided with general criticism of Prussian policy in the Czech and Polish discourse of the period. A special publication on "The Prussian Diet and the Moravians in Ratibor Duchy," written by the Catholic priest Jan Vyhlídal, appeared as the first volume of the series "Library of the Opavian Matice" (*Knihovna Matice opavské*) in 1909.[42] The second volume, composed by the same author and dedicated to the Czech population in Prussian Silesia in general, was released the following year.[43] However, the regional Czech press had already been observing the situation on the Prussian side of the border in the second half of the nineteenth century.[44] But besides representing, communicating, and imagining 'Czech-ness' in Silesia—the *Matice Opavská* propagated Czech literature, culture, and history in Silesia and aimed to spread its knowledge among the Czech inhabitants of the region—the *Matice* also made efforts in the opposite direction, to inform the Czech national public in Moravia, Bohemia, and especially in Prague about Silesia and the national movement there as well as the everyday lives of the Silesians. Through representations of Czech-Silesian material culture as well as of Silesian folklore and Silesian national activities, the country, the region, and its people were to be internalized in Czech national discourse as a specific, but important, integral, and respectable part of the national community and culture.

To be sure, this was both an attempt at national integration and a struggle for recognition on the part of the Czech-Silesians. Against this background the *Matice Opavská* reacted negatively to real or virtual signs of disrespect or misunderstanding from the national center, and looked on with suspicion when other national institutions tried to develop their own activities in the Silesian

---

41 Knapíková, 77–90.
42 Vyhlídal (1909).
43 Vyhlídal (1910).
44 Gawrecki (1989).

region; this was true especially for the Cyrilo-Methodian Matice (*Matice cyrilometodějská*) at Olomouc and the *Matice for People's Education* in Teschen-Silesia.[45] Such indignation on the part of the *Matice Opavská* could even concern other Moravian and Bohemian sister associations, despite the fact that the *Matice Opavská* was strongly inspired by *Matice*-societies in Bohemia, Moravia, and Slovakia and had cooperated closely with the *Moravian Matice* or the *Central School Matice* on various projects in its first decades. In claiming the right to be the primary and authentic representative of Czech-ness in Silesia, the *Matice Opavská* staked out a territory within the national discourse on a regional basis. In this context, regionality served as a principle of demarcation and competition without challenging the common national identity. The *Matice Opavská* instrumentalized Silesian (Opavian) regionalism as an ambiguous medium for both national integration and territorial difference.

3   Comparative Considerations

The cases of the Sorbian and Czech-Silesian *Matice*-societies represent different types of regionalization in the national context. Both institutions were established primarily as national associations. They combined ethnic-national and regional identities, but developed different forms of regionalism and different strategies for regionalist activities, as well as different understandings of regional agenda. Their basic divergence lay in the fact that the *Maćica Serbska* in Bautzen was founded rather as a typical 'central, nationwide' society similar to its Serbian or, above all, its Czech counterpart, but was from its very beginning in the 1840s forced to argue in an ethnic and regionalist manner with Saxon (and later Prussian and German) authorities, and to present the subject of its activities as a form of territorial and regional patriotism. In this way, the *Maćica* tried to avoid accusations of centrifugal activities or of the pan-Slavism which re-emerged during the Revolution of 1848. Another cause for the virtual regionalization of its activities was the inner dialectal, confessional, historical, and political disunity of the Sorbian territories, especially between Upper and Lower Lusatia. The foundation of the *Mašica Serbska* at Cottbus can be understood as an organizational expression of these circumstances despite the fact that it did not result in a break-up of the Sorbian movement. The *Maćica Serbska* at Bautzen had never abandoned its aspiration to represent the Sorbian movement and Sorbian culture as a whole. Using the role of the Czech Matice as a pattern, the *Maćica Serbska* was oriented primarily towards problems of

---

45   Knapíková, 30–31.

language and literature. It evolved continuously into a scientific institution organizing research on Sorbian subjects and publishing both popular and scientific literature. Its central press organ, *Časopis Maćicy Serbskeje* (Review of the Sorbian Maćica), aspired to become a scientific journal, and scientific sections were created in the first decade of the society's existence. This trend was not followed by the *Mašica* in Cottbus,[46] but in both cases, public and social activities remained the primary focus of the agenda. Generally, a certain rule of proportion can be observed between the regional character of the agenda on the one hand and the role of school education on the other: whereas the *Matice*-institutions in Prague, Brno, and Bautzen assumed a rather scientific and literary character, the idea of caring for Sorbian instruction and 'Wendish' (Sorbian) people's education (*Wendische Volksbildung*) remained important purposes of the Bautzen *Maćica* during its preparatory phase in the 1840s, and the issue did not disappear from the *Maćica's* horizon.[47] The Unity of Saints Cyril and Methodius at Brno, the *Mašica* at Cottbus, and all the *Matice*-societies in Austrian Silesia (the Czech ones in Opava and Teschen as well as the Polish *Macierz* at Teschen) were all active especially in this area. The Central School Matice (*Ústřední matice školská*) was even created to provide a kind of umbrella institution for local school *Matices* in various Bohemian and Moravian cities.

In the Czech-Sorbian comparison, a common pattern in the nineteenth century lay in the fact that the more 'regional' a *Matice*-association was, the more important was the role of the clergy as initiators, and the larger was the participation of non-elite groups (both social and intellectual) from outside the classical *Bürgertum*, and the more regional was its membership. Of course these observations are valid only to some extent, i.e., with limitations and exceptions, the causes of which should become a subject of further inquiry. But generally we can observe that because of the liberal and secular character of the Czech movement in Prague (not to mention the fact that some prominent Prague leaders like Palacký or Šafařík were non-Catholic), the importance of Catholic priests remained rather limited in the Czech Matice, whereas Catholic religiosity played a significant role in establishing a specific Moravian version of Czech-language patriotism.[48] At the same time, both conflicts and an intense cooperation with the clergy as changing tendencies marked the first decades of the *Matice moravská* in Brno. As we have seen, in Opava, Bautzen,

---

46   Noack and Schurmann, 20. Only after its new formation in 1993 did the *Mašica Serbska* obtain a scientific and cultural character; its members are now exclusively intellectuals, most of them researchers or teachers.
47   Kunze (1995), 102. For instruction in Sorbian see Kunze (2002).
48   Řepa, *Moravané*; see also Malíř.

and Cottbus the activities of the priests were even of decisive importance both as initiators and as leaders in the *Matice Opavská*, the *Maćica Serbska* (Bautzen) and the *Mašica Serbska* (Cottbus), even if they did not represent the largest part of their membership. As for the participation of non-elite groups, it remained limited in the central Czech Matice as well as in the semi-regional Matices in Brno and Bautzen, but was much stronger in the 'regional *Matica*-societies *par excellence*'—in Opava and Cottbus, where most of the membership was local. Yet, even from this perspective we can observe some correlation between centrality and regionality. In Prague the Czech Matice tried to win members in all the Czech regions and also abroad. In the Moravian Matice, the membership was very transregional at the beginning, as it had to be, with a significant role played by Bohemian national patriots in the first phase of the National Unity of Saints Cyril and Methodius. Further, the Unity tried to establish a network of members and associates throughout Moravia and Silesia, but later the membership of the Moravian Matice tended to be more limited in the territorial sense. In Bautzen, the largest group of members came from Saxon Upper Lusatia, but many of them were also from the Prussian territories of Upper and Lower Lusatia as well as from intellectual centers (Leipzig, etc.) and other localities outside of Lusatia. In spite of the fact that there were some Czech, Polish, and Russian members, the *Maćica* at Bautzen rather failed in its effort to win more members among the representatives of other Slavic nations.[49] Most of the members in Cottbus and in Opava came from the city and its country surroundings, even if a smaller share of the members of the *Mašica Serbska* originated from (but lived outside) that region—mostly in Upper Lusatia, but also abroad.[50] As far as the quantity of membership is concerned, the *Matice*-societies in the regional context appear to have been similar: they grew from a small group of initiators and founders to a membership of several hundreds during the second half of the nineteenth century.[51]

Bibliography

Achremowicz, Elżbieta, and Tadeusz Żabski. *Towarzystwo Literacko-Słowiańskie we Wrocławiu 1836–1886* [The Slavic Literary Society in Breslau 1836–1886]. Wrocław: Zakład Narodowy im. Ossolińskich, 1973.

---

49 Kunze (1995) 103, 193–204.
50 Noack and Schurmann, 20.
51 For Lusatia see Musiat, 67 and 188; Šołta *et al.*, 201.

Amborski, Jan Darosław. *O sławnym pisarzu J.I. Kraszewskim założycielu "Macierzy Polskiej"* [On the Famous Writer J.I. Kraszewski, the Co-Founder of the "Macierz Polska"]. Lwów: Macierz Polska, 1887.

Applegate, Celia. *A Nation of Provincials: The German Idea of Heimat*. Berkeley: University of California Press, 1990.

Belzyt, Leszek, and Hans-Werner Rautenberg. "Die Oberlausitz vom Wiener Kongreß bis zum Ende des Ersten Weltkriegs (1815–1918)." In Joachim Bahlcke, ed., *Geschichte der Oberlausitz: Herrschaft, Gesellschaft und Kultur vom Mittelalter bis zum Ende des 20. Jahrhunderts*. Leipzig: Universitätsverlag, 2nd ed., 2004, 181–220.

Chocholáč, Bronislav. *Matice moravská: Dějiny spolku od počátků do současnosti* [The Moravian Matice: A History of the Society from the Beginnings until Today]. Brno: Matice moravská, 1997.

Gawrecki, Dan, et al. *Dějiny Českého Slezska 1740–2000* [A History of Czech Silesia 1740–2000], vol. 1. Opava: Slezská univerzita v Opavě, 2003.

Gawrecki, Dan. "Czeska prasa w Opawie o Morawianach na Śląsku pruskim (1861–1883)" [The Czech Press in Opava on the Moravians in Prussian Silesia (1861–1883)], in *Studia Śląskie* 48 (1989), 157–196.

Gawrecki, Dan. "Opava znovu v čele Rakouského Slezska" [Opava again the Capital of Austrian Silesia]. In Karel Müller et al., *Opava*. Praha: Nakladatelství Lidové noviny, 2006, 234–270.

Grobelný, Andělín. *Slezsko v období národních táborů v letech 1868–1871* [Silesia in the Period of National Public Meetings, 1868–1871]. Ostrava: Krajské nakladatelství, 1962.

Habrmanová, Magda. "Slezská Matice osvěty lidové 1918–1938: Organizační vývoj a činnost" [The Silesian Matice of People's Education 1918–1938: Organizational Development and Activity], in *Časopis Slezského zemského muzea* 41 (1992), 52–72.

Haslinger, Peter, ed. *Regionale und nationale Identitäten: Wechselwirkungen und Spannungsfelder im Zeitalter moderner Staatlichkeit*. Würzburg: Ergon, 2000.

Haslinger, Peter. *Nation und Territorium im tschechischen politischen Diskurs, 1880–1938*. München: Oldenbourg Verlag, 2010.

Hroch, Miroslav. *Social Preconditions of National Revival in Europe: A Comparative Analysis of the Social Composition of Patriotic Groups Among the Smaller European Nations*. New York: Columbia University Press, 2000.

Jakubíková, Renáta. *Vznik a počátky Matice opavské* [The Formation and Beginnings of the Opavian Matice], in *Časopis Slezského zemského muzea* 43 (1994), 143–154.

Jan, Libor, and Bronislav Chocholáč, ed. *Dějiny Moravy a Matice moravská: Problémy a perspektivy* [A History of Moravia and the Moravian Matice: Problems and Perspectives]. Brno: Matice moravská, 2000.

Jenč, Rudolf. *Stawizny serbskeho pismowstwa* [A History of Sorbian Literature], vol. 1. Budyšin/Bautzen: Domowina, 1954.

Jermakova, Maja J. "Serbolužickaja matica." In *Slavjanskie maticy, XIX vek* [The Slavic Maticas, 19th Century]. Vol. 1. Moskva: Rossijskaja Akademija Nauk, 1996, 159–189.

Judson, Pieter M. *Guardians of the Nation: Activists on the Language Frontiers of Imperial Austria.* Cambridge: Harvard University Press, 2007.

Knapíková, Jaromíra. *Matice opavská. Spolek, osobnosti a národní snahy ve Slezsku (1877–1948)* [The Opavian Matice: The Association, its People, and National Efforts in Silesia (1877–1948)]. Opava: Matice slezská, 2007.

Konarski, Stanisław. "Parczewski, Alfons Józef Ignacy." In *Polski Słownik Biograficzny* [Polish Biographical Encyclopedia], vol. 25. Wrocław: Zakład Narodowy im. Ossolińskich, 1980, 201–06.

Krueger, Rita. *Czech, German, and Noble: Status and National Identity in Habsburg Bohemia.* Oxford: Oxford University Press, 2009.

Kunze, Peter. *Jan Arnošt Smoler: Ein Leben für sein Volk.* Bautzen: Domowina-Verlag, 1995.

Kunze, Peter. *Sorbisches Schulwesen: Dokumentation zum sorbischen Elementarschulwesen in der sächsischen Oberlausitz des 18./19. Jahrhunderts.* Bautzen: Domowina-Verlag, 2002.

Macierz Polska. Lwów: Macierz Polska, 1883.

Malíř, Jiří. *Morava na předělu (K formování národního vědomí na Moravě v letech 1848–1871)* [Moravia at a Watershed (On the Formation of National Consciousness in Moravia, 1848–1871)], in *Časopis Matice moravské* 109 (1990), 345–62.

Müller, Michael G., and Rolf Petri, eds. *Die Nationalisierung von Grenzen: Zur Konstruktion nationaler Identität in sprachlich gemischten Grenzregionen.* Marburg: Herder-Institut, 2002.

Musiat, Siegmund. *Sorbische/Wendische Vereine 1716–1937: Ein Handbuch.* Bautzen/Budyšin: Domowina-Verlag, 2001.

Myška, Milan. "Opava v polovině 19. století" [Opava in the mid-19th Century], in *Časopis Slezského muzea* 37 (1988), 113–133.

Myška, Milan. "Sociální a teritoriální skladba členů a příznivců Matice opavské v době jejího založení" [Social and Territorial Composition of the Members and Supporters of Matice Opavská in the Time of its Formation], in *Časopis Slezského zemského muzea* 38 (1989), 45–56.

Noack, Matina, and Peter Schurmann, eds. *Sorbische Kostbarkeiten / Serbskie drogotki.* Cottbus: Wendisches Museum, 2010.

Řepa, Milan. *Moravané nebo Češi? Vývoj českého národního vědomí na Moravě v 19. století* [Moravians or Czechs? The Evolution of Czech National Consciousness in Moravia in the 19th Century]. Brno: Doplněk, 2001.

Rettalack, James N., ed. *Saxony in German History: Culture, Society, and Politics 1830–1933.* Ann Arbor: University of Michigan Press, 2000.

Řezníková, Lenka et al. *Figurace paměti: J.A. Komenský v kulturách vzpomínání 19. a 20. století* [Figurations of Memory: Comenius in Cultures of Remembrance in the 19th and 20th Centuries]. Praha: Scriptorium, 2014.

Rozhlad: Serbski kulturny časopis [Rozhlad. Sorbian Cultural Review] 47 (1997).

Schattkowsky, Ralph, and Michael G. Müller, eds. *Identitätenwandel und nationale Mobilisierung in Regionen ethnischer Diversität: Ein regionaler Vergleich zwischen Westpreußen und Galizien am Ende des 19. und am Anfang des 20. Jahrhunderts.* Marburg: Herder-Institut, 2004.

Sergeevič Myl'nikov, Aleksandr. "Die Entstehung der Maćica Serbska und einige Fragen des historisch-vergleichenden Studiums der Kultur bei den Völkern Zentral- und Südosteuropas in der Epoche der nationalen Wiedergeburt," in *Lětopis: Jahresschrift des Instituts für sorbische Volksforschung* 26 (1979), 44–57.

Šołta, Jan, and Peter Kunze. "Die Maćica Serbska in Bautzen: Ihre Stellung in der nationalen Bewegung der Lausitzer Sorben im 19. Jahrhundert," in *Lětopis: Jahresschrift des Instituts für sorbische Volksforschung* 26 (1979), 31–43.

Šołta, Jan, et al., eds., *Geschichte der Sorben, vol. 2: von 1789 bis 1917.* Bautzen: Domowina-Verlag, 1974.

Stemler, Józef. *Dzieło samopomocy narodowej: Polska Macierz Szkolna, 1905–1935* [A Work of National Self-Help: The Polska Macierz Szkolna, 1905–1935]. Warszawa: Zarząd Główny Polskiej Macierzy Szkolnej, 1935.

Stone, Gerald. *The Smallest Slavonic Nation: The Sorbs of Lusatia.* London: Athlone Press, 1972.

Ther, Philipp, et al., eds. *Regionale Bewegungen und Regionalismen in europäischen Zwischenräumen seit der Mitte des 19. Jahrhuderts.* Marburg: Herder-Institut, 2003.

Traub, Hugo. "Dějiny Matice Moravské" [A History of the Moravian Matice], in *Časopis Matice Moravské* 34 (1910), 197–229 and 313–41, and 35 (1911), 60–102 and 154–192.

Tschernik, Ernst. *Die Entwicklung der sorbischen Bevölkerung von 1832 bis 1945: Eine demographische Untersuchung.* Berlin: Akademie-Verlag, 1954.

Völkel, Měrćin. *Trać dyrbi Serbstwo: 150 let Maćicy Serbskeje* [The Sorbs will survive. 150th anniversary of the Sorbian Maćica]. Budyšin: Domowina-Verlag, 1997.

Vyhlídal, Jan. *Pod perutěmi pruského orla. Obrázky ze života českého lidu v Prusku* [Under the Prussian Eagle's Wings: On the Life of the Czech People in Prussia]. Opava: Matice Opavská, 1910.

Vyhlídal, Jan. *Pruský sněm a Moravci na Ratibořsku* [The Prussian Diet and the Moravians in the Duchy of Ratibor]. Opava: Matice Opavská, 1909.

CHAPTER 5

The Slovenian Matica: The 'Foundation-Stone'

Marijan Dović

The Slovenian Matica was established in 1864, during the mid-nineteenth-century wave of the formation of similar associations throughout the Slavic world, following closely the foundation of the Dalmatian (1861) and Slovak (1863) Maticas. In the spirit of Slavic mutuality, it was explicitly modelled upon its predecessors (the Czech Matica in particular) and envisioned as one of the pillars of the Slovenian national revival. Especially prior to 1914—when there were practically no Slovenian scholarly institutions—its significance for the development of Slovenian intellectual life was substantial: the pretentious metaphor of a "foundation-stone" upon which the "edifice of Slovenian culture was built" might almost be taken literally in reference to this period.[1]

However, the Slovenian Matica was only one among the many factors that were advancing the 'cultivation' of Slovenian culture throughout the long nineteenth century. In order to assess its role justly, the Slovenian Matica needs to be observed in the context of general developments in Slovenian literary culture: its institutional settings, rival publishing enterprises (especially the St. Hermagoras Society), and the parallel media infrastructure. In such a context, the Matica turns out to be a phenomenon quite distinct from the isolated 'foundation-stone.' Nevertheless, a survey of its prehistory and its first five decades, when there were no universities or academies in major cities with Slovenian populations, should demonstrate that the Matica in this period did represent an indispensable nodal point for the advanced scholarly and publishing endeavours of the Slovenian national movement. Furthermore, even though it suffered a gradual decline in importance after the First World War, the *Slovenska matica* (initially the *Matica slovenska*) managed to survive the tempests of the twentieth century and has retained its vitality to this day.

1 Intermediary Structures of Slovenian Literary Culture and the Matica

Prior to the second half of the nineteenth century, the intermediary and institutional structures of Slovenian literary culture were relatively weak. However,

---

[1] See Lah, 3.

economic development—which increased the urban population, secured the growth of the bourgeois middle class, and advanced the functional differentiation of society—went hand in hand with the expansion of the media system, publishing, and institutional life. These intermediary structures began to prosper especially after the 1848 'springtime of nations' when the firm grip of censorship loosened. The emerging national media helped to foster the sense of a community along ethnic and linguistic lines, connecting the Slovenians, who were living politically and administratively detached in the traditional Habsburg lands of Carniola (where they represented a majority), Carinthia, Styria, and the Littoral, into a new framework of the national 'imagined community.' This expansion of the media was coupled with the strengthening and territorial spread of various national institutions (associations, reading rooms, gym societies, etc.). These various manifestations of an increasingly nationalistic character indelibly marked the second half of the nineteenth century, resulting also in a growing tension between the Slovenian and German communities.[2]

The expectations invested in the formation of Matica societies in the Slavic world were generally great and at the same time rather diverse. The Maticas were not simply understood as publishers; at the same time, they were supposed to function as centers of education, scholarship, enlightenment, media development, the spread of literacy, and preservation of the national heritage. In this respect, they were conceived of as substitutes for scholarly institutions such as universities, academies, and peer associations. The Slovenian Matica represents a typical case: at the time of its establishment, Slovenian scholarly institutions were practically non-existent. Thus, to understand the role of the Slovenian Matica in the context of institutional developments, it is necessary to give a brief overview of the Slovenian institutions that the Matica was attempting to 'replace.'

If one does not count the Slovenian Reformation movement in the sixteenth century, which was thoroughly repressed after 1600, the first modern scholarly association in Ljubljana was the *Academia operosorum*, the 'Academy of the Diligent' (1693–1725). But it was not until the age of Enlightenment, when the wealthy baron Žiga Zois had founded his Ljubljana circle, that the (informal) institution appeared with the stamp of a more distinct national character. Zois's circle (whose members included the poet Valentin Vodnik and the historian and playwright Anton Tomaž Linhart) was most active between 1780 and 1819, working simultaneously to educate the larger public (with calendars,

---

2 For details, see Vodopivec, 111–26; Dović 2007, 119–23; and the 'Slovenian' entries in *Encyclopedia of Romantic Nationalism in Europe* (Leerssen, ed.).

almanacs, a newspaper, and original poetry and plays) and striving for more far-fetched scholarly achievements, such as Anton Tomaž Linhart's history of Slovenia written in German, a new translation of the Bible, etc.[3]

Following the unfavorable era of the *Vormärz* regime, after 1848 institutional life intensified and became increasingly nationalized. The Slovenian Association (*Slovensko društvo*) in Ljubljana became active in organizing various national events, such as the highly ceremonial *béseda* (literally, a 'word') gatherings and commemorations of national figures.[4] After 1860 an efficient network of reading rooms (*čitalnice*) was spreading throughout the country.[5] In contrast, the development of scholarly institutions was anything but remarkable. It was not until after the downfall of the Habsburg monarchy that Ljubljana could establish its own university, which was founded in 1919 after the formation of the Kingdom of Serbs, Croats, and Slovenes (from 1929 the Kingdom of Yugoslavia), while the Academy of the Sciences and Arts was only established in 1938, on the eve of the imminent continental war. As there was no systematic provision of Slovenian school textbooks, the Slovenian Matica in its first fifty years (1864–1914) actually had to represent a number of different institutions. At the same time, it was supposed to be a central scholarly publishing house, a proto-university, and a scholarly peer association (proto-academy).

The post-1848 period was also marked by a media explosion triggered by the (temporary) abolition of pre-publication censorship. The newspaper *Kmetijske in rokodelske novice* (Agricultural and Handicraft News, published 1843–1902), edited by Janez Bleiweis, the political leader of the so-called Old-Slovenians, was joined by numerous newborn print media of every kind. A full-fledged Slovenian printed culture developed by the end of the century, including three dailies: the liberal *Slovenski narod* (Slovenian Nation), the conservative *Slovenec* (The Slovenian), and the Triestine *Edinost* (Unity). A number of other newspapers and magazines kept emerging in this lively period, including the major literary journals *Ljubljanski zvon* (The Bell of Ljubljana) and *Dom in svet* (Home and World). The rapidly expanding media system fostered the functional differentiation and professionalization of editorial and writing roles while at the same time stimulating the development of prose literature

---

3 See Dović 2007, 89–91, and Vidmar.
4 Among the first were the poets Valentin Vodnik and especially France Prešeren, the Slovenian national poet. For veneration of 'cultural saints' and their role in nation-building, see Dović and Helgason 2017. For an overview of over 1,700 memorials to various Slovenian literati, see Dović 2013.
5 See Perenič.

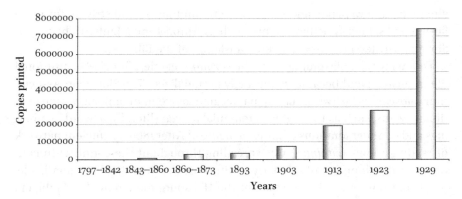

FIGURE 5.1 The quantitative growth of Slovenian-language newspapers (in copies printed) from the late eighteenth to the mid-twentieth century.
SOURCE: GABER 1937, ŠLEBINGER 1937

(fiction, feuilletons), advertising, etc. (see Figure 5.1).[6] All these magazines offered a platform for the development of Slovenian literature and criticism, but also for scholarship; in a way, they were complementing the activities of the Matica, but also competing with them.

Finally, it needs to be mentioned that the Slovenian Matica was neither the first publishing house for Slovenian books nor the one with the greatest reach and impact. In this respect, primacy should be given to the church-related fellowship of St. Hermagoras. Though the founding of the two institutions was connected to a certain degree, the latter definitely outweighs the Matica in terms of building a broad Slovenian 'reading nation.'

In 1845 the bishop Anton Martin Slomšek attempted to establish an association for educating ordinary people. In fact, his original idea was associated with the term *matica*. However, after official rejection in 1845, Slomšek designed a somewhat less ambitious project. His ideas were finally carried out in 1851 by Anton Janežič and Andrej Einspieler, two leading Carinthian intellectuals who were convinced that instead of an ambitious scholarly association (*matica*), a popular society similar to the Czech association *Dědictví sv. Jana* would better

---

6 Up until 1918, the estimated total of media published in all Slovenian territories amounted to 420 million copies of various newspapers on three billion pages, about 33% of them published in Carniola, 25% in the Littoral, 17% in Styria, 6% in Carinthia, and 14% in American exile. The extent of printed periodicals on the eve of the First World War drew the Slovenian newspaper-reading population closer to the most developed European areas (see Gaber, Vatovec, Šlebinger 1937, and Lapajne).

fit the requirements of the uneducated. In 1853 the provincial government in Klagenfurt (Celovec) allowed the formation of the Association of St. Hermagoras (*Društvo sv. Mohora*). This new association promptly set out to publish Slovenian books with predominantly religious contents (see Prijatelj 1956). After the association was transformed into a church fellowship and renamed the St. Hermagoras Society (*Družba sv. Mohora*), its rapid expansion began. Due to the highly efficient network for advertising and distribution offered by the social and infrastructural network of the Catholic Church (which at that time had no lay counterpart), the membership of the association in its first decade surpassed ten thousand subscribers. In three decades (1859–89), the most successful Slovenian publishing house managed to gather an astonishing eighty thousand subscribers, reaching its zenith on the eve of the First World War (see Figure 5.2). The subscribers, regularly referred to as 'limbs,' received a yearly package of Slovenian books through the ecclesiastical network. The contents of the books would usually fit within the triangle of morals-utility-leisure. The society was not intended as a medium for the dissemination of sophisticated scholarly projects or ambitious literary works; its production was often seen as predominantly trivial, though it often published the works of major writers as well. Nevertheless, its role was crucial in preparing the broader framework of the 'national revival' (see Simonič and Moder).

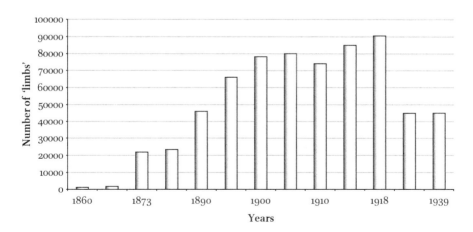

FIGURE 5.2   The growing number of subscribers to the annual book collection of the St. Hermagoras Society (1860–1939).
After World War I, the development of the society was interrupted by the new political and territorial reality. While the Klagenfurt branch was now a part of Austria, a Gorica (Gorizia) branch was founded within the Italian Kingdom (1924), while the Celje (1927) branch served the majority of Slovenian readers living in the Kingdom of Yugoslavia. All three branches have survived to this day.
SOURCE: HLADNIK 1982, MODER 1957

These readership figures are quite impressive: when the project was nearing its peak, the annual book collection reached about a quarter of a million readers.[7] It is thus quite appropriate to repeat the familiar saying that the *Mohorjeva* taught Slovenians how to read. More precisely: the Slovenian 'readership miracle' was produced by an alliance between religious and national ideas, and by utilizing the most efficient infrastructure offered by the Catholic Church.[8] Compared to the Slovenian Matica, the *Mohorjeva družba* harbored wider and more popular ambitions. However, the structure and functioning of both institutions were in principle very similar (membership, annual collections, 'limbs'). In many respects—especially regarding the publishing of fiction and popular educational books—the Catholic society was an *explicit rival* of the lay Matica; only its reach was greater.

2 The Founding of the Slovenian Matica: Prehistory 1845–1863

The history of the foundation of the *Slovenska Matica* is well researched.[9] There is no doubt that the first initiative was taken by the bishop Anton Martin Slomšek. With the assistance of Oroslav Caf, on 23 January 1845 Slomšek appealed to the authorities of *Ilirski gubernij* in Ljubljana for permission to found an association for the advancement of Slovenian books and literacy. According to Caf's writings in Bleiweis's *Novice* on 19 February 1845, the association's name would in fact be 'Matica,' but its actual character was supposed to be predominantly popular, oriented towards educating the broader masses. The literary historian Ivan Prijatelj assumes that the denomination was suggested by Caf, who was familiar at least with the Czech Matica. But the project was turned down—with no explanation or justification, as Slomšek complained.

---

7 This is a remarkable achievement given the fact that at the beginning of the nineteenth century the population of the territory of today's Slovenia had not reached one million (it rose to about 1,077,000 by 1846), and that by the end of the century this figure was about 1.3 million. The city population grew from some 6% in 1818 to roughly 16% in 1890, while illiteracy fell from 60% in 1830 to 15% by the end of the century.

8 After 1918 the role of the Society declined slightly, as other institutions and more regular publishing methods became competitive. After 1945, the Society was often hampered by the socialist authorities, but never really crushed. Today, *Mohorjeva družba* remains an important Slovenian publisher, still partly utilizing the original model of annual collections and advertising via the Church network. See also Hladnik; Dović 2007, 124–28.

9 This is perhaps no surprise, since one of the consistent features of the legacy of the Matica is its obstinate interest in its own history, etymology, trans-national connections, etc. This self-referential obsession is attested in numerous memorial records, histories, ceremonial speeches, and regularly issued publications with bibliographies.

Prijatelj assumes that Count Josef Sedlnitzky, the chief imperial censor, was in the background.[10]

After this first attempt failed, initiatives began to reappear in the Slovenian press after 1848. In 1850 a patriot from Celje, J. Šubic, proposed in *Novice* the establishment of a Matica based on Serbian, Czech, and Illyrian models, exclaiming at the end: "Let the Slovenian Matica rise!"[11] But in practice during the 1850s there were many conceptual dilemmas to be resolved regarding the founding of the Slovenian Matica. The major issue was whether the Matica should become distinctly Slovenian or should rather merge with the Illyrian Matica operating since 1842 in Zagreb. This was a crucial problem, since merging with the Illyrian Matica would result in a twin-track development: alongside the lively cultural developments in Slovenian, advanced scholarly projects would proceed in the Croatian language.[12] The hesitation was due to an awareness that the restricted financial powers of the young Slovenian bourgeois elites could not provide funds sufficient to generate adequate capital through annual interest, which was the desired model for the functioning of a Matica. At the same time, the pro-Illyrian intellectuals, especially in Carinthia, such as Janežič, Einspieler, and Majar, were in favor of merging with the Illyrian Matica.[13]

The constitutional changes in the early 1860s gradually brought more favorable conditions for establishing societies. In 1860, among the initiators of the Slovenian Matica were a Russian Slavophile, Ivan Aksakov, and Ferdo Kočevar (who published under the pseudonym Žavčanin), who argued that the establishment of such an institution, based on sufficient funding, was of vital interest for the national cause. In 1861 Janežič was still opposed to an independent Slovenian Matica project and maintained that merging with the Illyrian Matica would be a better solution. Many others, like Fran Cegnar in 1862, supported the idea of an independent Slovenian Matica. After the death of Slomšek in the fall of the same year, Franc Kosar reconnected this idea with the legacy of Slomšek's unsuccessful 1845 attempt; Kosar's Maribor lecture was promptly reported in *Novice*. At the beginning of 1863, when reading rooms were rapidly spreading across Slovenian territory and the millenary of the mission of Saints Cyril and Methodius into Moravia (in 863) was approaching, the

---

10   Prijatelj 1923, 3–5; Lah, 15–17.
11   Prijatelj 1923, 6.
12   Although the name suggested a broader South Slavic concept, the Illyrian Matica was in practice operating more or less in the Croatian language. In 1874, it was renamed the Croatian Matica (*Matica hrvatska*).
13   Even though at the very same time they had initiated a subscriber-based society for distributing Slovenian books, which later grew into the successful St. Hermagoras Society.

time finally seemed ripe. Fran Levstik, a writer and the future secretary of the Matica, promoted the cause in his *Naprej*, while the ingenious Lovro Toman, a poet and later a successful politician (and leader of the Slovenian deputies in the Vienna parliament) published an emotional appeal in *Novice* on 7 January connecting the Matica (as the mother-queen bee) with the idea of a bee-hive, and thus opening a potent metaphoric field which was later often exploited and expanded within the Matica discourse and nationalist discussions more generally. On 8 March 1863 a solemn *béseda* ceremony was staged in the Ljubljana reading room, including a plea by Toman and Bleiweis for the formation of a Matica that would allow "Slovenians to stand firmly among others in the family of nations."[14] The Illyrian dilemma seemed to be overcome, and the first patriotic florins for the independent Slovenian Matica soon began to flow in.

Toman, equally successful as an intelligent debater among the Vienna parliamentarians and as a poetic firebrand of his people's emotions at home, declared that the Matica was a "heart in the body of the nation" and that literature was its blood. Toman certainly knew how to write an appeal that would "find an echo in the hearts of patriotic donors."[15] The first to respond to proposals from Ljubljana were, surprisingly, the Styrian patriots from Maribor (Marburg) led by Janko Sernec and an energetic Czech immigrant, Emanuel Chocholoušek.[16] The Styrians managed to gather forty donors (each contributing the sum of 50 florins), and to send two encouraging letters to Toman and Bleiweis (all this correspondence was promptly published by *Novice*). Apart from the emotional charge—culminating in the metaphorical description of the Matica as the river Sava, collecting its streams to become a mighty current when it would join the great (Slavic) Danube—the letters sketched the general outlines of the organizational structure of the Matica; the second letter even included a proposal for the society's regulations. This practical gesture of initiative, wrapped up with the first money donations and draft rules, was passed on by the Maribor patriots (in a somewhat ritualized manner) to their Ljubljana compatriots. Toman, Bleiweis, and Etbin H. Costa, the mayor of Ljubljana, were the ones who had to take the following steps. The prospects for an independent Slovenian Matica seemed brighter now; after the short polemics

---

14 Prijatelj 1923, 18.
15 Ibid., 18–19. Contrary to the cold-hearted pragmatists, Toman was well aware of the mobilizing potential of the veneration of national poets and cultural saints. This is why he was so heavily involved in rituals, commemorations, and the designing of memorials to Vodnik and Prešeren (see Dović and Helgason, 111–22).
16 According to Prijatelj, Chocholoušek was among the fiercest patriots (1923: 20).

with Levstik, even the pro-Illyrian Janežič was now willing to take over the Carinthian committee.[17]

3 The Slovenian Matica: 1864–1914

As the enterprise gained momentum, the leading nationalist intellectuals in Ljubljana finished the Matica statute and formed a temporary committee consisting of forty members. While drafting the society's regulations, they considered all the available rules of the existing Slavic Maticas. The Emperor's decree of 4 February 1864 officially allowed for the foundation of the Slovenian Matica, but requested six minor adjustments in the proposed regulations. Among them, two are especially noteworthy: the addition of an explicit statement on the apolitical nature of the institution in §1, and the deletion of the word "Slavic" from the formulation "Slavic library" in §2. The adjusted version was finally approved on 6 June 1864. New members were invited to join: fifty florins (goldinars) were required for individual memberships and one hundred florins for institutions. Kaiser Franz Joseph I himself, the Ljubljana industrialist Fidelij Terpinc, and Baron Anton Zois each contributed five hundred florins, while the bishop from Đakovo in Croatia, Josip Juraj Strossmayer, even contributed one thousand florins. The business model was similar to that of the St. Hermagoras Society: members were supposed to receive the annual book collection for free, and other Matica-supported works with special discounts. According to the regulations, a part of the principal was to be invested for further development, and another part spent for the annual book production. On 11 April 1864 the founding meeting was held in the office of the Ljubljana Agricultural Association (which also hosted Bleiweis's *Novice*). Baron Anton Zois was elected as the first president. The nobleman soon withdrew due to ill health, leaving Lovro Toman to take over the presidency. The new secretary, with a monthly allowance of thirty florins, was Fran Levstik, a young writer and critic. Thus far, the total sum collected was four thousand florins, still far from

---

17   Toman, 146–47. Prijatelj's extensive interest in the prehistory of the Matica may itself be less striking than the enormous attention given to the issue of *primacy*. Later, especially Bleiweis and Toman were often accused of 'parasitism' and passive appropriation of what should be credited to the 'real' patriots. But this in fact is a part of a larger problem, namely the general discrediting of the so-called Old-Slovenians represented by Bleiweis and Toman. Fran Levstik's bitterly sharp comments, followed by the later communist rejection of these allegedly too conservative 'fathers of the nation,' need to be considered in order to explain the fact that their obviously invaluable contributions to the cause of nation-building (including the Matica) were later diminished and ignored.

sufficient for any serious enterprise. This is why a campaign to attract new members was launched immediately, leaning heavily upon the enthusiastic support of *Novice* and other newspapers.[18]

For the year 1865, a single book was prepared and distributed to the society's 'limbs' (among other things, members of the Matica shared this denomination with those of the St. Hermagoras Society). The *Calendar* (*Koledar*) included the Matica regulations, a short account of its history, and the membership list. Apart from the well known 'queen bee' and 'bee-hive' imagery, it introduced another inventive set of metaphors: an image of the family, consisting of fourteen Slovenian 'sisters' (the reading rooms), a 'brother' (the "Sokol" gym society), and a 'mother'—the Matica. The publication was supplemented with an interesting appendix, namely a "Map of the Slovenian Land and Provinces" donated by the lawyer and geographer Peter Kozler. This map's turbulent prehistory—the original print run and the copper plates were seized from the Vienna printer, and its author was even brought before a military court for alleged high treason in 1853—testifies that this piece of printed paper was loaded with explosive nationalist potential. The police ban had finally been lifted in 1861, so a broader audience could now view the map representing the territorial spread of Slovenian speakers (regardless of the administrative borders); moreover, the map used exclusively Slovenian toponymy and bore the self-confident expression "Slovenian land" in its title (see Figure 5.3).

On 5 November 1865 the first general assembly of the Slovenian Matica was held in Ljubljana. The somewhat ritualistic events of the day deserve a more detailed description. At 8:00 A.M. a solemn Catholic mass began in the Ljubljana cathedral as the bells rang festively.[19] Afterwards, the assembly moved to the Ljubljana city hall, made available to the Matica by the mayor, Costa. By that time, some seven hundred founding members had donated the sum of 26,000 florins.[20] The major dispute during the session was over whether the Matica needed a professional secretary or whether this work should be done

---

18 Lah, 27–40. These articles were often highly poetic, but also pretentious and hostile. Even prior to the founding of the Matica, Caf had expressed his wish that there should be no "wry Slovenian" (*spačeniga Slovenca*) who would not support such an endeavor (Prijatelj 1923, 4). Such exclusive rhetoric was later even intensified in the nationalistic discourse (see Lah, 40–41).

19 In the first years, there was no conflict between the Matica and the Catholic Church, although the latter was slightly concerned with its role in the new association: the bishop of Ljubljana stated that to the Matica "it will be a very sacred rule never to offend the Catholic faith in the published books" (Lah, 42). Obviously, unlike in the case of the St. Hermagoras Society, the Church could not exert any direct control over the Matica.

20 At the very same time, the rapidly expanding St. Hermagoras Society already counted over two thousand members.

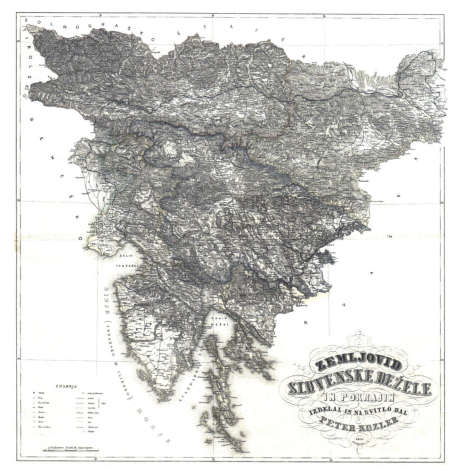

FIGURE 5.3   Peter Kozler, "Map of the Slovenian Land and Provinces." Supplement to the first annual Slovenian Matica collection, 1865.
SOURCE: ZRC SAZU INSTITUTE OF SLOVENIAN LITERATURE AND LITERARY STUDIES

by unpaid patriotic volunteers, as Josip Vošnjak and Janko Sernec proposed. Fran Levstik's professional position was supported by Davorin Trstenjak and Janez Bleiweis, and the idea of a professional secretary prevailed. A forty-member committee was elected. Among those who won almost unanimous support were Bleiweis, Zois, Toman, Costa, Terpinc, Kozler, and Trstenjak. The committee consisted mostly of all-round patriots rather than renowned scholars; nevertheless, it still could be described as a kind of a proto-academy. In the evening, a solemn *beseda* was staged, utilizing the standard repertoire of nationalist rituals: heated emotional speeches, national flags, the participation of the "Sokol" gym society, and the singing of the (unofficial) anthem *"Naprej, zastava Slave!"*[21]

In spite of the great expectations, the development of the Slovenian Matica was neither rapid nor steady. Among the counter-tendencies were—apart from the meager original production of Slovenian texts—the still present neo-Illyrian ideas, the rivalry with the St. Hermagoras Society, and the suspicions of some of the Catholic officials (such as Luka Jeran) towards the new institution. The evolution of the Matica in its first period, from 1865 to 1882, when it was led by the Old-Slovenians, is usually regarded as modest. The number of subscribers grew slowly and reached about fifteen hundred members in 1882. The main publication of the Matica was the annual *National Calendar* (*Narodni koledar*, 1865–68), later re-baptized as the *Chronicle of the Slovenian Matica* (*Letopis Matice slovenske*, 1869–98). The *Chronicle* was a hybrid publication consisting of scholarly contributions from very diverse fields mixed with literature, reports, membership lists, and other texts. For the most part, the literary works included in the Matica *Chronicle* were less significant than those published in contemporary magazines or even at Hermagoras. However, scholarly production in particular was progressing both in extent and relevance.[22]

Even if one sticks to the traditional view that the first two decades of the Slovenian Matica were not particularly successful, many achievements of this period remain unquestioned. In 1879 patriotic donors purchased an impressive building on Congress Square in central Ljubljana that remains the headquarters of the Slovenian Matica to this day. Other achievements include the publishing of Slovenian school textbooks, mostly adapted from German or Czech sources. After 1882, as the difficulties of the first period were overcome, the program of the Matica began to change. The talented editor Fran Levec joined the board, took up the function of a secretary, and from 1893–1907 led the company as its president.[23] The level improved and the membership increased: in

---

21   Simon Jenko's militant text, set to music in 1860 by Davorin Jenko, soon became an indispensable ingredient of Slovenian nationalist gatherings. *Slava* signifies both 'glory' and the 'Slavic world,' so the title means something like "Onward, the flag of the glorious Slavs!" See also Lah, 44–72.

22   In the 1890s, the decline of the miscellaneous *Chronicle* began as its components became emancipated. Since 1890, literature was no longer part of it. After the scholarly publications went their own way as well in 1899, only self-referential essays and documents remained for this once-central Matica annual publication (see Šlebinger 1930).

23   A gifted organizer, Levec halved the number of board members (from forty to twenty). In his period, the Matica's initially ceremonial assemblies gradually turned into (dull) operational business meetings.

the 1890s there were already about 2,000 subscribers, and this number rose to about 3,600 towards the end of his mandate. The 'Levec period' of the Slovenian Matica was marked by the establishment of special literary series. After 1886, Matica published the Leisure Library (*Zabavna knjižnica*) collection, which mostly consisted of original Slovenian prose works and other literary works in Slovenian translations. Soon, following a substantial donation, another series for literature was initiated. The Anton Knez Library (*Anton Knezova knjižnica*, since 1892) produced much quality original fiction (for example by Ivan Cankar) and some literary historical studies. In addition, a special series for literature in translation was published by the Matica from 1904 to 1907, thus broadening the literary horizons and the repertoire of the young literary culture.[24]

However, the ground-breaking achievements of the Matica in this period were the scholarly ones. Among them, of exceptional relevance are the eleven volumes of *Slovenian Folk Songs* (*Slovenske narodne pesmi*, 1895–1907) collected and edited by Karel Štrekelj. Among other major contributions, there were also a slightly contested *History of Slovenian Literature* (*Zgodovina slovenskega slovstva*, 1894–1900) by Karel Glaser; a *Slovenian Bibliography* (*Slovenska bibliografija*, 1903–05) by Franc Simonič; and *Slovenian Land* (*Slovenska zemlja*), a topographical-historical work published irregularly in separate volumes as of 1892. Apart from these, a number of scholarly monographs from all possible fields—from philosophy to geography, from linguistics to psychology—contributed immensely to the development of the individual scholarly disciplines and their terminology, thus paving the way for the later establishment of the university in Ljubljana. Compared to its beginnings in 1866, when Janez Trdina's pretentious nationalistic *Zgodovina slovenskega naroda* (*History of the Slovenian Nation*) was published, the scholarly level grew immensely during the next five decades.[25]

In 1914 the *Slovenska Matica* was banned because of Fran Maselj (pseudonym Podlimbarski)'s Slavophile novel *Mister Franjo* (*Gospodin Franjo*, 1913), which criticized the Austro-Hungarian occupation forces in Bosnia. The first period of the Matica was over.[26] In the final analysis, its half-century of

---

24   See Šlebinger 1930, 7–48.
25   See Šlebinger 1930. To do justice to Trdina, it should be noted that his work was written in 1850, when he was only twenty years old. In 1866, even this fervent nationalist was no longer inclined to publish his juvenile text; however, the Matica board owned the copyright (originally, the work was commissioned by Matica's predecessor, the Slovenian Association in Ljubljana) and decided to publish the book in spite of the author's reluctance (Dolinar, 174).
26   Mahnič 1998, 252.

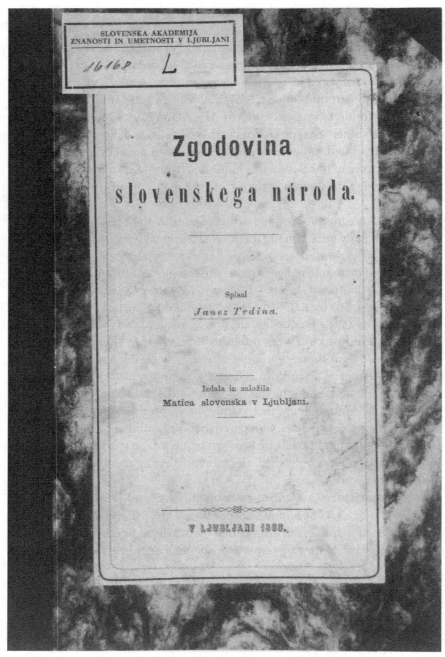

FIGURE 5.4　Janez Trdina, book cover of *History of the Slovenian Nation*, 1866. Even though the author—he wrote the book in 1850, when he was only 20—was not in favour of publication of his immature text any more, the young Matica felt a strong urge to come out with a Slovenian-written history.
SOURCE: ZRC SAZU INSTITUTE OF SLOVENIAN LITERATURE AND LITERARY STUDIES

activities proved invaluable, especially from the view of scholarly publishing and the co-ordination of scholarly work. The Matica also supported new original fiction (by awarding the Jurčič-Tomšič prize) and provided many Slovenian translations of world literature classics. As a publisher of literature, it was competing with the larger St. Hermagoras Society, a plethora of literary magazines, and a growing number of regular publishers and booksellers, such as the ambitious Lavoslav Schwentner.[27] On the other hand, the Matica was the first to demonstrate a concern for the systematic compiling and text-critical editing of national literary classics, thus forming the base of the vernacular literary canon. Apart from this, it took systematic care from the outset to cultivate the spirit of Slavic mutuality—the spirit that in fact marked its coming-into-being.[28]

After the collapse of the Habsburg Empire, the nearly one million Slovenians found themselves in the new political context of Royal Yugoslavia, experiencing a greater level of cultural autonomy in the new Slavic state.[29] In 1918 the work of the Slovenian Matica was resumed. Its confiscated property (though heavily depreciated) was returned, and the Matica regained the role of a central Slovenian scholarly publisher. With persistent criteria of high quality, it managed to publish an astonishing number of original and translated works from the humanities, social sciences, and literature. But inevitably, its previous roles were partly taken over by the University and later by the Academy of Sciences and Arts. After World War II, it was suspicious to the new Yugoslav communist authorities because of its bourgeois origins, but an attitude of tolerance prevailed and the Matica was allowed to remain on the thoroughly monitored cultural scene.[30] As a visible medium-sized Slovenian publisher, the Matica even enhanced its activities in the 1970s and 1980s by organizing

---

27 For more detailed analyses of Slovenian publishing history, see Moravec, Kovač, and Dović 2012.

28 From the very beginnings (organization, rules), the contacts with Czechs were especially important. In 1866 the Matica published the *Calendar*, Trdina's history, and the translated topographies of Carinthia and Carniola written in 1865 by a Czech geographer, Josef Erben. In 1867 the annual *Calendar* and the first two adapted textbooks were supplemented with Josip Marn's Czech grammar.

29 After the pressing issue of state borders was settled in 1920, more than four hundred thousand Slovenians found themselves living outside the borders of Yugoslavia (see Vodopivec, 173). In general, their cultural conditions soon became worse than they had been under Austro-Hungarian rule.

30 This unsettled period is thoroughly analysed by the historian Aleš Gabrič in a book (2015) issued on the occasion of the Matica's sesquicentennial in 2014. In 2018 Gabrič became the new chairman of the Matica.

symposia, lectures, and commemorations, partly siding with the dissident cultural stream and advancing Slovenian independence. After the establishment of the Republic of Slovenia in 1991, it continued its activities in the field of publishing but also in other areas.[31] Today, its membership and scholarly sections (on philosophy, natural sciences, history, and art history) still include highly renowned scholars, academics, publishers, and writers (such as Drago Jančar, a prominent Slovenian novelist and the chief editor of the Matica in the years 1981–2016).[32]

In the new millennium, the question of the relevance of such hybrid institutions imposes itself quite naturally—not only in Slovenia, but also in other (Slavic) cultures. One can assume that the times of the Maticas—at least as imagined by their originators—are ultimately gone. Yet it seems interesting that in many respects, the Maticas are still able to lean upon the obsolete nineteenth-century rhetoric. This is particularly visible in the cases of Croatian or Serbian Maticas that effortlessly legitimize themselves within the nationalist legacy, enjoying unanimous, virtually sacral reverence in their homelands; in this regard, the position of their Slovenian counterpart seems to be less exalted.[33] To be sure, the Slovenian Matica has also been claiming a privileged status in independent Slovenia, emphasizing its major historical role in culture, scholarship, and education. However, the state was not so eager to fulfil such desires, and in the period from 2001 to 2017, "the oldest Slovenian scholarly institution" found itself in serious economic difficulty as it was not receiving any special public financing.[34] The issue was finally resolved in November 2017

---

31 As the Matica describes its present role on its website (in Slovenian), it is "a scientific and cultural institution that organizes scholarly gatherings dealing with various problems of Slovenian culture and society and its future. At the same time, it is a publishing house responsible for publishing high-quality original works and translations in the humanities, social sciences, natural sciences, medicine, and technology" (http://www.slovenska-matica.si).

32 See the bibliographies and accounts in Bernik, Munda, Grafenauer, Mahnič 2004, and Jančar *et al.*

33 This impression was confirmed at the presentations in the Matica workshop organized by NISE in February 2012 in Budapest. It was also noted in the ceremonial oration by Milček Komelj on the 150th anniversary of the Slovenian Matica in 2014: according to him, some of the Slavic Maticas enjoy in their homelands the status of outright 'sacred things' (Komelj, 8), which is obviously not the case in Slovenia.

34 In this period, its major income was state subsidies for books—an area where it had to compete with other publishers. The discussions among publishers in this period revealed that many were not ready to recognize the work of the Matica as substantially different from the work of other (quality) publishers; for them, the required special privileges for Matica were perceived as unjust.

FIGURE 5.5 The main façade of the Slovenian Matica building in central Ljubljana (on the Congress Square) today. The building was purchased by the patriotic donors to serve as Matica headquarters in 1879 and has remained its seat till the present day.
SOURCE: THE SLOVENIAN MATICA ARCHIVE

when a new law was passed in the Slovenian Parliament, granting the Matica relatively bright future prospects.[35]

In 2014 the Slovenian Matica celebrated its 150th anniversary, marking the occasion with a set of high-brow celebrations and the publication of another major item in the series of self-referential works.[36] Once again, the anniversary displayed an excessive self-referential tendency—a feature shared by other Maticas as well; one could hardly find another institution that would focus so much on its own history, deal so obsessively with its own beginnings, collect all possible memorial accounts, publish bibliographies, record ceremonial speeches and lectures, or generate contests over primacy. Throughout its history, the Slovenian Matica has sometimes been an object of controversy, but

---

35 The law was ratified with remarkable unanimity (none of the deputies present voted against it). As of January 2018, the state acknowledges the special status of the Matica and is, among other things, obliged to provide the salaries of its three professional employees.

36 Apart from (scholarly) contributions to the Matica's history and bibliography, this volume also reproduces ceremonial speeches, memoirs, posters, the script of the solemn celebration in the Slovenian Philharmonia, and dozens of photographs of the ceremony's most eminent participants (see Jančar et al.).

also of enthusiastic statements, passionate actions, and national fervor. This is how the eminent art historian Milček Komelj, Matica president in the years 2008–18, opened his ceremonial oration on 4 April 2014:

> It has been written that the Slovenian Matica is the mother of the Slovenian nation, the mother of Slovenian culture and science, our first spiritually united Slovenia, the crown of all our precious endeavours, our most important national-defensive and cultural institution, our highest scholarly establishment, the representative of spiritual Slovenia, our little university, the barometer of Slovenian culture, our ancient house of privileges and culture; its founding charter was labelled as the great letter of Slovenian spiritual union and the magna carta of the cultivation of the entire Slovenian nation.[37]

Certainly, presenting (simply by 'quoting') the exultant Matica-discourse in such a condensed manner—in the physical presence of the Slovenian president and other influential politicians—can be seen as a legitimate strategy in the Matica's endeavours to secure its position in a world that is becoming overtly hostile to the humanities. Whatever course the future will take, it is not likely that the Slovenian Matica will ever (re)gain the status of a national 'sacred thing.' However, at least its historical relevance will (and should) probably remain undisputed. Indeed, as I would like to suggest in conclusion, the success of the Matica enterprise may in part be indebted to the rich metaphorical possibilities that the word *matica* itself conveyed.[38] The metaphors of a 'queen bee' (implying a field of diligent, industrious bees collecting the national honey), the notion of a 'treasure-house,' the 'motherly' aspects of the word, the metaphor of the 'foundation-stone,' and finally the comparison with the river (streams of Slavic tribes uniting into the great pan-Slavic hyper-river) have been powerful tools in mobilizing patriotic energies and funds, especially in the first decades of the Matica's history. In this way, the metaphorical landscapes of the *matica* often managed to transgress the boundaries of initially pragmatic and rational concerns and to anchor this poetic and self-referential discourse firmly in the embrace of a national ideology. After all,

---

37   Komelj, 5.
38   As the Budapest NISE conference in 2012 demonstrated, the reception of the term 'matica' was quite varied in different countries. Ivan Prijatelj, an influent Slovenian literary historian, maintained that the 'queen bee' meaning was misleading. According to his account, the Slovak Šafárik was the one who baptized the Serbian institution as 'matica,' referring to the Czech meaning of a 'treasury' or 'fund' (Prijatelj 1923, 2). However, Prijatelj's theory is hardly persuasive in the light of the fact that the image of a beehive was a part of the Serbian Matica sign from the outset.

this poetic appeal may also explain why other institutions labeled *matica*—covering such diverse areas as music (the *Glasbena matica*), exile (the *Izseljenska matica*), and mountaineering—kept emerging in the nineteenth and even in the twentieth century.[39]

Bibliography

Bernik, France, ed. *Slovenska matica 1864–1964* [The Slovenian Matica 1864–1964]. Ljubljana: Slovenska matica, 1964.

Dolinar, Darko. "Trdina in začetki slovenskega literarnega zgodovinopisja" [Trdina and the beginnings of Slovenian literary historiography]. In Marijan Dović, ed., *Janez Trdina med zgodovino, narodopisjem in literaturo*. Novo mesto, Ljubljana: Goga, Založba ZRC, 2005. 167–86.

Dović, Marijan. *Slovenski pisatelj: Razvoj vloge literarnega proizvajalca v slovenskem literarnem sistemu* [The Slovenian writer: the evolution of the role of the literary producer in the Slovenian literary system]. Ljubljana: ZRC SAZU, 2007.

Dović, Marijan. "Economics and Ideologies of Slovenian Literary Mediation." *Primerjalna književnost* 35:1 (2012), 121–40.

Dović, Marijan. "Memorials in the Slovenian Literary Culture." *Slovene Studies* 35:1 (2013), 3–27.

Dović, Marijan and Jón Karl Helgason. *National Poets, Cultural Saints: Canonization and Commemorative Cults of Writers in Europe*. Leiden and Boston: Brill, 2017.

Gaber, Ante. "Skozi stoletja za našim novinarstvom" [Our journalism through the centuries]. *Razstava slovenskega novinarstva*. Ljubljana: Jugoslovansko novinarsko udruženje, 1937. 179–223.

Gabrič, Aleš. "Slovenska matica v času politične netolerantnosti" [The Slovenian Matica in Times of Political Intolerance]. In Jančar *et al.*, eds., *Slovenska matica: 150 let dela za slovensko kulturo*. Ljubljana: Slovenska matica, 2015. 22–61.

---

[39] The *Glasbena matica* (Music Matica) was founded in Ljubljana in 1872 as a rival to the German-oriented *Filharmonična družba* (Philharmonic Society). Its aim was to publish and promote Slovenian compositions, collect ethnic music, and stimulate the (national) musical life. In 1882, the *Glasbena matica* music school was founded, which in 1920 became a conservatory and later the academy. In 1891 a quality choir was founded, and after 1900 its branches were also operating in Novo mesto, Gorica, and Trieste (a Maribor branch was founded in 1919). The *Izseljenska matica* (Exile Matica) was founded in Ljubljana in 1951 as an institution for coordinating the cultural activities of Slovenian emigrants around the world and connecting them with the homeland. Both maticas survive to the present day. Still active are also the mountaineering associations *Planinsko društvo* (PD) *Ljubljana-Matica* (since 1893), *PD Maribor-Matica* (since 1939), *PD Celje Matica*, and *PD Matica Murska Sobota*.

Grafenauer, Bogo. "Ob stodvajsetletnici Slovenske matice" [On the 120th Anniversary of the Slovenian Matica]. *Bibliografija Slovenske matice 1964–1983*. Ed. Jože Munda. Ljubljana: Slovenska matica, 1984. 5–14.

Hladnik, Miran. "Mohorjanska pripovedna proza" [The literary prose at the St. Hermagoras Society]. *Slavistična revija* 30:4 (1982), 389–414.

Jančar, Drago et al., eds. *Slovenska matica: 150 let dela za slovensko kulturo* [The Slovenian Matica: 150 Years of Work for Slovenian Culture]. Ljubljana: Slovenska matica, 2015.

Kovač, Miha. *Skrivno življenje knjig. Protislovja knjižnega založništva v Sloveniji v 20. stoletju* [The Secret life of books. Controversies of Slovenian book publishing in the twentieth century]. Ljubljana: Filozofska fakulteta, 1999.

Komelj, Milček. "150 let Slovenske matice" [150 years of the Slovenian Matica]. In Jančar et al., eds. *Slovenska matica: 150 let dela za slovensko kulturo*. Ljubljana: Slovenska matica, 2015. 5–9.

Lah, Ivan. *Začetki slovenske matice: Spominski spis k 50 letnici* [The beginnings of the Slovenian Matica: A memorial essay on the 50th anniversary]. Ljubljana: Slovenska matica, 1921.

Lapajne, Ivo. "Razvojne smeri slovenskega novinarstva" [The directions of development of the Slovenian journalism]. In Borko, Božidar, ed. *Razstava slovenskega novinarstva*. Ljubljana: Jugoslovansko novinarsko udruženje, 1937. 224–36.

Leerssen, Joep, ed. *Encyclopedia of Romantic Nationalism in Europe*. 2 vols. Amsterdam: Amsterdam University Press, 2018. (Online version: https://ernie.uva.nl)

Mahnič, Joža. "Razvoj Slovenske matice od njenih začetkov do prve svetovne vojne" [The Development of the Slovenian Matica from its Beginnings to the First World War]. *Jezik in slovstvo* 43:6 (1997–98): 247–54.

Mahnič, Joža. *Včeraj, danes, jutri: Slovenska matica 1965–2003* [Yesterday, Today, Tomorrow: The Slovenian Matica 1965–2003]. Ljubljana: Slovenska matica, 2004.

Moder, Janko. *Mohorska bibliografija*. Celje: Mohorjeva družba, 1957.

Moravec, Dušan. *Novi tokovi v slovenskem založništvu. Od Schwentnerja do prvih publikacij akademije* [New currents in Slovenian publishing. From Schwentner to the first publications of the Academia]. Ljubljana: DZS, 1984.

Munda, Jože, ed. *Bibliografija Slovenske matice 1964–1983* [Bibliography of the Slovenian Matica 1964–1983]. Ljubljana: Slovenska matica, 1984.

Perenič, Urška. "The Reading Societies Network and Socio-Geographic Dynamics." *Slavistična revija* 62:3 (2012), 383–400.

Prijatelj, Ivan. "Predzgodovina ustanovitve 'Slovenske matice'" [The prehistory of the establishment of the 'Slovenian Matica']. In Borko, Božidar, ed. *Razprave I*. Ljubljana: Znanstveno društvo za humanistične vede, 1923. 1–35.

Prijatelj, Ivan. *Slovenska kulturnopolitična in slovstvena zgodovina 1848–1895* (I) [Slovenian cultural-political and literary history 1848–95 (I)]. Ljubljana: DZS, 1956.

Simonič, Franc. *Slovenska bibliografija* [The Slovenian bibliography]. Ljubljana: Slovenska matica, 1903–05.

Šlebinger, Janko, ed. *Publikacije Slovenske matice od leta 1864 do 1930* [Publications of the Slovenian Matica from 1864 to 1930]. Ljubljana: Slovenska matica, 1930.

Šlebinger, Janko. "Slovenski časniki in časopisi. Bibliografski pregled od 1797–1936" [Slovenian newspapers and magazines. Bibliographical overview 1797–1936]. *Razstava slovenskega novinarstva v Ljubljani 1937*. Ljubljana: Jugoslovansko novinarsko udruženje, 1937.

Toman, Lovro. "O zadevah matice slovenske" [On Slovenian Matica Issues]. *Kmetijske in rokodelske novice* 21/19 (13 June 1863), 146–47.

Vatovec, Fran. *140 let slovenske žurnalistike* [140 years of Slovenian journalism]. Maribor: n.p., 1937.

Vidmar, Luka. *Zoisova literarna republika* [Zois's literary republic]. Ljubljana: ZRC SAZU, 2010.

Vodopivec, Peter. *Od Pohlinove slovnice do samostojne države. Slovenska zgodovina od konca 18. do konca 20. stoletja* [From Pohlin's grammar to the independent state: Slovenian history from the end of the 18th century to the end of the 20th century]. Ljubljana: Modrijan, 2006.

CHAPTER 6

Framing a Regional Matica, from Dalmatian to Croatian

Daniel Baric

The existence of a whole range of 'maticas' with a variety of names in the Croatian cultural space can be seen as a consequence of changing political contexts tending in the long run toward cultural unification.[1] An Illyrian matica was founded in Zagreb in 1842, which became a Croatian matica in 1874,[2] while a Dalmatian matica was founded in 1862 in Zadar, the administrative capital city on the Adriatic coast, and remained active under this name until the First World War. A Yugoslav matica existed during the interwar period. In 1951 the central institution in charge of Croatians living abroad was founded as a matica and it is still active, operating from Zagreb.[3] Shortly after the independence of Croatia, a matica of the citizens of Zadar was founded in 1993, just after the siege of the city by the Yugoslav army was lifted.[4] Such a variety of institutions and names implies a shift in the way their members and the population perceived the promising potential of maticas. The actual role of the maticas in shaping modern Croatian culture, understood mainly as the need for publishing books and periodicals, along with organizing conferences and other social events with a cultural content, displays parallel developments, with specific rules and targets. Beyond the acknowledged quest for a culture defined in

---

1 In the nineteenth century Croatia did not exist as a full-fledged state, nor as a territorial continuity. Continental Croatia was part of the Kingdom of Hungary, whereas Istria and Dalmatia were administered from Vienna. For an overview of the institutional and cultural context, see Goldstein and Ganza Aras.
2 See the successive histories of the matica of Zagreb published by its own presidents: Smičiklas and Marković; Ravlić 1963; Bratulić (ed.); Bratulić and Mažuran; Damjanović.
3 *Hrvatska matica iseljenika* (Croatian matica of Emigrants), the "Croatian Heritage Foundation" in its official English translation. http://www.matis.hr/index.php/en/about-us/history (accessed 28 March 2016).
4 According to the local newspaper on the occasion of the celebration of twenty years of activities of the *Matica Zadrana* in March 2013, it is "unique in Croatia as an association free of political parties," promoting "the culture of living in the city of Zadar and its Croatian identity." See: http://www.zadarskilist.hr/clanci/28032013/matica-zadrana---glas-zadarske-savjesti (accessed 28 March 2016).

terms of national identity, the maticas in Croatia can also be regarded as places of blurred national identities, especially in the cases of regional foundations.

The first maticas were founded in the South Slav area in a time of redefinition of the nation, hence there were competing terms in use. 'Croatian' originally referred to inhabitants of North-West Croatia around Zagreb, whereas other names were given to the populations living in the eastern part of what is nowadays Croatia ('Slavonians') and in Dalmatia, where the term 'Slavo-Dalmatians' differentiated Croats and Serbs from the Italian-speaking population. As elsewhere in Central and Eastern Europe, the cultural patrimony and feeling of belonging to a nation was increasingly shared beyond learned and aristocratic circles, by a population that was becoming acquainted with linguistic and cultural ties. Spreading this culture to a wider collectivity was the main aim of the maticas, and this goal was realized by supporting writers, critics, and journalists, publishing and thus canonizing poetry and novels, and promoting art exhibitions and public concerts.[5] The multiple engagement of the Croatian maticas mirrors the efforts made to cultivate and celebrate a distinctiveness within a multicultural environment.

Focusing on a regional matica, however, brings to the fore a particularism based not on a single nation but on a territory. If the movement to nationalization of the Dalmatian matica can certainly be traced through to the eve of World War One, resulting in a convergence with the Croatian matica in a virtual merging of both maticas, this union does not encompass all the various activities in which the Dalmatian institution engaged. Recognizing the regional dimension of the matica as a cultural phenomenon brings into relief the popularity of this kind of institution, which was dedicated not only to promoting exclusively national identities. From its very beginning, the Dalmatian matica indeed strove to promote a specific regional and transnational identity; but cultivating one national culture was not the main goal of the founders of the Dalmatian matica. Nor was it the aim of the incipient Croatian matica, which was founded under an ambiguous, large-scale programmatic Illyrian name, encompassing ideally all South Slavs, even if its overall evolution witnessed nonetheless the growing predominance of the Croatian element.[6] An integrative understanding of cultures emerges from a programmatic perspective in regional as well as national contexts, which raises the question of the

---

5   In these activities, the maticas in Zagreb and Zadar replicated models that began spreading all over Europe some decades earlier (see Thiesse). For an approach which showcases various European examples anticipating elements to be found in the Croatian case, see Hellmuth and Stauber (eds.).
6   See Baric 2002.

actual understanding of the aim of the institution among its targeted audience. The Dalmatian matica was a succession of projects coming from its members, but it was also inspiring projections from outside that together determined its social significance.

1 Letters to the Matica: A Vision from Outside

The vast majority of the members of the Dalmatian matica were inhabitants of the region. In 1862, when the association was founded, fifty of them lived in Zadar, eighteen in Dubrovnik, ten in Dobrota in the Bay of Kotor, and one each in some twenty-one other localities.[7] Their sociological background shows a wide range of occupations and social status, but they all had in common a permanent contact with written culture. There were noblemen (the Borelli princes in Zadar, or Prince Medo Pucić in Dubrovnik, who were socially active), Catholic and Orthodox priests, and the head of an Orthodox monastery, along with an archimandrite, a director of a gymnasium, a professor, student, journalist, merchant, typographer, head of the Slavic reading room in Dobrota, lawyer, president of court, public prosecutor, postman ...[8] The members who were residents in continental Croatia, especially in Zagreb, played an important role due to their social status. A significant sum of money was donated by Josip Juraj Strossmayer, Bishop of Slavonia (and patron of the future Yugoslav academy), as well as by another influential cleric, Juraj Haulik, Bishop of Zagreb, and the Ban (viceroy) of Croatia, Josip Šokčević. Further east, the poet and Austrian army officer Petar Preradović, who was posted in Zadar in the 1840s, was the correspondent (*povjerenik*) of the Dalmatian matica in Timişoara in the Banat.[9]

The Dalmatian matica was in charge of promoting, through a network of correspondents, the activities of the matica well beyond the borders of the city of Zadar and the region, as a possible source of patronage, as shown by letters sent to the directorate. Among the correspondents with the matica appear some would-be writers who had not yet been published and hoped for publication by the matica. A mixture of respectful distance, faith in the strength of that institution, and self-confidence characterized the way they defined their

---

7 From North to South on the Adriatic coast: Rijeka, Bribir, Novi Vinodolski, Senj, Mali Lošinj, Obrovac, Smoković, Benkovac, Biograd, Šibenik, Drniš, Sinj, Kozica, Orebić, Korčula, Komiža, Babino Polje, Trsteno, Cavtat, Lopud and Perast. Zagreb numbered three, Osijek in Slavonia sixteen, Vienna two, and Florence one member (list in Diklić 2002, 173–77).
8 Ibid.
9 Ibid., 178.

own relation to the matica. Those who wrote to the board of directors generally expressed precisely what they expected from them. Some obviously irrelevant demands required no discussion in depth, such as that of the otherwise unknown Steva Kluić,[10] who addressed a letter (beginning in Italian) in which he proposed to publish a biography of Leonardo da Vinci.[11] He obviously ignored the essentially Slavic dimension ascribed to the maticas, and also the specific Dalmatian context of cultural competition between the Italian- and Slavic-speaking populations.[12] The supposed purposes and duties of the Dalmatian matica were explained by the correspondents themselves. Ivan Hramelli, an officer from Zadar, wrote in justification of his request to be sent books for free:

> I would like to emphasize that it has not been possible for me until now to come into possession of good instructive books, because I did not have the means to purchase any, so that the Venerable Direction will make a remarkable patriotic gesture if as many books as possible are donated to me [...] since the scope of the Croatian and Dalmatian maticas is to spread culture among our Croatian people through its patriotic work.[13]

These explicit formulations of the goals of the Dalmatian matica indicate that it took some time for the matica to provide information about its activities to Dalmatians who could identify with them. Ivan Hramelli explained that he had been informed about the possibility of receiving books in the local newspaper *Narodni List*.[14] Whatever their internal debates might have been to elaborate a cultural program, in their replies to the letters received by the board the matica had to explain precisely what its actual scope was and what could and could not be accomplished.[15]

---

10   Steva Kluić is neither recorded in the catalogues of the Croatian National and University Library (Zagreb) nor of the Research Library (Zadar), apart from a translation from Czech into Croatian of a guide for foreigners (Pitlik).
11   Hrvatski Državni Arhiv Zadar, Fond Matica dalmatinska, 567, box 1, piece 34. Letter with no date.
12   Cattaruzza, 49–68.
13   Hrvatski Državni Arhiv Zadar, Fond Matica dalmatinska, 567, box 1, piece 34, 20 November 1914.
14   The bilingual newspaper *Il Nazionale/Narodni List* published in Zadar adhered closely to the program of the Dalmatian matica for promoting Slavic culture. Both were founded in 1862, and its first director Natko Nodilo (1834–1912) was a member of the matica. On the political impact of the newspaper, see Cetnarowicz, 69–73.
15   Unfortunately the replies of the matica were not preserved.

The fact that the Dalmatian matica became pivotal in the whole cultural life of Dalmatia, not only in the field of literature but also in the fine arts, appears clearly in a letter sent by Josip Cortellazzo, a doctor of law of local noble descent:[16]

> I happened to get acquainted in Drniš with Petar Bibić, the son of farmers in the village of Velušić. [...] They told me that he was an artist [...] He showed me some of his works: various decorative pieces in which he represents the tragic poverty of our black and merciless mountainous region. [...] All of this he did without any school, just following his genius, that elemental force which moves him. I am deeply convinced that Petar Bibić is a born artist, one of those who come from the womb of our people [*iz matice plemena našega*].[17]

The deeply regional value of his work was emphasized by the use of the term *matica* (in the sense of *matrix*), which conveyed the idea of a natural affinity with the institution itself. The arguments of this supporter were eloquent enough to convince the board of the Dalmatian matica to grant Petar Bibić (1893–1971) a stipend from the institution, and also to finance his studies in Prague. Bibić became an artist and eventually gained popularity, especially after World War Two for his sculptures representing partisans.[18]

Over time the Dalmatian matica became a central cultural institution even for the highest representatives of the state: Emperor Franz Joseph sent a letter of congratulation at the very end of the official existence of the Dalmatian matica in 1916, when the fiftieth anniversary of the Austrian naval victory over Italy in July 1866 at Lissa/Vis in Dalmatia was celebrated.[19] This event was an important element of Austrian imperial patriotic memory and needed to be remembered especially during the ongoing war. As one of its first editorial projects the Dalmatian matica had published a poem in honor of the battle that had significantly strengthened Austrian pride in the face of Italy, even if the diplomatic benefits were negligible. The author, Savo Matov Martinović,

---

16   http://hbl.lzmk.hr/clanak.aspx?id=8925 (accessed 29 March 2016).
17   Hrvatski Državni Arhiv Zadar, Fond Matica dalmatinska, 567, box 1, piece 34. Letter with no date, probably 1912.
18   *Likovna enciklopedija Jugoslavije*, t. 1 (Zagreb 1984), 123. Hrvatski Državni Arhiv Zadar, Fond Matica dalmatinska, 567, box 1, piece 25 holds the letters sent by Bibić to the matica from Prague in 1912.
19   Hrvatski Državni Arhiv Zadar, Fond Matica dalmatinska, 567, box 1, piece 33, 11 August 1916.

was a Montenegrin living in Zagreb.[20] From the very beginning, the regional mission of the matica was understood as an extensive one, which gained acknowledgment from a wide variety of social strata.

2   The Dalmatian Matica as a Regional Institution

The history of the Dalmatian matica has been interpreted, in accordance with changing political contexts, as a mirror of the then-current cultural situation which required retrospective study. However, compared with other similar institutions, the Dalmatian matica did not stimulate a number of historians to produce monographs. The history of the Croatian matica has been presented far more often in a detailed way, uncovering the history of what is still perceived as a central institution in the development of modern Croatian culture.[21]

The historiography of the maticas tends to be self-referential, and this applies to the Dalmatian case as well.[22] A history of the institution itself, which remains an invaluable source for research on that institution, was published by one of the secretaries of the matica, Petar Karlić.[23] Access to archival sources is difficult, since the documents on the Dalmatian matica were dispersed among different archival series in the early 1920s following its cessation of activities, mainly in the State Archives in Zadar. This material is far from complete. Many documents that could have helped in tracing the history of the institution have been lost in the aftermath of the tumultuous events following the end of World War One and the installation of Italian authorities in Zadar. The extant material does make it possible to identify some main topics, and raises questions concerning the contexts in which the Dalmatian matica was active. Its name suggests that it was merely a regional institution, but the profile of its members and its publications show a less clear-cut affiliation.

---

20   Martinović. See Ravlić 1972, 196.
21   *Vijenac*, one of the oldest journals on cultural issues, has been published since 1869 by the Croatian matica, which also publishes other cultural and scientific magazines for a wider audience.
22   Petar Karlić (1913) and Marjan Diklić (2002), who relies heavily on the first historian, have proposed a chronology for the internal organization of the matica: 1. The formative period (1848–62); 2. Foundation and activity from 1862 to 1874 under the presidency of B. Petranović; 3. The presidency of Miho Klaić (1875–96); and 4. Towards the merging with the Croatian matica. Historians of the Illyrian/Croatian maticas who are themselves involved in the functioning of these institutions have done the same. Nevertheless, scholarship from outside the institution has recently begun to develop (e.g. Aralica).
23   Karlić 1913, Part 1.

According to its goals, the Dalmatian matica achieved major editorial successes in its efforts to reach the South Slavic population. During the whole period of its existence, ties were maintained with many readers through the *National Calendar* (*Narodni koledar*) published every year from 1863 to 1900, and through the *Collection of Folklore* (*Narodna pjesmarica*) that was edited seven times between 1865 and 1912.[24] These books were distributed in the city of Zadar through a growing network of specialized libraries.

Publishing books in the local Slavic language and making them available to the general public was an issue of paramount importance to the founders. Confronting one of the highest rates of illiteracy in Austria-Hungary, the Dalmatian Slavic elites wished to stimulate the intellectual improvement of the population, and also to promote the development of an alternative to Italianate culture. This goal was especially important in Zadar, where most of the population spoke Italian, whereas the countryside and the other Dalmatian cities started in the 1870s to elect local Slavic representatives. The administration of the matica provided a network and an efficient supply chain for Slavic books, which were given to nascent cultural institutions on local levels. A 'National Reading Hall' (*Narodna čitaonica*) was established in 1862 under the aegis of the Dalmatian matica. Ivan Woditzka founded a lending library in 1869, followed by another one established by Franjo Wagner.[25] A Catholic lending library had beeen established between 1872 and 1876, followed in 1878 by both a Serbian reading room (*Srpska čitaonica*) and a German reading room. A Croatian reading room opened at the end of the century in the nearby Albanian-speaking suburb of Arbanasi.[26] In 1889 there were five bookshops in Zadar, with the Croatian one playing a leading role until World War One. The matica shared its premises with the Croatian reading hall from the beginning, and in 1903 followed its move to a more prominent and purpose-built accommodation on the new embankment in town.

Zadar occupied a specific place in Dalmatian culture, since it was the administrative and political center of a bilingual kingdom that was part of a multinational empire. A growing specialization of spaces according to linguistic demarcation lines was a reflection of the evolution of Dalmatia towards the nationalization of municipalities by Croatian parties, which began in the 1870s,

---

24 South Slavic *narod/narodni* can be translated as both nation/national and as people/popular. Other Slavic languages (Slovenian, Polish) use distinct terms (*narod/naroden* and *ljudstvo/ljudski* in Slovenian, *naród/narodowy* and *lud/ludowy* in Polish).
25 On the context in which the matica was working in Zadar, see Batović *et al.* (eds.), 221–37 and 864–72.
26 Diklić 1994, 95–106; Galić, 60–63.

with the sole exception of Zadar, which remained in the hands of parties in favor of Dalmatian autonomy and an Italian preponderance in public life. Public libraries and comparable associations promoting Italian culture were flourishing, like the *Lega nazionale,* the *Società Dante Alighieri,* and *Pro Patria,* established in 1887.[27] Still, amidst such a context of self-assertive national programs, the Dalmatian matica remained an institution that cultivated cross-cultural exchanges to some extent, and thus maintained a continuity with its foundation.

The original idea of establishing a Dalmatian matica was due to the counsellor at the Court of Appeal in Zadar, Božidar Petranović (1809–74), in the aftermath of the revolutionary movements in 1848–49 which articulated national programs demanding autonomy. Born in Šibenik into an Orthodox family, Petranović studied Law in Graz and Vienna, and in 1836 he launched the *Serbian-Dalmatian Magazine* (*Srbsko-dalmatinski Magazin*), gaining his first experience as an editor and cultural activist, at this point from a clearly Serbian perspective.[28] Inspired by the Czech example, he hoped to generate funds that would make it possible, as the Illyrian matica had done in 1842, to finance the publication of works of Renaissance literature, especially from Dubrovnik, as well as of practical books, in a language understandable for both Croats and Serbs.[29] All of them were to be published in the new orthography established by the Illyrian circles in Zagreb, which was supposed to spread more easily than the prestigious literature that was originally edited mostly in Venice, with transcriptions adopted from the Italian.[30]

After the end of the neo-absolutism of the Austrian Empire in the mid-1850s, which meant more freedom in the public sphere for collective initiatives, the regulations of the Dalmatian matica were sent to Vienna for approval, which was eventually given, so that the official opening of the Croatian matica could take place in July 1862 in Zadar.[31] The statutes made explicitly clear that the aim of the institution was to "publish useful national books, first of all those which intend to promote morality and civilization among the population, and when the capital interests of society will allow it, also those which

---

27   The Biblioteca Comunale Paravia was opened in 1857 in the Renaissance loggia on the main square in Zadar. http://www.zkzd.hr/hr/knjiznica/povijest (accessed 26 April 2016). See also Balić-Nižić, 16.
28   For biographical information see Perić; concerning the journal, see Prpa-Jovanović.
29   Karlić 1907, 8–11.
30   For questions of orthography and competing language standards in Zagreb and in Dalmatia, see Vince, esp. pp. 207–20.
31   Ravlić 1963, 92.

contain the works of our old classics."[32] The moral aspects were supposed to meet the expectations of the local government, as clearly appeared from the second article, which cautiously stated that "the matica is hence a purely literary society, and therefore any political discussion is to be excluded from its work."[33] Its activities were closely followed by the highest authorities. The statutes stipulated, after a correction in a different ink on the original document approved by the governor of Dalmatia, that in the deliberations of the sections an absolute majority of the present members was necessary. But "for a modification of the rules two-thirds of the votes are necessary and the approval of the sovereign," and not just the consent of the public authorities, this phrase being deleted.[34] A supplementary article was added by the authorities legalizing their right to keep an eye on the activities of the society: "The public authorities reserve to themselves the right to nominate a commissioner in order to keep watch on the compliance of the activities of the society with the rules, for which purpose he is entitled to make inspections."[35] Approval of the rules applying to the Dalmatian matica was linked to the right reserved for the highest imperial representatives in Vienna—not in Dalmatia—to control the content and the internal organization of the matica.

The constant scrutiny under which the Dalmatian matica was placed by the founding regulation originated in the cautious observation by the authorities of the potential trouble that could arise from the cultural orientation of the matica in Zadar. The belief in the unity of the South Slavs, which in Dalmatia meant Croats and Serbs, and which had been spreading ever since the beginning of the Illyrian movement in Zagreb in the 1830s, was regarded with unease in Vienna as a way of propagating Slavic solidarity and potentially an

---

32   Hrvatski Državni Arhiv Zadar, Fond Matica dalmatinska, 567, box 1, piece 36. The original rules, elaborated by "Dr Teodoro Petranovich," were approved on 24 June 1862. The documents were written in Italian and Croatian. The Italian version reads: "Regolamento della Società 'Matica dalmatinska,' visto ed approvato dall'i. r. Luogotenenza dalmata: 1. La Società della Matica dalmatinska in Zara è fondata allo scopo di raccogliere un capitale, che deve servire: 1) all'edizione di utili libri nazionali principalmente di quelli che intendono a promuovere la moralità e la civilizzazione del popolo, e quando le rendite della società lo consentiranno anche di quelli che contengono le opere dei nostri antichi classici."

33   "Da ciò consegue, che la Matica è una società puramente letteraria, e che quindi dalle sue trattazioni resta esclusa ogni discussione politica."

34   § 23: "per una modificazione del regolamento è necessario il voto di due terzi dei votanti e il consenso della pubblica autorità [deleted] e la sovrana approvazione."

35   § 26: "È riservato alla pubblica amministrazione di destinare un suo commissario, il quale sorvegli che l'azienda della società proceda secondo il regolamento, e per ciò ne possa prendere ispezione."

alternative political project.[36] The notion of cultural and linguistic unity as a prelude to a political one was expressed under the presidency of Petranović and of Miho Klaić (1829–96), the vice-president who took over the responsibility in 1875. Klaić was a professor of mathematics at the gymnasium of Zadar, a historian and active politician as a member of both the regional and the imperial parliaments. But the proclamation of political neutrality within the matica proved unsubstantial in reality, since the founding presidents articulated their convictions in the National Party (*Narodna stranka*). The activities of the Dalmatian matica were by no means politically neutral, but neither were they systematically explicit.

The common interest of the Croatian and Serbian maticas is evident from the names of the first donors who participated in the foundation of the new matica. The seal of the institution was logically inscribed in both Latin and Cyrillic letters. There were contacts between the institution and representatives of the Serbian association, who obviously did not consider the Dalmatian matica as purely Croatian, or at least as an exclusively Croatian club, even if some members clearly perceived its scope as chiefly Croatian: some letters end significantly "with Croatian greetings."[37] There were also signs of resistance to this interpretation. In the first pages of the literary magazine of the Dalmatian matica, *Glasnik Matice dalmatinske*, in May 1901, it was clearly announced that henceforth the magazine would publish regular updates about the literary scene in Serbia from their correspondent in Belgrade, the literary critic and prominent politician Jaša Prodanović (1867–1948).[38] This effort to bring information about recent Serbian literature to Dalmatia was seen as a positive element by one author (signing with the initials M.C.) who noted that publications in Cyrillic script used to go unnoticed by Croats in Dalmatia, who were simply unable to decipher books from the best publishing houses in Belgrade (*Srpska Knjižema Zadruga*), whereas Serbs in Dalmatia could read books published by the Dalmatian matica (though he admitted that he could not judge the situation in Serbia, with which he was not familiar). The author expressed the wish that reviews would help to "tear down the Chinese wall that separates Croatian from Serbian literature."[39] To give readers a chance to get acquainted

---

36   Rumpler, 196–200.
37   Croatian could also be endorsed by Serbs as a territorial denomination and not a national one. Petranović was openly in favor of the public use of what, at a meeting with Serbs of Dalmatia in Knin in July 1848, he called "our dear Croatian language." See Diklić 2002, 141.
38   On *Glasnik Matice dalmatinske* see Košutić-Brozović; V. Maštrović 1952; Milanja 1994.
39   M. C., "Srpska (iz novije književnosti)" (Serbian [recent Literature]), *Glasnik Matice dalmatinske* 1:2 (August 1901), 194.

with the other side of that wall was, he continued, in the uttermost interest of everyone.

In order to reduce the hindrance caused by a less familiar alphabet, the most popular periodical in Dalmatia, *Narodni Koledar* (the *National Calendar*), provided a table of concordance of the Latin and Cyrillic alphabets. As the eminent literary critic Jakša Čedomil noted, the publication of popular songs by the Dalmatian matica also went in this direction by displaying orally transmitted images of heroes that exemplified the struggle against the historical enemies, the Turks and Venitians.[40] These reflections on literature cannot be clearly understood outside of the political context in which a Croatian-Serbian coalition against the Italian-speaking autonomists was being elaborated at the time these texts were published, fostering the idea of a common interest in defending Slavic rights against those represented by Venice, namely by the Italian-speaking people of Dalmatia. Numerous texts recalled the black legend of Venice, whose memory was attacked as fiercely as it was cherished in contemporary Italian publications in Zadar. "Who can describe all the crimes of the Venetian rule in Dalmatia during four hundreds of years?" lamented the author of an article on the destruction of the forests in Dalmatia by the Venetians, a sensitive topic for a predominantly rural Slavic population. The message was conveyed with a national background: "Venice had annihilated every conscience in them (the Dalmatian Croats), every pride. The Dalmatians had forgotten that they are Croats, that they belong to the Croatian people. He (the Dalmatian Croat) thought he was created only to be a slave to the Venetians!"[41] The opposition to Venice had also the practical potential to unite all of the South Slavs, including the Bosnian Muslims. It is the merit of Luka Jelić (1864–1922), a Catholic priest and archaeologist, to have presented a Muslim from the hinterlands of Zadar as a hero for having fought against Venice and having allowed an inn to be constructed on the shores of Lake Vrana which Jelić described as the most beautiful piece of Dalmatian architecture in the seventeenth century.[42] As its main literary review clearly demonstrates, the Dalmatian matica functioned indeed as an intellectual forum that allowed

---

40   See Milanja 1993.
41   "Kako su Mletčani uništili dalmatinske šume" (How the Venetians Destroyed the Dalmatian Forests), *Narodni koledar za prostu godinu 1899* (National Calendar for the Year 1899), 55.
42   Luka Jelić, "Vranjanin začetnik kandijskoga rata (1645–1671 god.)" (Jusuf Mašković of Vrana, who Initiated the Cretan War [1645–1671])," *Glasnik Matice dalmatinske* 1:2 (August 1901), 113–29. After extensive renovation, this westernmost complex of Ottoman civil architecture was re-opened in July 2015. https://hr.wikipedia.org/wiki/Maškovića_Han (accessed 26 April 2016).

people to gather and mingle ideas and texts beyond confessional definitions that were becoming national, and thus contributed to the development of a regional identity understood as a matter of Slavic reciprocity. Dalmatia, however, was not a restrictive horizon.

3 The Dalmatian Matica as a Transnational Institution

With its membership and its material resources, as well its intellectual production, the Dalmatian matica was growing beyond the region. Approximately two hundred members formed the first network of the Dalmatian matica, extending well beyond the borders of Dalmatia and Croatia. The third paragraph of the founding text stated that interest in the activities of the matica could come from outside of Dalmatia and contribute financially to the constitution of the capital, and so it happened. Some members lived outside Dalmatia, in Slavonia, Slovenia, or Vienna. Letters arrived from all over the world, from Graz to Buenos Aires, expressing the wish to promote cooperation.[43] Though regional in its name, the matica of Zadar attracted interest in all Croatian regions and throughout the world, wherever there was a wish to establish a link with the land of the family origins. Dalmatia's poor economic development, linked with an acute phylloxera crisis in agriculture, entailed a demography characterized since the 1880s by the massive departure of some one hundred thousand emigrants, mainly to North and South America.[44]

In Dalmatia itself, social life in the matica was organized to disseminate knowledge among South Slavic readers, especially in the libraries. Among the most appreciated events organized by the matica were public readings by authors. These were social gatherings organized around publications, often by Croatian writers coming to Zadar.[45] Starting with its material organization, some models needed to be found for the Dalmatian matica. The very basic and essential matter of displaying, lending, and preserving books had as a consequence that furniture needed to be installed in the premises of the matica, that is, in a room inside the Croatian reading hall. It was part of the program of the matica in Zadar to propose books to readers, but also to provide bookshelves showing members that the South Slavs could provide an alternative to Italian

---

[43] Hrvatski Državni Arhiv Zadar, Fond Matica dalmatinska, 567, box 1, piece 18. Letters from the associations "Hrvatsko katoličko akademsko društvo Preporod" (Croatian Catholic Academic Associatation Revival) in Graz (31 May 1912) and "Hrvatska straža-Sociedad croata" (Croatian Watch-Tower) in Buenos Aires.

[44] Stipetić, 17.

[45] T. Maštrović 1990, 15–38.

intellectual and material culture. With this purpose in mind, in 1911 the directors of the matica appealed to the Slovenian matica in Ljubljana, which replied with contact details. Cabinet-makers from Slovenia were eventually hired to deliver the most important pieces of furniture. A cooperative of carpenters from Carniola (*Prva kranjska mizarska zadruga u Št. Vidu nad Ljubljano*) followed a model of cupboards provided by the Slovenian matica. Moreover, there was a correspondance with leading journals in Slovenia concerning the exchange of publications, so that readers in Zadar could take from the solid Slovenian wooden cupboard literary productions in Slovenian, such as its most representative *Ljubljanski Zvon* (1881–1941). To read Slovenian periodicals became possible by the time the furniture arrived, since the director of that Slovenian review, Janko Šlebinger, agreed in March 1912 to send copies of all issues and related publications.[46] The political landscape, however, was no longer the same. Illyrian hopes of South Slavic unity had been periodically rejected and regularly reactivated. What remained was a concentration on Croatian culture, with a distinctive interest in Serbian and Montenegrin cultures in Dalmatia.[47] The consequences for the maticas in both Zadar and Zagreb were obvious.

The Croatian matica established itself as the most prominent publisher of works dealing with Croatian culture. Some twenty years after the idea emerged, a specialized field was functioning in the editorial landscape of Croatia, with the Yugoslav Academy since 1866 publishing strictly academic works, whereas since 1868 the Society of Saint Jerome (*Jeronimsko društvo*) produced books with a definite Catholic character for a much wider audience. This form of shared publishing, as it functioned in Zagreb, was known in Zadar and a reduplication was attempted, with all the restrictions due to the situation in Dalmatia, including a smaller number of possibly interested and well-to-do readers. An agreement between the Croatian and the Dalmatian maticas dated 16 January 1911 was meant to solve the discrepancy between readerships in continental and maritime Croatia. This document has been interpreted as a major turning-point, and as effectively marking the end of the Dalmatian matica.[48] The Croatian matica in Zagreb was supposed to publish regularly for the Dalmatian matica in Zadar and to foster joint publications. However, the autonomy of the Dalmatian structure was maintained all the same. The Dalmatian matica was to "stay as it was, under its own administration, organized according to its own rules"; that is, it would remain autonomous in its main

---

46   Hrvatski Državni Arhiv Zadar, Fond Matica dalmatinska, 567, box 1, piece 33, 22 March 1912.
47   Roksandić, 83–90.
48   Karlić 1913; Diklić 2002.

prerogative, namely the editorial choices.[49] This was the first act of a merger with the Croatian matica. Both maticas agreed to cooperate in order to play a joint role in the development of Croatian culture, despite the long-standing administrative and cultural divide between Zagreb in Hungarian Transleithania and Dalmatia in Austrian Cisleithania. It seemed that the Croatian theme was gaining ground after the agreement between the maticas of Zadar and Zagreb, since the first book published by the Dalmatian matica in Zagreb was a work by the native Dalmatian writer Vladimir Nazor (1876–1949) entitled *Croatian Kings* (*Hrvatski kraljevi*). A history of Croatian literature was subsequently published by two authors, Vatroslav Jagić and Branko Vodnik (*Povijest hrvatske književnosti*), and there were numerous signs of activities aimed at exchanging books from the Dalmatian coast to the continental part of Croatia. This connection gained value in the eyes of the Croatian protagonists since it crossed the internal borders of Austria-Hungary. In doing so, it could realize what Croatian political leaders had sought in the last decades of the Habsburg monarchy: the association of the regions inhabited by South Slavs into a single coherent part of the empire.[50]

But the horizons of the Dalmatian matica developed well beyond the neighboring Slavic and Italian populations. The publications in the 1890s were no longer solely committed to a program of enlightenment and the promotion of the most recent Croatian literature. They also provided insights into other European literatures originating not only from Slavonic cultures. Correspondents from abroad were invited to deliver papers about Croatian, Serbian, Czech, and Polish, but also French, German, Dutch, Norwegian, and even Italian literature. This inflection towards more ambitious and international literary standards was due to the activism of Jakov Čuka (1868–1928), a former student of theology in Zadar and Rome, then professor of Croatian and theology at the Classical gymnasium of Zadar, who wrote under the pseudonym Jakša Čedomil in Croatian as well as in Italian, and read extensively in French and Italian. He was elected secretary of the matica in 1901, and is regarded as the founding father of modern literary criticism in Croatian.[51] The project was supposed to federate and emulate the entire literary scene in Dalmatia, which the Croatian matica had failed to reflect in the columns of its periodical published in Zagreb due to the existence of an alternative cultural institution, the association of writers, which heralded literary modernity in Zagreb. The Dalmatian literary review was fated to a brief existence, since its contract with the publisher, the

---

49   Diklić 1994, 162.
50   Stančić, 17.
51   Milanja 1985; Frangeš, 439–40.

Croatian bookshop (*Hrvatska knjižarnica*) founded in 1901, was not renewed. As a matter of fact, it turned out that there was a lack, and not a plethora, of readers for such contents in Dalmatia.

The publication had from 1901 to 1904 nevertheless offered an unprecedented widening of aesthetic and intellectual perspectives in the literary journals published in Croatia. A constant reflection revolved around the question of the specific place of Dalmatia in the world. An article by Ivo Tartaglia (1880–1949)—who later became mayor of Split and played an active role in interwar politics—about a play by the Dutch author Herman Heijermans, *Op Hoop van Zegen* (The Good Hope), showed the interest of the Dalmatian review in literary events far removed from local preoccupations. The article pointed out the tragic fate of fishermen on the Dutch coast who did not share the same understanding of the sea as in Dalmatia, where even tragedies, Tartaglia claimed, take place under a bright sky and do not completely annihilate the Mediterranean temperament.[52]

What was at stake with the series of notes on cultural events from abroad was a reflection on foreign literature, its benefits and potential dangers. Interweaving elements on regional cultural identity with reflections on cosmopolitan elements was the starting point for the search for a balance between "extreme nationalism and undefined cosmopolitanism, so that we learn from foreigners how to broaden our ways of thinking and sources of inspiration, [...] so that we multiply, not diminish our original creative energy."[53] The author (Marin Sabić) clearly formulated thoughts that were arising from the daily practice of the Dalmatian matica in its efforts to contextualize regional and national cultures in a multinational environment.

4   The End of the Regional Matica

After 1912 the activities of the Dalmatian matica as an autonomous body were diminished, first by the cooperation with the Croatian matica and then by the war. But it took a direct stroke to be expelled from Zadar. The way the Dalmatian matica ended reflects its multinational connections. Italy obtained the territory of Zadar in the Peace Treaty of Rapallo in 1920. Tensions rapidly

---

52   Ivo Tartaglia, "Holandeška: *Nada, Op Hoop van Zegen*: Primorska drama u 4 čina od Hermana Heyermana" (Dutch Literature: *The Good Hope*: A Sea-side Drama in Four Acts by Herman Heijermans), *Glasnik Matice dalmatinske* 1:4 (February 1902), 443–48.

53   Marin Sabić, "Narodna književnost i kozmopolitizam" (National Literature and Cosmopolitanism), *Glasnik Matice dalmatinske* 1:3 (November 1901), 357–69, here p. 368.

escalated in the city, now officially Italian in the middle of a predominantly Croatian- and Serbian-speaking environment on the other side of the new state border. Italians as well as South Slavs tended to feel that their rights had been infringed by the peace settlement. The former had hoped that the irredentist dream of an Italian Dalmatia would come true after the war, while the latter regretted that the regional center had become an Italian enclave.[54] After a first inspection of the Slavic books on the shelves in the Croatian reading room, where the matica was again functioning, the captain of the *carabinieri* who took control of the city in the name of the Italian government asked the person in charge of the institution to explain what kind of society this matica was exactly.[55] It was answered to the Italian officer that the Dalmatian matica was a purely literary society which had no political tendency whatsoever, as stated in its foundation charter. After a few months, an order was given to vacate the premises within twenty-four hours, which led to the rapid transfer of the volumes to the Serbian reading room, which agreed to house the reading stacks. The librarian of the Croatian reading room was then briefly informed that his duty was over. He left for Šibenik, in the territory of the South Slav Kingdom, so he could no longer look after the belongings of the matica in the rooms of the Serbian reading room. Shortly after this first transfer of books in 1922, some unidentified people forced their way into the Serbian reading room and started throwing the books down onto the main street of Zadar, while some others set about burning them. The *carabinieri* intervened and prevented a massive destruction. What remained from the bonfire, some fifteen hundred books, were transferred out of Zadar and housed in the rooms of a new institution, the Yugoslav matica in Šibenik, some seventy kilometers farther down the coast. Five pieces of the—probably Slovenian—furniture could also be salvaged: four cupboards and one table.

These events prove that the Dalmatian matica did exist for a short period of time in the interwar period, which is generally ignored by historians of the Croatian maticas who assume that the cooperation started in 1911 marked the end of the Dalmatian institution. But it was well remembered, first of all as a symbol, simply by its own existence in a completely new context, in a city now belonging to the Italian state. Even if its activities during the war and afterwards were not so numerous as in the preceding period of peace, the institution existed in the minds of the politically most active Italian-speaking people

---

54   Cattaruzza, 162–64.
55   Hrvatski Državni Arhiv Zadar, Fond Matica dalmatinska, 567, box 1, piece 1. Report of Mirko Perković on the fate of the Dalmatian matica in Zadar after the Italian occupation, 24 June 1927.

in Zadar, who saw in it precisely the instrument of their major political and cultural enemy, their Slavic neighbors in the town and in the newly established Kingdom of Serbs, Croats, and Slovenes. At this point, the Dalmatian matica could not survive, neither as a Slavic institution in a city that had become a stronghold of growing Italian irredentist anti-Slavic policy, nor in a region that had lost its autonomous status in the new South Slav state.[56] Nor could it survive as a regional institution, since Dalmatia was incorporated into a Slavic state with political options that excluded Dalmatian autonomy. The members and the material remnants of the institution were thus distributed among Croatian, Serbian, and Yugoslav affiliations.

Regional maticas are founded, may expand, and may disappear. They bear an inherent fragility in promoting a distinction at odds with the national paradigm. The Dalmatian matica was a place were regional identity was constantly enacted, but not with the aim of promoting a distinctive Dalmatian nation. If this distinction is the prelude to political independence, a matica is an important institution. As Montenegro gained its autonomy, a separate Montenegrin matica was founded in 1993, which played a role in defining Montenegrin culture as against Serbian and anticipated the independence of the state.[57] In the Czech case, a Moravian matica was among the first to be founded, in 1853, and after the period of loss of autonomy in Socialist Czechoslovakia it was reestablished in 1990, at a time of massive expectations for the democratization of culture.[58] Regional maticas emerge as the expression of a need to expose and spread a specific identity in the face of a dominant national culture. The Dalmatian matica can therefore be seen as much as a part of Croatian as of Dalmatian and of European cultural history.

Bibliography

Aralica, Višeslav. *Matica hrvatska u Nezavisnoj Državi Hrvatskoj* [The Croatian matica in the Croatian Independent State]. Zagreb: Hrvatski institut za povijest, 2009.

Balić-Nižić, Nedjeljka. *Talijanski pisci u Zadru pred Prvi svjetski rat* [Italian Writers in Zadar on the Eve of World War One]. Rijeka: Edit, 1998.

---

56   For the integration of Dalmatia into the South Slav kingdom, see Jakir (on the Yugoslav matica, see pp. 364–65).
57   http://maticacrnogorska.me/omatici.html (accessed 29 March 2016).
58   http://www.matice-moravska.cz/historie-a-soucasnost (accessed 8 October 2018). See also Chocholáč.

Baric, Daniel. "Der Illyrismus: Geschichte und Funktion eines übernationalen Begriffes im Kroatien der ersten Hälfte des 19. Jahrhunderts und sein Nachklang." In Jacques Le Rider, Moritz Csáky and Monika Sommer, eds., *Transnationale Gedächtnisorte in Mitteleuropa*. Innsbruck: Studien Verlag, 2002. 126–140.

Batović, Šime *et al.*, eds. *Zadar za austrijske uprave* [Zadar under Austrian Administration]. Zadar: Matica hrvatska, 2011.

Bratulić, Josip, ed. *Matica hrvatska: 1842–1997*. Zagreb: Matica hrvatska, 1997.

Bratulić, Josip, and Ive Mažuran. *Spomenica Matice hrvatske: 1842–2002* [Commemorative book of the Croatian matica]. Zagreb: Matica hrvatska, 2004.

Cattaruzza, Marina. *L'Italia e il confine orientale*. Bologna: Il Mulino, 2007.

Cetnarowicz, Antoni. *Die Nationalbewegung in Dalmatien im 19. Jahrhundert. Vom "Slawentum" zur modernen kroatischen und serbischen Nationalidee*. Frankfurt am Main: Peter Lang, 2008.

Chocholáč, Bronislav. *Matice moravská: Dějiny od počátku do současnoti* [The Moravian matica: A History from the Beginning to the Present Time]. Brno: Matice moravská, 1997.

Damjanović, Stjepan. *Matica hrvatska jučer, danas, sutra* [The Croatian matica Yesterday, Today, and Tomorrow]. Zagreb: Matica hrvatska, 2015.

Diklić, Marjan. "Hrvatska čitaonica u Arbanasima" [The Croatian Reading Room in Arbanasi]. *Zadarska smotra* 5–6 (1994), 95–106.

Diklić, Marjan. "Matica dalmatinska od osnutka do ujedinjenja s Maticom hrvatskom (1862–1912) povodom 140. obljetnice utemeljenja i 90. obljetnice ujedinjena" [The Dalmatian matica from its Foundation to its Unification with the Croatian Matica (1862–1912), on the Occasion of the 140th Anniversary of its Foundation and the 90th Anniversary of its Unification]. *Zadarska smotra* 1–2 (2002), 139–84.

Frangeš, Ivo. *Povijest hrvatske književnosti* [History of Croatian Literature]. Zagreb-Ljubljana: Nakladni zavod Matice hrvatske-Cankarjeva založba, 1987.

Galić, Pavao. *Povijest zadarskih knjižnica* [A History of the Libraries of Zadar]. Zagreb: Društvo bibliotekara Hrvatske, 1969.

Ganza Aras, Tereza. "Zašto Matica dalmatinska a ne Matica hrvatska u Dalmaciji?" [Why a Dalmatian and not a Croatian matica in Dalmatia?]. *Zadarska smotra* 5–6 (1994), 13–22.

Goldstein, Ivo. *Croatia: A History*. London: C. Hurst & Co., 1999.

Hellmuth, Eckhart, and Reinhard Stauber, eds. *Nationalismus vor dem Nationalismus?* In *Aufklärung* vol. 10, book 2. Hamburg: Felix Meiner Verlag, 1998.

Hrvatski Državni Arhiv Zadar [Croatian State Archive in Zadar], *Fond Matice dalmatinske* [Collection on the Dalmatian matica], classification mark: HDAZd 567, *kutija* (box) 1.

Jakir, Aleksandar. *Dalmatien zwischen den Weltkriegen: Agrarische und urbane Lebenswelt und das Scheitern der jugoslawischen Integration*. München: R. Oldenbourg Verlag, 1999.

Karlić, Petar. *Matica dalmatinska*, dio I, Osnutak i rad do izdanja *Narodnih pjesama* 1865 [The Dalmatian matica, Part 1: Foundation and Functioning until the Publication of the *Popular Songs* in 1865]. Zadar: Matica dalmatinska, 1907.

Karlić, Petar. *Matica dalmatinska*, dio I–III. Zadar: Matica dalmatinska, 1913.

Košutić-Brozović, Nevenka. "Značenje *Glasnika Matice dalmatinske* u književnom životu hrvatske moderne" [The Significance of the *Messenger of the Dalmatian Matica* in the Literary Life of Modern Croatia]. *Zadarska smotra* 5–6 (1994), 33–42.

Martinović, Savo Matov. *Viški boj* [The Battle of Lissa/Vis]. Zadar: Matica dalmatinska, 1867.

Maštrović, Tihomil. *Drama i kazalište hrvatske moderne u Zadru* [Drama and Theater of Croatian Modernism in Zadar]. Zagreb: Nakladni zavod Matice hrvatske, 1990.

Maštrović, Vjekoslav. "*Glasnik Matice dalmatinske* u Zadru (1901–1904)" [*The Messenger of the Dalmatian Matica* in Zadar (1901–1904)]. *Zadarska revija* 1:1 (1952), 19–26.

Milanja, Cvjetko. *Jakša Čedomil*. Zagreb: Sveučilište u Zagrebu-Liber, 1985.

Milanja, Cvjetko. "Jakša Čedomil (Jakov Čuka), kao sakupljač narodnih pjesama na Dugom Otoku" (Jakša Čedomil [Jakov Čuka], as a Collector of Popular Songs on Dugi Otok). *Zadarska smotra* 1–2 (Zbornik o Dugom Otoku, 1993), 362–82.

Milanja, Cvjetko. "Europski kriterij *Glasnika Matice dalmatinske*" [The European Criteria of the *Messenger of the Dalmatian Matica*]. *Zadarska smotra* 5–6 (1994), 43–50.

Perić, Ivo. "Kulturna i politička djelatnost Božidara Petranovića" [The Cultural and Political Activity of Božidar Petranović]. *Radovi Zavoda za hrvatsku povijest* 10:1 (1983), 45–96.

Petranović, Božidar. *Ustanova Družtva Matice dalmatinske* [The Institution of the Society of the Dalmatian matica]. Zadar: Matica dalmatinska, 1868.

Pitlik, Augustin. *Prag, glavni grad Češkoslovačke republike* [Prague, the Capital City of the Czechoslovak Republic]. Prague: Češkoslovački ured za strance, 1920.

Prpa-Jovanović, Branka. *Srbsko-dalmatinski magazin 1836.–1848.: preporodne ideje Srba u Dalmaciji* [The Serbian-Dalmatian Magazine 1836–1848: Ideas of National Renaissance among Serbs in Dalmatia]. Split: Kniževni krug, 1988.

Ravlić, Jakša. *Povijest Matice hrvatske, 1842–1962* [The History of the Croatian matica, 1842–1962]. Zagreb: Matica hrvatska, 1963.

Ravlić, Jakša. "Matica dalmatinska u podizanju narodne svijesti 1862–1870" [The Role of the Dalmatian matica in Raising the National Consciousness 1862–1870]. In Dinko Foretić, ed., *Dalmacija 1870*. Zadar: Matica hrvatska, 1972. 179–200.

Roksandić, Drago. *Srbi u Hrvatskoj od 15. stoljeća do naših dana* [Serbs in Croatia from the 15th Century to Our Own Days]. Zagreb: Vjesnik, 1991.

Rumpler, Helmut. *Österreichische Geschichte 1804–1914: Eine Chance für Mitteleuropa: Bürgerliche Emanzipation und Staatsverfall in der Habsburgermonarchie*. Vienna: Überreuter, 1997.

Smičiklas, Tade and Franjo Marković, ed. *Matica hrvatska od godine 1842. do godine 1892.: spomen-knjiga* [The Croatian matica from 1842 to 1892: A Commemorative Book]. Zagreb: Matica hrvatska, 1892.

Stančić, Nikša. "Hrvatski politički i društveni prostor u dugom XIX. stoljeću: segmentiranost i integracijska kretanja" [Croatian Political and Social Space in the Long 19th Century: Segmentation and Integrative Dynamics]. In Mislav Ježić, ed., *Hrvatska i Europa* [Croatia and Europe], vol. IV. Zagreb: HAZU-Školsla knjiga, 2009. 3–12.

Stipetić, Vladimir. "Stanovništvo Hrvatske u XIX. stoljeću (1800–1914)" [The Population of Croatia in the 19th Century (1800–1914)]. In Mislav Ježić, ed., *Hrvatska i Europa*, vol. IV. Zagreb: HAZU-Školsla knjiga, 2009. 13–24.

Thiesse, Anne-Marie. *La Création des identités nationales: Europe, XVIIIe–XXe siècle*. Paris: Éditions du Seuil, 1999.

Vince, Zlatko. *Putovima hrvatskoga književnog jezika: Lingvističko-kulturnopovijesni prikaz filoloških škola i njihovih izvora* [On the Roads of the Croatian Literary Language: Linguistic, Historical and Cultural Review of Schools of Philology and of their Sources]. Zagreb: Nakladni zavod Matice hrvatske, 2002.

CHAPTER 7

Macedonian Societies in the Balkan Context

Liljana Gushevska

In the 1880s, a number of cultural-educational and scientific-literary societies were established in the larger city centers in Macedonia (a part of the Ottoman Empire) as well as in the neighboring Slavic countries (notably Bulgaria). Their activities coincided with the period when Bulgarian propaganda intensified and gradually became dominant in the areas of culture, education, and religion in Macedonia, and when Serbian propaganda also intensified and was striving to position itself a little better and suppress any other claims. As a result, Macedonian separatism came to the fore and was promoted as a serious presence that became a subject of interest to the proponents of Bulgarian and Serbian propaganda.

We shall focus on two such societies through whose activities we can follow the development of a number of prominent intellectuals from Macedonia who were united around a common program and goals in this period, although later they would hold different—and even opposite—ideological and political positions.

In the Ottoman Empire the eighteenth century was a time when feudal relations were still undergoing transformation. In the area of foreign affairs, the Empire suffered more and more defeats by modern European armies; and with every peace agreement it lost parts of its territory, which in turn left it increasingly dependent on West European countries economically and politically. Besides Austria, Russia imposed itself more and more as the Empire's fiercest opponent (especially after the 1774 agreement) by profiling itself as the main supporter of the struggle of Orthodox Christians in the Balkans for freedom from Ottoman rule.[1]

As regards internal affairs, the situation became increasingly complex because of the growing power of the local feudal lords, who began to act independently of the central authorities. The crisis in Ottoman society and in the *timar-sipahi* system had the greatest impact on the peasants (the *raya*). Due to deficits in the state treasury, the central authorities increased the

---

1 Chepreganov, 148.

economic pressure on the *raya* by raising the existing taxes and introducing new ones.²

This anarchic situation of course also affected Macedonia, which was under Ottoman rule at the time. At the beginning of the eighteenth century, the consequences of the Great Turkish War (1683–99) were still being felt in its northwestern parts. In the western and central parts, numerous groups of bandits remained active, attacking and pillaging villages as well as travelers, caravans of merchants, monasteries, and even some of the larger towns. This unrest helped to increase the migration from the countryside to the cities and to changes in the demographic structure of urban settlements where the Macedonian Christian population became predominant. This trend continued until the first decades of the nineteenth century, when state reforms by the central Ottoman authorities calmed the situation to some extent.³

The last decades of the nineteenth century are characterized by large migrational movements in both the liberated and the non-liberated territories of the Balkan Peninsula.⁴ After the Congress of Berlin (1878), the position of the Christian population, which was mostly Macedonian, deteriorated. The economic conditions became particularly complex after the resettlement of tens of thousands of *muhajirs* (Muslims) who came to Macedonia from territories the Empire had lost in its wars or through decisions made by the Congress.⁵ The immense displeasure of the Macedonian people was manifested through organizing and starting uprisings and rebellions. The failure of these forms of organized armed resistance directed at the Ottoman Empire and the repressions undertaken against the civilian population increased the numbers of migrants even more. In 1878 in the Principality of Bulgaria alone there were 54,462 inhabitants who came from the Ottoman Empire, or rather from Macedonia. In 1893 this number increased to 66,971 people.⁶

---

2 Ibid., 148–49.
3 The *Hatt-ı Şerif of Gülhane* (Imperial Edict of Gulhane, 1839) proclaimed full equality of all citizens before the law, irrespective of their religious and ethnic affiliation, and guaranteed to all the subjects of the sultan the security of their persons and property. In February 1856, after the Crimean War, the *Hatt-ı Hümayun* (Imperial Reform Edict) was declared, an act which furthered the equality of all citizens of the Empire as regards their rights and duties. With these acts of reform, it was expected that the Empire would be transformed into a modern state of the western type (Chepreganov, 166–67).
4 Todorovski, 338. Russian and French diplomatic sources contain a number of accounts regarding the numerous Macedonian refugees at the time of the Russian temporary administration of Bulgaria. For more on this and on the fate of the Macedonian refugees, see Pandevska, 62–67.
5 From Serbia, Montenegro, and particularly from Bosnia and Herzegovina.
6 Todorovski, 339.

As regards religion, the church institution through which the 'millet system'[7] operated at this time on the territory of Macedonia and beyond, was the Archbishopric of Ohrid (which answered to the Patriarchate of Constantinople). What is characteristic is that it had its own church courts which settled disputes between Christians independently of the Ottoman courts.

In the eighteenth century, the Patriarch intensified his efforts to impose his own influence by increasing the use of Greek language at liturgies and in schools. This finally resulted in the abolition of the Archbishopric by an edict by the Sultan in 1767, and its eparchies were annexed directly to the Patriarchate.[8] After this, the Patriarchate began to intensify the Hellenization of the southern and south-western parts of Macedonia in particular, which led in the following period to an almost complete elimination of the use of the Church Slavonic language at liturgies and the folk language in schools in these areas. The Hellenization also affected the Vlachs, even though very few of the Vlachs and the Macedonians spoke Greek well.

Thus, an organized anti-Patriarchate action began around the mid-nineteenth century, especially in some of the larger Macedonian cities. Through the affirmation of their demands, the Macedonian citizenry was, among other things, trying to improve its position and to impose itself in the economic and social life within the state.

---

7 The essence of the millet system was the right of non-Muslim communities to regulate and manage their own internal affairs with respect to religion and other civil rights such as marrying, divorcing, property issues, education, etc. The religious representatives answered to the Ottoman authorities as regards their flock respecting the law. Immediately after the fall of Constantinople, three more millets, besides the Muslim millet, were legitimized in the Ottoman Empire: the Rum Millet (Orthodox), the Armenian Millet, and the Jewish Millet. All of the Orthodox population in the Balkans fell under the Rum Millet, the head of which was the Patriarch of Constantinople (Chepreganov, 157). For more on the term millet system, see Pandevska and Mitrova.

8 At that time the non-Muslim population was not covered by the educational system of the Empire. Therefore, the Archbishopric of Ohrid (especially the lower ranking clerics, who came mostly from Macedonia) played a significant role in preserving the religious and cultural identity of Orthodox Christians throughout the entire Balkans, and in spreading literacy among this population. In fact, the first schools were created in churches and monasteries, which were the only places where the Slavic script could be taught and clerics educated. Islamic education, on the other hand, was mostly of a religious character, though Eastern languages were also taught there, as well as Islamic philosophy and law, mathematics, etc. Education was conducted in the *mektebs* and *madrassahs* (the elementary and secondary Muslim schools). The Jews also had their own educational institutions; there were schools for children and adults within the synagogues. They had their own libraries, and their most important spiritual centre in this area was Thessalonica (Chepreganov, 161–62).

On the other hand, the struggle of the Macedonian and Bulgarian citizenry for church emancipation ended with the proclamation of the Bulgarian Exarchate with the Sultan's *firman* (decree) dated 28 February 1870. In accordance with the laws of the Empire, the Bulgar Millet was also recognized along with the existing millets. Hence, in order to acquire a legal status, the Macedonians were forced to join one of the two church institutions recognized by the authorities: either the Patriarchate or the Exarchate. Those who were included in the Patriarchate were registered as being Greeks in the various statistical records (much like the other Orthodox populations, for instance the Vlachs), while those included in the Exarchate were registered as being Bulgarians.[9]

One of the primary tasks of the Bulgarian Exarchate, especially after 1878, was spreading Bulgarian national and political influence in Macedonia, that is to say educating Macedonian youth in the spirit of the 'literate' culture of the Principality of Bulgaria. This category of pupils were expected later to seek an equivalence of cultural and political borders, i.e., to be annexed to the state whose *literate* culture they had adopted. Because of this, there was an early and active reaction against the *culture* sent out via the Exarchate.[10]

---

9   As regards the number and composition of the population in Macedonia, there are a number of statistics, mainly in the context of the statistics on the population in European Turkey. However, the numbers presented vary depending on the time period in which the statistical data was gathered, and depending on the origins of the author of a particular set of statistics, as well as on the definition of "Macedonia." To illustrate this, let us compare the reports by two Russian diplomatic representatives. Foreign advisor M. Petraiev explained that Macedonia encompasses the villayets of Thessalonica and Bitola, and about half of the Kosovo Villayet, and had a population of approximately 2,500,000 people. As regards the ethnic composition of the population, he presented the generally accepted view, supported by the official Turkish statistics as well, that the population was comprised of Turks, Albanians, Greeks, Bulgarians, Serbs, Kutzo-Vlachs, Jews, and Gypsies. But he was of the opinion that if one put aside the Turks, Jews and Gypsies as elements that had settled there additionally and had kept their individuality, then the rest of the population was a separate, mixed 'Macedonian' type that could not be placed under the heading of any of the known ethnographic groups. See: Notes by the foreign advisor Petraiev regarding the nationalities in Macedonia dated 17 December 1909, created in St. Petersburg (Dracul, 61–62). And this was the view of the Russian Consul Kalj: "Most of the authors that are researching the ethnography of Macedonia and are trying to present tables of its population belong to the nationalities and are interested in one of the existing propagandas; such is the case with: the Bulgarians—Shopov, Brankov, Knchev, Ishirkov; the Serbians—Cvijich, Ivanich, Gopchevich; the Greeks—Nikolaidis, Kazasis; the Romanians—Margariti, Duma, Diamandi; and others..." See: A short review to the First Department "Statistical and Ethnographic Accounts on the Population in the Villayet of Bitola," 19 February 1910 (Dracul, 97).

10 Kotlar-Trajkova, 183.

1 The Secret Macedonian Committee (SMC)

With such a constellation of relations in Macedonia (as part of the Ottoman Empire) and in its closest surroundings, the Secret Macedonian Committee was established in 1885 in Sofia by a group of Macedonian students (and not only students) at the University of Sofia. With its members originating from different parts of Macedonia, the Committee had its branches in other places as well.[11] The Bulgarian capital did not prove to be a favorable environment in which this society could develop its activities. According to data from the Bulgarian police, this group of about twenty young people promoted the idea of Macedonian separatism, that is to say that Macedonians were not Bulgarians but a distinct people with their own historical background. This was in collision with the fixed Bulgarian politics regarding any manifestation of a separate Macedonian identity. The police report[12] mentioned the following names of 'separatists': Dimitar Aleksiev (from v. Tresonche, Debar area), Kosta Ginovski (v. Galichnik, Debar area), Mihail Jordanov from Veles, Emanuil Georgiev from Kumanovo, Risto Chumerov from the village of Gjavato (Bitola area), Gjorgji Kostov from Prilep, Nikola Josifov from Tetovo, Vasil Karajovov from Skopje, Naum Evro from Struga, and Kosta Grupche (1849–1907) and Temko Popov (1855–1929), both from Ohrid. The Committee was uncovered and disbanded by the Bulgarian police; most of its members had to leave Bulgaria, and some of them went to Serbia.[13]

2 The SMC's Program Platform and the Activities Undertaken for Its Fulfilment

Four of the members of the Committee (Vasil Karajovov, Naum Evro, Kosta Grupche,[14] and Temko Popov) attended the negotiations with the Serbian government that took place towards mid-August 1886. They were supposed to make a plan for a mutual action in Macedonia that would include gathering sufficient funds for restoring the Archbishopric of Ohrid enabling the opening of church-school communities, taking the necessary steps for issuing

---

11 Ristovski 2011, 43.
12 The report is dated 18 December 1885 (Dimevski 1977, 195).
13 Dimevski 1977, 195.
14 Kosta Grupche came from the ranks of the Ohrid Educational and Students Society 'Saint Clement' and had close relations with Grigor Prlichev, one of the most prominent national activators and agitators in the fight for the suppression of Graecism in Ohrid.

a magazine *Macedonian Voice* in Macedonian in Constantinople, opening schools throughout Macedonia and appointing teachers who would teach in the Macedonian language, as well as printing books in Macedonian for the needs of the schools and the Macedonian people.[15]

After that, Evro, Grupche, Karajovov and Popov began their mission to realize these goals.[16] Thus, Temko Popov was employed as an economist at the boarding school of the Bulgarian Exarchate Gymnasium in Salonica. He became active on the social and political scene after the arrival of the first Consul, Petar Karastojanovich, at the newly opened Serbian Consulate in Salonica. The Serbian Consul responded positively to the requests for an independent cultural and political development of the Macedonians. In a letter dated 21 May 1887, he declared: "I have never missed an opportunity to assure them that by holding onto Bulgarians and Russia, they will never achieve what they want, but that they will reach their goal if they turn to Serbia."[17]

The Serbian Consul asked Popov to draw up a program that the Serbian government would support. And so the Provisional Program, submitted to the Consul by Popov in June 1887, was created. It consisted of four items: (1) as soon as the academic year 1887/1888, twelve teachers to teach in the Macedonian language are to be appointed in cities throughout Macedonia, preferably in their native cities;[18] (2) an article is to be published in Macedonia in which the political situation in Macedonia after the establishment of the Exarchate and the Principality of Bulgaria will be presented; (3) a Macedonian reading room is to be opened in Salonica that will later turn into a central association with branches in the more important places around Macedonia; (4) to get the

---

15 Dzambazovski 2006, 505.
16 Their plans faced a number of obstacles. For example Grupche, who was supposed to travel throughout Macedonia and submit a report on the situation there to the Serbian government via the Serbian representative in Constantinople, was arrested by the Bulgarian police on his way to Stara Zagora for being a Russian spy. Only after the intervention of the Serbian diplomatic representative in Sofia were he and Evro allowed to leave for Constantinople, which they reached on 1 May 1887 (for more on this, see Dzambazovski 2006, 206 and 509–10).
17 Dzambazovski 1964, 242.
18 The first item stated that, firstly, they should conduct their classes in a Macedonian dialect if possible, and secondly, all their efforts should be directed towards awakening people from the delusion of making Bulgaria whole and introducing a new and completely opposite idea: "MACEDONIA FOR THE MACEDONIANS" [in capitals in the original]. In the fourth item, the church issue is mentioned again, just as the restauring of the Archbishopric of Ohrid. The Provisional Program was published by Dr. Kliment Dzambazovski (1964, 243–44).

Ottoman government in Constantinople to approve the publishing of a weekly in the Macedonian language.

In the following period, the members of the SMC tried to realize these goals by engaging in two directions—through the institutions of the Ottoman Empire and by acquiring financial aid and other logistics from the Serbian government.[19] Thus, in the application they submitted to the Grand Vizier in June 1887 for permission to publish the journal, they clearly declared their loyalty to the Ottoman authorities and the Sultan and gave assurances that the journal would contain mainly historical and philological topics, and not so many political topics.[20] After receiving no reply to their two applications, Evro and Grupche also submitted an application to the Sultan. Once again left without a reply, their attempts to issue a magazine in Macedonian ended in failure.[21] However, Novakovich's diplomatic correspondence shows that the Ottoman authorities pointed to the involvement of the Patriarchy of Constantinople in

---

19 In fact, these two directions were intertwined in certain segments. For example, the Serbian diplomatic representative Stojan Novakovich had requested instructions from his Ministry of Foreign Affairs even before Evro and Grupche's arrival in Constantinople to organize their further activities. Getting carte blanche for his plans regarding Macedonia, he suggested to them to acquire a permit for publishing a literary weekly and bi-weekly magazine in a Macedonian dialect. However, the arrangement was that they would appear before the authorities independently, as Ottoman citizens (Dzambazovski 2006, 511). As a matter of fact, Serbian diplomat, public figure and scholar Stojan Novakovich (1842–1915) acted as the person in charge of carrying out the Serbian interests in Macedonia at the time. Makedonka Mitrova describes Novakovich's so-called 'Macedonism' as a "political-assimilation project," an ideological-political platform of the action of the Serbian propaganda activities (Mitrova 2018, 53–66).

20 The official program contained the following items: "a) *Makedonski glas* (Macedonian Voice) would deal with historical and philological matters, and less with politics, within the framework of the interests of the Ottoman state; b) it would preach to our compatriots unconditional and faithful obedience to sceptre of Abdul Hamid II, and respect of his glorious authority over our fatherland at the cost of our lives; c) it would let everybody know that our fatherland has nothing in common with the Bulgarians nor any of the other small states and therefore would preach avoidance and strict caution of their intrigues; d) it would preach about the need for joint work with the Turks, disregarding faith and nationality, in the interest of our common fatherland. The journal will be published once a week in a medium format" (*Documents on the Struggle*, vol. I, doc. 196, 301). Besides this official program, Evro and Grupche arranged with S. Novakovich another program which again stressed the loyalty to the Turks, contained measures for preventing Bulgarian propaganda, and stressed the usage of the Macedonian dialect without adding the Bulgarian definite articles and with a complete and ever-increasing mixing of the Serbian language (Dzambazovski 2006, 209–10 and 511–13).

21 Ibid., 210; 513–14.

this case.[22] He also acknowledged the fact that the Turkish censorship followed everything written about Macedonia very carefully, and that as soon as they saw the word *Macédoine* written anywhere, their eyes were wide open.[23]

Hence the belief that despite the implemented reforms and the promises proclaimed by the Ottoman authorities regarding the equality of citizens, the circumstances for even a Macedonian cultural affirmation were rather unfavorable. The Empire's weakness was being used by the Great Powers (notably Russia and Austria-Hungary) interested in dominating the Balkans, and also by the Balkan states interested in acquiring parts of Macedonia, which made the position of the Macedonian population ever more complex.

Seeing that the realization of the goals of their program was not possible, Evro and Grupche made an attempt to attract the attention of the Great Powers by sending a memorandum to their diplomatic representatives in Constantinople on 26 July 1887 in which they stated that the neighbouring Balkan states' aspirations towards their homeland Macedonia ('our fatherland of Macedonia') were also a threat to peace in Europe; and therefore stressing that

> in order to do away with such a situation, the illusions of the aforementioned little states should be eradicated, and this can only be carried out by the Macedonian population, which should announce to the world that they are also a separate people, with a separate history, features, and customs, and that they have nothing in common with the surrounding little states. Consequently, no one has the right to aspire to Macedonia. And it remains to the Macedonians—but in order to achieve this, the Macedonian population should be informed. And in order to start going

---

22 In one of his letters to the Serbian Minister of Foreign Affairs, Novakovich gives a detailed report on the persistance of Grupche and Evro in acquiring any information as to whether the printing of the journal had been approved or not by corresponding with different institutions of the Ottoman Empire during November and December 1887. In the letter he expressed his doubts regarding this explanation, and therefore personally turned to the Patriarchate upon which he received a reply that they did not know anything and that the Turks never asked for their advice in such matters (Dzambazovski 1987, doc. 29, 96–97).

23 Ibid., 98. The latter can be linked to the Decree on the New Administrative Division of the Empire into vilayets that resulted in partition of the geographic entirety of Macedonia into three vilayets—the Skopje Vilayet, the Bitola Vilayet, and the Salonica Vilayet (for more, see: Dimeski 1981, 63). According to the high order of the Sultan dated 25 '319 AH / 7 April 1903 "it is categorically forbidden to use the term (name) Macedonia, mentioned as a local name, in the written submissions and announcements related to the affairs of the Imperial Vilayets in Rumelia" (Stojanovski, 317–18).

along that road sooner, there is a great need to publish a Macedonian journal here, in the capital.[24]

The realization of the other two items from the program, as well as the compilation of primers in the Macedonian folk language with the aim of making them comprehensible for children, depended on the direct logistics of the Serbian government. Elements from the Serbian language were supposed to be inserted into them gradually, and they would then be more easily accepted by the population in general.

In order for the job to be done more successfully, a request to make a primer was given to Grupche and Evro, and also to Despot Badzovich, a Macedonian in the service of the Serbian government, as well as to the Serbian writer Milojko Veselinovich (in consultation with the academician Ljubomir Kovachevich).[25] Evro and Grupche finished their task in a short time and wrote the *Macedonian Primer*, and in June 1888 it was sent to Belgrade for evaluation.[26]

But the *Macedonian Primer* was not published primarily because of the predominant Macedonian language element in it.[27] And so, instead of the primer written by Evro and Grupche, the one written by M. Veselinovich was chosen and printed in seven thousand copies that were distributed throughout the schools in Macedonia. This meant that another item from the SMC's program was not realized in spite of the efforts to implement it.

Activities regarding the engagement of Macedonian teachers also ended in failure. As an economist in the Bulgarian Exarchate Gymnasium, Popov was working on recruiting and transferring Macedonian students from the

---

24   *Documents on the Struggle*, vol. 1, doc. 197, 301–03.
25   Македонски буквар, 49. This edition contains facsimiles of the primers written by Evro and Grupche and the one by Badzovich as well as, in part, the primer by Veselinovich. A comparative analysis of the three primers mentioned is given by Trajko Stamatoski (1986, 103–116).
26   Dzambazovski 2006, 286.
27   Regarding the language, it is notable that the writers were trying to create a standard based on the dialects of western Macedonia, with some minor compromises with respect to the Serbian language. In this respect, the Macedonian linguist Stamatoski states that Evro and Grupche's primer was rejected because it did not adhere to the instructions given by Novakovich, underlining that the authors were fully aware of the extent to which they could go without disturbing the integrity of the Macedonian language. He concludes that this primer "expresses the position of the Secret Macedonian Committee, is written in that spirit, i.e., it follows a quiet line and policy" (Stamatoski 1986, 115). For more on the linguistic analysis of this primer, see also Gushevska 2011, 178–88.

gymnasium to the Kingdom of Serbia.[28] But the sending of Macedonian teachers did not go as planned. Temko Popov mentioned this, among other things, in a letter to Despot Bazhovich dated 9 May 1888. He stated that the seven teachers who were engaged, all graduates of the Salonica Exarchate Gymnasium, did not receive the promised funds, and that therefore he found himself in a very difficult position.[29] The problems that arose from not sending the funds for the teachers' salaries were mentioned again in the correspondence of Novakovich with the Serbian Minister of foreign affairs. He wrote that he had been approached by a "certain Temko Popov or Popovich, a Macedonian from Ohrid, who has been working as an economist at the Bulgarian gymnasium in Salonica since last year."[30] Popov complained that neither he personally nor the twelve teachers he had persuaded to leave their jobs as Bulgarian teachers were paid anything.

Popov himself referred to these events in a much calmer tone in one of his letters from 1889.[31] He expressed regret that the involvement with the teachers failed at a time when it was just about to be finally realized, with the result that the eight teachers who had been hired were all discharged, and he himself suffered the most.[32]

Popov also attempted to realize the second item from the Provisional Program and in 1889 wrote the article in question, which was programmatic in both its contents and its language.[33] Criticizing the Bulgarian Exarchate harshly for the conditions in Macedonia, as well as his fellow citizens for allowing it to take over the folk schools, Popov ended his article with the following words: "Here is the way according to which, in my opinion, we would be able to: firstly, have our own popular bishops and organized schools in a short period, without the need of mercy from outside, for a harsh and a bitter fate awaits people who expect their spiritual food from foreign hands and have entrusted the

---

28   Dzambazovski 2006, 229.
29   Stamatoski 1998, 49–68. The letter is given in its integral form in the article, accompanied by a facsimile of the first page (63–68).
30   This letter is dated 29 March 1888.
31   This is the letter dated 5 April 1889 addressed to the Serbian Chairman of the Ministerial Council and Minister of Foreign Affairs at the time, Sava Gruich.
32   In this letter he explained what his 1887 Program consisted of. In fact, he presented a program that contained four items, but partly changed, because here Popov wrote about the opening of a Serbian trade or technical school, and also about getting funds for bribing influential people in Macedonian municipalities (Dzambazovski 1987, doc. 153, 375–76).
33   For more on this, see Stamatoski 1986, 94–102.

mission to such hands; secondly, with the settlement of this so thorny Church question, we shall earn the confidence of the Government, put an end to the intrigues, both external and internal, and so shall live peacefully under the paternal wing of His Imperial Majesty, our Master, Sultan Abdul Hamid II."[34]

3 Sources of Funding for Members of the SMC

The complete documentation (mostly diplomatic correspondence) that has been published so far with regard to the activities of the members of the SMC shows that the funding of a part of the activities of its members (in fact, the names of the three most prominent figures of this Committee are mentioned: Popov, Grupche, and Evro) was supplied by the Serbian government. In a letter dated 6 October 1888, the Serbian diplomat Stojan Novakovich sent a request to the Minister of Foreign Affairs of Serbia to cover the financial claims, among other things, of the Macedonians (this refers to Evro and Grupche).[35] The funding went smoothly in those segments where Novakovich expected the listed activists to serve as Serbian propagandists and agitators. But when a specific realization of Serbian promises was demanded (as in the case of the teachers), serious problems in communication emerged, and it became obvious that the Serbian state representatives were not prepared to support these activities financially. The same can be seen in the fact that they were not prepared to finance the publishing of a Macedonian primer by Evro and Grupche.

4 Understanding and Promoting Macedonian Identity

As we have already noted, the SMC was established by Macedonian emigrants in Sofia. Its program and the individual strivings of its members represented a direct reaction to the great expansion of Bulgarian propaganda in Macedonia. Hence, it is no coincidence that the SMC was active for a relatively short time and that it was banned by the Bulgarian authorities. However, it appears that all the essential activities of its most prominent members, who put great effort

---

34 *Documents on the Struggle*, vol. 1, doc. 202, 313.
35 Six hundred dinars a month were set aside for them (Dzambazovski 1987, doc. 98, 238–39). A detailed report on the funds reserved for this purpose was provided in a letter from Novakovich to the Serbian Minister of Foreign Affairs dated 9 January 1889 (Ibid., doc. 130, 325–27).

into the realization of the program goals they had established, occurred in the period from 1885 to 1889. The Serbian propaganda was persistent in its efforts to position itself in Macedonia, in circumstances when it had lost all its influence in this region, and it recognized the Macedonian National Cause as a means through which it could suppress the Bulgarian presence. It proceeded through gradual action and a policy of tolerance for this movement in the beginning, while at the same time trying to impose a sense of Serbian national feeling on the population. At the same time, even though they decided to act mostly on the cultural-educational plan, the goals of the SMC remained unrealized for purely political reasons, as a result of which their activities did not influence the masses directly and did not have a wider mobilizing effect on the people.

The key requests and motives for their activities, on the other hand, were very clearly pointed out by Popov in his letter to Badzovich with the slogan: "The main task is to make Macedonia Macedonian."[36] The members of the SMC strove to realize this aim by meeting the basic educational and cultural needs of the population, for example by organizing classes taught by local teachers who would use teaching aids in the Macedonian folk language. Therefore he sought help from the Serbian side: "Having no philologists of our own, where are the Serbian ones, who should know our language and write these elementary and indispensable books with such impartiality that they would use Serbian words, instead of additional ones, only if they could not find Macedonian words; and who would not be guided by blind patriotism and, instead of writing Macedonian textbooks, create purely Serbian ones."[37]

Although in some of the documents Macedonians are clearly characterized as having a "separate history, features and customs,"[38] this is a case where in defining cultural and ethnic particularities the issue of language relations and its treatment should be considered separately. Of course, it is not our intention to contest Anthony D. Smith's assertion that language is just one of the elements that in correlation with others creates ethnic identity,[39] but rather to take into consideration H.L. Shtepan's view that "Language is the main argument for the alleged proof to justify the pretensions to Macedonia. Those most insistent on this topic are the Bulgarians who are trying to stir the world into

---

36 Letter from Temko Popov to Despot Badzovich (*Documents on the Struggle*, vol. I, doc. 198, 304).
37 Ibid., 303–04.
38 In the above-mentioned *Memorandum*.
39 Smith, 27.

thinking that language is a force that could turn Macedonians into Bulgarians."[40] Hence, to paraphrase Benedict Anderson, it is more important to point out the capacity of language to create an 'imagined community.'[41]

The evolution of thought on the significance and physiognomy of a language is undoubtedly seen in Popov himself. The Provisional Program was created while he worked as an economist at the boarding-school of the Bulgarian Exarchate Gymnasium in Salonica; and the fact that he uses primarily the Bulgarian language and orthography is no surprise. But in his letter to Badzovich he used his native Ohrid dialect, while the debate *Who is to Blame?* is in fact a specific application of a fully developed concept for a literary language which in itself is of great significance regarding the history of the codification of modern standard Macedonian. In this regard, Blazhe Koneski notes: "With Temko Popov, in the 80s, we already have a full transmission to an alphabetical and orthographic system which is close to our system nowadays, and which is also close to Misirkov's system, and so Misirkov has his predecessors in Temko Popov and in the other people."[42]

Macedonian historiography recognizes the beginnings of Macedonian separatism in the activities of the SMC and its members in this period.[43] The views of Popov are also interpreted in this respect: "Let us not lie to ourselves, Despot, the national spirit in Macedonia has reached such a stage today that even if Jesus Christ had come to the Earth, he would not have been able to persuade the Macedonian that he was a Bulgarian or a Serb, excepting those Macedonians in whom Bulgarian propaganda has already taken root."[44] The ideological and programmatic determinations of the SMC largely corresponded with those stated by the Macedonian societies that acted at a later date.[45]

---

40   Shtepan, 50.
41   In *Imagined Communities*, Benedict Anderson states that it is much more important to appreciate the capacity of language to create imagined communities, to build *specific solidarities*, than to treat it as a mere feature of national affiliation (Macedonian translation, 190).
42   Koneski, 23.
43   Some of the former members of SMC remained active in the social-cultural field, as well as in the field of politics in various locations. Thus, Popov performed for a while the function of Mayor of his native Ohrid, which after the First World War became a part of the Kingdom of Serbs, Croats, and Slovenes.
44   Letter from Temko Popov to Despot Badzovich (*Documents on the Struggle*, vol. 1, doc. 198, 304).
45   Blazhe Ristovski (2011, 43) has noted that the program of the journal *Macedonian Oaoer* (as it is also called in scientific literature) corresponded with the points presented by the Macedonian Students' Society 'Vardar' (1893) and the Macedonian Club in Belgrade, as well as that of the Macedonian Scientific and Literary Society in St. Petersburg (1903).

5   The Young Macedonian Literary Society (YMLS)

The Young Macedonian Literary Society was established in 1891 by the Macedonian emigration in Sofia as a kind of cultural and educational society. Program-wise, it was a continuation of the Young Student Society (YSS), an illegal association of Macedonian students established in Sofia in 1890 which, among other things, advocated the publishing of a magazine in which the Ottoman terror, as well as the activities of various propagandas that they faced most directly while studying in Belgrade and Sofia, would be denounced.[46]

Among the more prominent members of the YMLS were: Petar Pop Arsov, Gjorgji Balaschev, Dimitar Mirchev, Hristo Popkocev, Kliment Karagjulev, Evtim Sprostranov, Kosta Shahov, Dame Gruev, Hristo Matov, Ivan Hadzi Nikolov, Naum Tufekchiev, and Toma Karajovov.

The monthly magazine *Loza* (The Vine) was the organ of the YMLS, giving them the name *lozari*. The first issue was printed in January 1892 in Sofia, and its leading article contained the Program Principles of the YMLS. It began with a quote from *Sophocles*: "He is a villain who has a better friend than his fatherland." The sacredness of patriotic love was expressed quite poetically and with heightened pathos in the introduction. At the same time, the situation in Macedonia was analysed in light of the events in the Balkans at the time, and it was noted that only the common efforts of its people could protect the future of their fatherland.[47] The article continued:

---

46   In his book *On Macedonian Matters*, their contemporary Krste Petkov Misirkov—the most important Macedonian intellectual of the end of the era, the linguist who set the principles for codifying the Macedonian language—described the founders of the YMLS and the circumstances in which it was established: "The idea of national unification for the Macedonians—albeit under a Bulgarian mask—began in 1890. At the end of 1889 thirty to forty Macedonian students from Belgrade moved to Sofia. These students were the heart and soul of all that has happened in Macedonia from that time till the present day. They were well acquainted with Serbia and Bulgaria, with their cultures and their aspirations in Macedonia. They were also aware of the danger that would arise if Macedonia were to be partitioned between these two states, that is, of course, if the Macedonians did not take to arms themselves and by their own strength and with their own means win freedom and so prevent the partition. It was upon their initiative that in the eighteen-nineties a nationalist-separatist movement was first formed with the aim of divorcing Macedonian interests from those of Bulgaria by introducing a Macedonian tongue which would serve as the literary language of all Macedonians. The mouth-piece of this Macedonian separatist movement in Bulgaria was the magazine *Loza*; Stambolov's authorities in Bulgaria, however, did not look favorably upon this spiritual movement and banned further publication of the magazine" (Misirkov 2003, 161).

47   What is noticeable here are the similarities with the positions expressed in the *Memorandum* by Grupche and Evro.

This should be the striving of every sensitive Macedonian, wherever he may be. The Young Macedonian Lit[erary] Society has exactly this aim in view. It is obvious that this is an enormous task. And indeed, it greatly exceeds the powers which are at the disposal of the Society for the time being. But at the same time, the Society believes it will not be long isolated by the patriots. To attain this aim, the Society issues its journal *Loza*. We leave it to those who are interested to assist us with moral and material aid, by which, among other things, they will instigate an undertaking of a literary nature as well.[48]

A total of six issues of the magazine *Loza* were printed: numbers 1 and 2 and the double issue 3–4 printed in the first half of 1892, and two more in the second half of 1894. Its contents were in the areas of literature, science, and social life, mostly in connection with Macedonia.

The Statute of the YMLS was published in the first issue of *Loza*. It contains six chapters with a total of eleven Articles regulating the organization, management, and activities of the society. These are the chapters that refer to the goals, membership, duties and the ways of funding the YMLS:

Article 1. The objectives of the Society are as follows:
- a) To publish a magazine the name, the program and direction of which shall be determined by decree;
- b) To set up a reading room in the capital, and when there are enough funds, decorate it; and
- c) When the Society has enough means, it shall do other good deeds in accordance with its objectives, like for example supporting students and other things.

B. Composition

Article 2. Members are:
- a) Active, who participate fully in the publishing of the magazine in every way and are accepted into the Society;
- b) Supporters, who put into the Society's cashbox any kind of aid; and
- c) Honorary, who are declared such by the Society for services provided directly to it or for Macedonia in general.

---

48   *Documents on the Struggle*, doc. 208, 324–26.

C. Funds

Article 3. The funds are comprised of:
- a) Voluntary payments that are paid every month by the active members;
- b) Voluntary contributions made by the members/supporters; and
- c) Various sources that the Society shall come up with.
[...]

E. Duties

Article 5. The administrative council shall have regular sessions every week.
Note 1. Decisions are made with a majority of votes.
Note 2. Regular sessions are valid if at least 1/3 of the active members who live in Sofia are present, and extraordinary ones if there are at least 1/ .[49]

Article 6. The chairman, and in his absence the vice-chairman, is the head planner of sessions and determines the order of the sessions.

Article 7. The administrator regularly takes minutes at the sessions and is responsible for the bookkeeping of the Society.

Article 8. The treasurer collects the payments by issuing vouchers signed by him and by the Chairman. He keeps accurate accounts of the incomes and expenses.
Note. The Society shall keep the unused funds in a current account in a "mutual cashbox of the Macedonians."

Article 9. The administrative council shall make its report public at the end of every year.
[...]
Sofia, 1892.[50]

---

49 The denominator is lacking in the original printed version of the paper.
50 Устав на Младата Македонска Книжовна Дружина во Софиа, Лоза, година I, книга I (іануари, 1892) (The Statute of The Young Macedonian Literary Society in Sofia, *Loza*, year I, book I (January, 1892)), 47–48.

The Statute did not express a national program for the Society, but as a concept it served as a model for many Macedonian societies later on.[51] Also, it is believed that in addition to the articles published in *Loza*, the members also had a secret program and a secret Statute of the Society that were taken to Romania to be printed there, but that they had burned there together with the printing house.[52]

The first issue of the magazine provoked harsh reactions, first and foremost in the Bulgarian press, but the discussion was also taken up by some Serbian and Greek newspapers as well. In fact, there was a great debate over the applied orthography based on the phonetic principle, which deviated greatly from the official Bulgarian orthography, and over the Macedonian words that were used in the texts, in particular in Ezerski's text, *Several Notes*.[53] The separatist ideas and strivings were, on the other hand, recognized in the program's principles. The loudest and harshest criticism came from the Sofia newspaper *Svoboda*, the official organ of the Bulgarian government of Prime Minister Stefan Stambolov, which published its first reaction on 18 February 1892.[54] The editors of *Loza* tried to reply to these attacks, but their reply was not published in *Svoboda*. Therefore they published it in the second issue of their own magazine, where they stated that the orthography they were using did not mean that they were working on the creation of a new Macedonian language, nor did they have any aspirations toward political separatism.

D.T. Levov also joined in the attacks and the condemnation of *Loza*,[55] and again, in the pages of *Svoboda*,[56] he fixed his attention on the first two articles in the first issue:

> From the article "Several Notes" on p. 5, it can be seen that it [the Society—note by Levov] belongs "to today's dominant Slavic element," that the name of that element is "Macedonians," that Macedonia is their fatherland and that it is "a separate Slavic (?!) region, the past of which was covered in glory, especially at the time of Philip and Alexander the Great, but has died down with their successors" (!!) [...] The "Young Society" pursues, under the veil of literature, not the goal of the realization and propaganda of some fantastic fictional phonetic orthography but

---

51 Ristovski 1983, 486.
52 Ibid., 501.
53 In fact, a text by Gj. Balschev lies behind the pseudonym. In this article, he discusses the travel notes of various foreigners in an effort to demonstrate the independent development of the Macedonian people (Ibid., 489).
54 Stamatoski 1998, 69–84.
55 This was a pseudonym used by Lev Dramov, a Stambolovistic publicist.
56 This issue was dated 13 April 1892.

tendencies and goals that are curious as much as repulsive, disgraceful and dangerous. The goals pursued by the "Society" [...] can be seen in the foreword of *Loza*.[57]

Towards the middle of 1892, Stambolov's government officially banned the work of the YMLS, and its members were forced to dissipate in order to avoid persecution from the government.[58] However, given the great influence the magazine had among the Macedonian emigration, there was an attempt to renew it in 1894, but with a new editor (I.K. Bozhinov) and using the official Bulgarian orthography. But, after just two issues, the magazine completely died out.

One of the founders of the YMLS and its president, Kosta Shahov, made an attempt to renew the YMLS through the Young Macedonian Society in 1894. This society developed its activities widely, and was joined by the gymnasium literary circle "Macedonian Unity" established by the founder of contemporary Macedonian dramatic literature and the Macedonian theater Vojdan Chernodrinski,[59] who organized literary/musical and other plays. In any case, the main core of the YMLS had been destroyed two years earlier.

6   The Place and Influence of the YMLS

The YMLS was active during a period of a heightened effort by a number of subjects who comprised the Macedonian national movement, where it represented a significant segment. But this was also a time when Macedonia was more often the subject of scientific interest, not only of domestic but also of foreign scholars, notably distinguished Slavists, who were especially interested in studying old manuscripts of Macedonian origin, and who pointed out the particularities of Macedonian dialects. For example, the book by one of the most prominent European researchers of Macedonia, Karl Hron, *The Nationality of the Macedonian Slavs*, was published in Vienna in 1890; and in 1891/1892 Vatroslav Oblak conducted extensive dialectological research on Macedonian

---

57   Quoted from Ristovski 1983, 492–93.
58   Serious criticsm of Stambolov's regime is given in the study Стамболовщината въ Македония и нейнитѣ прѣдставители (*Stambolovism in Macedonia and its Representatives*), published in Vienna in 1894. For safety reasons, the Macedonian publicist, philologist and revolutionary Petar Pop Arsov (1868–1941)—one of the associates and editors of *Loza*—used the pseudonym Vardarski.
59   This was a period when a big rift formed within the lines of the Macedonian emigration in Sofia, and these processes demand a separate study. For more on these events, see Bitovski, 16–18. Chernodrinski discusses these events in his play *The Macedonian Emigration* (Aleksiev, 901). See also Gushevska 2014, 171–82.

soil that in 1896 would result in the book *Macedonian Studies*.[60] Under such circumstances, although it existed for a relatively short time and its organ *Loza* was published (by the original editors) for only six months, the YMLS managed to exert a major influence, especially on the Macedonian emigration. At the same time, its activity had a strong echo and was followed and commented on within the wider Balkan area. The YMLS strove, to the best of its ability, to find the necessary funds for its functioning and for publishing the magazine in order to secure its independence, and later on to develop other activities, for example, to provide financial support for students.

Some of the members of the YMLS appeared as significant actors in later forms of organized activity within the Macedonian National Movement, while others played an important role in the social-political life of Bulgaria. In fact, the ideological divisions between former members of the YMLS appeared at the time of the restoration of *Loza*, an effort in which some of the old collaborators became involved, among them Andrej Ljapchev, Dimitar Rizov, Toma Karajovov, Naum Tufekdziev, and Nikola Naumov. Some of them completely accepted the idea of the population in Macedonia having a Bulgarian affiliation, and became direct opponents to the ideologists of the Macedonian Revolutionary Organization. Rizov, for example, even became a Bulgarian diplomat and was one of the initiators of the Serbian-Bulgarian collaboration on the eve of the Balkan Wars, conspiring to divide the territory of Macedonia after the fall of the Ottoman Empire. On the other hand, Dame Gruev, Petar Pop Arsov, and Ivan Hadzi Nikolov were among the founders of the Macedonian Revolutionary Organization;[61] Kosta Shahov was the editor of a number of magazines and the author of belletristic and publicistic books;[62] Evtim Sprostranov was a prolific historian, linguist, etc.

---

60   Oblak was, in fact, a student of the renowned Croatian linguist Vatroslav Jagich, who promoted the so-called Macedonian theory on the dialectal basis of the Old Slavonic language. For more on the studies of Macedonian language materials and manuscripts conducted by the most eminent philologists and linguists in the last decades of the nineteenth and the beginning of the twentieth century, see Pandev.

61   The prominent leader of the Macedonian national liberation movement Gjoche Petrov (1864/65–1921) held a positive opinion of the Lozari movement, underlining that it was a reaction against the aspirations of the Exarchate to direct public life in Macedonia and the first step towards self-initiative on the part of the progressive intellectuals of the *Loza* circle. In his *Memoirs* he wrote: "At the beginning the same people who led the struggle against the Exarchate were the first and foremost participants in the revolutionary cause" (*Documents on the Struggle*, doc. 209, 326).

62   Shahov shared the idea of cultural-political autonomy for Macedonia even though he did not dismiss the idea of its joining the Bulgarian Principality.

Generally speaking, the YMLS was treated by the Macedonian researchers as an organization with a concealed separatist orientation that appeared at the junction between two eras of Macedonian history and represented a direct introduction into the revolutionary action taken by the Macedonian people. At the same time, the 'Lozars' appeared as protectors of the Macedonian people and the Macedonian language, rallying the Macedonians to unify with the slogan "Let's join together."[63] The magazine *Loza*, despite its publicly declared position of compromise regarding the language issue, once again promoted a clearly elaborated and implemented concept for the language. The language difference came to the fore once again and became the basis for opposition to the official authorities in an environment that did not acknowledge this difference.

7   Conclusions

This analysis has focused on two significant Macedonian societies corresponding to the *maticas* of the Slavonic countries in the Balkans (for instance Serbia, Croatia, and the Bulgarian Literary Society in Braila). These societies unquestionably shared an orientation towards cultural-educational and scientific areas of activity (at least ostensibly), and their ambition to publish an appropriate journal. In any case, the Macedonian societies were not only formed later, but they also emerged, first and foremost, at a time of completely changed social-political circumstances in the Balkans, when the propagandas of neighboring countries used different mechanisms to completely organize and control the cultural-educational and the religious life of the Macedonian population. The difficult economic conditions and the inability to acquire an appropriate education in their native environment, notably in Macedonia as part of the Ottoman Empire, sent Macedonian students to the neighboring countries which, on the other hand, proved an unfriendly environment in which to organize the social-cultural life of the Macedonian emigration. At the same time, using the attribute *Macedonian* in naming the newly formed societies undoubtedly had a distinctive effect regardless of whether it was used in a territorial, cultural, or ethnic sense. Still, any manifestation of Macedonian distinctiveness provoked a strong reaction from the authorities and impeded a society's more durable existence and the development of versatile activity even when it was envisaged in the program goals.

---

63   Mironska-Hristovska, 93–108.

Hence, in the years to come, when some of the maticas grew into national academies with diversified and multiple activities, what remained of topical interest in Macedonia was the demand for education in the Macedonian folk language, the creation of literature in that language, and an independent church organization. Most of the societies proclaimed these goals in their programs. However, it is important to remember that they were also the continuation of organized actions carried out by the Macedonian citizenry starting in the 1850s with regard to the anti-Patriarchate and in the 1870s to the anti-Exarchate fight, as well as the activities of the church-educational communities. On the other hand, the later societies—those that proclaimed the idea of Macedonian separatism ever more clearly, as well as the idea of autonomy—were a continuation of these earlier activities.

Bibliography

Алексиев, Александар. "Драмското творештво за дејноста и разбивањето на 'Младата македонска дружина'." Сепарат на *Современост*, xx, 8–9 (октомври–ноември 1970). [Aleksiev, Aleksandar. "Dramatic Testimony on the Activities and the Disbanding of the 'Young Macedonian Society'." Offprint of *Sovremenost* xx, 8–9 (October–November, 1970)]: 875–905.

Андерсон, Бенедикт. *Замислени заедници: размислувања за потеклото и ширењето на национализмот* (ревидирано издание). Превод Ема Маркоска-Милчин. Скопје: Култура, 1998. [Anderson, Benedict. *Imagined Communities: Reflections on the Origin and Spread of Nationalism*. Revised Edition. Translated by Ema Markoska-Milchin. Skopje: Kultura, (1998)].

Битовски Д-р, Крсте. *Македонија и Кнежевството Бугарија (1893–1903)*. Скопје: Институт за национална историја, 1977. [Bitovski, Dr. Krste. *Macedonia and the Principality of Bulgaria (1893–1903)* Skopje: Institute of National History, (1977)].

Вардарски. *Стамболовщината въ Македония и нейнитѣ прѣдставители*. Виена: Печатница на Бр. Попеви, 1894. [Vardarski. *Stambolovism in Macedonia and its Representatives*. Viena: Popevi Brothers' Printing Shop, (1894)].

Гушевска, Лилјана. "Јазичните особености на *Македонскиот буквар* од Наум Евро и Коста Групче," *Спектар* xxix, 57 (2011). [Gushevska, Liljana. "Language Particularities of the *Macedonian Primer* by Naum Evro and Kosta Grupche," *Spektar* xxix, 57 (2011)]: 178–88.

Гушевска, Лилјана. "Навраќање на драмата 'Македонска емиграција' од Војдан Чернодрински," *Историја*, xlix, 1 (2014). ["A Review of the Play 'Macedonian Emigration' by Vojdan Chernodrinski," *Journal of History* xlix, 1 (2014)]: 171–82.

Димевски, Славко. "Некои форми на здружување на македонското граѓанство и интелигенцијата во 80-те години од XIX век." *Годишник на Институтот за социолошки и политичко-правни истражувања* 1, III (1977). [Dimevski, Slavko. "Some of the Forms of Association of the Macedonian Citizenry and Intelligentsia in 1880s." *Institute of Social and Political-Legal Research Yearbook* 1, III (1977)]: 183–201.

Димески Д-р, Димитар. *Македонското националноослободително движење во Битолскиот вилает (1893–1903)*. Скопје: НИО Студентски збор, 1981. [Dimeski, Dr. Dimitar. *The Macedonian National Liberation Movement in the Bitola Vilayet (1893–1902)*. Skopje: JPO Studentski zbor, 1981].

Documents on the Struggle of the Macedonian People for Independence and Nation-State, volume I. Skopje: University of "Cyril and Methodius," 1985.

Дракул, Д-р Симон (избор, превод, редакција и коментари). *Македонија меѓу автономијата и дележот (Зборник руска дипломатска документација—1894–1913)*, седми том 1909, 1910–1913. Скопје: Селектор, 2006. [Dracul, Dr. Simon (selection, translation, editing, and commentary). *Macedonia between Autonomy and Division (A Compilation of Russian Diplomatic Documentation—1894–1913)*, seventh volume 1909, 1910–1913. Skopje: Selektor, 2006].

Конески, Блаже. "Македонскиот писмен јазик во XIX век," In *Македонскиот XIX век. Јазични и книжевно-историски прилози*. Скопје: Култура, 1986. [Koneski, Blazhe. "Macedonian Literary Language in the 19th century." In *The Macedonian 19th Century. Linguistic and Literary-Historical Articles*. Skopje: Kultura, 1986], 21–24.

Котлар-Трајкова, Наташа. "Антиегзархиската борба како афирмација на македонскиот идентитет." In *Македонскиот идентитет низ историјата*. Скопје: Институт за национална историја, 2010. [Kotlar-Trajkova, Natasha. "Anti-Exarchate Struggle as an Affirmation of the Macedonian Identity." In *Macedonian Identity throughout History*. Skopje: Institute of National History, 2010], 177–189.

Лоза, година I, книга I (Iануари 1892). [*Loza*, year I, book I (January 1892)].

Македонскибуквар. Редактори Д-р Катерина Тодоровска, Кирил Јорданоски. Скопје: Менора, 2008. [*A Macedonian Primer*. Editors Dr. Katerina Todorovska, Kiril Jordanoski. Skopje: Menora, 2008].

Миронска-Христовска, Валентина. "Историските пораки на 'лозарите' за национална, културна и политичка слобода." In *Македонската преродба*. Скопје: Институт за македонска литература, 2007. [Mironska-Hristovska, Valentina. "The Historical Messages Given by the 'Lozars' on National, Cultural and Political Freedom'." In *The Macedonian Revival Movement*. Skopje: Institute of Macedonian Literature], 93–108.

Мисирков, Крсте П. "Националниот сепаратизм: земіишчето на коіе се имат развиіено и ке се развиіат за однапред," in *За македонцките работи*. Фототипно издание по повод *100*-годишнината од излегувањето на книгата. Приредил Блаже Ристовски. Скопје: Македонска академија на науките и уметностите, 2003. [Misirkov, Krste P. "National Separatism—the Soil on Which It Has Grown and Will Continue to Grow in the Future," in Blaže Ristovski, ed., *On Macedonian Matters. On the Occasion of the Hundredth Anniversary of the Publication of the Book.* Translated by Alan McConnell. Skopje: Macedonian Academy of Sciences and Arts, 2003].

Митрова, Македонка. *Дискурсот на српската интелектуална елита за османлиска Македонија*. Скопје: Институт за национална историја, 2018. [Mitrova, Makedonka. *Ottoman Macedonia in the Discourse of the Serbian Intellectual Elite*. Skopje: Institute of National History, 2018].

Пандев, Димитар. *Вовед во македонистиката*. Скопје: Македонска реч, 2009. [Pandev, Dimitar. *An Introduction to Macedonistics*. Skopje: Makedonska Rech, 2009].

Пандевска, М-р Марија. *Присилни миграции во Македонија во годините на Големата источна криза (1875–1881)*. Скопје: Институт за национална историја—Книгоиздателство Мисла, 1993. [Pandevska, Marija. *The Forced Migration in Macedonia in the Years of the Great Easter Crisis (1875–1881)*. Skopje: Institute of National History—Misla Publishing House, 1993].

Пандевска, М-р Марија. и Македонка Митрова. "Речниците и толкувањето на поимот милет." In *Прилози од Четвртиот меѓународен конгрес "Исламската цивилизација на Балканот."* Истанбул: IRCICA, 2015. [Pandevska, Marija, and Makedonka Mitrova, "Dictionaries and the Interpretation of the Term Millet." In *Proceeding of the Fourth International Congress "Islamic Civilation in the Balkans."* Istanbul: IRCICA (Research Centre for Islamic History, Art and Culture), 2015], 315–28.

Ристовски, Блаже. "'Лозарите' во развитокот на македонската национална мисла." In *Македонскиот народ и македонската нација*, 1. Скопје: Мисла, 1983. [Ristovski, Blazhe. "The 'Lozars' in the Development of Macedonian National Thought." In *The Macedonian People and Macedonian Nation*, 1. Skopje: Misla, 1983], 469–510.

Ристовски, Блаже. *Избрани дела во десет тома. 1. Крсте П. Мисирков (1874–1926)*. Скопје: Матица македонска, 2011. [Ristovski, Blazhe. *Selected Works in Ten Volumes. 1. Krste P. Misirkov (1874–1926)*. Skopje: Macedonian Matica, 2011].

Smith, Antony David. *The Ethnic Origins of Nations*. Oxford: Blackwell Publishers, 1986.

Стаматоски, Трајко. *Борба за македонски литературен јазик*. Скопје: Мисла, 1986. [Stamatoski, Trajko. *The Struggle for a Macedonian Literary Language*. Skopje: Misla, 1986].

Стаматоски, Трајко. *Континуитетот на македонскиот литературен јазик.* Скопје: Просветно дело, 1998. [Stamatoski, Trajko. *The Continuity of the Macedonian Literary Language.* Skopje: Prosvetno Delo, 1998], 69–84.

Стојановски, Александар. *Македонија под турска власт (статии и други прилози).* Скопје: Институт за национална историја, 2006. [Stojanovski, Aleksandar. *Macedonia under Turkish Rule (Articles and Other Supplements).* Skopje: Institute of National History, 2006].

Тодоровски, Глигор. *Демографските промени во Македонија од крајот на XIV век до балканските војни: со посебен осврт на турското колонизирање, исламизирањето, потурчувањето, албанизацијата и миграциите во Македонија.* Скопје—Мелбурн: Матица македонска, Институт за национална историја, 2000. [Todorovski, Gligor. *Demographic Changes in Macedonia from the End of the Fourteenth Century until the Balkan Wars: with Special Attention to Turkish Colonization, Islamization, Turkish Assimilation, Albanization, and Migrations in Macedonia.* Skopje—Melbourne: Matica Makedonska, Institute of National History, 2000].

Џамбазовски, Академик Климент. *Културно-општествените врски на Македоните со Србија во текот на XIX век (второ дополнето издание).* Скопје: Институт за национална историја, 2006. [Dzambazovski, Academician Kliment. *Cultural-Social Relations of Macedonians with Serbia in the 19th Century* (second revised edition). Skopje: Institute of National History, 2006].

Џамбазовски, Д-р Климент (приредил). *Граѓа за историјата на македонскиот народ од Архивот на Србија,* том *IV,* книга *III (1888–1889).* Београд: Архив на Србија, Архив на Македонија, 1987. [Dzambazovski, Dr. Kliment (compiler). *Materials on the History of the Macedonian People from the Archives of Serbia, volume IV, book III (1888–1889).* Belgrade: Archives of Serbia, Archives of Macedonia, 1987].

Џамбазовски, Д-р Климент. "Нови прилози за 'македонското сепаратистичко движење'." *Гласник на Институтот за национална историја,* VIII, 2 (1964). [Dzambazovski, Dr. Kliment, "New Articles on the 'Macedonian Separatist Movement'." *Glasnik, Institute of National History* VIII, 2 (1964)]: 241–258.

Чепреганов, проф. Д-р Тодор (Уредник). *Историја на македонскиот народ.* Скопје: Институт за национална историја, 2008. [Chepreganov, Prof. Dr. Todor (Editor). *History of the Macedonian People.* Skopje: Institute of National History, 2008].

Штепан, Ханс Лотар. *Македонскиот јазол* (второ издание). Скопје: Аз-Буки, 2005. [Shtepan, Hans Lothar, *The Macedonian Knot* (second edition). Skopje: Az-Buki, 2005].

CHAPTER 8

Language, Cultural Associations, and the Origins of Galician Nationalism, 1840–1918

Xosé M. Núñez Seixas and Alfonso Iglesias Amorín

The Galician movement, also known as *galeguismo* (Galicianism), is an example of delayed evolution, with its transition from a cultural to a political movement not taking place until after the outbreak of World War I.[1] The advent of the liberal revolution in Spain and the consolidation of the workers' movement made it more difficult for latecomers among national movements to gain the support of the majority of their purported compatriots. In fact, the Galician movement was born in the 1840s, alongside its Catalan or Breton counterparts. Its first political claim was to restore what had been the Galician regional unity of the Ancien Régime. This unity had been undermined by the 1833–34 territorial division into provinces, implemented by the Spanish liberal government as it adopted a centralized model inspired by the French one: its new territorial demarcations, also called *provinces*, broke up the 'Ancient Kingdom' of Galicia into four new provinces. Far from responding to the ideal type of a national movement, evolving from a starting period of cultural revival followed by a phase of political agitation, the first stages of the Galician movement were clearly political. Its first actors were people actively engaged in politics, who claimed that Galicia had been a territorial unity legitimized by a common history, rooted in the Middle Ages, as well as by a common culture and ethnographic traits. All this served as a basis for encouraging the study of past Galician 'glories' and lost 'independence,' and for protests against the economic backwardness of the country, seen as a result of being marginalized by the Spanish State. The first Galicianists advocated some form of self-government for the country, not flanked by a parallel effort to reconstruct its language and history.

This situation changed at the end of the 1850s, as a new generation of intellectuals focused their activity on crafting a 'national history' for Galicia. They were the historians Verea y Aguiar, Benito Vicetto, and above all Manuel Murguía, who laid the foundations of the historical narrative of Galician

---

1 For an introduction to the history of the Galician movement, see Beramendi and Núñez Seixas (in English), Núñez Seixas 1996 (in German), and Gemie (for the general context).

nationalism in his monumental *Historia de Galicia* (*History of Galicia*) published in five volumes between 1865 and 1913. In a similar vein, some writers recovered and enhanced the literary use of Galician, a romance langugage sharing roots with Portuguese in the Middle Ages. Authors such as Rosalía de Castro, Manoel Curros Enríquez, and Eduardo Pondal were the main figures of what was called the 'Resurgence' (*Rexurdimento*) or literary revival, which manifested itself first in minor literary genres, then in poetry, and from the last decade of the nineteenth century in prose. The literary production and the cultural endeavours of the Galicianist elites were accompanied by an unstable network of cultural associations, as well as by some institutions, all of them attempting to create a solid basis for the diffusion of the movement's tenets and particularly to broaden the social and public use of Galician.

The Galician movement, like many other Western European cases of substate nationalist movements, was not characterized by the adoption of a *Matica* model, that is, a core institution that served as a center for all endeavours related to the language, culture, arts and politics of the national movement. The institutional and associative network set up by Galicianists was ideologically undefined, and it was never able to compete politically with the republican and traditionalist associations and clubs. However, there was a certain line of continuity in the foundation and existence of Galicianist associations of a cultural and political nature.

1   The Literary Academy of Santiago de Compostela

The first cultural institution related to the nascent political 'Provincialism' was the Literary Academy in Santiago de Compostela, founded in 1840 by a group of university students. Among them stand out one charismatic leader, Antolín Faraldo, who shortly afterwards would become a main theoretician of the first Galician movement, together with José María Posada, the later founder of the newspaper *Faro de Vigo*, and the journalist and writer Antonio Neira de Mosquera. Some civil servants and professionals could be found amongst the first members of the Literary Academy, while its first president was also a member of the Catholic clergy.[2] Most of the Academy's literary activities took place at the members' own houses, as the radical democratic affiliation of a majority of them was not particularly welcomed by local authorities. Its Galicianist commitment was still diffuse and limited to emphasizing the historic and literary recovery of the Galician regional past.

---

2   Beramendi, 75.

In fact, the Literary Academy was not particularly active throughout its first years of existence. During its sessions, speeches were given, poetic pieces were presented and recited, and diverse projects on the regional arts were undertaken and subjected to collective discussion. The Academy also published some short-lived journals and several books. Not all the topics treated were specifically related to Galicia, though some of them were amazingly modern, such as Faraldo's defence of the legal equality of women and men.[3] According to the president of the association in 1842, Vicente M. Cociña, the Academy consisted merely of a "scientific lunch" at which steps were taken towards "describing the place reserved for our province [Galicia] among the world's nations."[4] He also pointed out that the Academy was unique in attempting to shape a real "literary unity" in Galicia.[5] Apart from the Literary Academy, the young Galicianist Neira de Mosquera attempted to set up a new cultural institution related to Galicianism, the Galician Archaeological *Diputación* (council), with an "exclusively scholarly" character. However, this endeavour failed shortly after its start in 1843. The number of activists around the Literary Academy was reduced and rarely exceeded one hundred fifty individuals, almost all of them belonging to the urban middle classes.[6]

During the 1850s, a new association replaced the Literary Academy: the *Liceo de la Juventud* (Youth Club), which had already been founded in April 1847. Its objective was to foster literary and artistic sociability among the university students, including leisure.[7] Its several activities took place at a central religious establishment that had been secularized by the liberal state, and were attended by some later relevant writers and historians who played a major role in the articulation of the Galician literary and historical revival. This was the case with the historian Murguía, the poets Aurelio Aguirre, Eduardo Pondal and Rosalía de Castro, and the lawyer Juan M. Paz-Nóvoa.[8] Their activities were

---

3   Varela Jácome 1954, 151–55.
4   Vicente M. Cociña, *Discurso pronunciado por el presidente de la Academia Literaria de Santiago en la Sesión Jeneral de reposición de cargos del año 1842* [Speech made by the president of the Literary Academy before the General Assembly of 1842] (Santiago de Compostela: Imprenta de la V. e H. de Compañel, 1842), 10.
5   Ibid., 9. See also J. Mª Posada, *A la Academia Literaria en el día de la reposición de cargos del año de 1842* [To the Literary Academy on the day of the renewal of its leadership, 1842] (Santiago de Compostela: Imprenta de la V. e H. de Compañel, 1842).
6   Beramendi, 74.
7   Antonio Neira de Mosquera, *Discurso pronunciado en el Liceo de la Juventud* [Speech at the Youth Club] (Santiago de Compostela: Imp. de Juan Rey Romero, 1849), 8.
8   Beramendi, 136.

aimed at influencing university students, as well as some local intellectuals and professionals, through the promotion of the regional arts.[9]

Several cultural institutions for university and high-school students promoted by the first regionalists also emerged through the second half of the nineteenth century. Most of them were located at the University town of Santiago de Compostela, ranging from the *Unión Escolar y Artística* in Santiago (Scholarly and Artistic Union, 1861) to the *Ateneo Escolar Gallego* (Galician Scholarly Athenaeum, 1881).[10] However, none of these associations played a major role in the Galicianist movement as they were not organically linked to its political and cultural activities.

2 The Literary Contests (*xogos florais*)

As in other European peripheries, literary contests provided a model for the development of minority culture. The first Galician literary contests, directly modelled after those held in Catalonia in 1859, were performed in the city of A Coruña in 1861. However, the language of an overwhelming majority of the pieces was Castilian and not yet Galician. The parallel contests celebrated in Pontevedra saw an increasing presence of the Galician language. No fewer than twenty-four literary contests were organized between 1861 and 1891, although only three of them exclusively admitted literary pieces in the Galician language (Ourense 1877, Pontevedra 1886, and Tui 1891).[11] The Literary Contest held in Tui in 1891 marked a peak moment, as the whole ceremony was held in Galician and it was mandatory that all the compositions had to be presented in that language.[12]

Nonetheless, a scarcely political engagement still prevailed, and the place reserved for the Galician language was not yet acknowledged definitively. Several years later, in August 1907, the regionalist weekly *A Nosa Terra* referred to the contests held in Lugo that same year, lamenting the fact that all the participants were required to present their texts in Castilian except in the section devoted to comic poetry, "as if in Galician love, faith and homeland could not be sung and referred to as respectfully and artistically as they are in Castilian."[13] Even in 1918, when the Language Brotherhoods had emerged and Galician

---

9   Neira de Mosquera, 7.
10 Barreiro Fernández, 362.
11 Hermida Gulías, 240 ff.
12 Monteagudo 1999, 365.
13 *A Nosa Terra*, 18 July 1907.

nationalism had been introduced into the public sphere, the literary contests held by the Language Brotherhood from the small town of Betanzos still admitted pieces presented in Castilian, something that caused the main Language Brotherhood from A Coruña to refrain from supporting the ceremony.[14] Some political leaders, like the liberal politician Eduardo Vicenti, proposed already in 1891 to found a new type of organization, a Galician 'Land League' of Irish inspiration, whose objective should consist in "replacing the so-called Literary Contests and regionalist associations, created as leisure social clubs to entertain and give shelter to diverse groups of writers who aim to touch us with their songs and poems."[15]

Remarkably, the promotion of Galician theater was never a major concern for the promoters of the literary contests. In most of them, there were no prizes for dramas. One possible explanation for this absence is that regionalists and language activists alike were concerned above all with the recovery of Galician as a language of high culture, which should be written properly in the major genres. Therefore, and quite paradoxically so, the diffusion of Galician in popular theater—mostly represented in Castilian—received hardly any attention.[16]

3 The *Literary Galicia* Association (Madrid)

Not all the cultural endeavours linked to the Galician movement were born on Galician soil. Some clubs and associations emerged in Latin America, particularly in Havana and Buenos Aires, places where a great number of Galician migrants had settled since the 1870s. Some initiatives around outstanding Galician writers were to be found also in Madrid. This was the case with the *Galicia Literaria* (Literary Galicia) association founded in 1875 by Teodosio Vesteiro assisted by the writers Añón de Paz, Manoel Curros Enríquez, the brothers Andrés and Jesús Muruais, and Victorino Novo. The objectives proclaimed by the new association were rather vague: it would be "an association of Galicians residing in the Spanish capital, in order to strengthen links among them, to mutually encourage the cultivation of the Arts, and to constitute a nucleus of good Galicians working for the honor and prosperity of the country."[17] They

---

14   Torres Regueiro, 107.
15   Beramendi, 293.
16   Tato Fontaíña, 23.
17   University Library of Santiago de Compostela, Manuscripts section, Ms 321: *Acta de fundación y Actas de las reuniones de la Sociedad Galicia Literaria, 1875–1876*—"Acta de

also proclaimed Galicia's "moral and material" interests and promoted the study of regional literature among the Galician people, focusing on topics related to the Arts and Literature. Politics and religion were excluded from public discussion. However, the members of the association admitted their liberal-progressive and even openly Republican inclinations, and enthusiastically adhered to the principles of the French Revolution.[18] The *Galicia Literaria* held meetings on a regular basis, and commemorated holidays such as the anniversaries of prestigious Galician writers, beginning with that of the eighteenth-century erudite and friar Benito J. Feijoo (1676–1764). The members of the association recited poems and novels, and attempted to set up a library on topics related to Galician history and culture.

The *Galicia Literaria* was short-lived (around one year and a half), and its existence was marked by several internal quarrels between progressive and conservative members, particularly following the publication of the book *The Galicians Portrayed by Themselves*. Vesteiro, the founder of *Galicia Literaria*, returned to Galicia and committed suicide shortly afterwards (1876).[19] In spite of its short lifespan, this association was considered crucial for the ideological evolution of some of its most prominent members, who continued to be linked to the Galician movement.

4   The Association of Galician Folklore

By the end of the nineteenth century, several 'folklore associations' had been founded in different parts of Spain, imitating the example offered by contemporary English and French folklore societies.[20] They celebrated the conservation and promotion of folklore and local tradition, establishing a link between regional and local culture and state national identity. This was also the case with the *Sociedad del Folklore Gallego: Sociedad del Popular Saber de Galicia* (Galician Folklore Association), founded in 1883 and headed by the Galician writer Emilia Pardo Bazán, a representative of literary realism in Castilian. Even though she was by no means close to the Galician movement—she published in Castilian—many of those joining the association were somehow related to the movement, from the writers Galo Salinas and Andrés Martínez-Salazar to

---

Fundación de la Sociedad Galicia Literaria" [Proceedings of the Foundation of the Literary Galicia Association].

18   *Acta de fundación y Actas de las reuniones de la Sociedad Galicia Literaria, 1875–1876*—"Bases de la Sociedad 'Galicia Literaria'" [Rules of the Literary Galicia Association], 5–6.
19   Álvarez de la Granja, 31; see also Varela Jácome 1949.
20   See Baycroft and Hopkin.

the poet Francisco M. de la Iglesia. The objectives of the new association were merely antiquarian: to "Recover those traditions that get lost, those uses that are forgotten, and those vestiges from ancient times that risk vanishing forever," with the aim not to revive them, but simply to "store them," to keep their remembrance alive and bring them together in a "universal museum, where intellectuals may study the whole history of our past."[21] The field of interest of the *Folklore Gallego* ranged from popular sayings and games to recipes, as even such "negligible and banal things," according to Pardo Bazán, were a part of Galician folklore.

The Galician Folklore Association was able to broaden its activities and set up a central office, the rudimentary beginnings of a museum, a library, and a network of members and collaborators, which enabled it to become one of the most 'flourishing' folklore associations in Spain and in all of Europe, as Galo Salinas summarized in his 1885 annual report.[22] Its non-political character also allowed the association to gain financial support from several local institutions and to move its central headquarters to an emblematic building in the city of A Coruña.[23] In the following years the Galician Folklore Association issued some books on popular music, regional traditions, religious devotions and sanctuaries, as well as local gastronomy. A scientific method was also developed and implemented to collect pieces of folklore systematically. In 1889 a Galician contest on 'popular science' was held in A Coruña.[24]

Although a substantial part of its members were linked to the Galician movement and shared regionalist ideas, the Folklore association never took up an openly pro-Galicianist stance; quite the opposite, as it loudly proclaimed its loyalty to the Spanish nation and made frequent use of the colors of the Spanish flag (red and yellow) on the covers of its publications. This caused some of the most prominent Galicianist intellectuals, such as the historian Manuel Murguía, to distance themselves from the association's activities.

In January 1895 the Folklore Association was disbanded, with the purpose of founding a Galician Academy as a continuation of its activities. This was a project suggested since the 1880s by some regionalist activists led by the former Republican Curros Enríquez from Havana; in the Caribbean a campaign

---

21 Emilia Pardo Bazán and Salvador Golpe, *El Folk-Lore Gallego en 1884–85. Sus actas y acuerdos y discursos de Emilia Pardo Bazán, presidente y Memoria de Salvador Golpe, Secretario* [Galician Folklore in 1884–85. Its proceedings and agreements, as well as speechs by its president Emilia Pardo Bazán and its secretary Salvador Golpe] (Madrid: Establecimiento Tipográfico de Ricardo Fé, 1886), 6.
22 Salvador Golpe, "Memoria" [Memory], in Pardo Bazán and Golpe, *El Folk-Lore Gallego*, 24.
23 Ibid., 28.
24 See Saurín de la Iglesia.

carried out by Galician journals and associations achieved considerable success. Nevertheless, frequent quarrels among some of its founding intellectuals prevented the Galician Academy from being firmly established. The disputes particularly pitted those who, like Murguía, favored a more politically engaged Galicianist commitment of the new Academy, against those like Pardo Bazán, who were supporters of an extremely mild regionalized Spanish nationalism, whose main vehicular language should continue to be Castilian.[25]

5 The Celtic Cavern of A Coruña

The 'Celtic Cavern' (*Cova Céltiga*) was the popular nickname of a social circle that, in the last years of the nineteenth century, assembled A Coruña's most important Galician regionalists. Meeting in a bookstore owned by the writer Uxío Carré, they discussed topics related to Galician history and politics. It became the most active and consistent cultural group of the city. Its promoters were also active at the political level. In 1897 they founded the *Liga Gallega* (Galician League), led by the prominent national historian Manuel Murguía and later on by the liberal regionalist Waldo Álvarez-Insua, who had returned from Havana in 1899, where he had been active in the internal politics of the Galician immigrant community. The most important writers in the Galician language, both poets and novelists, were also members of this circle, from Murguía and Eduardo Pondal (who wrote the lyrics of the Galician anthem, which was first played in 1907 in Havana) to the musician Pascual Veiga (the composer of the anthem's music) and the linguist Eladio Rodríguez-González.[26] Among the main objectives of the Galician League, the "promotion and defence of Galician language and culture" stand out.[27]

Moreover, the group of activists of the Celtic Cavern also promoted the foundation of other associations, such as the Regional School of Declamation and the *Revista Gallega* (Galician Review), a bilingual weekly published since 1895 by the writer Galo Salinas. Amongst the main tenets of the new magazine were the diffusion of Galician language and literature, the promotion of the standardization of the Galician language, and its introduction into the school system. Finally, according to some of its members, the project of founding an

---

25   Xosé Filgueira Valverde, "A *Sociedad del Folklore Gallego* abríu a cancela da recuperación cultural de Galicia" [The Galician Folkore Association paved the way for Galicia's cultural recovery], *La Voz de Galicia*, 30 December 1982.
26   See Ferreiro and López Acuña.
27   Beramendi, 310 and 320.

Academy of the Galician Language emerged from the discussions and projects exchanged at the Celtic Cavern. In fact, some of its most active members promoted the foundation of the Academy in 1906.[28]

6 The Regional School of Declamation and Other Theatrical Endeavours

In contrast to the scarce attention that the nineteenth-century literary resurgence had given to theater, the literary production of theatrical works in Galician took a noteworthy step forward at the beginning of the twentieth century. Both existing and new theater associations and groups now devoted their efforts to writing and performing plays in Galician. Among them stands out the Regional School of Declamation, founded in the city of A Coruña in 1903 by Salinas, who was soon replaced by the younger writer Manuel Lugrís. This initiative gained enthusiastic support from some actors and theater directors too.[29] Amidst a theatrical environment that was overwhelmingly dominated by the presence of the Castilian language, the School managed to initiate performances of Galician theater in several towns, particularly A Coruña and Ferrol, usually staging works written by regionalist authors. Some of these, like the drama ¡Filla...! (Daughter!) by Salinas had been performed for the first time in the Galician migrant community of Buenos Aires in 1894.[30]

Although the School ceased its activity in 1905,[31] it set an inspiring example that was soon followed by other groups, such as the *Bellas Artes* theater association (1905), the first Galician Dramatic Company (1908), and the Galician Dramatic School (1913), which all enjoyed remarkable successes in Galicia. Similarly, in 1910 some university students from Santiago de Compostela set up the *Joven Galicia* (Young Galicia) association, inspired by a reformist creed opposed to the overwhelming dominance of political clientelism in Galician public life. Their initiative also promoted theater performances in Galician, as well as private courses in the Galician and Portuguese languages, and the demand to create a Chair of Galician-Portuguese Language and Literature at the University of Santiago de Compostela.[32]

---

28   Quoted by López Varela, 33.
29   Tato Fontaíña, 47.
30   Rabuñal Corgo, 161–69.
31   Tato Fontaíña, 55.
32   Beramendi, 364; Tato Fontaíña, 62.

7 The Galician Royal Academy

Galician regionalism lacked the support of the regional clergy, the upper classes, and the rural nobility; at the other end of the social spectrum, the leaders of the movement completely ignored the workers and peasant classes. Therefore, and despite noteworthy ideological and cultural developments, *galeguismo* entered the twentieth century deeply afflicted by an extreme political weakness. Nevertheless, cultural and political activities coexisted during this period: Galician regionalists never confined their activities to the cultural field alone, but established separate organizations that launched political agitation. However, until the 1930s their cultural successes overshadowed their political visibility by far.

After several failed attempts, the old project of setting up an Academy for the promotion of the Galician language succeeded in 1905–06. The participation of some intellectuals and leaders from the Galician immigrant community in Havana proved to be decisive. In the Cuban capital, the typographer Xosé Fontenla Leal and the writer and journalist Manoel Curros Enríquez, alongside other activists, fostered in 1905 the constitution of an Association devoted to "initiating and boosting" the Galician Academy, and soon gathered several hundred members.[33] Not only the idea came from overseas, the necessary financial resources were also collected amongst the Galician emigrants in Cuba, where the "Initiation and Patron Association of the Galician Academy" experienced a noteworthy success, attracting members from several towns.[34]

The definitive founding of the Galician Academy took place in A Coruña in September 1906. Its main objective was to bestow on Galician the status of a full-fledged 'language' and to achieve its standardization by means of "publishing a Grammar and a Dictionary,"[35] as well as promoting Galician literature, researching folklore, and studying the arts, history, and sciences related to the country, including its religious traditions. According to its first statutes, the Academy's objective was to "cultivate the Arts in general, particularly those studies that could best contribute to the knowledge of the history, antiquities and language of Galicia,"[36] as a "cultivated corporation of genuine regional character, to which outstanding and prominent Galician persons belong."[37] Local and provincial authorities enthusiastically supported the foundation of

---

33 Núñez Seixas 1992, 87–90.
34 López Varela, 45.
35 "Constitución de la Academia" [Constitution of the Academy], *Boletín de la Real Academia Gallega*, 2 (20 June 1906).
36 "Constitución de la Academia," *Boletín de la Real Academia Gallega*, 3 (20 July 1906).
37 "La Academia Gallega" [The Galician Academy], *La Voz de Galicia*, 30 September 1906.

the Academy. Nevertheless, in spite of the fact that the Galician Academy received the label 'Royal' from the Spanish Monarchy in August 1906, a privilege supposedly in recognition of its contribution to overall Spanish culture, no representatives of the central state organs attended the Galician Academy's first meetings.[38]

The new Academy was in many respects a successor to the Association for Galician Folklore and perpetuated its interest in ethnography and folklore. In fact, prominent members of that association, such as Pardo Bazán and Ramón Pérez Costales, were given honorific posts at the institution. However, the Academy's concern for the Galician language was intended to be of a different nature. Perhaps because of this distinct character, it was not able to collect institutional partnerships as important as those of its predecessor: the provincial council of A Coruña did not pay its fee until 1909, whereas the Central State did not defray its contribution until three years later. Only the money remittances sent by its supporters and associates in Cuba enabled the institution to survive during its first years of existence. Until 1920 the Academy had a small and modest flat as its headquarters; that year, the institution was allowed to move to a part of the magnificent building housing the town hall of A Coruña, and to set up a small museum. Its meetings were regularly held at different places and towns.[39] Yet, lack of financial resources remained a constant concern, limiting the Academy's activities.[40]

At least in theory, the production of a Dictionary and a definitive grammar of the Galician language constituted the main objective of the Academy. Its members collected versions and meanings of different Galician words, and compiled a linguistic archive based on the record cards filled in by themselves or by earlier scholars of the language who donated their private collections. The first results were published in 1912, consisting of a fascicule distributed amongst Academy members and their supporters, with subsequent issues published until 1928, when the Dictionary was interrupted at the word "C." The results were even more disappointing with regard to a definitive standardization of the Galician language. In 1907–08, the Academy organized some courses on "Galician Grammar", which actually also included notions of Archaeology, History, Literature, and Philology and were attended mainly by "a majority of Galician girls."[41] However, no steps were taken to unify the scientific criteria

---

38 See López Varela, 47; "Constitución de la Academia," *Boletín de la Real Academia Gallega*, 5 (20 September 1906).
39 López Varela, 147.
40 "Memoria" [Recollection], *Boletín de la Real Academia Gallega*, 32 (20 January 1910).
41 "El curso de la Academia" [The Academy's course], *A Nosa Terra*, 19 February 1908.

needed to establish a written standard of the Galician language. Although not without interruptions, from its foundation the Academy published a monthly bulletin which kept its members informed about the institution's activities. The bulletin also published articles related to Galician History, Ethnography, Literature, and the Arts. However, until 1923, most of the essays were published in Castilian, Galician being almost exclusively reserved for poetry and theatrical pieces.

Leisure activities that were intended to foster contact between scholars and their countrymen were also developed for Academy members. These activities were a mixture of sociability and the cultivation of culture, and entailed ethnographic excursions to collect words, popular songs, traditions, and other expressions of Galician folk culture.[42] The Academy also participated in the organization of the Literary Contests, which continued to be held on a regular basis, as well as the 1909 Regional Fair celebrated in Santiago de Compostela. However, apart from these activities, the internal life of the Academy mostly limited itself to organizing tributes to those of its most prominent members who had passed away, as was the case with Curros Enríquez, whose corpse was repatriated from Havana after his death in March 1908.

During its first years of existence, the Galician Academy aroused the interest of the most vehemently regionalist sectors, who expected it to take the lead of the Galicianist movement and to act as a multifunctional initiative devoted to the promotion of its cultural and political objectives. However, many of them increasingly detached themselves from the new institution, as they soon realized that its active involvement with the Galician language and culture was less intense, and more inclined towards the traditional understanding of a folkloric and antiquarian legacy than they had expected. The Academy's interest in the Galician past was mostly antiquarian, ignoring the new criteria dictated by the principle of nationalities *en vogue* since World War I, which aimed at modernizing the inheritance of the past in order to construct a modern national culture. Those, like the young Republican journalist Antón Villar Ponte, who were now interested in pushing the Galician movement in a nationalist direction according to the influential models of the Irish or the Catalan movements, considered that the Academy was merely controlled by "academics, erudite scholars and archaeologists" who "devote[d] themselves to studying old things of our country as if it was a dead country, whose singularity was sunk into a sterile Castilianism. If they develop a dictionary, this will become a

---

42   "Excursión al Bréamo" [Trip to the Bréamo], *Boletín de la Real Academia Gallega*, 15 (20 October 1907); "Excursión al Bréamo", *A Nosa Terra*, 25 August 1907.

pantheon of our language. And their bulletin has become a dead echo of past things. The members of the Academy just look backward."[43]

In fact, before the Galician movement entered its nationalist stage in 1916–18, and until the moment in which the younger generation of nationalist intellectuals and writers began to join the Academy from the mid-1920s, it can be argued that it continued to operate chiefly as a pseudo-traditional folklore association. The institution was mostly dominated by traditionalist regionalists, whose main concern was to study Galicia's past, as well as to vindicate the specifically Galician contribution to Spanish national culture. The absence of an efficiently self-propelled dynamic of cultural nationalism explains why the Academy initially failed to achieve its founding aim: the standardization and modernization of the Galician vernacular, which would not be realized until the 1930s, and this process could not be completed before the outbreak of the Spanish Civil War in July 1936.[44]

8   The Language Brotherhoods and the Ideological Shift to Nationalism

In 1916, influenced by the spread of the nationality principle during World War I, the Galician movement entered a new stage of evolution, leaving behind its regionalist phase and opting for a nationalist self-definition. At the beginning of that year, Villar Ponte, a journalist and returnee from Havana, published the booklet *Galician Nationalism: Our Regional Vindication*, in which he advocated (still in Castilian) the proclamation of the existence of Galicia as a nation, and that it should be invested with the right to self-determination. Furthermore, he linked the recovery of the language and the 'national spirit' of the country to its political emancipation, now regarded as a necessary precondition for the creation of a modern Galician culture. He also claimed that Galicia should be one of the Iberian nations to shape a new Spanish federation, later to merge with Portugal into an Iberian confederation made of the *true* ethnically defined nationalities (Galicia, Portugal, the Basque Country, Catalonia, and Castile).[45]

---

43   Quoted by Monteagudo 1999, 380. See also Insua 2006.
44   See Núñez Seixas 1997; Monteagudo 2006.
45   Antón Villar Ponte, *Nacionalismo gallego. Nuestra afirmación regional* [Galician Nationalism: Our Regional Vindication] (A Coruña: Imp. La Voz de Galicia, 1916). On the history of the Language Brotherhoods, see a complete description by Insua 2016 and Cochón.

Villar Ponte was trying to promote the constitution of a League of Language Friends, which became effective as the *Irmandade dos Amigos da Fala* (Brotherhood of Galician Language Friends) was founded in the city of A Coruña, where its first assembly was called at the headquarters of the Galician Academy. Shortly afterwards, new Brotherhoods emerged in other Galician towns (Santiago de Compostela, Monforte de Lemos, Pontevedra, Vilalba, and Ourense). The founding objectives of the A Coruña Language Brotherhood focused on cultural matters; leaving politics aside, its main goal was the promotion of the oral and written use of the Galician language among its members, and their commitment to promote it in Galician society through the publication of newspaper articles, as well as publishing a mouthpiece of its own. A knowledge of popular culture had also to be fostered among the *irmandiños* ('brothers') through excursions to the countryside, meeting its inhabitants and listening to Galician folk music. Other local brotherhoods also maintained this cultural line; however, alongside this, they also aimed at active intervention in local politics. All in all, the first steps of the Language Brotherhoods made them appear as a fluid network of cultural associations rather than as a nationalist or regionalist political party with explicit aims.[46] The weekly activities first deployed by the organization were of an overwhelmingly cultural character, such as weekly lectures on various topics on Saturday evenings,[47] courses in Galician language and literature, literary soirées, the establishment of choral societies (such as the *Follas Novas* choir in Santiago de Compostela), the performance of theatrical and musical pieces in the Galician language, folklore festivals, and excursions to the countryside in search of the supposedly 'authentic roots' of Galician culture.

The commitment to the Galician language was now the most decisive feature of the new organization, as the Brotherhoods used the language exclusively for all their activities and publications. In May 1917, *A Nosa Terra* (Our Homeland) summed up the main activities developed by the Brotherhoods during their first year of existence, citing organized excursions to the countryside; the teaching of Galician language courses for urban middle-class Castilian-speakers who did not speak it; ceremonies to honor nineteenth-century Galician writers (Curros Enríquez and Eduardo Pondal), as well as to Pedro Pardo de Cela, the Galician aristocrat executed in 1483 by the Castilian Kings and now regarded as a symbol of lost Galician independence, and to the 'martyrs' of the 1846 Provincialist uprising in Carral (a village near A Coruña); the launching of the publication of the monthly bulletin; the fostering of

---

46 Beramendi, 434.
47 "Novas da causa" [News of the movement], *A Nosa Terra*, 25 December 1916.

performances of Galician theater; and the diffusion of the Galician anthem and flag—symbols that had become more recognizable owing to the commitment of the Galician movement.[48] Unlike the East-Central European *Matica* model, the movement did not have a single 'house' or headquarters but rather several centers devoted to the task of spreading the new cultural creed in the main Galician cities and in their surrounding countrysides.

The fostering of Galician culture, and theater in particular, as well as the promotion of choral songs and dances, constituted an important part of the Brotherhoods' efforts. The new nationalists created choral associations, which partly reunited previous groups, and founded new ones, such as *Cántigas da Terra* in A Coruña or *Cántigas e Agarimos* in Santiago de Compostela, *Airiños da Miña Terra* and *Toxos e Flores* in Ferrol, and the *Coral de Ruada* in Ourense. Their artistic performances ran parallel to the Brotherhoods' political and cultural activities, and also attracted new adherents to the movement by promoting a primary feeling of attachment to Galician culture.[49] Theater companies also developed under the patronage of the Brotherhoods, whose associates frequently supported the formation of new dramatic groups. Theater was seen as an efficient instrument to influence public opinion, as well as to gain new supporters. As the Brotherhoods initially lacked any clear-cut political orientation, the regional Conservative and Catholic elites alike were attracted by its proud commitment to the Galician language. Therefore, they approached the organization and collaborated closely with some of its activities.[50] As a consequence, the number of theater performances in the Galician language increased dramatically: in 1918, twenty-one new Galician dramas had their premières. Although almost all theater groups included Castilian pieces in their repertoire, some theater groups close to the workers' movement or to the associations of the lower middle classes started using the Galician language in their performances. This was the case in 1917 with the Association of Shop Assistants of the town of Ferrol, led by a member of the local Language Brotherhood, as well as with the theater group of the same town's Workers' trade union

---

48 "O primeiro ano da Irmandade" [The first year of the Brotherhood], *A Nosa Terra*, 20 May 1917. On the 'invention' of the Galician national symbols, see Núñez Seixas 2012. See also Villares.

49 See Costa Vázquez-Mariño.

50 The nationalist weekly *A Nosa Terra* informed in December 1916 on the performance of several Galician dramas of Lugrís Freire at the Catholic Workers' Circle in Santiago de Compostela.

the following year.[51] In 1918 the Language Brotherhoods decided to set up an annual theater contest in Galician.

Theater in the Galician language made evident steps forward. However, the weekly *A Nosa Terra* stressed in 1919 that the topics dealt with in Galician had to evolve from historic dramas to more contemporary concerns of the middle and popular classes, from social reform and cheap housing to the question of female suffrage. It was with this objective that the Declamation Group of the National Conservatorium of Galician Arts, created by A Coruña's Language Brotherhood, set out its activities in April 1919 and performed Galician theatrical pieces once a week.[52] However, it mainly addressed the educated middle class.

The Language Brotherhoods started as a multifunctional center of sociability committed to fostering the literary and public presence of the Galician language. In subsequent years, they ended up being a political party. Their first adherents were recruited among the younger members of the urban liberal professions and middle classes, with a minor yet meaningful participation of the lower middle classes and skilled manual workers. University students also formed a good percentage of the first Brotherhoods' members. Until the beginning of the 1920s the membership figures of the Brotherhoods remained relatively low and did not surpass six hundred affiliates, most of them concentrated in the towns of A Coruña and Santiago de Compostela.[53] The powerful nationalist organisation of Havana (the *Xuntanza Nazonalista Galega*) was also able to gain an outstanding presence among Galician immigrants in Cuba.[54] Their internal organization was democratic; women were also given a place in their activities (as members of a 'female section' of the Brotherhoods, they were also entitled to found Brotherhoods wherever the number of male members was insufficient); and they were increasingly coordinated at the Galician level, as expressed in their First Assembly held in Lugo (November 1918). At this assembly, a first political program was approved, based on the adoption of the new label 'Galician nationalists' and the definition of Galicia as a separate nation entitled to enjoy all the rights entailed by the nationality principle. However, as a strategic aim the organization campaigned for the federal restructuring of the Spanish State as a multinational polity, in which Galicia would be one of the units. One consequence of this was that the Catholic

---

51   Tato Fontaíña, 72–75.
52   Monteagudo 1999, 481.
53   Beramendi, 444.
54   See Núñez Seixas 1992, 111–13.

Church withdrew its support from the Galician cause, and lay Regionalists who disagreed with the Galician movement's new nationalist orientation established weak separate organizations, which disappeared within a few months.

Before taking this political step, the Language Brotherhoods had been little engaged in politics, and had mainly concentrated on cultural tasks and the promotion of the vernacular. Their apparent political neutrality made it possible that their endeavours were welcomed at first by large sectors of the Galician public sphere, both right- and left-wing, also including provincial and state institutions as well as the Catholic hierarchy. In fact, the local clergy even attempted to take control over the organization in 1918 by attracting the new Galicianists to a 'Regionalist week' held in Santiago de Compostela, which was attended by several Traditionalist leaders who were more or less sympathetic towards regional decentralization. During the Language Brotherhoods' first two years of existence, the nationalist leadership had attempted to hide its ideological orientation. However, from November 1918 this was no longer possible, and the open shift of the Brotherhoods towards ethnonationalism caused some of the initially receptive sectors to distance themselves from those who came to be regarded as separatists. That same year, the most important local Brotherhood, that of A Coruña, inaugurated its new headquarters and established the achievement of home-rule and self-government for Galicia as one of its main goals, alongside the continuation of its cultural agitation. *A Nosa Terra*, also published by the Brotherhood of A Coruña, became the regular mouthpiece of the Galician movement, its one to two thousand copies being distributed all over Galicia and also sent to the Galician migrant communities of Cuba and Argentina.

Although it did not reach a mass audience, the weekly journal *A Nosa Terra* definitively established the exclusive public use of Galician as a distinctive feature of the Galician movement (now a national movement) and steadily became a political journal, while Galician cultural nationalism found other channels of expression in the 1920s. On the occasion of the second anniversary of the foundation of the Brotherhoods, their journal stated that "During the last two years, a cultivated Galician has been more extensively spoken than in the whole preceding century."[55] Ever since 1916–18, Galician culture, the definitive standardization of the Galician language, and the broadening of its public and literary use have remained linked to the evolution of the Galician national movement, and have determined the shaping of a linguistically-based political culture that continues to be a distinctive feature of Galician nationalism in the twenty-first century.

---

55   "O segundo aniversario da fundazón das Irmandades," *A Nosa Terra*, 30 May 1918.

Bibliography

Álvarez de la Granja, María. *Teodosio Vesteiro Torres. Aproximación á súa vida e á súa obra* [Teodosio Vesteiro Torres: An introduction to his life and work]. Vigo: Instituto de Estudos Vigueses, 1998.

Barreiro Fernández, Xosé Ramón. *Historia da Universidade de Santiago de Compostela* [History of the University of Santiago de Compostela]. Vol. II: *O século XIX* [The 19th century]. Santiago de Compostela: USC / Parlamento de Galicia, 2002.

Baycroft, Timothy, and David Hopkin, eds. *Folklore and Nationalism in Europe during the Long Nineteenth Century*. Leiden: Brill, 2012.

Beramendi, Justo. *Galicia, de provincia a nación. Historia do galeguismo político, 1840–2000* [Galicia, from province to nation. A History of the Galician movement]. Vigo: Xerais, 2007.

Beramendi, Justo, and Xosé M. Núñez Seixas. "The Historical Background of Galician Nationalism (1840–1950)." *Canadian Review of Studies in Nationalism* XXII: 1–2 (1995), 33–51.

Cochón, Luis, ed. *Arredor das Irmandades da Fala: Pensamento, política e poética en Galicia (1914–1931)* [On the Language Brotherhoods: Thought, politics and poetics in Galicia]. Vigo: Xerais, 2016.

Costa Vázquez-Mariño, Luís. "La formación del pensamiento musical nacionalista en Galicia hasta 1936" [The emergence of nationalist musical thought in Galicia until 1936]. Ph. D. Thesis, University of Santiago de Compostela, 1999.

Ferreiro, Manuel, and Fernando López Acuña. "O Himno: historia, texto e música" [The anthem: history, lyrics and music]. In Xosé Ramón Barreiro Fernández and Ramón Villares, eds., *Os símbolos de Galicia* [The symbols of Galicia]. Santiago de Compostela: Consello da Cultura Galega/ Real Academia Galega, 2007. 105–92.

Gemie, Sharif. *A Concise History of Galicia*. Cardiff: University of Wales Press, 2006.

Hermida Gulías, Carme. *Os Precursores da normalización: Defensa e reivindicación da lingua galega no Rexurdimento (1840–1891)* [The forerunners of cultural normalization: Claim and vindication of the Galician language during the Resurgence period]. Vigo: Xerais, 1992.

Insua, Emilio. *Antón Villar Ponte e a Academia Galega: contributos para a historia dunha institución centenaria* [Antón Villar Ponte and the Galician Academy: a contribution to the history of a centennial institution]. Vilaboa: Eds. do Cumio, 2006.

Insua, Emilio. *A nosa Terra é nosa! A xeira das Irmandades da Fala (1916–1931)* [Our land belongs to us! The trajectory of the Language Brotherhoods]. A Coruña: Baía, 2016.

Leerssen, Joep. *National Thought in Europe: A Cultural History*. Amsterdam: Amsterdam UP, 2006.

López Varela, Elisardo. *Unha casa para a lingua: A Real Academia Galega baixo a presidencia de Manuel Murguía (1905–1923)* [A home for the Language: The Galician

Royal Academy under the presidency of Manuel Murguía]. A Coruña: Espiral Maior, 2001.

Monteagudo, Henrique. *Historia social da lingua galega* [A social history of the Galician language]. Vigo: Galaxia, 1999.

Monteagudo, Henrique. "A Academia, o idioma e o nacionalismo, 1906–1936: Notas para unha historia" [The Academy, the language and nationalism, 1906–36: Some notes for a history]. *Grial* 171 (2006), 26–37.

Núñez Seixas, Xosé M. *O galeguismo en América, 1879–1936* [The Galician movement in America]. Sada–A Coruña: Eds. do Castro, 1992.

Núñez Seixas, Xosé M. "Die galicische Nationalbewegung (1840–1939): Ein historischer Überblick". *Lusorama-Zeitschrift für Lusitanistik* 30 (1996), 91–110.

Núñez Seixas, Xosé M. "Idioma y nacionalismo en Galicia en el siglo XX: un desencuentro histórico y diversos dilemas en el futuro" [Language and Nationalism in 20th-century Galicia: A historical misunderstanding and some dilemmas for the future]. *Revista de Antropología Social* 6 (1997), 165–91.

Núñez Seixas, Xosé M. "Sobre símbolos y conmemoraciones del galleguismo, 1890–2011" [On symbols and commemorations of Galicianism]. In Ludger Mees, ed., *La celebración de la nación. Símbolos, mitos y lugares de memoria en el discurso nacional* [Celebrating the nation: Symbols, myths and sites of memory in national discourse]. Granada: Comares, 2012. 191–213.

Rabuñal Corgo, Henrique. "No centenario da 'Escola Rexional de Declamación' (1903–2003)" ["One hundred years of the 'Regional History of Declamation'"]. *Anuario Galego de Estudos Teatrais* (2002), 161–69.

Saurín de la Iglesia, María Rosa. "Emilia Pardo Bazán y la Sociedad del Folklore Gallego (1885–1893)" [Emilia Pardo Bazán and the Galician Folklore Association]. In José M. González Herrán, Cristina Patiño Eirín and Ermitas Penas Varela, eds., *La Literatura de Emilia Pardo Bazán* [The Literature of Emilia Pardo Bazán]. A Coruña: Fundación Caixa Galicia, 2009. 677–96.

Tato Fontaíña, Laura. *Historia do teatro galego. Das orixes a 1936* [A History of Galician Theater: From its origins to 1936]. Vigo: A Nosa Terra, 1999.

Torres Regueiro, Xesús. "A Irmandade da Fala de Betanzos. 1917–1930" [The Language Brotherhood in Betanzos. 1917–1930]. *Anuario Brigantino* 14 (1991), 91–138.

Varela Jácome, Benito. "Vesteiro Torres y la *Galicia Literaria*" [Vesteiro Torres and *Literary Galicia*]. *Cuadernos de Estudios Gallegos* 4:12 (1949), 73–93.

Varela Jácome, Benito. "La Academia Literaria de Santiago en 1842" [The Literary Academy of Santiago in 1842]. *Cuadernos de Estudios Gallegos* 28 (1954), 151–55.

Villares, Ramón. *Identidades e afectos patrios* [Identities and love for the fatherland]. Vigo: Galaxia, 2017.

CHAPTER 9

Félibrige, or the Impossible Occitan Nation

Philippe Martel

The nineteenth century in Europe was the century of nation-builders. This was true not only in Central and Eastern Europe, where 'nationalities' tried to emerge from under the rule of old Empires (Austrian, Russian or Ottoman), but also in the western part of the continent: in Spain with Catalonian and Basque revendication, and in the United Kingdom with Celtic revivals from Ireland to Wales and Scotland. In some respects, Italian unification may be conceived as a successful variant of this general process, which is conveniently symbolized by a well-known formula, the 'Springtime of Peoples' of 1848, even if in fact it began before this date.

Within this general framework, the situation of France is paradoxical. On the one hand, the French Revolution and the Napoleonic wars (each in its own way!) played a role in the diffusion of an aspiration to both national and social emancipation, through the efficient blows they inflicted on old absolutist states and traditional feudal loyalties. On the other hand, as far as the French internal situation was concerned, both Revolution and Empire led to a considerable acceleration of unification: economic unification implying the constitution of a national market; social unification, at least theoretically, with the proclamation of civic equality inside the whole community of (male) citizens; and cultural unification at last, with the increasing diffusion among the lower classes of a French national language which until 1789 had been the privilege of the upper classes. During the nineteenth century, the revolution in industry and transport and the creation of a rather efficient educational system completed the process. The political instability of this same century, with its succession of monarchist, Bonapartist, and republican regimes, did not weaken the general trend towards the homogenization of French society around national identification: right and left, 'reds' and 'whites,' clerical and anticlerical parties might sometimes fight each other with considerable violence, but their common adherence to the French nation was never questioned, and was even a source of pride.

Therefore, one would expect the utter disappearance of older particular cultures linked to peripheral territories that the regular expansion of the French state had successively absorbed and subdued throughout the centuries: Breton-, Occitan-, or Basque-speaking areas, and, at least until 1870,

German-speaking Alsace; all these alloglott regions were bound to forget their own indigenous language for the benefit of a unitarian academic French. And indeed, each of these languages began at this time to lose ground to monolingual francophony. By the middle of the century, most observers could predict the impending disappearance of what was in ordinary French called the *patois*.

But this unification met unexpectedly with reactions in some regions where revival movements began. This was the case in Britanny as early as the 1830s: Hersart de la Villemarqué's Breton folk-song anthology (the *Barzaz Breiz*) was published in 1839. In Occitan-speaking southern France, this reaction was embodied by an association whose aim at first was merely literary, but which would later try to go farther under the direction of its main animator, Frédéric Mistral: the provençal Félibrige. The question is: to what extent would this association succeed in leading the Occitan revival—in Hrochian terms—from the nation-building phase A to phase B?[1]

1   The Meaning of Félibrige

Félibrige is an association whose members are called the *Félibres*. The first characteristic of this word—found by Mistral in an old religious song about the meeting between the young Jesus and the doctors of the synagogue (*li set felibre de la lèi*, the seven "*félibres* of the law")—is that it had no meaning in any language before 21 May 1854, when, according to tradition, a bunch of young Occitan-speaking and -writing poets decided to choose it as their emblem. The mentor of this group was then Joseph Roumanille, the elder, but very soon the true leader would be Frédéric Mistral. At first a confidential and informal club with little influence even in its native Provence, the Félibrige gradually became the leading force of the Occitan renaissance following the success of Mistral's first great poem, *Mirèio* (1859).[2]

Of course, this small group did not appear in a desert. The French Revolution had thoroughly modified the ways in which French authorities dealt with linguistic and cultural plurality on their territory. The old monarchy did not pay much attention to what was spoken by the lower classes, because it did not accord them any place in political life, nor listen to anything they might have to say. Therefore there was no need, from such a point of view, to diffuse largely a minimal knowledge of a common language. On the contrary, education for the masses was considered by many persons of distinction as a threat to social

---

[1] See Hroch 1985.
[2] See Mauron.

order, as defined by Divine Providence and tradition (everyone in his right place). From 1789 onward, the new system considered that citizenry—that is, the freshly acquired right for ordinary people to take part (at least to some extent) in the political life of the 'nation'—implied the mastery of official French as the only language fit for all practical purposes, while any other language was considered inappropriate for the expression of Reason, or worse, as a remnant of the Old World, antagonic to the new order. If at the beginning there was some tolerance for a pedagogic—or rather propagandistic—use of *patois*, very soon, and decisively during the Terror (1793–94), an imperative diffusion of French and the eradication of everything except French became the rule. Henri Grégoire was the best known among those who designed and tried to apply this rule.[3]

The revolutionary power lacked the practical means and tools to enforce the linguistic policy it envisioned. But these principles would now be widely accepted by most of the governments that would follow; and the new regimes, whether constitutional-monarchist or Bonapartist or republican, all shared the same conviction that linguistic unification was not only an administrative necessity but a social and political one as well, if not an almost religious obligation. Gradually, whole sectors of the Breton, or Alsacian (before 1870), or Corsican, or Occitan societies were led to adopt French as the normal medium in family transmission. The upper classes went first in this process as early as the beginning of the century; the middle classes followed after the middle of the same century; and eventually the linguistic shift affected the lower classes, first the urban, then the rural. This evolution was slow—it is not finished even today—but it was steady enough to gradually displace the various non-French languages previously spoken in France. Language death therefore became a common topic in literary and journalistic discussions, as an obvious and unavoidable consequence of modernity.

But if many observers accepted this death with resignation, and sometimes with enthusiasm, others perceived it as a tragic loss. For some of them, grief and nostalgia gave way to engagement in support of the preservation of their doomed language. Their motives were not homogenous. Some, particularly in the old nobility and the Catholic clergy, considered the *patois* as a shield against 'the language of Voltaire' and the subversive ideas it expressed, giving at the same time a justification to those who, in the other camp, had since Grégoire's time condemned *patois* as fatally bound up with obscurantism and feudal reaction. Such an ideological position was largely observable in the cases of Breton or Basque, and was not totally unknown in the Occitan regions.

---

3   De Certeau; Boyer and Gardy (eds.).

Others may have had different motivations. Grégoire's famous survey launched in 1790 as the basis for his great 1794 report had paradoxical effects its promotor had not foreseen: his forty-three questions included precise, nearly scientific inquiries about the phonetics, lexicality and history of the various *patois*, and therefore led those who agreed to answer them to study their local language, to try to find its genealogical links with French or other European languages, or the literary 'monuments' whose vectors they could once have been. For the Abbé Gregoire *patois* was a target; but for some of his correspondents, it became a scientific object: some of them even sent specimens of *patois* literature, or dialect grammars, compelling Grégoire in his official report to acknowledge for instance the value of 'provençal.' This tendency was strengthened during the First Empire by a second and much more extensive survey by Jean Antoine Coquebert de Montbret which moved many more respondents to discover their provinces' cultural heritage.[4] At the same time, some nationally recognized scholars discovered elements of this heritage to be of great cultural importance. François Raynouard, a former colleague of Grégoire in revolutionnary assemblies and an Academician, became the first true editor of Occitan troubadour poetry.[5] Some years later (1823), the first great historian of 'liberal' sensibility, Jean de Sismondi, popularized for the enlightened public of his time the notion of a 'Midi,' or better of a 'Provençal' people whose medieval culture united literary excellence (the troubadours), socio-economic growth, and political progressism, along with a tolerance which allowed heretical thinking to develop freely, at least up until the time when a grisly alliance between clerical fanaticism and feudal brutality led to bloodshed in the Albigensian Crusade. This was to become a widespread cliché during the whole century and even later.[6]

Therefore, it is easy to understand how some young Southerners with a certain cultural capital could point to a strange paradox created by national intellectual production: the much-loathed *patois* had been the poetical medium of the first great occidental renaissance, around 1200; and the distant, marginal, underdeveloped 'Midi' of their own time had once been the blessed fatherland of a first attempt, during the Dark Ages, to invent something that made it the precursor of modern democracy. By a not so strange contradiction, it was precisely those who had freshly acquired access to offical French culture who acquired at the same time the intellectual tools that would permit them to question this official culture. After all, Mistral, the son of a well-to-do peasant

---

4   See Merle.
5   Martel 2008.
6   Martel 1982, 2002.

(but a peasant nonetheless) had earned a law degree at Aix-en-Provence, and had a fair command not only of French but of Latin and Greek as well, that is to say, the basis of the recognized culture of his time. Not all his followers could boast of the same academic achievements, but most of them had mastered French and acquired a minimal culture. What is true of the *Félibres* is also true of their precursors of the first half of the nineteenth century. The protagonists of the Occitan revival were never ignorant of the official language and culture, not marginal survivors of monolingual rural societies alien to contemporary cultural evolutions; on the contrary, they were often excellent former pupils of the French educational system who were unwilling to sacrifice their own original culture.

And thus the keen perception by those individuals of what threatened the very survival of their native speech, together with the discovery of its eminent, albeit long-forgotten dignity, led some of them to a conscient renaissancist activism. This process is evident from the quantitative growth of printed works in Occitan, especially in Provence, where urbanization simultaneously hastened the retreat of Occitan as a universally spoken medium and created the social conditions that would allow those who wanted to fight this retreat to come together. As early as the 1850s, some 70% of what was printed in Occitan was written in provençal dialect. No wonder then that it was in Provence that the first collective institution devoted to this goal appeared.[7]

Of course, the beginings of this strangely named *Félibrige* were modest, if not utterly invisible (comprising roughly 5% of the total number of Occitan editions published between 1855 and 1860). This changed after 1859, with the success of Mistral's first long poem, the 'rustic epic' *Mirèio*. Critics adored this poem, enough to forget and forgive the language in which it was written—Mistral had cleverly supplied a French translation. He did not understand at this time that for many of these so enthusiastic critics, what made the success of *Mirèio* was first of all its exotic flavor: many of them saw it as a specimen of primitive popular poety, linked to a strange southern tribal society, a repository of ancient medieval folklore. At another, more polemical level, this "fresh, rustic, charming" story (to cite the most frequently used adjectives in their newspapers) could be considered as a counter-attack against certain new literary trends of the time, as embodied for instance by Charles Baudelaire. From this point of view, Mistral was not recognized truly as, with his language, a part of the authorized French literary landscape, but was rather used in a struggle—esthetic and political—that was really none of his business and had no positive implications for the recognition of Occitan as a legitimate literary language.

---

7   Martel 2001.

It is significant that most critics added to their enthusiastic compliments a note of reserve: why did this Mistral use his boorish *patois* instead of writing like everybody else in the only true language, French?[8] From the beginning, thus, we find the Félibrige simultaneously taken grudgingly into account to some extent, but not fully accepted. And this was only a beginning.

2   The Félibrige as an Organization

In its first years, the Félibrige was nothing more than a small informal club of good friends in the same neighborhood. With the so-called triumph of *Mirèio*, such an informal arrangement could not last. The association needed a charter, and would in fact have four different charters before the death of its leader in 1914.

The first statutes (1862) identified forty-nine *Félibres* plus one president: the *capoulié*—Mistral, unsurprisingly. They were co-opted (i.e., chosen at first by Mistral), perpetual, and distributed among seven sections: two for the *gai sabé*, that is, for writers, and five for historians, philologists, artists, scientists, and 'friends': those who could not fit into the canonical sections but nonetheless deserved a place in the academy. Alphonse Daudet, for instance, was one of the 'friends': he had written mostly in French and lived in Paris, but he possessed two major qualities: he was a good friend of Mistral, and could be (and might in fact have been) a useful ally and relay posted in the very heart of the Parisian literary scene.[9]

The model here is obvious: the Institut de France, with its various academies for *sciences, inscriptions et belles-lettres, arts, sciences morales et politiques* ... and the Académie Française above all. Clearly, the idea was to gather those who in every region of the 'Midi' were the foremost in their domains; the Félibrige was a shadow-academy, one could say.

But there was a problem. In the way the French system worked—and for that matter still works—anyone in Southern France who enjoyed some kind of pre-eminence in the sciences, or historical knowledge, or arts, or whatever, did not need the benediction of the Félibrige; he would rather seek recognition from some national academic entity, or at least from one of the scientific, literary, or 'archaeological' societies that every major provincial city could boast of. There were at that time a number of historians or local scholars who could have found a place in the carefully designed Félibrian organigram, but they

---

8   Martel 2010, 176–209.
9   Jouveau 1984, 155–59.

simply had no interest in it and saw no social advantage to be gained by joining the team of these *patois* writers. For instance, the Toulousan scholar Adolphe-Félix Gatien-Arnould would have been a valuable recruit: a professor and member of the old-fashioned but still prestigious Académie des Jeux Floraux, he was the editor of a monument of medieval Occitan culture, the *Flors del Gay saber*, a fourteenth-century manual for linguistic and rhetorical correctness. Moreover, his militancy for a decentralized republic could have led him to meet Mistral when he himself began to dream of such a political ideal. But Gatien-Arnould never showed any interest in the Félibrige, and perhaps he was not even invited to join. From the beginning therefore, the link between the Occitan renaissance and what remained of a general intellectual life in the southern provinces could not be established.

In 1876 the second Félibrian charter appeared.[10] Mistral preserved the idea of an academic summit—the *Counsistori*, with fifty *majourau* co-opted for life and the *capoulié* elected by them—but he abandoned the interdisciplinary pretense of the former organigram: most of the *majourau* would now be writers, and the rest would be persons of merit who deserved (at least from Mistral's point of view) to be associated with the small leading elite, according to various criteria: their social standing, or their national (that is, Parisian) connections, or their regional origins. It was strategically important to have representatives of the western and northern Occitan-speaking regions (like Gascogne or Limousin) to compensate for the initial preponderance of Provence. Their political tendencies were also important: at every 'election' Mistral made sure to preserve a balance between right and left, priests and freemasons.

But what was new is that under this elite, the charter gave a place to average Occitan patriots, ordinary people interested in the Occitan language who might one day hope to be received among the happy fifty few. These ordinary members, the *manteneire*, those who 'maintain' (borrowed from the traditional terminology of the Académie des Jeux Floraux in Toulouse, one of the most prestigious of those provincial societies that kept a safe distance from the Félibrige), were deployed in regional sections, the *mantenènço*, comprising the main provinces and dialectal divisions of the Occitan area: Provence, Languedoc, Aquitaine, and later Guyenne-Perigord, Limousin, and Auvergne. For a while there was also a Catalan *mantenènço*, and Catalan *majourau*, but not for long (not later than 1893), since Catalans in Spain had their own agenda and their own preoccupations that were not easily compatible with those of the Occitans. And beneath this regional level, the charter recognized local groups, the *escolo* (schools), at the dimensions of a city or a French departement. These

---

10   Jouveau 1970, 25–35.

escolo numbered five the first year, mostly in Provence: Aix, Avignon, Forcalquier, Marseille, and Montpellier. By 1914 there were fifty-two of them, covering most of the Occitan-speaking area.

This 1876 charter attempted to establish a compromise between the élitism of the first charter and another choice that would permit a larger, more democratic recruitment, gathering the good will of every part of what Mistral had learned to consider as the great *Miejour*, the South from the Atlantic to the Alps, far beyond the original limits of his provençal homeland. Of course the two directions were contradictory, especially given that in the gestion of the whole of the association, only the *Counsistori*, the *majourau*, were entitled to decide. Actually, as the *Counsistori* held only one annual gathering; daily affairs were in the hands of the board, the *burèu*: the *capoulié* and the *cancelié* (secretary), with 'assessors' and 'syndics' as representatives of the various *mantenènço*. In fact, for most of the time of his *capoulierat* until 1888 and even afterwards, Mistral was the one who ultimately decided.

In 1905 a new charter was designed by the then *capoulié*, Pierre Devoluy. It introduced potentially drastic changes: the fifty *majourau* would remain, but the *manteneire* and the *mantenènço* would disappear.[11] Central in the new system were the local groups, the *escolo*, conceived as the normal interface between the Félibrige—to which they were contractually bound—and Occitan society at large. In Devoluy's conception, these local associations could consist not only of the traditional Félibrian groups, interested mainly in language and literature, but of any group involved in local life in all its dimensions, cultural or not, including trade unions. Next to the old *Counsistori*, the new charter instituted a *Counsèu Generau*, with representatives of every associated local association. Had the scheme worked, and had many associations joined the new organization, the direction of the Félibrige would have been in the hands of these delegates, an emanation of the 'field.' At a time when a law of 1901 imposed elected directorates for associations, this was a real opportunity for a larger base of average *Félibres* and an extension of their field of action through the admission of new actors.

The reality was far less ideal. In fact, this new organization met with fierce opposition from the old *Félibres* and solid indifference from the ordinary southern associations. No more than a dozen local *escolo* gave their assent to this new Félibrige, and all of them were in fact traditional Félibrian associations, far from the real associative life of the Occitan regions in all its variety. In 1909 Devoluy was compelled to resign.

---

11 Jouveau 1970, 320–27.

In 1912 a new charter re-established the old system for all practical purposes, with its *majourau*, its *mantenènço*, and its *manteneire*, the only innovation was perhaps the introduction of a new and unexpected denomination for the *Miejour* soon to be a subject of internal polemics: *la nacioun oucitano*.

Beyond the regulations, what was the real life of the Félibrige?[12] We know the size of its membership from the irregularly published yearbook of the Félibrige, the *Cartabèu de Santo Estello*. Before 1914 it did not exceed one thousand for the core of the association, the *majourau* and *manteneire* (the *manteneire* numbered 228 in 1877, 441 in 1882, and 928 in 1914). One can add a little more by taking into account those who belonged to the local *escolo* without asking to become *manteneire*: not more than five or six thousand by 1914. Compared with the whole population of the Occitan-speaking regions, roughly ten million, one can estimate the real weight of the Félibrige. Furthermore, following individual trajectories reveals a high turnover rate: only one out of ten *Félibres* remained in the association for twenty years.

This evaporation of adherents was not the only problem for the Félibrige. Its financial situation was not particularly bright. The *manteneire* had to pay a subscription, a rather high one, according to the 1876 statute: ten francs a year, at that time not a small sum (three times the daily wages of an industrial worker). Later, after the 1912 reform, the subscription fee was lowered to three francs. The available annual balance-sheets reveal a gap between the theoretical numbers of members and the actual numbers of subscriptions registered by the treasurer (in 1914 only 517 of the 928 adherents are recorded as having paid). Except for these subscriptions, the Félibrige had no real source of income. The result was clear: in 1879–81, the *Cartabèu* anounced a figure for the Félibrige's receipts of 1,732 francs. In 1908, at a time when the *manteneire* no longer existed, the receipts had fallen to 885 francs, and to 615 by 1910. That same year, to give a point of comparison, the local *escolo* of Dordogne, *Lou Bournat* (the beehive), received 4,769 francs. A comparison with the resources of other meridional literary and scientific societies, usually limited to one department instead of the roughly thirty of the Occitan area, shows the same gap. And sometimes it was Mistral who helped the association more or less discreetly with portions of the literary prizes from which he benefited regularly.

The consequences were clear: with such modest resources, the Félibrige was unable to build an efficient administrative organization: no permanent staff, not even a stable, registered office where its archives could be kept safe. Gratuitous devotion was the rule for its administrators. Therefore, the association had no real capacity for editing: sometimes it could issue its yearbook

---

12   Martel 2010, 87–119.

(the *Cartabèu*, with membership lists, decisions by the *Counsistori*, and financial reports), but there are no *Cartabèu* for the years between 1882 and the beginning of the twentieth century. There was an annual publication, the *Armana Prouvençau*, a cheap booklet—an almanac—including poems, prose, and 'official' notices from the directors (for instance, the annual speech of the *capoulié* during the Santo-Estello feast); but for all practical purposes any *Félibre* who wished to publish his work had to rely on private editors, most often at his own expense. Among the first historical *Félibres*, two were professional publishers: Théodore Aubanel and the veteran Joseph Roumanille, associated with François Seguin and, like Aubanel, one of the foremost printers in Avignon. In fact, the number of Occitan titles issued by both of them does not make up more than 2% of their total production. There are Félibrian journals, of course; but they were edited most often by a local *escolo*, if not in fact the property of a particularly devoted and eminent *Félibre* who paid for them— and, of course, chose what he wished to publish—such as the *Revue Félibréenne* of Cancelié Paul Mariéton from 1885 until his death in 1909; or *Lou Felibrige* (1887–1912) of his *vice-cancelié* and notwithstanding concurrent Jean Monné; or the *Occitania* (1911–14) of Christian de Villeneuve-Esclapon, who had made a first attempt in 1877 with *Lou Prouvençau*, or *Prouvenço*, later *Vivo Prouvènço* (1905–14), the journal of Pierre Devoluy. Each of these publications was at one time the official organ of the Félibrige, for lack of a regular official one.[13] Of course the implication is clear: how could such privately held papers be the bearer and expression of a collective project? Private and local initiative was also what allowed the Félibrige to hold its annual celebration, the Santo Estello, coinciding with a meeting of the *counsistori* and the moment when the *capoulié* delivered a speech meant to tell members what kinds of action was expected from them, while poets competed for literary awards. This annual meeting was the foremost if not the only opportunity for *Félibres* from distant regions to get in touch with each other and with the local Occitan-speaking population they claimed to represent and serve, and their main opportunity to express publicly what they wanted.

3   The Program of the *Félibres*

Did the Félibrige have a common program, accepted by everyone, which all its members supported and diffused? Except for certain principles in common, there was more than one single program.

---

13   See Bonifassi.

The initial project as conceived by the small original group was relatively simple—which did not mean it was modest. These young lovers of Provençal poetry and language shared certain basic convictions: that Provençal was not a mere *patois* but the rightful heir, albeit weakened, to the great troubadourish literature, and that it might therefore someday, in spite of its present state, recover the high status it had once enjoyed. To achieve this goal, it needed a thorough epuration and normalization, that is, a coherent orthography, the suppression of the numerous French words that had invaded it during the last centuries, and the building of a literary register able to compete with the great literary languages of the time. Where other writers could satisfy themselves by writing familiar or burlesque songs and poems, the *Félibres* were more ambitious: Mistral's *Mirèio* is an epic, he himself claimed to be the "humble pupil of Great Homer," and he sought recognition of his talent in Paris. This strategy of conquest, built upon a reference to the glorious troubadours freshly rediscovered by Paris, marks a fundamental difference from what occurred with the other regional languages of France. Villemarqué's *Barzaz Breiz*, mentioned above, does not present itself as a personal creation but as a collection of popular songs; and if Villemarqué and his followers regularly expressed their certitude about the existence, once, of a great medieval Breton literature similar to Welsh and Irish counterparts, they were unable to offer any actual proof of its existence.[14]

The second conviction, soon acquired by the first *Félibres*, was that they were not alone. Beyond their little Provençal countryside there was a larger world where closely related dialects were spoken from the Atlantic to the Alps, and from Limousin to the Pyrenees. By 1860 the first *Félibres* had discovered Catalan and its strong similarities with Occitan in spite of its inclusion in a different state. The record of the old Troubadours gave the Occitan renaissance its chronological depth; the discovery of Catalan gave it its spatial amplitude: it was no longer a provincial problem, but something far broader.

At this point, Mistral and some of his friends might have begun to conceive of a wider project for their renaissance. The Occitan-Catalan area crosses the official 'national' boundaries. Both Catalonia and 'Provence,' which for Mistral encompassed the whole of southern France—the term 'Occitan' was still largely ignored—shared not only a common language, but a common history as well: after all, both had suffered a common defeat at Muret (1213) against a French feudal army. Both were from that moment separated and included each in a different state, and both were therefore submitted to a foreign power

---

14   See Le Berre.

irrespective of their proper identity. Having met some Catalan politicians engaged in what would soon become a powerful national revendication, Mistral dreamed at one moment of the possibility of developing something similar in Southern France. He did not go too far, of course; national separatism was not in his mind—and the disciples who would follow him on that road would also reject any separatism—so strong by that time was the acceptance of France as the only legitimate national identity. What they dreamed of was a real decentralization, if not a federal system, possibly extended beyond the national boundaries to the whole of Europe—or at least of 'Latin' Europe, where small peoples could obtain recognition and the revival of their indigenous languages. This was Mistral's dream, at least during the first years after the success of *Mirèio*; he lost some of his illusions later. But others took up the challenge at the end of he century. Some were left-wing militants, associating federalism with direct democracy, such as Louis-Xavier de Ricard, a former militant in the 1871 Paris Commune, and the theorician in 1877 of a Latin and republican federalism including South American nations. Others preferred the provincial system of the old Ancien Régime, among them a young Provençal called Charles Maurras, who at the beginning of the nineties led a significant federalist group where he learned a good deal about politics that he would later put to use—outside the Félibrige, of course.[15]

The Félibrian movement and later in the twentieth century its Occitanist offspring have oscillated regularly between two positions: one merely literary and cultural, alternating with a recurrent temptation to political action, not only for the language but for the people and the country of the language as well, with no success in either case, and always against the opposition of friends who rejected any deviation of Félibrian action toward politics. The only claim that could be shared even by those elements hostile to federalism or decentralization was the revendication for Occitan at school, precisely at a time when the French state was developing an obligatory primary school system for all children, with French as the only teaching language of course, and no place for a *patois* duly expelled from the classroom—Grégoire's dream at last fulfilled.

The Félibrige was notably absent in some areas where it could have been present, as were other similar movements all around Europe at the same period. During the early years it was difficult for the Félibrige to find partners in the academic field. In France at that time there were scholars at the university or in the provincial scientific societies who worked on Occitan matters:

---

15 Martel 2010, 484–525.

dialectologists or philologists like Paul Meyer (École des Chartes, Collège de France), specialists in medieval literature, and collectors of popular lore—songs and tales—and what would soon become ethnology. There were also historians who studied provincial history, but generally speaking, with few exceptions, they were not *Félibres*. In the best of cases, they ignored the Félibrige and went on with their careers as if it did not exist, never mentioning it. Sometimes they considered it as a nuisance, and even fought against it. Since the great survey of French popular songs by Hippolyte Fortoul (1853), there were some scholars in every Occitan-speaking region, most of them amateurs, who devoted themselves to collecting the oral literature of their countryside: Damase Arbaud in Provence, Jean-François Bladé in Gascogne, Félix Arnaudin in Landes, and others everywhere. Bladé was the only one to have had occasional contacts with the Félibrige (he was a *majourau*, but does not seem to have been much involved with the association). Conversely, if Mistral himself had an acute interest in popular literature, he was not a collector; he might use a popular legend as the core of one of his own productions, and did the same with old songs, but his own work always came first. Only at the end of his life did he become engaged in a great ethnographic undertaking with the Museon Arlaten, perhaps because by that time he no longer believed in a possible revival of Occitan literature, and turned toward a nostalgic recuperation of tools and various items linked to the rural society of his childhood, a society he considered anyway as doomed. At the same time, the Félibrige took a position in favor of the promotion of traditional costumes that were about to be discarded by those who used to wear them—most of the Félibrian *escolo* after World War I would be folkloric groups wearing more or less reinvented local costumes. In the field of historical studies, only around the end of the century did the Félibrige acknowledge the need for a specific work on Occitan history, at a time when French schools were diffusing a basic knowedge of national history that left no place for regional particularities. Devoluy took up the challenge and produced an *Istòri naciounalo de la Prouvènço e dou Miejour* (A National [*sic*] History of Provence and the Midi), but it remained unpublished for nearly a century afterwards.

In fact, the original choices allowed no space for any alternative functions. Literature, and particularly poetry, was the royal way to recognition in the small Félibrian world. And the goal of this literature was not to valorize popular rural culture, but rather to build a truly high culture, in potential concurrence with the French official culture, but anyway alien to the familiar popular culture of the Occitan-speaking classes. Little wonder that these classes showed no real interest in what the *Félibres* kept claiming in their confidential feasts and journals. What, then, was the social basis of this movement?

4 The *Félibres* and the World around Them

The *Cartabèus* list the *Félibres* and allow us to have an idea not only of their numbers but also of their locations and, most of all, of their social status. It is furthermore possible through other sources to have an idea of their social origins, at least for the most eminent ones, the writers and *majourau*. The results are instructive.[16]

From a geographical point of view, the Félibrige clearly recruited its members in the south-eastern part of Occitan territory, in Provence and oriental Languedoc, roughly between Toulon and Béziers (55% of the total in 1876, still 45% in 1914). The weight of this south-east was still more important among the *Counsistori* (with respectively 66% and 52% membership in the same years). The western part, beyond Toulouse, was affected only by the end of the century. As for the northern part, in Limousin, Auvergne, and the Alps, membership remained small. This is not surprising, since the movement originated in the lower valley of the Rhône; but this is not the whole explanation. What the *Cartabèu*s reveal is the importance of towns: most of the *Félibres* were town-dwellers, a fair proportion living in big cities (in 1914, 40% in cities with populations of more than twenty thousand), and some even in Paris, and these were not the least active members. Here we have an apparent paradox: Occitan society at this time was largely rural and would remain so up to the middle of the twentieth century. Furthermore, the peasantry was the stronghold of Occitan-ophonia at a time when towns were beginning to shift to French. But the actual distribution of most *Félibres* is utterly contradictory.

Here comes our second paradox: the Félibrige did not recruit among monolingual Occitan peasants. On the contrary, peasants appear to represent only a small minority (less than 5% of the movement in 1914), and they were of course bilingual. The industrial workers were still fewer (actually they do not represent an important fraction of the Occitan population as a whole, due to the relative underdevelopment of the Occitan economy). Thus the Félibrige presented itself as the natural spokesman for Occitan-speaking popular classes that were absent from its ranks. But this absence of the common folk was not compensated by a real investment on the part of the leading classes: they were also not particularly numerous in the *Cartabèu*s. We know of course that in the whole of French society they were few; but they were proportionally fewer still in the Félibrige, particularly with regard to their counterparts in the Breton movement for instance, where the clergy and aristocracy were prominent. Ever since Mistral first journeyed to Paris in order to be recognized by the elite, in

---

16   See Martel 2010, 484–525.

Paris first and in 'the provinces' later, this had been a permanent strategy for the Félibrige, in contradiction to its pretense to be linked with the popular classes. The strategy failed; the upper classes in the Midi chose French as the only fitting language for them, and saw no interest in the preservation of a *patois* they only happened to use with their servants in the best of cases. On that point they were in complete agreement with the Parisian elites and the state authorities. No comparison was possible either with the Breton movement—which was favored by what remained of the old aristocracy and clergy—nor with the Catalan *Renaixença* in Spain, in which the bourgeoisie of Barcelona played a leading role. This allegiance explains the early turn to nationalist politics—and a relatively successful politics at that—which characterized Catalonian claims as early as the eighties, when the city's bourgeoisie chose to contest the weakened power of Madrid.

Who, then, were the *Félibres*? Mostly middle-class professionals—physicians, lawyers, executives (around 20% during the period 1876–1914), often bound to the French administration (20%), and later clerks or salesmen. There were no notabilities, or very few: a handful of members of Parliament, from left or right, generally most cautious, and not particularly active in their Félibrian militancy when in office. The most prominent of them, Maurice Faure, a radical-socialist senator, may have been a (modest) Occitan writer and the efficient animator of the Parisian Félibrige (whose main activities were feasting and occasionally inaugurating patriotic monuments in southern towns). But as Minister of Public Instruction for six months between 1910 and 1911, he found no interest or opportunity for any practical measures in favor of Occitan at school. A good half of those writers whose social background is identifiable through biographical data were born in the lower classes (and in villages for roughly 35% of the whole panel) and later gained—in the towns—a more or less higher status. Moreover, they were born to Occitan-speaking families but later acquired a fair command of written and spoken French.

The implication seems clear. The Félibrige did not recruit in the social sectors that still held to the old language, and who formed the mass of Occitan society. Nor did it recruit in the higher spheres among the happy few who were in charge. Its members had no social power, no real prestige. In the highly hierarchical French society of the time—despite the official egalitarist and republican phraseology—they carried no weight. They were not recognized as part of the common people, who anyway were not interested in the literary defense of a language they spoke daily, without being proud of it, for they hoped that at least their own children would master French, the only language of social promotion. To these people the Félibrige had nothing to say. But at the same time, the *Félibres* were not perceived by the elites as belonging to their world. This is evident from what Parisian critics had to say about Mistral: he was at best described as a picturesque gentleman-farmer, at worst as a provincial whose accent when speaking French was laughable. As for the language he used and tried to impose as a legitimate literary vector, it was just a preposterous pretense; this was clear as early as 1859. And Mistral, at least, had been greeted and celebrated by Alphonse de Lamartine himself. What could be said of the others who had not even had the benefit of such a chance? They were triply insignificant: as provincials, as middle-class quidams, and as *patois*-fanatics.

Last of all, they had no real possibility to strike back, to launch a national rebellion, a revenge for the Albigensian Crusade. Why should they, after all? At their level, they were a part of those to whom the modernization of French society had given a chance to escape the rural poverty of their ancestors. They were stuck halfway between the ancient world, whose language they could still master, and the new one, that gave them the cultural capital and the literary skill that enabled them, once they adapted to the new language, to write their poems. And their children would perhaps ascend higher still—leaving the old language behind. At that time there were very few examples of familial or intergenerational transmission of the Félibrian cause, perhaps because most of those who were themselves involved saw their commitment as a purely personal choice, if not a mere hobby.

5 An Occitan or a French Exception in the Field of Nation-Building?

Comparison of the Félibrige with other 'nation-building' movements all across nineteenth-century Europe reveals some common points, but the differences are far stronger. Such movements classically arose in the apparently Arcadian realm of pure knowledge. Intellectuals, more or less young, were everywhere devoting themselves to arid research about the language of their territory as a token of their people's identity. This meant a great deal of work and thought: reflexion, first of all, about the recognition of the popular common speech of the countryside (always considered as more 'pure' than its urban cousins) as an autonomous language, clearly distinct from others with which it came in contact. Comparison with a totally alien language is of course far easier (of Celtic with Anglo-Saxon, for example, or Slavic as against Magyar or German). The problems begin when the local idiom is compared with more or less closely related varieties of the same linguistic group. Instructive from this point of view is the case of Slovak, and the debate beween the supporters of an 'old Slovak' closely related to Czech and those advocating a 'new Slovak' built upon divergent rural forms. The same process occured with Ukrainian and Russian, and with Macedonian, with a difference in this last case: namely, the debate here was not only a grammatical one, but a clearly political one: the territory of Macedonia was claimed by both Serbia and Bulgaria, so the degree of kinship between local Slavic dialects and the standards of the two neighboring and rival states could have serious consequences.

Questions about a proper language imply a particular effort of standardization as soon as the 'national' language has been duly identified. Sometimes the language builders may rely on models provided by ancient written forms inherited from past times when political conditions permitted the rise of an indigenous norm. This is the case for insular Celtic, Ireland Gaelic, and Welsh, which are able to claim a prestigious medieval past that endows them with graphic principles—and even a particular alphabet for Irish—as well as formal literary models and lexical resources that may be mobilized in a process of purification. The history of Breton is quite different, and in fact the normalization of the language here followed different paths. The same situation occurred in Central Europe for languages whose literary traditions were scarce or nonexistent. In such cases everything had to be invented, from the choice of the alphabet (Cyrillic or Latin?) to the choice of what would become the authorized standard: a local form considered as more pure or original than the others, or a geographically 'central' variety (such as 'Serbo-Croatian'), or a synthetic language borrowing its various elements from distinct parts of the dialectal landscape? The next problem would be to make this new 'national' language acceptable to its would-be speakers.

The Occitan situation was ambiguous: the ritual reference (and reverence) accorded the courtly language of the Troubadours was not sufficient to compensate for the fact that the graphic principles of medieval *scripta* had been forgotten since the fifteenth century, and that since that time, the only graphic and linguistic model available for those who mantained a literary use of Occitan came from French. The absence of any institution able to define and diffuse a norm everywhere on the vast Occitan territory led to a complete graphic anarchy; every author wrote according to his own fantasy, on the basis of French orthographic conventions, in spite of the fact that these conventions were unadapted to the Occitan phonological system (for example, the diphthongs which no longer exist in French but are frequent in Occitan: [p'aure], [d'eure], [pl'oure] ("poor, must, to rain"), written *paouré, déouré, ploouré*). At the beginning of the nineteenth century, while re-discovering the previously inaccessible troubadourish texts, some authors tried to work out a more convenient system, restoring some medieval graphemes and privileging etymology at the expenses of phonetics, a choice which exposed them to charges of pedantic archaism. Mistral and Roumanille joined forces to elaborate a kind of compromise between a broadly phonetic spelling suited to their own dialect (eliminating for instance consonantic finals like the plural mark in -s) and the restoration of medieval notation for diphthongs (*paure, deure, ploure*). This compromise would later be criticized and rejected by a fraction of the Félibrige, but this is another story. What is important is the fact that this new orthographic system was imposed on anyone who wished to be recognized and published by the Félibrian reviews. Whoever did not accept the rule was excluded from the mainstream.

Beyond these orthographic problems lies a second one, more problematic still: the question of a supradialectal norm. As previously said, Mistral and his friends used and promoted their own native variant, the Provençal dialect of the southern Rhône valley. Their natural tendency was later, when the initial circle began to broaden, to consider the 'language of *Mirèio*' as the foremost incarnation of what a resurrrected 'Provençal' should be for the whole of the Occitan-speaking area, from the Atlantic to the Alps. Of course, this pretense met with strong opposition in regions with the most distinct dialects—in Languedoc, Gascony, and Limousin—and anyway could not be supported by any institutional power, neither political nor socio-cultural. Mistral's indisputable and undisputed prestige was not sufficient to gain the assent of all those writers everywhere to whom he had shown the way of the Occitan renaissance. At that time and still today, there is consequently no recognized unitarian form of Occitan, and every one writes his own variety, but this situation does not hinder interdialectal circulation.

A second difference from other 'nation-building' movements is the place given to historic records. While other 'peoples' could boast of a national past embodied in a state or a kingdom (or kingdoms, as in the insular Celtic situation), or a dukedom (as in Britanny up to 1532), Occitania as such, and under that name, was never a political entity. What was historically observable was an array of 'provinces' (Guyenne, Béarn, Languedoc, Vivarais, Provence, Dauphiné, Auvergne, Limousin, Rouergue, etc.), each with its own history and ruling dynasty before annexation, and its own chronology (namely, its own date of 'attachment' to France). The only moment of relative unity, at least culturally and to some extent also politically (and including Catalonia as well), was the celebrated time of the Troubadours before the Albigensian Crusade in the thirteenth century, a time brutally put to an end when the Northerners devastated and conquer the future Languedoc for the final triumph of the French monarchy. The implication was clear: Mistral and his friends might write vivacious and indignant poems on this topic, but did not dare to use them as justification for a contemporary 'revenge' against France. Language was at the foundation of 'Meridional' identity far more than history.

In the same line of reflexion, the most interesting point of comparison with other minority situations is the political dimension, that is, the nature of the political projects nurtured by the *Félibres*, whenever they attempted to pass from Hroch's phase A to phase B. To put it simply: was there any temptation or actual attempt to promote a clearly nationalist, or even separatist action? As indicated previously, there were moments when the Félibrige, or rather only some of its militants (and herein lies a good part of the problem) considered the possibility of a political claim. We have seen that Mistral dreamed of it after the success of *Mirèio* and his encounter with the Catalans, who were at the same time beginning their own renaissance. Later there was at some moments the rekindling of a federalist revendication, or at least an aspiration to a true decentralization of the French state. But unlike what was observable in Britanny for instance as soon as the very beginning of the twentieth century, this aspiration did not lead to the creation of a real party, and of course, those who believed in it never took part in any electoral campaigns, or anyway not under the Félibrian colors. The need for effective 'action' was frequently proclaimed, but it remained for all practical purposes a purely literary formula, if not a mere slogan.

Several explanations may account for this failure to cross the threshold of political activism. First, the heterogenous composition of the Félibrian community, which cannot be ascribed as a whole to a particular sector of opinion. Right and left, republicans, monarchists, socialists, all these tendencies cohabited more or less cordially according to the general climate of the moment. Unlike other situations, in Ireland, Britanny, or Slovakia for instance, the religious question had no real importance, in spite of the virulence, at the beginning of the twentieth century, of some reviews clearly defending a Catholic revendication at the moment of the separation of Church and State. Anyway, the charters, whatever their evolution may have been during this period, all shared a rejection of political and religious debates inside the association. There was a moment between 1876 and 1879, at a time when the right-left conflict was particularly intense at the national level, when republican *Félibres* could have broken off and created their own organization, but ultimately this did not happen. Faced with local and national opinion, the *Félibres* most of the time took great care not to antagonize anyone and gave voice to an ecumenical discourse, putting the stress upon consensual notions such as love for their 'little fatherland' as an indispensable complement to love for France, the 'Great Fatherland.'[17]

---

17   See Pasquini.

6 The Paradoxical Félibrige

Apparently the Occitan renaissance could rely on a discourse provided with all the canonical elements that were conducive—elsewhere—to nation-building: a proper language with a rich literary heritage, and a territory, an ancient province with long-established historical boundaries (though less readily identifiable than Brittany or the island of Corsica). Though it lacked a common history shared by its various regions, Occitania could at least valorize one dramatic episode from its past, the Albigensian Crusade, and thus gain the opportunity to identify a hereditary enemy: the Northern Frenchman, the barbarous 'Francimand.' Not all the small peoples who took up the cause of nationhood in the nineteenth century could marshal such a set of arguments, but this did not hinder their progress, their self-affirmation, and their capacity to gain the support of a large part of their society. Why did 'Occitania' fail to follow such an example?

First, one cannot underestimate the strength of the identification with France among the Occitan population, which had begun with monarchy, under the form of dynastic loyalty, and was amplified by the revolutionnary process, when the lower classes became directly involved in political life and struggles. Here is the great difference from most of other countries of the same period. The revolution of 1789 transformed the old kingdom, the familial patrimony of a dynasty, into a new kind of political community based on the rights of the Sovereign People. The former 'subjects' would henceforth be 'citizens,' that is, agents of their own history, and, at some level, co-owners of the new 'Nation.' In the numerous conflicts of the two following centuries, they may have taken antagonistic positions, sometimes to the point of civil war; but this antagonism remained within the circle of national debate. To put it in nineteenth-century terms, there are two 'Frances'—one of Order, and the other of Movement—but each is France in its own way. This does not mean that the relation to politics works the same way in the North and in the 'Midi.' Parisian observers at that time clearly identified (and denounced) a peculiar attitude towards the State among the southern population, namely an old tradition of sometimes violent contestation of fiscal pressure, or a strong refusal of military conscription leading to massive desertion, and generally speaking, a tendency to collective as well as individual violence unknown elsewhere in France—all elements which determine the diffusion during the first half of the century of a particularly negative image of the 'Meridional.'[18] But this reluctance to accept the rules imposed by the modern state did not involve any

---

18 See Ploux.

longing for another national identity. By the end of the century, national acculturation had begun to reduce the gap between the official national norm and deviant southern behaviour. There was a general acceptance of France which left no room for the promotion of any national Occitan claims beyond the demand that more recognition should be accorded to the proper language of the 'Midi.'

But there is another element of this integration of the national French ideology that could be understood sociologically in terms of alienation: to begin with, the fact that the Félibrige had no more success in the higher classes that in the lower ones. At the top of southern society, the not particularly active bourgeoisie and what remained of the old nobility had no respect for the language of the lower classes. They were therefore not interested in middle-class intellectuals who were struggling for the sake of the *patois*. As for the average Occitan-speaking peasant, his priorities lay elsewhere than in the reclamation of his native language, not to speak of abstract matters such as decentralizaton, federalism, the Albigensian Crusade, etc. Ironically enough, the only moments when one can observe a fragile contact between the *Félibres* and ordinary people, on some parts of the Occitan territory at least, was for instance when the government decided to forbid bullfights in the lower Rhône Valley. Mistral's presence in the arenas of Nîmes in this context (as in 1894) may have gained him the sympathy of *aficionados* of the corrida, but this support went no farther and was promply forgotten. Worse yet: when in 1907 a severe overproduction crisis brought the wine-growers of Languedoc to the verge of insurrection, and while some of their leaders evoked the record of their Albigensian ancestors and tried to involve Mistral in their protests, Mistral and his fellow *Félibres* did not follow: this economic revendication was no concern of theirs. What these Occitan-speaking peasants—hundreds of thousands of them—were demanding was not the defense of the Occitan language but the protection of the French state for wine production and commercialization.

In sum, the Occitan renaissance lacked a social dynamic that could lead a significant part of the local society to use the arguments poetically displayed by the *Félibres* in a global strategy of distantiation from a State in which they felt unwillingly included. This kind of dynamic was at work in the old Habsburg domains, and even more in the decaying Ottoman Empire. In another context, Catholic Irishmen had quite good reasons to seek revenge against the dominant English. Catalans, those brothers of the Occitan people, may have had their own reservations about the archaic and inefficient government in Madrid. One way or the other, all these peoples were frustrated, and national revendication was for them not only a possible but a concretely useful and promising way to obtain satisfaction. Nothing of the sort occurred in the Occitan situation, not even for the *Félibres* themselves: as indicated above, the socioeconomic evolution of French society did not make them the losers of the game. Individually speaking, most of them enjoyed a more or less significant social promotion during their lifetimes. Why should they feel frustrated and resentful of a France where, after all, they had their place? They possessed a rich set of cultural, linguistic, and historical justifications for a potentially vigorous revendication, but they used them carefully to argue for quite moderate demands: a minimal recognition of both the value of their language and its compatibility with French culture and identity. All the pieces of the nation-building weapon were on hand and ready to work; what was lacking was the finger on the trigger, since no one really felt the need to shoot.

Under these conditions, the Félibrige should have disappeared after the death of its prophet, Frédéric Mistral. But it did not disappear. It survives to this day, along with a more recent form of Occitanism born as a reaction against its impotence. The Occitan renaissance has continued, in part because the social evolution that was at its origin also went on during the twentieth century, leading ever more individuals out of the lower classes up into the middle class, and leaving them sufficiently at ease with French not to consider Occitan as a hindrance, yet able to take issue with the French common sense that imposed the repudiation of the original languages. And so for each generation the cause of Occitanism could find new champions, partly because after all, what this renaissance did best was to create literature—and a worthy literature too—and also partly because the official monolingualism of French society could not overcome the resistance of linguistic and cultural plurality on its own territory. Here is our last paradox: the Occitan resistance is not strong enough to reverse the steady process of linguistic substitution, but French efforts to achieve total monolingualism and cultural uniformity have not yet succeeded in wiping it out entirely.

Bibliography

Bonifassi, Georges. *La presse régionale de Provence en langue d'Oc—Des origines à 1914*. Paris: Presses de l'Université Paris-Sorbonne, 2003.

Boyer, Henri and Philippe Gardy, eds. *Dix Siècles d'Usages et d'Images de l'Occitan: Des Troubadours à l'Internet*. Paris: l'Harmattan, 2001.

De Certeau, Michel, Dominique Julia, and Jacques Revel. *Une Politique de la langue. La Révolution française et les patois: l'enquête de Grégoire*. Paris: Gallimard, 1975.

Hroch, Miroslav. *Social Preconditions of National Revival in Europe: A Comparative Analysis of the Social Composition of Patriotic Groups Among the Smaller European Nations.* Cambridge: Cambridge University Press, 1985.

Jouveau, René. *Histoire du Félibrige, 1876–1914.* [Nîmes: n.p.], 1970.

Jouveau, René. *Histoire du Félibrige, 1854–1876.* [Nîmes: n.p.], 1984.

Le Berre, Yves. *Qu'est-ce que la littérature bretonne?* Rennes: Presses Universitaires de Rennes, 2006.

Martel, Philippe. "Les historiens du début du XIXe siècle et le Moyen Age occitan: Midi éclairé, Midi martyr, ou Midi pittoresque." *Romantisme* 35 (1982), 49–71.

Martel, Philippe. "Le petit monde de l'édition en langue d'oc au temps des félibres." *Bibliothèque de l'École des Chartes* 159 (2001), 153–70.

Martel, Philippe. *Les Cathares et l'histoire: Le drame cathare devant ses historiens (1820–1992).* Toulouse: Privat, 2002.

Martel, Philippe. "The Troubadours and the French State." In Dirk Van Hulle and Joep Leerssen, eds., *Editing the Nation's Memory: Textual Scholarship and Nation-Building in 19th-Century Europe.* Leiden: Brill, 2008, 185–219.

Martel, Philippe. *Les félibres et leur temps: Renaissance d'oc et opinion, 1850–1914.* Bordeaux: Presses Universitaires, 2010.

Mauron, Claude. *Frédéric Mistral.* Paris: Fayard, 1993.

Merle, René. *L'écriture du provençal de 1775 à 1840.* Béziers: CIDO, 1990.

Pasquini, Pierre. *Le pays des parlers perdus.* Montpellier: Presses du Languedoc, 1994.

Ploux, François. *Guerres paysannes en Quercy.* Paris: La Boutique de l'Histoire, 2002.

CHAPTER 10

Educational, Scholarly, and Literary Societies in Dutch-Speaking Regions, 1766–1886

Jan Rock

Looking for an equivalent of the nineteenth-century Slavic *matica* in the Dutch-speaking regions of Europe, one finds not a single institution but a collection of societies that were involved either in the philological study of old language, literature, and culture, or in its public dissemination. Attempts to combine these two activities, as the *matice* did, were always short-lived.

What equivalents of the *matica* are to be found? The Slavic *matice* were themselves divergent, though they shared some common features. On the one hand they facilitated national philological studies by setting up scholarly infrastructures for the nation-wide study of history, language (including spelling), and literature. On the other hand, they spread scholarly products among their members and to the broader public: they set up printing houses and publication series, they organized education in schools and elsewhere, and they made funds and stipends available to students. It was essential that such initiatives should come 'from below,' from civil society, and not from any central or imperial government.

These three characteristics—philological, intermediating, and non-governmental—are also typical of many societies in the Dutch-speaking area. Societies in the fields of education, philology, and literature in Dutch appeared from the end of the eighteenth century onwards and determined the pivotal role of language, history, and culture in building national identities. During the revolutionary era and the nineteenth century they interacted with the political establishment and the modernization of successive states: the Dutch Republic, the Habsburg Netherlands and the Prince-Bishopric of Liège (until 1795), the United Kingdom of the Netherlands (1815–30), and the Kingdoms of the Netherlands and Belgium (from 1830 onwards).

Two of these societies will be discussed first, because they were (and still are) many-branched and highly influential: the *Maatschappij tot Nut van 't Algemeen* (Society for the Common Benefit, from 1784) in the Dutch Republic and later the Netherlands, and the *Willemsfonds* (Willems Fund, from 1851) in Belgium. Both were preoccupied with education and the spread of philological and other knowledge through books in Dutch. The Dutch language and history had a very long tradition of study at universities since around 1600 and at academies from the eighteenth century onwards. These scholarly institutions were either established or acknowledged by central governments, and differ in this sense from the *matice*; yet they shared a common object of study and were never completely indifferent to public dissemination. Two such major philological and academic societies will thus be considered here: the *Maatschappij der Nederlandsche Letterkunde* (Society for Dutch Letters, from 1766) in the Dutch Republic's oldest university city, Leiden, and the Imperial Academy (from 1772) in Brussels, the capital city of the Habsburg Netherlands. In addition, several societies throughout the nineteenth century maintained complex relations with official recognition and debated questions of academic or artistic-literary autonomy. Some scholarly societies from the Netherlands and literary societies from the United Kingdom of the Netherlands and Belgium will also be discussed at the end of this chapter.

This chapter focuses on Dutch-speaking societies that had either their philological activities or a concern for education and public dissemination—or both—in common with the *matice*. For each society the most important studies are discussed below, followed by the most relevant elements of their establishment and activities. The ideological base for each society is sketched in terms of constellations of ideals of civic education, socialization, and nationalist ideas of history, language, and literature. Some relevant developments in the societies' histories are also mentioned briefly. The societies introduced here have already been studied thoroughly, and I rely heavily on these studies; yet many aspects of these societies, in particular their mutual contacts and transfers, still need to be mapped.

1   One Language, Two States, Many Nations

Though the Dutch-speaking regions shared a common language, its regional variants were always meaningful both to men of letters and to everyday users in linguistic, political, and psychological respects. In its varying forms, the Dutch language served agendas of unification and regional particularism alike. Along with their common language, these regions had maintained close and complex interrelations from medieval times onwards, culminating in a century of Dutch revolt against the Spanish king (1548–1648).[1] They shared a common history up to a certain point, but most historians agree that from the Treaty of Münster in 1648 onwards, the northern provinces unified in the Dutch Republic

---

1   Cf. Blom and Lamberts.

and the southern provinces under Habsburg rule need to be considered as separate regions. This was indeed the conclusion of the most renowned Dutch historian, Johan Huizinga:

> Two nationalities came into being instead of one. The Southern Netherlands became in almost all respects the genuine outgrowth of the Burgundian state, but pruned back on both sides. They formed a state and a nationality, but for two and a half centuries they lacked the property that makes state and nationality complete: freedom. The Northern Netherlands formed a nationality in a higher sense than their neighbours, because they had freedom. But they could hardly be called a state, so dominated were they by the principle of provincial autonomy.[2]

Separated during the proto-national phase, the Dutch Republic and the Habsburg Netherlands developed differently into modern nation-states.

At the end of the eighteenth century, the Dutch Republic lost its leading position in Europe regarding its form of government, colonial trade, and the international prestige of its science, scholarship, art, and its free printing press. For decades it had witnessed conflicts between Republicans and Orangeists (supporting the hereditary succession of the Princes of Orange as stadholders, at times resulting in monarchic ambitions). Now it fell into step with European modernization: it witnessed constitutional revolutions in 1794, became part of Napoleonic Europe in 1806 under Louis Bonaparte, King of Holland, and from 1810 was a full part of the First Empire. During these years nationalist resistance grew, and in 1813 Willem Frederik of Orange-Nassau proclaimed himself sovereign monarch. At the Congress of Vienna in 1814–15 he was confirmed as King William I and his kingdom was united with the former Habsburg Netherlands. From this United Kingdom of the Netherlands the southern provinces separated in 1830. In 1848 the (northern) Kingdom of the Netherlands became a constitutional and parliamentary monarchy. This political creation of a Dutch national state was preceded and paralleled from the second half of the eighteenth century by a national cultural community of citizens sharing the Dutch language, the Protestant religion, forms of sociability, and a common understanding of the Republic's past. During these decades, a foundational myth of the ancient Batavians came to be accompanied by the image of a seventeenth-century Dutch Golden Age, enabling the modern state of the

---

2   Johan Huizinga, *Verzamelde Werken* II, ed. L. Brummel (Haarlem: Tjeenk Willink, 1948), 158, cited in Wils 2005, 77. All translations are my own.

Netherlands to create a political and cultural continuity with the old Republic centred around the provinces of Holland, Utrecht, and Zeeland.[3]

In the provinces of the Habsburg Netherlands and the Prince-Bishopric of Liège the creation of such a continuity may have seemed less self-evident. Their stately forms had been determined by the rule of the Habsburg Empire and the Holy Roman Empire. A proto-national consciousness rose nevertheless within the imperial contexts during the eighteenth century.[4] The initial events of the French Revolution in 1789 had their impact first in the Prince-Bishopric, where a revolutionary republic was proclaimed (and the cathedral next to the principal palace was demolished from 1794 onwards). Meanwhile, in the Habsburg Netherlands, discontent with the centralization policies of the Austrian Emperor Joseph II led in 1790 to the Brabant Revolution and a confederation named the United States of Belgium. Both the former Habsburg Netherlands and the Prince-Bishopric saw some Restoration politics and military interventions, and became part of the French Republic in 1795. At the time of the United Kingdom of the Netherlands, dissatisfaction grew in the southern provinces with central policies regarding language, education, religion, and economy, and with the authoritarian rule of King William I, resulting in the Belgian Revolution of 1830.

Together with the proclamation of a Belgian constitutional and parliamentary monarchy and a coalition between Liberal and Catholic political elites, the cultural construction of a Belgian nation began. Nationalistic culture flourished, initially in order to distinguish the new state from the Kingdom of the Netherlands, but after a few months also in order to preserve the new state from political and military, but also cultural threats from Paris. In particular, a national Belgian history was created, going back to the Celtic Belgians and with an overarching myth of consecutive foreign occupations. Paintings, theater plays, and novels with historical subjects were produced, together with all other varieties of nationalistic culture, mostly at official academic and artistic institutions.[5] Thus, a Liberal and Catholic elite, in both the political and cultural sense, created a new nation-state; but the language for this new nation-state remained under discussion. The political and religious powers used mainly French, although the Dutch language and the Flemish, 'northern' character of the new nation was never repudiated, and during the nineteenth century would become a distinctive element of Belgian-Flemish literature abroad.[6]

---

3   See Blom and Lamberts; Kloek and Mijnhardt; and Van Sas.
4   See Koll.
5   Deprez and Vos (eds.); Dunthorne and Wintle (eds.).
6   Van den Berg and Couttenier; Verbruggen.

During this process of Belgian nation-building and the contest over a national language, the 'cultivation'[7] of Flemish culture and the Flemish variant of the Dutch language grew as a more or less distinct national movement, with an increasing popularity channelled through cultural and student societies. Eventually, after World War I, Flemish nationalism became separatist in principle.[8]

Even much abridged historical accounts such as this suggest that the nationalistic processes in the Dutch-speaking areas are too divergent to bring together in a single comprehensive overview. This article does not aim to provide a full account of all the forms of nationalism in both nation-states. The movements among the Walloon or French-speaking population, the Frisians, and the German-speaking territories in Belgium after the First World War will not be discussed, nor will ephemeral and transnational territories and identities such as those in the Grand Duchy of Luxemburg (from 1815), French Flanders, Limburg, or Neutral Moresnet (1816–1920). It should also be noted that this article takes the Dutch-speaking area as a whole not in a *pan*-Dutch sense—such a movement was a historical reality at several moments, e.g. during the United Kingdom, also after 1830, and especially in the twentieth century.[9]

The issue in question is the search for an equivalent of the Slavic *matice*, their organizational forms and their activities; in other words, a search for the forms of sociability assumed by a scholarly and educational interest in the Dutch language. For this reason, and notwithstanding the politically diverse realities, a comparison of societies from the whole of the Dutch-speaking regions is legitimate. Mutual personal and institutional contacts existed, in particular during the United Kingdom in the 1820s. This was a determining decade for the realization of the Herderian presupposition of national thought: the identification of language, people, and identity. Later on, every state had its own ambitions, and the cultural, social and political movements and realities within them diverged. In short: the limits of this survey are merely geographical, chosen to make possible a broad comparison with the *matice*.

2 The *Maatschappij tot Nut van 't Algemeen*

The organization in Dutch-speaking areas most similar to the Slavic *matica* was the *Maatschappij tot Nut van 't Algemeen* (Society for the Common Benefit), though it dates back to 1784. Its history has yet to be studied comprehensively,

---

7   Leerssen 2006.
8   Deprez and Vos (eds.).
9   Wils 2009, 171–82.

though its branches ('departments') and libraries in some cities have received historiographical attention,[10] as have its protagonists Jan Nieuwenhuyzen and his son Martinus, and the school books its members published.[11] The place of the 'Nut' in the context of Dutch sociability is discussed in much-acclaimed studies of Dutch cultural and scientific societies in the eighteenth and nineteenth centuries by Wijnand Mijnhardt, who describes their ideals of education, communication, and human development. He exposes the eighteenth-century Enlightenment roots of the idea that scholarship and public education serve social reform. The ideals held by the 'Nut' were those of human rationality, education, and sociability, while its organization tried to transcend the traditional urban and provincial limits that bound other societies, in line with the unifying tendencies in Dutch politics during the revolutionary era.

The *Maatschappij tot Nut van 't Algemeen* was founded in November 1784 in Edam, a town in the province of Holland, by the physician Martinus Nieuwenhuyzen and the pastor J.A.S. Hoekstra, who relied on the ideas of Nieuwenhuyzen's father Jan, an Anabaptist pastor in the nearby town of Monnikendam. The latter had identified a need for cheap educational books in order to disseminate the growing knowledge of other recently established societies. His son added a vision of an improved education and a national school system. This double diagnosis by the Nieuwenhuyzens needs to be seen against the background of the Fourth Anglo-Dutch War (1780–84) and the economic decline from the 1770s onwards, which became distinct in the pauperization of even the most industrialized cities in Holland, such as Amsterdam, Haarlem, and Leiden, and a political debate that was increasingly violent and culminated in a civil war during the last decades of the century. While patriotic ideals called some to arms, they made others exploit a blossoming literary culture. The Nieuwenhuyzen's ideas indeed had potential, given the wide popularity in Holland of reading societies and newspaper tables in coffee houses,[12] and the region's high degree of literacy (68% in 1800).[13] The Edam founders sought similar minds in the rest of the country by sending out one thousand invitations among their contacts, first in Edam and Amsterdam, where Martinus Nieuwenhuyzen and Hoekstra were known for their journal *De menschenvriend (The Philanthropist)*. Their initiative resulted in the establishment of local branches, the first in Amsterdam (1785), which would become the central

---

10 See Eerenbeemt and Hake.
11 For Nieuwenhuyzen and his son see Helsloot and Dodde; for school books see Buijnsters and Buijnsters-Smet.
12 See Kloek and Mijnhardt.
13 Helsloot and Dodde, 68.

department in 1787 following attempts by the Orangeist municipal government of Edam to gain control over the society and its policy of membership. From that year onwards, the society had its seat in culturally the most important city in the country. Other local branches were founded throughout Holland: in Waterland, Zaandam, and Haarlem; and in other provinces, e.g. in Bergen op Zoom (1890).

The activities and meetings of the 'Nut' were always centered around education and publishing. The initial plans mentioned that manuscripts of new school books would be selected in open competitions. This procedure appeared to be too slow, however, so members of the 'Nut' began to write them themselves. In particular, the founder Martinus Nieuwenhuyzen produced school books for learning to read and write, arithmetic, and religious and civic duties. Some of his books reveal an early interest in the national past: his *Levensschetsen van Vaderlandsche mannen en vrouwen* (1788, with Adriaan Loosjes Pz.), was a collection of short biographies of men and women from the national past.[14] Nicolaas Anslijn wrote *Brave Hendrik* (1810) and *Brave Maria* (1811), two readers that became the most successful texts in the Netherlands up until World War I. These and other books were at first published by the 'Nut' itself, but because of the high costs they were handed over to publishers around 1790, which meant losing control over the price and the reach of the books. Cheap books nevertheless remained a core element in the society's vision of national education, as recorded by Nieuwenhuyzen in *Ontwerp eener schoolbibliotheek* (*Plan for a school library*, 1787), and for the greater part adopted by a commission of the society as *Algemeene denkbeelden over het nationaal onderwijs* (*General Thoughts on National Education*, 1796). These plans were executed as the 'Nut' founded schools and *kweekscholen* (training schools) from 1795 onwards, and rewarded pupils with prizes. Overall, the Haarlem branch, founded in 1789 by Loosjes, can count as exemplary: a school for adults was set up, a training school, a sewing school, a savings bank, and—most importantly—the first public library in the Netherlands that allowed readers to take books home (1794).

The educational ideas of Nieuwenhuyzen and the 'Nut' were practical and moderate interpretations of the ideals of the Enlightenment. A good education would enable individual citizens to take a position of their own, both towards powers bigger than they and towards other individuals. Such an education would develop rationality and a love of consistent truth and beauty; it would stimulate scientific practice; and it would lead to personal happiness. The Anabaptist background of Nieuwenhuyzen became clear in the role he reserved for

---

14   Mathijsen 2013, 150.

religion. He saw the search for reason as a divine order and as a contribution to harmony, truth, and happiness; he prescribed that "one must in all cases further men's true happiness, and that this can never happen except through the propagation of wisdom and Christian virtue."[15] Such a happy and reasonable as well as religious individual had to contribute to harmonious communities, starting with family and including school and country. Educating the individual citizen thus meant edifying the nation.

Reading and writing in the mother tongue played a central role in this view of national education through individual development and of society as a conglomerate of virtuous and useful individuals, but not because they were the essence of the national character—as they would become in more Romantic ideas of the nation. Reading and writing were primarily of instrumental interest: language was a vehicle for social cohesion, and reading was a pedagogic instrument for citizenship. Here again, Nieuwenhuyzen put forward his combination of moderate Enlightenment ideals and religious duties as a characteristically *Dutch* combination. For example, he described a hierarchy of authority based on reasonability, also at school, in his *Schoolboekjen van Nederlandsche deugden* (*Little School Book of* Dutch *Virtues*, 1788, my emphasis). Nieuwenhuyzen and the 'Nut' combined, in short, the Enlightened pedagogical thoughts of John Locke, Jean-Jacques Rousseau, and others, with views familiar in Holland since the seventeenth century, such as those of Jacob Cats, to establish an educational infrastructure with a crucial role for reading in a Dutch nation-state to be created during the nineteenth century.

3   The *Willemsfonds*: Education in the Flemish National Language

A similar interest in the education of the people, with a particular interest in books in Dutch, developed more than sixty years later in the *Willemsfonds*, in the political context of the new state of Belgium. This fund was established in 1851 in Ghent, in the Dutch-speaking province of East-Flanders. Its initial aim was to publish books in Dutch in order to facilitate education and self-education for Dutch-speaking Belgians. This would help to (re)create a Flemish cultural life of a prestige equal to that of the French-speaking political elite and the dominant francophone culture in Belgium. For the greater part of the nineteenth century, the *Willemsfonds* grew in terms of membership, local branches, and activities organized. The history of this nineteenth-century growth was written as early as 1906–09 by the Belgian historian Paul Frédéricq;

---

15   M. Nieuwenhuyzen in *De Menschenvriend*, cited in Helsloot and Dodde, 60.

more recent studies were published mainly by or in collaboration with the Liberaal Archief in Ghent and Harry Van Velthoven, among others.[16]

The *Willemsfonds* was established by a small group of men of letters from Ghent and Brussels with both Catholic and Liberal political views. The names of the three first presidents are well known in the philological and literary 'phase A' of Flemish nationalism: Jules de Saint-Genois (president 1851–55), Ferdinand Augustijn Snellaert (president 1855–62) and Frans Rens (president 1862–74). They were literary historians, poets, and journal editors. The fund was named after another philologist and poet, Jan Frans Willems (1793–1846), a public servant living in Antwerp and Ghent, who already during the United Kingdom of the Netherlands had advocated using the vernacular language as an official language in the provinces of Flanders and Brabant. In his *Verhandeling over de Nederduytsche Tael- en Letterkunde, opzigtelyk de Zuydelyke Provintien der Nederlanden* (1819), Willems defended the value of the Dutch language in his own time by exposing its long history of literary production.[17] The scope of the *Willemsfonds* was not limited to philological interests; from the beginning, its activities and organization were aimed at a broader public and political influence. By 1856, the fund had 185 members, also outside Ghent, mostly from the middle classes. The Ghent base remained important: not only was the fund accommodated by the city government (in the *Lakenmetershuis* at the Vrijdagmarkt), but the Ghent members were represented by statute in the general committee (*Algemeen bestuur*) and were elective only for the executive committee (*Dagelijks bestuur*), which included the president, the secretary, and the treasurer.

Like their eponymous philologist, the initiators identified the social inferiority of a group of citizens with some of the group's cultural particularities and practices. They diagnosed social oppression among the poor and mainly rural population in the Dutch-speaking provinces of Belgium. This region had even been famine-stricken in the preceding decade, following a potato disease, and people were leaving "poor Flanders" (*arm Vlaanderen*) for the highly industrialized Walloon regions (in the south of Belgium), and for America. The initiators also diagnosed cultural oppression in a double sense: Flemish culture was oppressed by the francophone industrial elite, which was also a political elite thanks to census suffrage; and it was oppressed by the Catholic Church, which controlled most institutions of education and culture, again mainly in French. Additionally, the Dutch language as spoken in Flanders was considered nothing more than a scattered collection of local dialects, not suited for any

---

16 See Frédéricq; Bots *et al.*; Van Velthoven and Tyssens.
17 See Willems and De Smedt.

Bildung—thus reinforcing the social retardation of those who did not speak the dominant French language. In the words of Van Velthoven: "One was poor because one spoke Flemish."[18]

The cure proposed by the *Willemsfonds'* initiators was to re-evaluate Flemish history and to make the Dutch language instrumental for social education. Their main instrument in the first years was—as noted above—the publication of books in Dutch. Another main concern was to improve the educational quality of state schools, and to avoid the influence of bishops; older members were expected to practice self-development through civic virtues such as diligence, providence, and thrift. Additionally, from 1870 onwards the *Willemsfonds* put forward a historical image in which the figures of the Beggars (*Geuzen*), the combatants on the side of the Protestants and local nobility during the Dutch Revolt against the Spanish royal army, played a central role. The Beggars' religious motives were not stressed, but rather their Liberal ideals and their violent persecution by the Inquisition. This image contrasted with the one propagated by clergymen in which the Flemish people had maintained a Catholic essence throughout the centuries together with their language. In short, the *Willemsfonds* used official schools, laicized self-education, and a refined Dutch language as implements for a "civilizing offensive,"[19] which was thus as Flemish as it was Liberal—as reflected in the much-used double slogan *Klauwaard en Geus*, referring to the two historical images of the Flemish heraldic lion and the Beggar.

After 1862, the year Julius Vuylsteke became the fund's secretary and the dominant figure for decades, the *Willemsfonds* tried to extend its influence beyond Ghent and the province of Eastern Flanders by diversifying its activities and expanding its organizational structure. The fund kept on publishing books, but it also set up libraries and organized public lectures and courses, with striking success: between 1865 and 1896 the library in Ghent lent 1,819,951 volumes to 39,740 readers.[20] Local branches were set up, initially in the major cities of Flanders: a local branch in Ghent next to the central organization (1868), in Antwerp (1871), in Bruges (1872), in the capital Brussels, and in Lier (both 1873). Later branches were limited to small towns and to a few Liberal rural communities. Accordingly, the members of the *Willemsfonds* and volunteers in the local branches were recruited mainly from the middle classes; farmers and laborers were almost absent. This organizational expansion contributed to the *Willemsfonds'* success: every Flemish province had local branches, and membership

---

18   Van Velthoven and Tyssens, 17.
19   Ibid., 21.
20   Ibid., 25.

grew by 1884 to 4,544, consisting for the greater part of public servants (mainly teachers) and office workers, but also craftsmen, entrepreneurs and traders, and professions like lawyers, notaries, doctors, and artists. Ghent remained the center of the *Willemsfonds* during this expansion, and was the place where members from all local branches assembled every October.

The growth of the *Willemsfonds* also laid bare some internal political differences. The ideological neutrality of the initial founders was soon replaced with a mild Liberal stance, which was not explicitly Masonic but nonetheless anticlerical. At the same time, the *Willemsfonds* tried to maintain neutrality in party politics and did not affiliate with the Liberal political party, nor with the Liberal pillar then under construction. This did not mean that it stayed out of everyday politics; petitions about legislation over language and education even became one of the *Willemsfonds*' preferred means of action.[21] It was precisely these issues and the preparation of the language law of 1883 which divided the *Willemsfonds* into opportunists and radicals. Additionally, in the last decades of the century, debates on social issues and the question of universal suffrage revealed a cleavage between doctrinaire and progressive Liberals, both outside and within the *Willemsfonds*. When in 1884 the Catholic party obtained an absolute majority in Parliament and formed a government alone, the *Willemsfonds* experienced some revanchist measures, since it had profited in earlier decades from subsidies from the national government. The *Willemsfonds*' membership declined for the first time, though it remained a determining factor in the history of Belgium, if only through its Catholic pendant, the *Davidsfonds*, established in 1875.[22]

4 The Society of Dutch Literature in Leiden

Years before the *Maatschappij tot Nut van 't Algemeen*, scholarly and literary societies in the Dutch Republic were occupied with the past and the language of the country, with the aim of educating their members to become proper citizens of the Dutch Republic. Though at first sight they seem to be more exclusive in nature than the 'Nut,' a closer examination of their activities reveals a concern for the public interest beyond educational initiatives. This is why one of them has a place here: the *Maatschappij der Nederlandsche Letterkunde te Leiden* (Society of Dutch Literature in Leiden). This society also combined Enlightenment ideals with civil socialization and with nationalist ideas about

---

21 Van Velthoven 2008.
22 See Wils 1977–89.

language, literature, and history. These ideas existed in the Habsburg Netherlands as well, long before their application to 'poor Flanders' by the *Willemsfonds*. Initial traces can be found in the Imperial Academy founded under Empress Maria Theresa in 1772. The Academy was concerned in the first place with philology, but it also addressed the public.

Literary societies grew from below in the Dutch Republic, from the middle of the eighteenth century onwards. In almost every town they served a local market, as they were populated by the town's political and cultural elite, or by university students. Their principal aim was less the philological study of national culture than mere sociability and a form of active citizenship.[23] For some of them, however, ambitions grew as they tried to address literary men beyond the city walls and tried to organize a joint scholarly study of the Dutch language. The first to do so was the *Maatschappij der Nederlandse Letterkunde te Leiden*. F.H.K. Kossmann outlined some of the major episodes at the Society's centenary in 1966, and studies of the Society's history and social engagement have been published more recently.[24] The Society grew out of a students' society in the 1760s and became a central institution for the study of (old) Dutch literature. It had important features in common with the *matice*: it set up a scholarly infrastructure for nation-wide philological study, it tried to spread knowledge among its members and to the broader public, it published books, and it was not established as a government initiative.

The Society's emergence from civil society deserves some attention, since its predecessor among the Leiden students determined in large measure its organization and practices. In 1757 a students' society was established under the name of *Linguaque animoque fideles* (*Companions in both language and spirit*), changed in 1761 into *Minima crescunt* (*Tiny things grow*). The members indeed wanted small things to grow, including themselves. They all were the sons of notable Leiden families, had learned Latin, and studied theology or law at the city's university. Their society was a training ground for literacy and the elegant use of the Dutch language in treatises, poetry, and eloquence. The students met fortnightly to discuss each other's work. Each member was required by the statutes to read aloud a linguistic or historical treatise, or a poem of his own making, and he also had to submit fifteen linguistic commentaries on the language of a Dutch poet, one from the classic seventeenth century or a younger one. The seventeenth-century Amsterdam poet Joost van den Vondel was especially favored, as in almost all works on eloquence, grammar, and

---

23 Singeling; De Vries.
24 See Kossmann; Honings; Van Kalmthout *et al.* (eds.).

linguistics during the eighteenth century.[25] Fellow members were required to comment on all of the pieces. Those who failed to submit work, or who remained silent or made only "insulting, childish or superfluous" comments, were fined.[26] Their collaborative work resulted in mainly linguistic treatises and some poems published in the society's journal, *Maendelijksche by-dragen ten opbouw van Neer-land's tael- en dicht-kunde* (*Monthly Contributions for the Advancement of Language and Literature of the Netherlands*; 1758–62), later renamed *Nieuwe bydragen tot opbouw der vaderlandsche letterkunde* (*New Contributions to the Advancement of National Literature*; 1763–66).

Such common literary exercises in Dutch were considered as a means to promote civil socialization, as would later be the case for the *Maatschappij tot Nut van 't Algemeen* as well. The students' attention to old poets and history was more a classical education in rhetoric, a training in eloquent use of the Republic's language of public affairs and sermons, than a study of national roots in language and history. Here again, we see Enlightenment ideals of education and citizenship combined with an interest in local culture and history. In this respect, a treatise by student-member Rijklof Michaël van Goens entitled *Vrymoedige bedenkingen over de vergelyking der oude dichteren met de hedendaegschen* (*Frank Considerations on the Comparison of Ancient with Contemporary Poets*) and published in the society's journal, is particularly remarkable. At the age of eighteen, he became involved in the ongoing *querelle des anciens et des modernes*, an originally French quarrel about the quality of modern literature as compared to classical Roman texts. Van Goens stated that every literary text had to be judged in terms of its own historical context, and denied the existence of universal standards for literary beauty.[27] At the core of civic self-education, the earliest traces of a historicist view of Dutch literature emerged at roughly the same time it began to spread throughout Europe following the success of Ossian's poems.[28]

Minima Crescunt merged in 1766 with societies in Utrecht and Hoorn to form the Society of Dutch Literature in Leiden. On the one hand, this new Society continued the students' societies; its meetings and activities were organized in the same way, and the by-laws remained more or less the same. Old Dutch poets and history were still studied collectively. The members still had to submit treatises on Dutch language and literature, on archaeology, or on national history. The system of reviews, comments, and corrections persisted,

---

25 See Rutten.
26 Honings, 23.
27 Honings, 25; Johannes.
28 Leerssen 2004.

only the publication series was now called *Werken* (*Works*). On the other hand, the Society's ambitions went well beyond those of students, and rigidly so: students were no longer allowed as members. Instead, some Leiden professors joined, like Johan Lulofs and Everhardus Scheidius, and renowned historians and linguists like Jan Wagenaar and Balthasar Huydecoper. They added to the initiators' symbolic capital and enabled Frans van Lelyveld, one of them, to present the Society as a forum for individual philologists, societies *and* their public, all over the nation: "A number of enthusiasts and some societies favoring language and antiquities, in various regions of our Netherlands, have come to the noble decision to unite in a general Society, and to join hands together, in order to present the fruits of their exercises, under a more general heading and scope, to the scholarship-loving Fatherland."[29] The study of language, literature and history had to be disseminated all over the 'scholarship-loving Fatherland': the Society now had a national interest; it was no longer a mere educational club in Leiden.

In order to meet this ambition, from 1774 onwards the Society organized competitions that were open nationwide. The subjects were chosen by the annual general meeting during the summer. These competitions were a way of coordinating philological studies in the Dutch Republic. The same was true for the Society's library, which grew slowly at first but acquired an important collection of linguistic works, ancient books and manuscripts bequeathed by its member Zacharias Henrik Alewijn in 1788. From that moment on, the Society's library became one of the best equipped workshops for philologists.[30] From 1770 onwards, members also made plans for a Dutch general dictionary. The benefits of such a work were clearly stated during an annual meeting: it would shed some light on "already worn-out customs and habits of our honest Forefathers; their former simple and sincere way of life; lost arts; changed judicial procedures; and abolished national laws."[31]

With this justification for a dictionary the Society repeated a typical mix of reasons for studying the domestic past and the vernacular which could be heard all over Europe: a vague respect for the old and a quest for lost purity and sincerity were linked to concrete matters of changing jurisdiction, customs, vocabulary, and local topography. The work for this important dictionary was also organized collectively, and some of the members began to collect words and definitions. Though it did not result in a dictionary, their work was used for other philological purposes. It served, in particular, the first scholarly edition

---

29   Cited in Honings, 25.
30   Rock 2009.
31   *Jaarvergadering*, in Honings, 31.

of a thirteenth-century chronicle of the world and of the Netherlands entitled *Spiegel historiael* compiled by Jacob van Maerlant and Lodewijk van Velthem after Vincent of Beauvais' *Speculum historiale*, which was edited by the Society's members Jan Steenwinkel and Jacob Arnold Clignett from 1784 onwards. Clignett and Steenwinkel were the first in the Netherlands to promote medieval literature not only for its historical value, as accounts of the early history of the Low Countries, but also for its literary merits. They appreciated the simplicity of Maerlant's language, which lacked the frills of later ages, thus applying Van Goens' literary-historicist view to medieval literature.[32]

To sum up: the Society for Dutch Literature in Leiden originated as a civic initiative, revaluated literary history, and undertook its philological activities collaboratively through open competitions and publication series. All of this makes it kindred to the Slavic *matice* in terms of its activities, its way of working, its social composition, and its concern for public dissemination. One major difference in its political context, however, becomes clear in view of its official recognition: stadholder William V granted the Leiden Society a patent and his patronage in 1775. The Society offered him a golden medal in exchange for his classic political support for cultural sociability.

From the 1780s onwards, during the political instabilities in the Republic, in France, and in the rest of Europe, the now officially recognized learned Society of Dutch Literature had serious difficulty pursuing its collaborative philological work. The contributions to the dictionary stopped, and literally no one participated in the open competitions. Instead, the Society, now under the chairmanship of Matthijs Siegenbeek, professor in Dutch rhetoric at Leiden University, focused on the public dissemination of its expertise. A new series of publications, the *Verhandelingen* (*Treatises*), was launched in 1806, and new meetings were held during the winter from 1804 onwards, where one could attend readings on the Society's fields of interest. These meetings were open for members and, on payment of an entrance fee, for all others—including women. In other words, the public part of the Society's plan remained active, but not the philological part. In addition, the official recognition was disputed after the French Emperor Napoleon Bonaparte installed his brother Louis Napoleon as King of Holland. King Louis also granted his patronage. The Leiden Society, grown from below as a students' society, thus became in time officially acknowledged by both the ancient and the revolutionary regimes for its practicing of Dutch eloquence, linguistics, poetry and history, as well as its addressing of the public in general.

---

32   Rock 2006, 290–93; Rock 2015, 41–45.

5 The Imperial Academy in Brussels

Most of the Slavic *matice* propagated the history and culture of a region within the Habsburg empire in order to supplement cultural policies from the central state. However, in the Austrian Netherlands, the Habsburg government itself founded an Imperial Academy in Brussels and entrusted it with studying the history of the land. Cultural historian Tom Verschaffel argues that the work of the historians attached to this Academy can rightly be described as early contributions to a national history of the Habsburg Netherlands initiated by the imperial government.

The Imperial Academy was founded in 1772 as the institutional precipitation of a new intellectual climate that flourished after the beginning of Empress Maria Theresa's reign in 1740. In particular, her minister Count Cobenzl (in function from 1753 until his death in 1770) initiated an active policy to stimulate cultural and intellectual life in and around Brussels, the administrative capital of the Austrian Netherlands. Cobenzl tried to structure and unify some of the existing intellectual activities. Although his attempts were also aimed at strengthening control over society at a time when Enlightenment ideas were spreading from nearby Paris, he found some cooperation among local authors. This resulted at first in traditional historiographical work, such as descriptions of the imperial dominions from a historical perspective, for crown prince Joseph's benefit. At the university library in Louvain, however, the attention to the history of the Low Countries, and especially of the Dutch Revolt, resulted in a collaborative undertaking coordinated by university librarian C.F. Nelis with J.F. Paquot, "Her Majesty's historiographer" (*historiographe de sa Majesté*) from 1762 onwards. They formed an elaborate network of correspondents to collect information from local experts. Out of this network in 1769 a Literary Society (*Société littéraire*) emerged with Cobenzl as its president. It was reformed into the Imperial Academy, following the example of the Academy in Mannheim (Kurpfalz). Johan Daniel Schöpflin, the head of the Mannheim Academy and also professor of history at the University of Strasbourg (France), acted as an adviser in this process. Empress Maria Theresa decreed the Academy's foundation in June 1772. Thus, the Academy, created after a German example by the central authorities, gave the existing local networks of intellectuals an institutional and official status acknowledged by the central powers in Vienna.

Who were these local intellectuals? Not one of the members of the Academy was a professional historian, since history was not a separate field of study at the University of Louvain—the only university in the Austrian Netherlands—as it was in the latter half of the eighteenth century at some German universities, especially Göttingen. The members mostly had a traditional humanist profile: they had degrees in law or medicine; they were clergymen or noblemen, merchants, teachers, or public officers. Admittance to the Academy was, in spite of the lack of a full education in history, a way of being officially acknowledged as a historian.

Both the production and dissemination of historical knowledge were notably modernized by the Academy. Next to more traditional activities on the production side—notably the publication of historical documents, and the mutual communication and discussion among the members via letters or at meetings—new sources for historical knowledge were opened up: the imperial library in Brussels, for example, was made public for the Academy's benefit. New contributors (new human resources) were found in a system of open competitions. Participants had to present a written and elaborated answer to a historical question posed by the Academy members. These competitions were not only a "breeding ground" (Verschaffel's term), another way of recruiting historians all over the country; they also fostered the genre of the historical treatise as a form of dissemination. The treatise met the requirements of a well-reasoned answer to a given question, making individual contributions fit into collective research plans: it was concise, it presented arguments and historical evidence, and it had a more or less standardized form. Winning treatises were published in the Academy's *Mémoires*. As Verschaffel notes, the system of open competitions thus made the Academy not only an official institution for historians, but also a "public forum" for all the interested contributors whose historical treatises it published.

The Academy's questions for open competitions suggest, as Verschaffel argues, a research plan for a hitherto unwritten history of the Southern Netherlands, with a general, even national outline. In this respect too, the Academy did some traditional historical research: it still focused mainly on the Dutch Revolt and its effects in counties and cities all over the Low Countries, as many historians had done before. For the period after the Revolt, the Academy took a new geographical entity as its subject: the southern part of the Low Countries, which was predominantly Catholic and remained under the royal sovereignty of Philip II of Spain and his Habsburg descendants. From this perspective, the Academy in a way adapted—somewhat belatedly—a tradition of regal historiography to the new political situation. But its treatises also focused on the difference between the Habsburg dominions and the now independent northern Republic of the Seven United Provinces, and aimed at a general view of the history of the southern dominions as a whole. This view was needed to replace the separate histories of each of the constituent provinces and main cities as they had been written up until the last decades of the eighteenth century. This general scope had been used before in bibliographies produced by book printers in the cities of Brussels, Louvain, and Antwerp (like Custis and Paquot), and at the Academy around 1800 it resulted in new general histories, like those of Du Chasteler and Jean des Roches, in whose books the relatively young political entity of the Austrian Netherlands was given a history of its own.

According to Verschaffel, these first general histories of the Southern Netherlands prove that the Imperial Academy was important not only as a facilitating society for scholars, not only as a centralized and open forum for historians, but also as an institution creating a national history, precisely because of its official status: it was at the Academy, in its meetings and *Mémoires* in the last decades of the eighteenth century, that traditional forms of regal and ecclesiastical historiography were turned into a collective, problem- and evidence-based way of doing historical research on the national past without losing any intellectual or societal status. The status of the domestic historiographical tradition was assured by the title of Academy, which put it in line with older academies like the Académie des Inscriptions in Paris (1663) or those of German cities like Göttingen and Mannheim. In short, as Verschaffel's thesis on the study of national history in the Southern Netherlands says, "the burgeoning national consciousness is more a result than a cause of national history."[33]

The Imperial Academy thus took a particular position compared to most *matice*: it was initiated by the imperial Habsburg government and nevertheless contributed to the creation of a national history and identity in the Austrian Netherlands. After 1830, the now Royal Academy remained an official center for the study of Belgian national history. Throughout the nineteenth and twentieth centuries, however, it lost some of its organizational influence as history became a modern university discipline from the 1860s onwards. The development of an autonomous sphere for scholarship and science had become clear earlier, in the academy-like Royal Institute in Amsterdam.

6   National Philology and Academic Autonomy in the Netherlands (1806–82)

In certain other institutions similar to the *matice*, a tension between official recognition and a striving for scholarly or artistic autonomy became

---

[33]   Verschaffel, 98.

particularly clear throughout the nineteenth century. This was the case for certain philological societies in the Netherlands and for a collection of literary societies in the new kingdom of Belgium.

In 1806, King Louis Napoleon founded the Holland Institute, later to become the Royal Institute. Though it was a new institution in a new state, the Kingdom of Holland, many similarities with the older Society for Dutch Literature in Leiden are evident, as well as with academies in Brussels and elsewhere in Europe. The Holland Institute also operated collectively: its members met in sessions, they had a library at their disposal, they had plans for a dictionary (and realized a few reference works on seventeenth-century authors), they organized open competitions, set up publication series that putatively addressed the whole country, and they were supported by the government.[34] The Leiden Society actually continued to exist, competing with the new Institute in various ways: some of its members refused to pay their contributions once they became members of the Institute. The work on the edition of the *Spiegel historiael*, which was started by two of the Society's members and benefitted greatly from its collective expertise, was continued by the Institute in 1812. Nevertheless, the two institutions co-existed as long as the Napoleonic regime lasted, and when the United Kingdom was founded in 1815, both the Leiden and the Amsterdam institutes were officially recognized by King William I (as was the Brussels Academy). Between 1806 and 1830, the institutional field thus multiplied, and both old and new players were officially recognized by subsequent political regimes. They all spoke in the official "voice of scholarship," also regarding Dutch history and culture.[35]

More important than this multiplication of institutes, however, was a qualitative change in the philological work. During the 1810s and 1820s, the attention to historical documents and the Dutch language, dating back to the Leiden Society, found a connection with German nationalist thought. Jacob Grimm corresponded with the Holland Institute on the Dutch version of *Reineke Fuchs* and the recently discovered Comburg Manuscript.[36] The young August Heinrich Hoffmann von Fallersleben visited the Low Countries, consulting among others the Royal Library in The Hague and the library of the Society for Dutch Literature in Leiden.[37] The institutional forms that philological study had taken in both the Habsburg Netherlands and the Dutch Republic made it possible

---

34 Van den Berg; Van Berkel.
35 Van Berkel.
36 Leerssen 2006.
37 See Brinkman.

for German philologists to communicate with them and thus inspired them to give their scholarly work nationalist overtones.[38]

This nationalization of philology was not only an imported product, however. The philological research and college life at Leiden University by late humanists like Justus Josephus Scaliger (1540–1609) and Justus Lipsius (1547–1606) were suited for reclaiming the German novelty of nationalist philology as a homeland tradition. The protagonist in this exchange of ideas was Willem Bilderdijk, a controversial poet, theologian, historian, and philologist, a politician, royal teacher, and *Privatdozent*, and a famous patient. He gained access in 1780 to the Society for Dutch Literature through an open competition on the relation between poetry and philosophy. Between 1809 and 1818, he was the president and secretary of the philological section of the Holland Institute, and he came into contact with German philologists—much to his discontent. He disapproved of what he called a philological contest among the Germans and their refusal to communicate about newly discovered manuscripts.[39] Around 1820, he even tried to close the Dutch-German border to all philological traffic. He had made some critical notes on the edition prepared by the German professor Friedrich David Gräter of *Van den vos Reynaerde*, a much-discussed medieval tale among Dutch, German, and French philologists.[40] He refused, however, to publish these notes, "that every Dutchman can see at my place, but which I for my part will keep secret from the Germans until a new edition is carried out again by one of us [Dutchmen], for which purpose I will readily share them."[41] Bilderdijk thus linked the study of an old text to citizenship, and even doubted the sincerity of German scholarship, for "one knows how uncommunicative Scholars are in a country that treats Study not as a Pleasure, but as Profit."[42] Bilderdijk thus made a qualitative and ethical distinction between German and Dutch philology. Earlier in his life, he had already favored Leiden's first university librarian, Janus Dousa (1545–1604), a nobleman and leader of the civil resistance against the Spanish occupation of Leiden in 1573–74.[43] By linking early modern universities with modern institutions through Dutch philology, Bilderdijk gave scholarship a nationalist importance, thus realizing German ideas of cultural nationalism by opposing them.[44]

---

38 See Rock 2009.
39 Leerssen 2006, 29–30.
40 Ibid., 75–95.
41 Bilderdijk, 146.
42 Ibid., 145.
43 See Van Eijnatten.
44 Rock 2010, 277–87 and 301–02.

Bilderdijk's vision of the national value of philology was widely shared by other men of letters, but it competed more and more with ideals of modern academic scholarship. In the period of the United Kingdom the government still assembled philologists from both the northern and the southern provinces, and even Germany, to form a new official philological commission. The commission on *Rerum belgicarum scriptores* was named after one from the 1770s which had existed within the Imperial Academy. Its mandate was to publish the most important accounts of the history of the new Kingdom—the kind of work that still was being carried out by the other institutions. It bore little fruit, since the kingdom split up in 1830. In Belgium, its work was taken over by a *Commission royale d'histoire* (Royal Commission of History), which after some decades was swallowed up by the Royal Academy.

In the northern Kingdom of the Netherlands, comparable work was done by a new students' society, the *Vereeniging ter bevordering der oude Nederlandsche letterkunde* (Association for the Advancement of Old Dutch literature).[45] The ambition of this generation of students, however, was no longer to integrate educated citizens into society or to practice nationalist philology; they sought to establish Dutch philology as an academic discipline. Two of the Association's founding members, Willem Jonckbloet and Matthias de Vries, succeeded in obtaining chairs in Dutch history and eloquence in the 1840s. The latter founded a lexicographical school (later institute) in Leiden, where he and his collaborators finally carried out the plans for a general Dutch dictionary previously formulated by the Society of Dutch Literature in Leiden and the Holland Institute. Between 1882 and 1998 it published the *Woordenboek der Nederlandsche Taal* (*Dictionary of the Dutch language*).[46]

This dictionary was not the achievement of some philological society; it was a product of the modern academic discipline of lexicography. Meanwhile, and in spite of the acknowledged national value of their work, the real public realm was becoming less and less a concern of these learned societies. They merely published old texts, but no longer organized open competitions or public lectures, nor did they pursue official acknowledgment. Philology, though it was considered of national importance by Bilderdijk and others, was now carried out in specialized institutions without explicit concern for public dissemination. Together with the modern academic disciplines, scholarly autonomy had come into view.

---

45 See Mathijsen 2008.
46 Rock 2010, 305–74.

7 Flemish Literary Societies in Belgium (1815–86)

Along with the proliferation of scholarly institutions accompanied by both nationalist and autonomist philological scholarship, literary societies multiplied too, and in their turn claimed autonomy for their artistic activities. In the Dutch Republic, literary societies had known their heyday between c. 1750 and 1800,[47] and they instigated a long-lasting literary culture centered around individual authorship. King William I did not reduce governmental support for local literary societies in both parts of his United Kingdom (and he continued to support scholarly societies from previous regimes). In the southern provinces he used literary societies in a policy of acculturation to traditions in the former Republic—as the literary historian Janneke Weijermars has recently pointed out.[48] After the provinces separated in 1830, the surviving societies, together with similar new ones, transposed the use of the Dutch language and literature in the creation of a national identity to the new Belgian state. As the nineteenth century progressed, however, Flemish literary societies questioned their political role, as cultural historian Greet Draye has shown. Both the cultural politics of William I and the literary societies in Belgian debates on national identity and literature are the subject of this final section. Such literary societies also propagated the creation of national poetry, just as the *matice* did, but in a different relation towards state powers.

While literary societies multiplied in the Dutch Republic, in the Austrian Netherlands an older tradition of *rederijkerskamers* (chambers of rhetoric) was kept alive, in particular in the larger cities, like *De Wyngaerd* (The Vineyard) in Brussels or *De Fonteine* (The Fountain) in Ghent. Their institutional forms and activities were more traditional than in the societies of the Republic: they were private and limited to a single city, they organized various tournaments, mostly for drama and to a lesser extent for poetry, and they recruited from lower social segments. Between 1819 and 1825 William I tried to overcome this difference in his United Kingdom by giving his support in the southern provinces to new literary societies in the northern style, like Concordia in Brussels and the *Maatschappij van Nederlandsche Taal en Letterkunde 'Regat Prudentia Vires'* in Ghent. These new societies followed the example of literary societies in the northern provinces; sometimes they were even founded by people from the north. The initiators were mostly professors and judges, while the members were local public officers and teachers. Their activities were identical: the members held meetings and public readings on literature and history, they

---

47 Singeling; De Vries.
48 See Weijermars 70–76, 121–42, 183–86.

published miscellanies, and they managed a library (including newspapers and magazines). They also organized open competitions, the entries for which were mostly judged by scholars from the Royal Institute in Amsterdam. The fields of interest of these societies, poetry, history, and some philosophy, were not noticeably innovative.

The governmental *cachet* they all nevertheless shared is remarkable. King William I acted often as a patron or honorary member, or he supplied a starting capital, mostly promised even before their actual foundation. An attempt by the Society for Dutch Literature in Leiden to set up a central society in the northern provinces failed, though some members saw the Antwerp educational society *Tot Nut der Jeugd* (For the Benefit of the Young) as such a body. Governmental support seems also to have served as an intelligence network, since the leading members maintained correspondence with ministers, rather than as an infrastructure for philological research and national education similar to the *matice*. Some contemporaries indeed saw the societies as an attempt by the mainly Holland-oriented government to dominate culturally local traditions. Only some faithful supporters of the new kingdom, like the above-mentioned Jan Frans Willems, favoured the new Holland-style societies, though he also explicitly noted the differences in language and culture between Holland and the southern province of Brabant. In all such cases, whether a municipal or a governmental initiative, support and patronage were in favor of the various *matice*-like philological, educational, and literary societies. At least during King William's reign, however, official recognition remained an impediment for the literary societies to find general acceptance among the public in the southern provinces.

This finding by Weijermars is the more striking, since after 1830, when Belgium was established with a dominantly French-speaking government and administration, Dutch-speaking Belgian nationalists chose the Holland-style literary society as an important organizational form.[49] Newly founded literary societies, such as *De Olyftak* (The Olive Branch) in Antwerp (1835–79) or *De Tael is Gansch het Volk* (Language is the Whole People) in Ghent (1836–93), continued to look very much like King William's unpopular societies. The organizational elements were similar: the members (seldom more than thirty) were mostly public officers and teachers, they organized meetings where they were obliged to give lectures (or pay fines), and they had a library with papers and magazines at their disposal. Thus Belgian Dutch-speaking nationalists during the philological phase took over a form of cultural policy used by the expelled King William.

---

49   See Draye, *passim*.

Yet two major differences between the societies before and after Belgium's independence have to be stressed. Firstly, the Dutch language had become a prominent issue. The first admission requirement for De Olyftak was to have a command of the Dutch language and be able to use it in poetry, while the metonymical name of the Ghent society speaks for itself. The importance of the Dutch language was now no longer self-evident, nor an object of official cultural policy as it had been during the United Kingdom. Secondly, these societies did not have governmental backing. All of them were founded, like most of the *matice*, by Flemish nationalists themselves, rallying support among likeminded men of letters. In fact, their efforts embodied the official acknowledgment of the Dutch language they cultivated, and thus of the Flemish nation. Both differences can be explained by the Flemish societies' *raison d'être*, according to Draye: these societies were literary societies in order to effect political change. Sociability was again not a goal in itself, or a form of educating the members, but a political means. Of course their members wanted to be poets, but they wanted even more to be intermediaries between their culture and political change. Therefore, when literary societies in Belgium no longer enjoyed political patronage or recognition after 1830, it became their first goal to reclaim it.

This primacy of politics over literature in the Flemish literary societies explains their attempts to establish a centralized *matica*-like institution in the Dutch-speaking part of Belgium. Some of these were very short-lived, mostly because of political dissension: the *Maetschappy ter Bevordering der Nederduitsche Tael- en Letterkunde* (Society for the Advancement of Dutch Language and Literature, 1836) existed for only five years, and the *Nederduitsch Taelverbond* (Dutch Language Union) never really came to full force. As I have shown, two coordinating organizations aimed at public dissemination did flourish: the *Willemsfonds* and its Catholic counterpart the *Davidsfonds*; yet they did not have a coordinating function in philological matters. That remained for decades the prerogative of the now Royal Academy in Brussels, and of more and more of the universities. Therefore, a complementary philological institution for the Flemish movement was founded in Ghent in 1886, the *Koninklijke Academie voor Nederlandse Taal- en Letterkunde* (Royal Academy of Dutch Language and Literature), at the instigation of the philologist Willem De Vreese and others. Compared to both the *Willemsfonds* and the *Davidsfonds*, this Academy was never really connected with the by now increasingly popular nationalist movement in Flanders. At the same time, new ideals of modern, autonomous literature became dominant at the end of the century, as elsewhere in Europe. By the 1880s, it was not only scholarship that claimed a separate place in the Belgian and Dutch societies; literature did so as well.

8 An Overview

Societies equivalent to the Slavic *matice* are not hard to find in the Dutch-speaking areas of Europe, though none of them has every feature in common with a *matica*. One major difference lies in the political contexts and therefore in the nature of governmental support.

For the Dutch Republic it is notable that already during its closing decades, from the middle of the eighteenth century onwards, cultural societies existed that cultivated national history and literature. These were the result of private initiatives and tried to reach their members and a broader public through publications and open competitions. The Society of Dutch Literature in Leiden (1766) was the first literary society to do so on a nationwide scale and became the most important until about 1800. It tried to find a wider public over the years, through its publication series, open competitions, and eventually public lectures. An overtly educational agenda was found in the *Maatschappij tot Nut van 't Algemeen* (1784), which gave up competitions and publishing activities in favor of the foundation of schools and public libraries, and writing school books. It was organized throughout the country in local branches. Both societies were officially acknowledged by the central government. After 1800, in the Napoleonic Kingdom of Holland and the subsequent (United) Kingdom of the Netherlands, neither society lost its official status. A new central scholarly institution was established in 1806, the Holland (later Royal) Institute, where philological activities were given a nationalistic *élan*, while philological societies and modern academic disciplines pursued scholarly autonomy in the second half of the nineteenth century. The early occurrence of cultural and educational societies in the Dutch Republic explains why Enlightenment ideals of education and citizenship were more apparent than essentialist ideas about national history and literature. Most societies therefore never became opposed to the political contexts in which they operated.

In the Habsburg Netherlands at the end of the eighteenth century, the political context for the pursuit of history and literature in societies was in at least one respect unlike that in the Dutch Republic: the Habsburg government itself initiated an Imperial Academy in Brussels in 1772. It studied the history of its own regions, among other things disseminating its work through publication series and organizing open competitions to enable collaboration throughout the provinces. This (later Royal) Academy kept on playing an important role in nationalistic history writing, in particular after the creation of the Belgian state. Meanwhile, important renewals had taken place in the literary field, in particular in the period of the United Kingdom of the Netherlands. It was after the involvement (or at least support) of the central government, in this case King

William I and his ministers, that new literary societies were established in the former Austrian provinces. These societies copied their organization from existing societies in the northern provinces and used the same instruments for public dissemination of literature, such as open competitions and lectures. After 1830 and in the new political context of Belgium, these forms were continued by Dutch-speaking men of letters who often sought official recognition from the Belgian state. Within these literary societies, members debated the Flemish character of the Belgian state, but, as the nineteenth century progressed, also the question of literary autonomy. In the meantime, an important new fund was established in 1851: the *Willemsfonds*. Like the *Maatschappij tot Nut van 't Algemeen*, it focused on education through the production of cheap books and the establishment of public libraries, and its local branches covered most of the country. It also had a political ambition: it enjoyed governmental support and tried to influence everyday politics through petitions. The *Willemsfonds'* idealistic connection between language, history, and social reform was more elaborate than was the case for the 'Nut' almost seventy years earlier.

Bibliography

Bilderdijk, Willem. "Kort verslag wegens gevondene brokken van een oud Hollandsch rijmwerk." In Bilderdijk, *Taal- en dichtkundige verscheidenheden*. Rotterdam: J. Immerzeel Jr., 1820. 135–64.

Blom, J.C.H., and E. Lamberts. *History of the Low Countries*. Trans. James C. Kennedy. New York / Oxford: Berghahn, 1999.

Bots, Marcel, Harry Van Velthoven, A. Deprez, L. Pareyn, J. Daelman, and J. Dewilde, eds. *Het Willemsfonds van 1851 tot 1914*. Bijdragen Museum van de Vlaamse Sociale Strijd 9. Gent: Provinciebestuur Oost-Vlaanderen / Liberaal Archief, 1993.

Brinkman, Herman. "Hoffmann von Fallersleben and Dutch Medieval Folksong." In Dirk Van Hulle and Joep Leerssen, eds., *Editing the Nation's Memory: Textual Scholarship and Nation-Building in Nineteenth-Century Europe*. European Studies 26. Amsterdam / New York: Rodopi, 2008. 255–69.

Buijnsters, P.J., and L. Buijnsters-Smets. *Bibliografie van Nederlandse school- en kinderboeken 1700–1800*. Zwolle: Waanders, 1997.

De Smedt, M. *De literair-historische activiteit van Jan Frans Willems (1793–1846) en Ferdinand Augustijn Snellaert (1809–1872)*. Koninklijke Academie voor Nederlandse Taal- en Letterkunde. Reeks VI. Bekroonde werken. Gent: Secretariaat van de Koninklijke Academie voor Nederlandse Taal- en Letterkunde, 1984.

Deprez, Kas, and Louis Vos, eds. *Nationalism in Belgium: Shifting Identities, 1780–1995*. Basingstoke: Macmillan / New York: St. Martin's Press, 1998.

De Vries, Marleen. *Beschaven! Letterkundige genootschappen in Nederland 1750–1800*. Nijmegen: Vantilt, 2001.

Draye, Greet. *Laboratoria van de natie: Literaire genootschappen in Vlaanderen, 1830–1914*. Nijmegen: Vantilt, 2009.

Dunthorne, Hugh, and Michael Wintle, eds. *The Historical Imagination in Nineteenth-Century Britain and the Low Countries. National Cultivation of Culture*. Leiden / Boston: Brill, 2013.

Eerenbeemt, H.F.J.M. van den. *Streven naar sociale verheffing in een statische stad: Een kwart eeuw arbeid van de Maatschappij tot Nut van 't Algemeen in Bergen op Zoom, 1791–1816*. Nijmegen: Centrale Drukkerij, 1963.

Frédéricq, Paul. *Schets eener geschiedenis der Vlaamsche Beweging*. Uitgave van het Victor de Hoon-Fonds. 3 vols. Gent: Vuylsteke, 1906–09.

Hake, B.J. "The Pedagogy of Useful Knowledge for the Common Man: The Lending Libraries of the Society for the Common Benefit in The Netherlands, 1794–1813," *History of Education* 29 (2000). 495–515.

Helsloot, P.N., and N.L. Dodde. *Martinus Nieuwenhuyzen 1759–1793: Pionier van onderwijs en volksontwikkeling*. Amsterdam: De Bataafsche Leeuw, 1993.

Honings, Rick. *Geleerdheids zetel, Hollands roem! Het literaire leven in Leiden 1760–1860*. Leiden: Primavera Pers, 2011.

Johannes, Gert-Jan. *De lof der aalbessen: Over (Noord-)Nederlandse literatuurtheorie, literatuur en de consequenties van kleinschaligheid 1770–1830*. Nederlandse cultuur in Europese context. Monografieën en studies 10. Den Haag: SDU, 1997.

Kloek, J., and W. Mijnhardt. *1800: Blueprints for a National Community. Dutch Culture in a European Perspective*. Basingstoke / New York: Palgrave Macmillan, 2004.

Koll, Johannes. *"Die belgische Nation": Patriotismus und Nationalbewußtsein in den Südlichen Niederlanden im späten 18. Jahrhundert*. Niederlande-Studien 33. Münster / New York / Berlin: Waxmann, 2003.

Kossmann, F.K.H. *Opkomst en voortgang van de Maatschappij der Nederlandse Letterkunde te Leiden: Geschiedenis van een initiatief*. Leiden: Brill, 1966.

Leerssen, Joep. "Ossian and the Rise of Literary Historicism." In Howard Gaskill, ed. *The Reception of Ossian in Europe*. London: Thoemmes, 2004. 109–25 and 416–18.

Leerssen, Joep. *De bronnen van het vaderland: Taal, literatuur en de afbakening van Nederland, 1806–1890*. Nijmegen: Vantilt, 2006.

Mathijsen, Marita. "Stages in the Development of Dutch Literary Historicism." In: D. Van Hulle and J. Leerssen, eds., *Editing the Nation's Memory: Textual Scholarship and Nation-Building in Nineteenth-Century Europe*. European Studies 26. Amsterdam / New York: Rodopi, 2008. 287–303.

Mathijsen, Marita. *Historiezucht: De obsessie met het verleden in de negentiende eeuw*. Nijmegen: Vantilt, 2013.

Mijnhardt, Wijnand. *Tot heil van 't menschdom: Culturele genootschappen in Nederland 1750–1815*. Nieuwe Nederlandse bijdragen tot de geschiedenis der geneeskunde en der natuurwetenschappen. Amsterdam: Rodopi, 1988.

Rock, Jan. "Literary Monuments and Editor's Jokes: Nationalism and Professionalisation in Editions of Lodewijk van Velthem's *Spiegel Historiael* (1727–1906)," *Variants: The Journal of the European Society for Textual Scholarship* 5 (2006). 285–313.

Rock, Jan. "Gewonnen perkament, gewaarborgde kennis: Joannes Clarisse en de bibliotheek van de Maatschappij der Nederlandse Letterkunde als geleerde werkplaats." In *Jaarboek van de Maatschappij der Nederlandse Letterkunde te Leiden 2007–2008*. Leiden: Maatschappij der Nederlandse Letterkunde, 2009. 58–73.

Rock, Jan. *Papieren monumenten: Over diepe breuken en lange lijnen in de geschiedenis van tekstedities in de Nederlanden 1591–1863*. Ph.D. diss., University of Amsterdam, 2010.

Rock, Jan. "Refashioning Poets, Fashioning Readers: Explorations of the Self-Fashioning of Jacob Arnout Clignett and Jan Steenwinkel, 1781–1784," *De achttiende eeuw* 47 (2015). 34–48.

Rutten, Gijsbert Johan. *De Archimedische punten van de taalbeschouwing: David van Hoogstraten (1658–1724) en de vroegmoderne taalcultuur*. Uitgaven Stichting Neerlandistiek VU 52. Amsterdam: Stichting Neerlandistiek VU / Nodus Publikationen, 2006.

Singeling, C.B.F. *Gezellige schrijvers: Aspecten van letterkundige genootschappelijkheid in Nederland, 1750–1800*. Amsterdam / Atlanta: Rodopi, 1991.

Van Berkel, Klaas. *De stem van de wetenschap: Geschiedenis van de Koninklijke Nederlandse Akademie van Wetenschappen*. Vol. 1: 1808–1914. Amsterdam: Bert Bakker, 2008.

Van den Berg, Willem. "De Tweede Klasse: een afdeling met een problematische missie (1808–1816)." In W.P. Gerritsen, ed., *Het Koninklijk Instituut (1808–1851) en de bevordering van wetenschap en kunst*. Amsterdam: Koninklijke Nederlandse Akademie van Wetenschappen, 1997. 61–88.

Van den Berg, Willem and Piet Couttenier. *Alles is taal geworden: Geschiedenis van de Nederlandse literatuur 1800–1900*. Geschiedenis van de Nederlandse literatuur. Amsterdam: Bert Bakker, 2009.

Van Eijnatten, Joris. *Hogere sferen: De ideeënwereld van Willem Bilderdijk (1756–1831)*. Hilversum: Verloren, 1998.

Van Kalmthout, Ton, Peter Sigmond, and Aleid Truijens, eds. *Al die onbekende beroemdheden: 250 jaar Maatschappij der Nederlandse Letterkunde*. Leiden: Leiden University Press, 2016.

Van Sas, N.C.F. *De metamorfose van Nederland: Van oude orde naar moderniteit, 1750–1900*. Amsterdam: Amsterdam University Press, 2004.

Van Velthoven, Harry. *Tussen opportunisme en radicalisme: Het Willemsfonds en de Vlaamse kwestie in 171 petities (1860–1913)*. Gent: Academia Press / Liberaal Archief, 2008.

Van Velthoven, Harry and Jeffrey Tyssens. *Vlaamsch van taal, van kunst en zin: 150 jaar Willemsfonds (1851–2001)*. Gent: Willemsfonds Algemeen Bestuur / Liberaal Archief, 2001.

Verbruggen, Christophe. *Schrijverschap in de Belgische belle époque: Een sociaalculturele geschiedenis*. Nijmegen: Vantilt / Gent: Academia Press, 2009.

Verschaffel, Tom. *De hoed en de hond: Geschiedschrijving in de Zuidelijke Nederlanden 1715–1794*. Hilversum: Verloren, 1998.

Weijermars, Janneke. *Stepbrothers: Southern Dutch Literature and Nation-Building under Willem I, 1814–1834*. National Cultivation of Culture 8. Leiden: Brill, 2015.

Willems, Jan Frans. "'Introduction' to the *Treatise on Dutch Language and Literature, with regard to the Southern Provinces of the Netherlands* (1819–24)." In Theo Hermans, ed., with Louis Vos and Lode Wils, co-eds., *The Flemish Movement: A Documentary History 1780–1990*. London / Atlantic Highlands, NJ: The Athlone Press, 1992. 67–70.

Wils, Lode. *Honderd jaar Vlaamse beweging*. 3 vols. Leuven: Davidsfonds, 1977–89.

Wils, Lode. *Van Clovis tot Di Rupo: De lange weg van de naties in de Lage Landen*. Historama 1. Antwerpen / Apeldoorn: Garant, 2005.

Wils, Lode. *Van de Belgische naar de Vlaamse natie: Een geschiedenis van de Vlaamse Beweging*. Leuven / Den Haag: Acco, 2009.

CHAPTER 11

A Century of Change: The Eisteddfod and Welsh Cultural Nationalism

Marion Löffler

The early modern history of Wales laid the foundations for the form its cultural nationalism took in the nineteenth century.[1] Politically, the Principality of Wales was incorporated into England with the Acts of Union of 1536 and 1543, an event celebrated by many because it afforded Welshmen equal rights with their English neighbours as subjects of the English Crown.[2] However, the preamble to the Act of Union of 1536 established English as "the natural Mother tongue used within this Realm," ruling that

> from henceforth no Person or Persons that use the Welsh Speech or Language shall have or enjoy any manner Office or Fees within the Realm of England, WALES, or other the King's Dominion, upon Pain of forfeiting the same Offices or Fees, unless he or they use and exercise the English Speech or Language.[3]

In the wake of the union, native religious customs bound up with Catholicism disappeared as King Henry VIII established the Anglican Church as a state church; the native legal system was superseded by English law; and the medieval bardic system decayed due to the increasing Anglicization of the Welsh nobility and gentry.[4] However, in 1563, Queen Elizabeth I passed an Act for the Translating of the Bible and the Divine Service into the Welsh Tongue, which led in 1588 to the publication of the first complete translation of the Bible into Welsh. On the basis of this translation, Welsh became the main medium of religion in Wales, and it developed a lively print culture. This latter phenomenon, which was absent for the other Celtic languages in the British

---

1 A wide range of Welsh-language literature on aspects of Welsh culture is available in published form, but in this essay, English sources have been favoured. I am grateful to the financial support of The Leverhulme Trust, which enabled me to conduct research connected with the subject matter of this chapter.
2 Jenkins 2007, 129–30.
3 Bowen, 75; see also Löffler 1994, 34–36, 198.
4 See Lewis.

Isles,[5] was crucial for the development of a Welsh-language national cultural movement in the nineteenth century.[6]

The immediate roots of Wales's nineteenth-century cultural nationalism lie in its cultural and religious renaissance in the eighteenth century, when patriotic Welshmen began to establish societies for the preservation of their culture and to gather and print medieval poetry and prose, and when Dissenting Protestantism and Methodism (then still a part of the Anglican state church) turned the Welsh towards reading as a form of religious observance.[7] Socially, the men who participated in this cultural renaissance comprised members of the gentry and civil servants of the Crown, businessmen, artisans, Dissenting ministers and Anglican priests. Since Wales was an overwhelmingly rural country with no capital, no town with more than ten thousand inhabitants, and no institutions of higher education, these early efforts mostly emanated from or were connected with the capital, London, where expatriate Welshmen were concerned about their home country. The French Revolution boosted their efforts, as radical political ideas were linked to Enlightenment values, fostering a new pride in Welsh culture and history.[8]

In the course of the nineteenth century, Welsh cultural nationalism slowly relocated to Wales itself geographically, and away from radicalism politically.[9] As the state administration of what by then had become the United Kingdom of Great Britain and Ireland extended into every social domain, the Welsh, while keen to preserve their national characteristics through the Welsh language and through the Protestant Nonconformist denominations which had seceded from the Anglican state church, were also eager to prove themselves worthy members of the growing British Empire.[10] Their concern with respectability and improvement became especially pressing after 1847, when a very unfavourable government *Report on the State of Education in Wales* blamed the Welsh language for the perceived immorality and ignorance of the Welsh nation.[11] This explains the transition from romanticism to a 'scientific modernism' within parts of the movement, and perhaps also why Welsh men and women focused their efforts not on a sustained campaign for political independence,

---

5 "Bible, in the Celtic languages," in Koch, vol. 1, 206–11.
6 Bowen, 149ff.; Löffler 1994, 47–51, 205–6; Jones and Rees.
7 G. Williams, 21–25; Morgan 1992, 43–100; Morgan 1981.
8 Kidd; Löffler 2012.
9 G. Williams, 25–28.
10 Morgan 1997.
11 I.G. Jones 1992; Tyson Roberts.

but on cultural and religious nationalism.[12] Radical political elements in the fast-growing industrial areas of south Wales increasingly turned towards socialist ideologies in the course of the nineteenth century, which stressed internationalism and spurned any nationalist efforts.

1 The Evolution of Cultural Societies

The first London-Welsh society, the Honourable and Loyal Society of Ancient Britons, was founded in 1715 as a charitable institution for Welsh families in London.[13] Its title is paradigmatic for Welsh cultural nationalism until the Second World War insofar as it attempted to express political loyalty to the British state while stressing the cultural distinctiveness of the Welsh. More important was the Honourable Society of Cymmrodorion (1751), which became a model for future societies. Resurrected twice, in 1820 and 1873, it exists to this day.[14] From the mid-eighteenth century it convened monthly meetings in London, which mixed Welsh entertainment with scholarly papers and furthered research into Welsh history, literature, and antiquities. Its constitution, published in 1755, stressed the importance of the Welsh language to Wales and vowed:

> To cultivate [...] a Language so excellent in itself, so fruitful in many venerable and undoubted Monuments of Antiquity, so highly useful and indeed necessary, to the Restoration and Improvement, not only of the History of Great Britain and Ireland, but likewise of several Countries upon the Continent, and to make it more generally understood.[15]

---

12 Political nationalism in Wales expressed itself through the short-lived *Cymru Fydd* movement founded in 1886 and first culminating in an unsuccessful Bill for Home Rule introduced to the British House of Commons by the ironmaster and MP Ernest Thomas John in 1912. A Welsh nationalist party, *Plaid Cymru*, was founded in 1925. In 1998, Wales established *Cynulliad Cenedlaethol Cymru* (The National Assembly for Wales), which has law-making powers within the political structure of the United Kingdom (E.W. Williams; H.M. Davies).

13 Jenkins and Ramage, 12–13. This volume provides detailed lists of membership in this and the subsequent London societies for the nineteenth century.

14 For the Hounourable Society of the Cymmrodorion, see http://www.cymmrodorion.org/ (last accessed 28 September 2018).

15 "Constitutions of the Honourable Society of Cymmrodorion in London (1755)," in Jenkins and Ramage, 227–30.

This passage distills the aims of most nineteenth-century cultural societies in Wales. Although its constitution also referred to the "improvement of trade and manufacture in Wales," nothing much was done in this vein.[16] Science was likewise neglected. The society published the famous *British Zoology* by Thomas Pennant,[17] but furthering scientific endeavours was not a priority until the latter half of the nineteenth century. The membership of the society was socially so humble that one of its prime movers, Lewis Morris, the overseer of Crown mining rights in Cardiganshire, recommended that "their titles be disguised as much as possible, that every English fool may not have room to laugh in his sleeve."[18] The society admitted 'corresponding members' from Wales itself, which established its leading role, and that of the societies which followed, in the exchange of ideas and knowledge between London and Wales. After its second resurrection in 1873, in which the civil servant Sir Hugh Owen was a key figure, the London Cymmrodorion assumed a greater role in Wales itself. It is due to their efforts that a National Eisteddfod Association was founded in 1881, and it was then that they decided to hold annual meetings at the National Eisteddfod itself to serve "as a focus of patriotic aspirations and activities for Welshmen, irrespective of differences of party or creed."[19] The "Cymmodorion Section" of every National Eisteddfod held after 1880 became a starting point for many reforms and initiatives in late Victorian Wales.

As the number of Welshmen in London increased, other societies were founded. In 1770, the Gwyneddigion Society was established, most of whose members (as the name indicates) came from north Wales.[20] Its main patron was the affluent businessman Owen Jones (Owain Myfyr), without whose generous financial support the society could not have pursued its work, but its members also included radical writers and poets like Thomas Roberts (Lwynrhudol) and John Jones (Jac Glan-y-Gors).[21] Influenced by the ideas of the French Revolution and socially plebeian, the Society's rules required every member to be Welsh-speaking and to be partial to Welsh poetry sung to the harp, the national instrument of Wales. Despite its decline by the early years of the nineteenth century, its impact on Welsh culture was significant. It initiated the movement to publish Welsh medieval literary treasures and, most

---

16   Ibid., 86.
17   Biographies of most of the people mentioned here may be found at "Welsh Biography online" on the website of the National Library of Wales, http://yba.llgc.org.uk/en/index.html (last accessed 28 September 2018).
18   J.H. Davies, vol. 2, 386.
19   Evans 1890, 42; Jenkins and Ramage, 177–8.
20   See Davies Leathart.
21   Jenkins and Ramage, 93–7 and 110–12; Phillips; J.B. Edwards.

importantly, it revived the nearly moribund eisteddfod, remodelling it as a proto-national institution.

The Cymreigyddion Society, founded in 1795, was even more democratic in membership than the Cymmrodorion and the Gwyneddigion, and aimed at maintaining "the Welsh language pure and undefiled" and at "promoting the development of mental powers; always avoiding, however, such topics as promote theological or political argument."[22] In the difficult political climate of the late 1790s, during which all societies worked within the constraints of repressive political legislation in Britain, this was probably wise. Nevertheless, its members appear to have discussed less poetry and more church and secular politics than their predecessors, and even listened to lectures on astronomy in the Welsh language.[23] The society petered out in the 1850s,[24] bequeathing its name—Cymreigyddion—to most of the local societies which were being founded in Wales. By then the cultural momentum had shifted firmly from the capital of the world's largest empire to Wales itself.

The end of the Napoleonic Wars in 1815 brought a new beginning to Welsh cultural nationalism as men with less radical religious and political leanings established 'Cambrian' cultural societies in Wales itself. Many of them were Anglican priests operating with the blessing of Thomas Burgess, who had become Bishop of the diocese of St David's in 1803. Keen on strengthening the Anglican state church against the growing influence of Nonconformist denominations such as Methodism, Baptism, Presbyterianism and Unitarianism, Burgess founded schools and colleges and began to appoint Welsh-speaking clerics to Welsh parishes. Most importantly, he supported these clerics in their antiquarian and literary efforts. Men like David Rowland (Dewi Brefi) in Carmarthenshire, William Jenkins Rees (Casgob) in Radnorshire, and John Jenkins (Ifor Ceri), Walter Davies (Gwallter Mechain), and David Richards (Dewi Silin) in Montgomeryshire became central to the Cambrian societies which continued the eisteddfod tradition of the Gwyneddigion.[25] In October 1818, Bishop Burgess and his circle, together with Edward Williams (Iolo Morganwg), the only Nonconformist there, established the Cambrian Society in Dyfed, whose aim was to promote "the preservation of Ancient British literature, poetical, historical, antiquarian, sacred, and moral, and the encouragement of national

---

22   Jenkins and Ramage, 129.
23   Ibid., 132–33. The University of Wales Press series of books on 'Wales and the French Revolution,' published from 2012, presents poetry, prose, and drama from the period.
24   Ibid., 136.
25   B.L. Jones; Miles, 75.

music."[26] They were followed by similar societies for the remaining three ancient parts of Wales: Powys (1819), Gwynedd (1820), and Gwent (1822).[27] Among the aims of the societies were cataloguing and publishing Welsh manuscripts, placing Welsh manuscripts in the British Library, and gathering books published in the Welsh language in the library of the Honourable Society of Cymmrodorion in London as a national repository until Wales would have its own National Library.[28] Most of the energy of the societies, however, was spent on organizing a series of eisteddfodau in Wales itself between 1819 and 1834. Following the lead of the Cambrian societies, local societies were founded all over Wales from the 1820s onwards, in rural areas as well as in the rapidly industrializing south, to which Welsh men and women seeking work were migrating in increasing numbers. This internal migration (in which Wales differed from Celtic countries like Ireland and Scotland, whose inhabitants were forced to leave their native countries, mostly for America) led to the emergence of a Welsh-speaking, Nonconformist culture centered on chapels and Sunday schools as well as on choirs and local cultural societies.[29] These societies, often led by the local minister, schoolmaster, and members of the lower middle class, encompassed a large part of the Welsh-speaking population.[30]

2 The National Eisteddfod of Wales

The eisteddfod movement is central to cultural nationalism in nineteenth-century Wales. A majority of the men and women connected with the struggle for the Welsh language contributed to its development or received encouragement and patronage from it. Most of the societies, clubs, and initiatives in the field of native culture, whether in literature, language reform, history, or social and educational reform, were either initiated at an eisteddfod or utilized the institution as a meeting place and focus point.

First documented in 1176, when the Lord Rhys ap Gruffudd held a competition at Cardigan in west Wales, the eisteddfod was a medieval cultural competition of poets and musicians, patronized by the nobility and intended to

---

26 Ibid., 77.
27 Ibid., 84–94.
28 Ibid., 78.
29 I.G. Jones 1980, 47–71; G.H. Jenkins 1998.
30 In 1871 a private language survey counted 71.2% of the population of Wales as Welsh-speaking. When the decennial "Census of Population for England and Wales" included a question on the Welsh language in 1891, this figure had fallen to 54.5%. See D. Jones 1998, 223, 225.

license poets and uphold the standards of Welsh literature.[31] By the second half of the eighteenth century the institution had declined into occasional poetic meetings of amateur bards held sporadically at inns and taverns.[32] It was the Gwyneddigion Society which provided the ideological impetus and the financial stimulus for the revival of the institution, when it began to organize and sponsor eisteddfod competitions in north Wales from 1789, for which it announced prizes for poetry and prose essays in the Welsh language, for singing, and for the playing of national instruments. Their series of eisteddfodau held between 1789 and 1804 greatly stimulated the production and publication of Welsh poetry and prose.[33]

Following a gap during the Napoleonic Wars, the first eisteddfod of the Dyfed Cambrian Society, held in July 1819, was extensively reported in the by then thriving Welsh periodical press. The official 'auditor' W.J. Rees ensured that the eisteddfod, together with its newly invented governing body, the Gorsedd of the Bards of the Isle of Britain,[34] was remembered as an apolitical cultural event which united Welshmen across religious divides. The report on the audacious move by Edward Williams to make Bishop Burgess a member of the Druidic Order was especially important, for it announced a union of Nonconformity, the Anglican state church, and ancient Celtic druidism:

> The old Bard of Glamorgan [...] approached the Bishop, telling him that he had been authorized (or urged, because I could not hear him very clearly) to dress his Lordship with the Druidic Order: Well, said the Bishop, I will bow to everything which you consider appropriate; at this point the Bard attached a white ribbon to the Bishop's right arm. This caused prolonged and general applause. This revealed that religious prejudice had been left outside the audience by the mighty and the common. To see the *Bishop of St David's* thus honoured by an old *Dissenter* was a sight a thousand times more beloved by the proponents of love and general goodwill, and opponents of prejudice and partisanship, than had the Arch-Bishop of Canterbury, with all his robes and his Archiepiscopal pomp been seen fulfilling the same task.[35]

---

31   H.T. Edwards 1990.
32   Morgan 1992, 56–58.
33   Morgan 1981, 64–66; Jenkins and Ramage, 125–26.
34   The Gorsedd had been devised by Edward Williams in the early 1790s and became part of the nation's festive inventory during the nineteenth century. See Charnell-White; Löffler 2007, 41–77.
35   Löffler 2007, 44. The original Welsh may be found there.

The following series of what have been named 'provincial eisteddfodau,' organized by the Cambrian societies until 1834, greatly furthered the production and publication of Welsh literature, yet also transformed the festival into an event dominated by the English language—which was understood by the gentry whose patronage and financial backing was sought and obtained—and by the popular music which attracted large numbers of paying spectators.[36]

The new eisteddfod tradition was re-Cymricized between 1834 and 1853 by the Abergavenny Cymreigyddion Society and especially its founder and main patron, the influential Augusta Hall, Lady Llanover (Gwenynen Gwent), wife to Sir Benjamin Hall, MP.[37] Her efforts to promote the Welsh language, to record Welsh folk songs and encourage the playing of the triple harp, and to further the development of the Welsh woollen industry and of a Welsh national costume, all left a lasting legacy.[38] Apart from patronizing native scholars, such as the Vicar Thomas Price (Carnhuanawc) and the Chemist Thomas Stephens, the Abergavenny eisteddfodau gave the Welsh festival an international dimension by furthering the beginnings of Pan-Celtic association and by attracting scholars from Germany and France to prestigious essay competitions on Welsh and Celtic philology.[39] They bridged the gap between the provincial and local eisteddfodau of the first half of the century and the National Eisteddfod of Wales which emerged in its second half.[40]

In the absence of conventional national institutions, in the second half of the nineteenth century, the eisteddfod and gorsedd were reshaped until they met the requirements of a modern national focus, thereby deflecting English criticism of Welsh backwardness and warding off the threat of cultural annihilation. The first eisteddfod of Wales to call itself 'national' was the Grand National Eisteddfod, Llangollen of 1858, organized by the Anglican priest and antiquary John Williams (ab Ithel) and made possible by the coming of the railways to Wales, which could now carry increasing numbers of competitors and visitors to hitherto isolated parts of the country.[41] At Llangollen in 1858 a meeting of poets and literati decided that a national festival should be organized annually, to be held alternately in north and south Wales.[42] It also discussed a petition to found a National Library of Wales (established at Aberystwyth in 1907) and first assembled a committee for the standardization of

---

36 H.T. Edwards 2000, 293–316; Miles, 105–08.
37 Morgan 2007; Thomas, 1–12; Löffler 2007, 47.
38 Thomas, 6–7.
39 Löffler 2006; Thorne.
40 Miles, 94–96.
41 For a short sketch on the railway in Wales, see D. Jones 1995.
42 Löffler 2007, 55–58; H.T. Edwards 1980, 4–6.

the Welsh orthography.[43] In the wake of Llangollen, a General Eisteddfod Council was established which organized national eisteddfodau from 1860 until 1868. As published in the newspaper *Y Faner* (The Flag), membership of the National Eisteddfod was to be open to:

> 1. Our prince. 2. Our nobility. 3. Our gentry. 4. Our clerics. 5. Our merchants, and the masters of our workers. 6. Our civil servants. 7. Our people. 8. Last, but primarily, our poets; that is, there should be a lay, poetic, and literary membership.[44]

Every class of member was to pay a particular fee, with the interest from this fund used to sponsor further eisteddfodau.[45] Beginning in 1861, the revered civil servant Sir Hugh Owen furnished this National Eisteddfod with a 'Science Section' that inaugurated social and educational reform. In 1863 for instance, it started the Welsh University Movement which led to the establishment of the University College Wales, Aberystwyth in 1872 and to the establishment of a federal University of Wales in 1893.[46] The romantic Gorsedd was retained as a festive part of the national event, a colourful link with a past that appeared to rival the antiquity of most of Wales's larger European neighbours. This first attempt to create a permanent National Eisteddfod ended in 1868 when the institution went bankrupt.[47]

A second national series between 1869 and 1880 proved more permanent, since it led to the founding in 1881 of the National Eisteddfod Association which organizes the national festival to this day.[48] Its early history and aims were laid down in the first of its *Transactions*, published in 1887. Its first president was The Most Honourable the Marquess of Bute, a coal industrialist and probably the richest man in Wales at the time; the forty-five vice-presidents encompassed Welsh gentry and most of the Welsh Members of Parliament, but

---

43 Miles, 111–12.
44 *Y Faner*, 8 May 1861 (my translation).
45 Between 1860 and 1868 various "Regulations of the Eisteddfod" citing differing membership categories were published. The regulations attached to the *Programme of the Chester Eisteddfod, 1866*, for instance, lists "ordinary members, life members, honorary members, and delegated members," the first "composed of three classes [...] those paying 21s. per annum, [...] those paying 15s. per annum, [...] and those paying 10s. or 5s. per annum."
46 H.T. Edwards 1980, 53–112; H.T. Edwards 2001.
47 Statistics on the National Eisteddfod from 1861, on Welsh publishing and on library lending may be found in D. Jones 1998, 475–518. Unfortunately, this volume does not feature financial statistics.
48 Löffler 2007, 59–60.

the fifty-five-member Council was of humbler origin.[49] More than a thousand pounds were to be raised from subscriptions annually, and it was proposed to "widen the range of the subjects for competition by embracing to a greater extent than has yet been attempted, works of art, the productions of the manufacturer and the handicraftsman."[50] Henceforth, the National Eisteddfod of Wales served as a focus for Welsh-language culture as well as an instrument for furthering social and educational reform in the country on an ever-increasing scale. Whereas 187 competitors took part in 41 competitions in Aberystwyth in 1865, by the Liverpool Eisteddfod of 1900 these figures had risen to 1,410 and 107, respectively.[51] The *Transactions*, published annually since 1887, contain reports on important meetings and texts of the winning poetry and prose entries, along with valuable essays on the literature and history of Wales, folklore collections, novels, poems, short stories, and songs. Since the 1860s the National Eisteddfod of Wales has developed into a week-long annual focus for the nation, held alternately in north and south Wales, which encompasses almost all aspects of the national culture (and by now sub-cultures).[52]

The National Eisteddfod of Wales and its Gorsedd have also become focal points for cultural nationalists well beyond Wales, inspiring cultural nationalists in Ireland, Scotland, Brittany, and Cornwall to devise similar institutions. The constitution of *An Comunn Gaidhealach* (The Highland Association), founded in 1891, "followed closely the lines of the great Welsh Association," the Eisteddfod.[53] Welsh delegates were present at the first Scottish *Mòd*, a cultural festival held from 1891, and the Gorsedd was invited to preside over the Irish cultural festival, the *Oireachtas*, in 1897. Both Brittany and Cornwall followed the Welsh example by founding their own Gorsedd assemblies, in 1900 and 1928, respectively.[54] Following a meeting at the Blaenau Ffestiniog National Eisteddfod of 1898, a Pan-Celtic organization was discussed which came into being on 12 October 1900 in Dublin, and proceeded to hold three congresses and publish a periodical.[55] Their understanding of what constituted a nation was strictly dependent on culture, and indeed on language, as editorials in

---

[49] E.V. Evans 1887, vii–ix; J. Davies.
[50] W.E. Davies 1887, x–xvi.
[51] D. Jones 1998, 487–88, 493–97. Note that a whole choir, for instance, would have counted as one competitor.
[52] For the history of the National Eisteddfod Association, see R.T. Jenkins. The National Eisteddfod of Wales has its own website: www.eisteddfod.org.uk (last accessed 28 September 2018).
[53] National Library of Wales Manuscripts, D. Rhys Phillips Papers, 362.
[54] Le Stum, 41–60; Miles, 215–31.
[55] Löffler 2006, 146; Löffler 2000.

their periodical *Celtia* made clear more than once, with reference to Eastern Europe:

> Events during the nineteenth century have been tending in the direction of the evolution of national units on the basis of language. Greece, Italy, and Germany are conspicuous examples of such an evolution. Language is the most powerful bond between nations as between individuals. Sometimes its efficiency is marred by historical, political or dynastic accidents, or by geographical configuration or distance. Austria-Hungary, Switzerland, and the United States have been quoted as the exception to the rule "No language, no nation." But nobody can seriously maintain that there is such a thing as an Austro-Hungarian "nation."[56]

Irish and Welsh Pan-Celts measured themselves against Slavic cultural efforts. The university of Prague, where every subject could be studied through the medium of Czech, was praised in comparison with the University of Wales, founded in 1893, where English was the only medium of education. The efforts of Douglas Hyde, the leader of the Gaelic League, were likened to the work of František Palacký on behalf of Czech half a century earlier.[57] News reports highlighted the cruel linguistic oppression of Polish children in towns like Poznań, and letters discussed this 'Polish question.'[58] At the first Congress of the Pan-Celtic Association in August 1901, the Warsaw barrister Alfons Parczewski delivered a paper on "The Slavonic Society for the Dissemination of National Literatures: an Example for the Celtic Nations," and at the second Congress in 1904 he spoke on "A Survey of the Language Map of Europe." The latter was not only reprinted in full in *Celtia*, but re-published as a pamphlet.[59] Vehicles for Western and Eastern European cultural nationalism like the Eisteddfod and the Matica were thus connected in their efforts on behalf of their indigenous languages.

3   Publishing the Treasures

The first volume of the *Cambrian Register*, an ambitious journal published by the London Gwyneddigion in 1796, opened by noting that

---

56   *Celtia*, I:2 (February 1901), 1.
57   *Celtia*, VIII:2 (February 1908), 23.
58   *Celtia*, II:2 (February 1902), 18–21; Ibid., II:6 (June 1902), 123.
59   *Celtia*, I:9 (September 1901), 137; Ibid., IV:Congress Number (1904), 107; *Celtia Congress Supplement* (1904), 5–12; Parczewski.

> Since the revival of learning in Europe, most nations have been emulous of bringing forward their respective stores of ancient memorials, in order to enrich the common stock; but a vast treasure is contained in the Welsh language, in manuscripts, and the oral traditions of the people, of which barely a notice has hitherto been given to the world.[60]

Gathering the literary and historical treasures hidden in manuscripts and making them available to the Welsh was a major preoccupation of nineteenth-century Welsh nationalism. Similar passages occur in the prefaces to all the early historical-literary periodicals of the movement, which (unlike the many religious Welsh-language periodicals that appeared during the nineteenth century) were often in English.[61] Sponsored by civil servants like Lewis Morris and wealthy artisans like Owen Jones, scholars like William Owen Pughe and Edward Williams laid the foundations for Welsh learning by copying, editing, and publishing ground-breaking collections of Welsh manuscripts which influenced Welsh writing well into the twentieth century. It is thanks to their efforts that *Barddoniaeth Dafydd ap Gwilym* (a collection of the poetry of Dafydd ap Gwilym, Wales's most innovative medieval poet) was published in 1789,[62] and that the three-volume *Myvyrian Archaiology of Wales* made a large amount of medieval Welsh poetry and prose available to a public readership for the first time.[63] However, Edward Williams, who supplied much material for both undertakings, was not only intimately familiar with the literary traditions of his country; he was also a highly gifted forger. Therefore, both these and following publications, used widely during the nineteenth century, were seen by later generations as tainted, their existence spurring the move towards 'modernizing' Welsh culture.[64] These early efforts were continued in the antiquarian and patriotic journals of the 1820s and 1830s, which reprinted ancient laws, stories, descriptions of monuments, and Welsh poetry; through eisteddfod competitions on collections of cultural artefacts and historical essays; and by the Cambrian Archaeological Association and the Welsh Manuscripts Society.

---

60   "Preface," *Cambrian Register* I (1796), v.
61   So, for instance, in the *Cambro-Briton and General Celtic Repository* and the *Cambrian Quarterly Magazine and Celtic Repertory*.
62   See Jones and Owen.
63   See Constantine.
64   Löffler 2007, 144–45. Between 2000 and 2008 a project on "Iolo Morganwg and the Romantic Tradition in Wales" at the Centre for Advanced Welsh and Celtic Studies produced a series of works on Iolo Morganwg. See www.iolomorganwg.wales.ac.uk (last accessed 28 September 2018).

In 1836, six members of the Abergavenny Cymreigyddion (among them the historian Thomas Price) founded the Welsh Manuscripts Society "for the purpose of transcribing and printing of the more important of the numerous bardic and Historical Remains of Wales."[65] Between 1840 and 1862, the society published eight volumes of sources for the study of Welsh culture, such as W.J. Rees's *Lives of the Cambro-British Saints*, as well as editions of the earliest Welsh epic *Y Gododdin* and the Welsh medieval chronicles *Brut y Tywysogion* and *Annales Cambriae*. However, the editors of these volumes did not possess the learning nor, at times, the wish to distinguish between authentic sources and forgeries, which diminished the value of their work.[66] The society's work was continued on a sounder basis by Edward Owen, a civil servant who spent sixty years researching in the British Museum and published the fruits of his labours in the *Catalogue of the MSS Relating to Wales in the British Museum* (1900–22).[67] In 1908 he was appointed as the first Secretary of the Royal Commission for the Ancient and Historic Monuments of Wales, Aberystwyth, which still exists.[68]

The Cambrian Archaeological Association was founded with similar objectives by H. Longueville Jones and John Williams in 1846. A year earlier, they had established the journal *Archaeologia Cambrensis*, which found it difficult to escape the lure of the forged material in circulation until 1853 when, following a public split, John Williams founded a rival journal, the *Cambrian Institution*. This freed the Cambrian Archaeological Association and its periodical to pursue a more scientific approach.[69] It was here that Thomas Stephens published ground-breaking articles debunking the forgeries of previous generations.[70] The Cambrian Archaeological Association is still active in Wales, though its role declined with the foundation of the Royal Commission for the Ancient and Historic Monuments of Wales.

4   A National Historiography

By the end of the eighteenth century, the Welsh "no longer appeared to have a distinct history, but only traditions which were either discredited or merely

---

65   The aims of the Welsh Manuscripts Society were reprinted in each of the volumes it published, together with the names of its members.
66   Löffler 2007, 81–82. For the role of the forgeries, see R.J.W. Evans 2005.
67   See Owen.
68   For its website, see http://www.rcahmw.gov.uk (last accessed 28 September 2018).
69   See Bowen Thomas.
70   Löffler 2007, 134–37.

contributory to English traditions."[71] Their medieval authors were doubted by English scholars, and their manuscripts rotted in the libraries of their alienated gentry. It comes as no surprise that the efforts to revive a Welsh national culture encompassed the resurrection of a national history. As in other European countries, this process began with the rediscovery and invention of traditions,[72] followed, after 1850, by the pursuit of a strategy of scientific 'self-correction' to pre-empt criticism by the hegemonic power.[73]

Late eighteenth- and early nineteenth-century Welsh historians had concentrated on three historical strands: the beliefs that the Welsh (as the original 'British') were the earliest settlers of the British isles, that (a Proto-Protestant) Christianity had been practised by these early Britons long before it was reintroduced by Saint Augustine of Canterbury in the sixth century, and that Welsh culture was based on the druidic traditions first described by Roman authors.[74] In pursuit of these assumptions they refused to entertain any doubts about the authenticity of the sources on which they relied, sometimes even against their own better judgement.[75] By the 1840s, however, those historians who may be counted among the founding fathers and mothers of Welsh history, such as Jane Williams (Ysgafell), Thomas Price (Carnhuanawc), and Robert Pryse (Gweirydd ap Rhys), began to attempt Welsh histories based on authentic sources, both in Welsh and in English.[76] Their works complied with the principles endorsed by Thomas Stephens, the amateur scholar who initiated the process of self-correction and set the parameters for modern Welsh history-writing. His famous *Literature of the Kymry*, the winning essay of the Abergavenny Cymreigyddion eisteddfod of 1848, published in 1849, announced that he aimed to provide a "*rational* account" of Welsh literary history,[77] demanding "a rigid examination of the sources of our national history, and to submit our records to the test of an honest and searching, yet kindly criticism."[78] The following decades were marked by a process during which this new school of Welsh history-writing, increasingly dominated by professional scholars, clashed with the amateur adherents to a romantic history of a Wales filled with ancient druids and local folklore.[79] Alongside them, younger writers, such as

---

71   Morgan 1981, 17.
72   Morgan 1992, 43–44.
73   David Smith 54; Harvie 235–36. For the European aspect, see R.J.W. Evans 2013.
74   Morgan 1992, 45–46, 62–69.
75   Löffler 2007, 98–108.
76   See Price; J. Williams; ap Rhys.
77   Stephens, vii.
78   Löffler 2013.
79   Löffler 2007, 137–42.

A CENTURY OF CHANGE   247

the journalist Owen Rhoscomyl and the civil servant Sir Owen M. Edwards, published popular histories like *Flame Bearers of Welsh History* and periodicals like *Cymru* and *Wales*, which attempted to bring history to the common Welsh people. In 1911, John E. Lloyd, Professor of Welsh History at the University College of Bangor (North Wales), published *A History of Wales from the Earliest Times to the Edwardian Conquest*, the first history of Wales which adhered to professional standards but set out to serve the Welsh people. Tellingly, its story ends with the loss of Wales's political independence.[80]

5 A Language Fit for Modern Life

Although the translation of the Bible and its use in the Protestant liturgy prevented Welsh from dissolving into a number of mutually unintelligible dialects, it was considered past its prime in the seventeenth and eighteenth centuries. English authors considered it "a grotesquely ugly, guttural tongue [...] spoken as a patois."[81] The few Welsh scholars and poets who attempted to cultivate it were resigned to the fact that

> To Languages as well as dominions (with all other things under the sun) there is an appointed time; they have had their infancy, foundations and beginning, their growth and increase in purity and perfection; as also in spreading and propagation; their state of consistency, and their old age, declinings and decays. And thus it pleased the Almighty to deal with us Brittains; for these many ages hath eclipsed our power and corrupted our language, and almost blotted us out of the books of records.[82]

However, during the course of the eighteenth century, the output of Welsh literature increased steadily, and with it the esteem in which the Welsh language was held. Dictionary makers like Thomas Richards and John Walters published works of increasing bulk in the second half of the century, as the veneration shown the language by the London Welsh societies translated itself into efforts on its behalf.[83] The first attempt to assemble a definitive dictionary of the Welsh language came from William Owen Pughe, a member of the Gwyneddigion Society who received much support from Owen Jones. His *Geiriadur*

---

80   See Pryce.
81   Morgan 1992, 69.
82   T. Jones, ii.
83   Morgan 1992, 70–71.

Cymraeg a Saesoneg: A Welsh and English Dictionary published between 1793 and 1803, encompassed over one hundred thousand words, forty thousand more than Samuel Johnson's *Dictionary of the English Language* of 1755. Unfortunately, Pughe was influenced by late eighteenth-century ideas of composing vocabulary from a limited number of 'elementary words' (223 in the case of Welsh), which, combined with his zeal to simplify Welsh orthography, diminished the value of his works and occasioned a vicious orthography war in the first half of the nineteenth century.[84] The early efforts at language improvement, in adapting the vocabulary to changing societal conditions, left coinages such as *pwyllgor* (committee), *geiriadur* (dictionary), *gweriniaeth* (republic) and *chwyldro* (revolution), which are still in use. Over the course of the nineteenth century, authors, publishers, and editors came to focus less on the antiquity of the Welsh language and more on its future functionality.

Many activists in the cultural movement therefore produced dictionaries designed to translate new terminology from English and thus equip the Welsh language to serve the modern nation. Between 1800 and 1920, over twenty dictionaries of the Welsh language appeared. The most important among them were the works of Daniel Silvan Evans, *An English and Welsh Dictionary*, assembled for and published in two volumes by Gwasg Gee between 1852 and 1858, and *A Dictionary of the Welsh Language* [...] *Geiriadur Cymraeg*, published in five parts by W. Spurrell and Son between 1887 and 1906.

National print languages are of central importance to emerging nations, and the booming Welsh print culture of the nineteenth century required a standardized orthography.[85] At its first resurrection in 1820, the London Cymmrodorion had included standardizing the orthography of the Welsh language among its "leading objects." From the 1820s to the late 1840s, eisteddfod competitions regularly offered prizes for essays on subjects such as "to fix the orthography of the Welsh language which is to be brought back as nearly as possible to the standard of the Welsh Bible."[86]

In the face of these discussions and the various orthographies used by different authors, Welsh publishers began to assemble lists of 'difficult words' for the aid of printers. At the Llangollen eisteddfod of 1858, a group of fifty Welsh writers commissioned Thomas Stephens and Robert Pryse to circulate questionnaires on these 'difficult words' to all Welsh publishers, printers, and

---

84   Carr 2000; Idem 2005. His dictionary was nevertheless reprinted in 1891 (Pughe).
85   P.H. Jones 2000. Figures for the circulation of newspapers and periodicals may be found in D. Jones 1998. Details for the development of Welsh orthography until 1928 are sourced from Löffler 1997.
86   "Dyfed Cambrian Society, 1825," in Jenkins and Ramage, 157.

editors of Welsh periodicals. On the basis of their replies they drew up an *Orgraph yr Iaith Gymraeg* (*Orthography of the Welsh Language*), which was brought out by the leading publisher Gwasg Gee in 1859.[87] Unfortunately, the publication in 1861 of a rival orthography by the well-known author and later Professor of Welsh, Daniel Silvan Evans, prolonged these discussions. The 1860s were a difficult decade for the Welsh language. The eisteddfod, in financial difficulties and exposed to vicious attacks by the English press, concentrated on modernizing itself. The London Cymmrodorion, which could have provided guidance, was defunct; not until 1885 did it initiate the foundation of the Society for the Utilization of the Welsh Language, which later became known as *Cymdeithas yr Iaith Gymraeg* (The Welsh Language Society).[88] Together with members of *Cymdeithas Dafydd ap Gwilym* (The Dafydd ap Gwilym Society), a Welsh student association at Oxford University, this society resumed work on a Welsh standard orthography in 1886.[89] The new orthography, developed by John Morris-Jones, later professor of Welsh at Bangor University College, was vigorously discussed in popular periodicals and newspapers. Its main principles were deemed so important that they even appeared as an appendix to *Cymru Fydd*, the journal of the short-lived political movement for Welsh independence. The National Eisteddfod of 1889 declared orthographic reform a main point on its agenda. All efforts were brought together in the report of the 'Orthographical Committee' of the Society for the Utilization of the Welsh Language in 1893. Since this committee had included influential publishers and writers like Owen M. Edwards, its work came to be accepted widely in school books and by private publishing houses. The resulting *Orgraff yr Iaith Gymraeg* (Orthography of the Welsh Language), published in 1928, is the basis for the standard used at present.

The long nineteenth century was decisive for the history of the Welsh language and Welsh culture in more ways than one. The partial industrialization of Wales meant that those parts of the population that could no longer live off the land did not have to emigrate, but instead moved to south or north-east Wales, where they often settled in tightly-knit communities according to their areas of origin. The Welsh language was thus not, like Irish, dispersed into a diaspora, but concentrated in new, urban communities. While it had no overt prestige as a language of government or power (this was reserved for English), Welsh dominated Nonconformist Christian churches attended by the vast majority of the Welsh, which also organized much of Wales's cultural life.

---

87 See Löffler 1997.
88 Jenkins and Ramage, 212–14.
89 The Dafydd ap Gwilym Society now has a digital presence as a facebook group.

Nonconformity and Welsh thus became twin national symbols. Nationalism in nineteenth-century Wales as a result mainly concentrated on culture; on the preservation, development, and extension of the Welsh language and its literature; and on Welsh history. Initiated and led by the lower middle class and by Anglican and Nonconformist clerics, the long nineteenth century therefore witnessed a reworking of Welsh cultural traditions into a national culture without which the Welsh language would not have survived the challenges of the twentieth century.

Bibliography

ap Rhys, Gweirydd. *Hanes y Brytaniaid a'r Cymry. Cyfrol 1*. [A History of the Britons and the Welsh, Volume 1]. Llundain, Caerlleon, ac Abertawe: William Mackenzie, 1872.

Bowen Thomas, Ben. "The Cambrians and the Nineteenth-Century Crisis in Welsh Studies, 1847–1870," *Archaeologia Cambrensis* 127 (1978), 1–15.

Bowen, I., ed. *The Statutes of Wales*. London/Leipzig: T. Fisher Unwin, 1908.

Carr, Glenda. "William Owen Pughe and the London Societies." In Branwen Jarvis, ed., *A Guide to Welsh Literature c. 1700–1800*. Cardiff: University of Wales Press, 2000. 168–86.

Carr, Glenda. "An Uneasy Relationship: Iolo Morganwg and William Owen Pughe." In Geraint H. Jenkins, ed., *A Rattleskull Genius: The Many Faces of Iolo Morganwg*. Cardiff: University of Wales Press, 2005. 443–60.

Charnell-White, Cathryn. *Bardic Circles: National, Regional and Personal Identity in the Bardic Vision of Iolo Morganwg*. Cardiff: University of Wales Press, 2007.

Constantine, Mary-Ann. "Welsh Literary History and the Making of 'The Myvyrian Archaiology of Wales'." In Dirk Van Hulle and Joep Leerssen, eds., *Editing the Nation's Memory: Textual Scholarship and Nation-Building in Nineteenth-Century Europe*. Amsterdam: Rodopi, 2008. 109–28.

Davies Leathart, William. *The Origin and Progress of the Gwyneddigion Society of London Instituted M.DCC.LXX*. London: Hugh Pierce Hughes, 1831.

Davies, Hywel M. *The Welsh Nationalist Party 1925–1945: A Call to Nationhood*. Cardiff: University of Wales Press, 1983.

Davies, John H., ed. *The Letters of Lewis, Richard, William and John Morris, of Anglesey (Morrisiaid Môn) 1728–1765*. Aberystwyth: n.p., 1909.

Davies, John. *Cardiff and the Marquesses of Bute*. Cardiff: University of Wales Press, 2012.

Davies, W.E. "The National Eisteddfod Association." In E. Vincent Evans, ed., *Eisteddfod Genedlaethol y Cymry: Cofnodion a Chyfansoddiadau Buddugol Eisteddfod Aberdar,*

1885 [The National Eisteddfod of the Welsh: Minutes and Compositions Aberdare 1855]. Caerdydd: Llys yr Eisteddfod, 1887.

Edwards, Hywel Teifi. *Gŵyl Gwalia: Yr Eisteddfod Genedlaethol yn Oes Aur Victoria 1858–1868* [Gwalia's Festival: The National Eisteddfod during Victoria's Golden Age]. Llandysul: Gwasg Gomer, 1980.

Edwards, Hywel Teifi. *The Eisteddfod.* Cardiff: University of Wales Press, 1990.

Edwards, Hywel Teifi. "The Welsh Language in the Eisteddfod." In Geraint H. Jenkins, ed., *The Welsh Language and its Social Domains 1801–1911.* Cardiff: University of Wales Press, 2000. 293–316.

Edwards, Hywel Teifi. "The Merthyr National Eisteddfod of 1901," *Merthyr Historian* XIII (2001), 19–26.

Edwards, J.B. "John Jones (Jac Glan-y-Gors): Tom Paine's Denbighshire Henchman?" *Denbighshire Historical Society Transactions* 51 (2002), 95–112.

Edwards, Thomas. *A Brief Analysis of Welsh Orthography.* Denbigh: Gwasg Gee, 1847.

Evans, E. Vincent, ed. *Eisteddfod Genedlaethol y Cymry: Cofnodion a Chyfansoddiadau Buddugol Eisteddfod Aberdar, 1885* [The National Eisteddfod of the Welsh: Minutes and Compositions Aberdare 1855]. Caerdydd: Llys yr Eisteddfod, 1887.

Evans, E. Vincent. *The Ninth Annual Report of the National Eisteddfod Association.* Cardiff: Llys yr Eisteddfod, 1890.

Evans, R.J.W. "'The Manuscripts': The Culture and Politics of Forgery in Central Europe." In Geraint H. Jenkins, ed., *A Rattleskull Genius: The Many Faces of Iolo Morganwg.* Cardiff: University of Wales Press, 2005. 51–68.

Evans, R.J.W. "National Historiography, 1850–1950: The European Context." In Neil Evans and Huw Pryce, eds., *Writing a Small Nation's Past: Wales in Comparative Perspective, 1850–1950.* Farnham: Ashgate, 2013. 31–47.

Harvie, Christopher. "Anglo-Saxons into Celts: The Scottish Intellectuals 1760–1930." In Terence Brown, ed., *Celticism.* Amsterdam: Rodopi, 1996. 231–56.

Hughes, R.E. "Aspects of Welsh Lexicography in the Nineteenth Century with Special Reference to the Contribution of Daniel Silvan Evans." Unpublished MA thesis, University of Liverpool, 1941.

Jenkins, Geraint H., ed. *A Social History of the Welsh Language. Language and Community in the Nineteenth Century.* Cardiff: University of Wales Press, 1998.

Jenkins, Geraint H. *A Concise History of Wales.* Cambridge: Cambridge University Press, 2007.

Jenkins, R.T. and Helen M. Ramage. *A History of the Honourable Society of Cymmrodorion and of the Gwyneddigion and Cymreigyddion Societies (1751–1951).* London: Honourable Society of Cymmrodorion, 1951.

Jenkins, R.T. "Hanes Cymdeithas yr Eisteddfod Genedlaethol" [The History of the National Eisteddfod]. *Transactions of the Honourable Society of Cymmrodorion 1933–34–35* (1936), 139–55.

Jones, Bedwyr Lewis. *Yr Hen Bersoniaid Llengar* [The Old Literary Parsons]. Penarth: Gee Dros Wasg yr Eglwys yng Nghymru, 1963.

Jones, Dot. *The Coming of the Railways and Language Change in North Wales 1850–1900*. Aberystwyth: Centre for Advanced Welsh and Celtic Studies, 1995.

Jones, Dot. *Statistical Evidence Relating to the Welsh Language 1801–1911*. Cardiff: University of Wales Press, 1998.

Jones, Ieuan Gwynedd. "Language and Community in Nineteenth-century Wales." In David Smith, ed., *A People and a Proletariat: Essays in the History of Wales 1780–1980*. London: Pluto Press, 1980. 47–71.

Jones, Ieuan Gwynedd. "1848 and 1868: 'Brad y Llyfrau Gleision' and Welsh Politics." In I.G. Jones, *Mid-Victorian Wales: The Observers and the Observed*. Cardiff: University of Wales Press, 1992. 103–65.

Jones, Owen, and William Owen, eds. *Barddoniaeth Dafydd ab Gwilym* [The Poetry of Dafydd ab Gwilym]. Llundain: H. Baldwin, 1789.

Jones, Philip Henry, and Eiluned Rees, eds. *A Nation and its Books: A History of the Book in Wales*. Aberystwyth: National Library of Wales, 1998.

Jones, Philip Henry. "Printing and Publishing in the Welsh Language 1801–1914." In Geraint H. Jenkins, ed., *The Welsh Language and its Social Domains 1800–1911*. Cardiff: University of Wales Press, 2000. 317–47.

Jones, Thomas. *Y Gymraeg yn ei Disgleirdeb. Neu helaeth Eir-lyfr Cymraeg a Saesoneg / The British Language in its Lustre Or a Copious Dictionary of Welsh and English*. London: Mr Lawrence Baskerville, 1688.

Kidd, Colin. "Wales, the Enlightenment and the New British History," *The Welsh History Review* 25:2 (2010), 209–30.

Koch, John T., ed. *Celtic Culture. A Historical Encyclopedia*. 5 vols. Santa Barbara: ABC-Clio, 2006.

Le Stum, Philippe. *Le Néo-druidisme en Bretagne: Origine, Naissance et Développement, 1890–1914* [Neo-druidism in Brittany: Origin, Birth and Development]. Rennes: Ouest-France, 1998.

Lewis, Ceri W. "The Decline of Professional Poetry." In R. Geraint Gruffydd, ed., *A Guide to Welsh Literature c. 1530–1700*. Cardiff: University of Wales Press, 1997. 29–74.

Löffler, Marion. *Englisch und Kymrisch in Wales. Geschichte der Sprachsituation und Sprachpolitik* [Welsh and English in Wales: History of the Linguistic Situation and of Language Policies]. Hamburg: Kovač, 1994.

Löffler, Marion. "Nationalismus und Sprachentwicklung: Die Orthographie des Kymrischen im Neunzehnten Jahrhundert," unpublished manuscript, Second Congress of Celtic Studies in Germany, Bonn, 1997.

Löffler, Marion. *'A Book of Mad Celts': John Wickens and the Celtic Congress of Caernarfon 1904*. Llandysul: Gwasg Gomer, 2000.

Löffler, Marion. "Pan-Celticism around 1900." In Sabine Rieckhoff, ed., *Celtes et Gaulois dans l'Histoire, l'Historiographie et l'Idéologie Moderne* [Celts and Gauls in History, Historiography and Modern Ideology]. Glux-en-Glenne: Bibracte, 2006. 143–53.

Löffler, Marion. *The Literary and Historical Legacy of Iolo Morganwg, 1826–1926.* Cardiff: University of Wales Press, 2007.

Löffler, Marion. *Welsh Responses to the French Revolution. Press and Public Discourse.* Cardiff: University of Wales Press, 2012.

Löffler, Marion. "Failed Founding Fathers and Abandoned Sources: Edward Williams, Thomas Stephens and the Young J.E. Lloyd." In Neil Evans and Huw Pryce, eds., *Writing a Small Nation's Past: Wales in Comparative Perspective, 1850–1950.* Farnham: Ashgate, 2013. 67–81.

Miles, Dillwyn. *The Secret of the Bards of the Isle of Britain.* Llandybïe: Dinefwr, 1992.

Morgan, Prys. *The Eighteenth Century Renaissance.* Llandybïe: C. Davies, 1981.

Morgan, Prys. "From a Death to a View: The Hunt for a Welsh Past in the Romantic Period." In Eric Hobsbawm and Terence Ranger, eds., *The Invention of Tradition*, new ed. Cambridge: Cambridge University Press, 1992. 43–100.

Morgan, Prys. "Early Victorian Wales and its Crisis of Identity." In Laurence Brockliss and David Eastwood, eds., *A Union of Multiple Identities: The British Isles, c. 1750–1850.* Manchester: Manchester University Press, 1997. 95–109.

Morgan, Prys. "Lady Llanover (1802–1896), 'Gwenynen Gwent'," *Transactions of the Honourable Society of Cymmrodorion*, new series 13 (2007), 94–106.

Owen, Edward. *Catalogue of the MSS. Relating to Wales in the British Museum.* 2 vols., 4 pts. London: The Honourable Society of Cymmrodorion, 1900–22.

Parczewski, Alfons. *A Survey of the Language Map of Europe and a Sketch of an International Peace Union for the Protection of Linguistic Minorities.* Caernarfon/Paris: Paul Geuthner, 1904.

Phillips, Geraint. "Forgery and Patronage: Iolo Morganwg and Owain Myfyr." In Geraint H. Jenkins, ed., *A Rattleskull Genius: The Many Faces of Iolo Morganwg.* Cardiff: University of Wales Press, 2005. 203–23.

Price, Thomas. *Hanes Cymru* [A History of Wales]. Crughywel: Thomas Williams, 1836–1842.

Pryce, Huw. *J.E. Lloyd and the Creation of Welsh History: Renewing a Nation's Past.* Cardiff: University of Wales Press, 2011.

Pughe, William Owen. *Geiriadur Cenhedlaethol Cymraeg a Saesneg—A National Dictionary of the Welsh Language.* Denbigh: Gwasg Gee, 1891.

Stephens, Thomas. *The Literature of the Kymry: Being a Critical Essay on the History of the Language and Literature of Wales during the Twelfth and Two Succeeding Centuries.* Llandovery: William Rees, 1849.

Thomas, Mair Elvet. *The Welsh Spirit of Gwent.* Cardiff: University of Wales Press, 1988.

Thorne, David. "Cymreigyddion Y Fenni a Dechreuadau Ieitheg Cymharol yng Nghymru" [The Abergavenny Cymreigyddion Society and the Beginnings of Comparative Linguistics in Wales], *Cylchgrawn Llyfrgell Genedlaethol Cymru / National Library of Wales Journal* 27:1 (1991), 97–107.

Tyson Roberts, Gwyneth. *The Language of the Blue Books: the Perfect Instrument of Empire.* Cardiff: University of Wales Press, 1998.

Williams, Emyr W. "Liberalism in Wales and the Politics of Welsh Home Rule, 1886–1910," *Bulletin of the Board of Celtic Studies* 37 (1990), 191–207.

Williams, Glanmor. *Religion, Language, and Nationality in Wales.* Cardiff: University of Wales Press, 1979.

Williams, Jane. *A History of Wales Derived from Authentic Sources.* London: Longmans, Green, and Co., 1869.

CHAPTER 12

"Racy of the Soil": Young Ireland and the Cultural Production of Nationhood

Roisín Higgins

In 1842 the prospectus of the newspaper *The Nation* determined that its aim should be "to aid and organise the new movements going on among us; to make their growth deeper and more 'racy of the soil'; and above all, to direct the popular mind and the sympathies of educated men of all parties to the great end of Nationality."[1] *The Nation* was a publishing sensation, selling more than ten thousand copies a week at sixpence per copy and with an estimated readership of over a quarter of a million.[2] It was the organ of a group of men who would become known as "Young Ireland" and was a central part of a complex matrix through which they attempted to create and transmit a sense of Irish nationhood.[3] The Young Irelanders were an intellectual coterie who wanted to educate and politicize their fellow-countrymen. This was neither an original aim nor was it specifically Irish. However, it was undertaken in a decade during which revolution in France and famine in Ireland added sharper edges to Irish politics.

1 Society and Politics

Ireland entered the nineteenth century as part of the United Kingdom. The Act of Union between Britain and Ireland, which came into effect in 1801, dissolved the Irish Parliament and created a legislative union based in London. Ireland's immediate cultural outlook did not look robust. The removal of some political and literary figures to London following the dissolution of the Irish parliament greatly reduced Ireland's intellectual class, and the extension of English copyright laws to Ireland threatened the native publishing industry.[4] However,

---

1 *Prospectus of the Nation*, October 1842.
2 O'Sullivan, 44. Ann Andrews has argued that *The Nation*'s publication "heralded one of the most important developments in the history of Irish nationalism" (Andrews, 17).
3 The founders of *The Nation* were Thomas Davis, John Dillon, and Charles Gavan Duffy. For a comprehensive academic study of Young Ireland, see Quinn.
4 Tilley, 465.

educational and political developments in the 1820s and 1830s meant that Irish nationalists nevertheless reached the middle of the nineteenth century politically and culturally alert.

The early decades of the nineteenth century witnessed significant strides in the development of a more regular education system. Religious organizations expanded educational opportunities by setting up schools, and in 1831 a national school system of primary education was established. The state set up a National Education Board to promote, control, and largely finance education in Ireland. Within two years, almost eight hundred schools with over one hundred thousand pupils had been set up within or were brought within the state system. By the end of the century it catered for over half a million pupils. Denominational schools responded with their own expansion and catered for one hundred fifty thousand children by 1845. As a result, illiteracy levels were estimated at 51% of the population in 1841, and further reduced to 45% by 1845.[5] The ability to read was primarily associated with the young, non-rural population and with the English language. This literate, urban population was a vital audience for the Young Ireland agenda.

This period was also one of important political changes. The 1790s had been a pivotal decade in Irish history. The Society of United Irishmen had conjoined the ideas of Irish republicanism and separatism, and their armed insurrection in 1798 became an important touchstone for future Irish revolutionaries.[6] One of the crucial legacies of the campaign of the United Irishmen was that it politicized large sections of the Irish population. Heavily influenced by the politics of the French Revolution, radicals in Ireland saw 'the people' as central to their campaign and used popular culture to shape public opinion by employing genres which overcame the literacy barrier, such as ballads, prophecies, toasts, and oaths. These genres provided interfaces between the formal, private, written word and the more public oral tradition.[7] Catholics in Ireland (80% of the population) were further politicized by the campaign for Catholic emancipation led by Daniel O'Connell in the 1820s. The significance of O'Connell's campaign lay, not in its winning the right for Catholics to sit in Parliament (in 1829), but rather in its method. O'Connell created the first peaceful mass movement in Europe. A political sense of Catholic consciousness was formed through an emphasis on the power of demographic numbers and a concentration on shared grievances. The organization was funded by the 'Catholic rent': a subscription of one penny a month which was collected in

---

5 Boyce, 160.
6 Bartlett, 206.
7 Whelan, 72.

parishes throughout Ireland. By harnessing the infrastructure of the Catholic Church in this way, O'Connell brought large sections of the population—and a great deal of money—into the political movement.

2 Networks of Association

The key intellectual figure in the early years of the Young Ireland movement was Thomas Davis (1814–45), a young Dublin Protestant. He saw reading as a political act which was a vital part of national regeneration. Espousing knowledge as power, he argued that "a man could as well dig with his hands, as govern, or teach, or lead, without the elements of knowledge."[8] Davis had been active in his College Historical Society and suggested the founding of an 'Irish Lyceum' to cultivate the study of Irish language, literature, and history.[9] He was part of an intellectual culture in which men sought to create associations and clubs that would further their understanding of Ireland through the study of its science and arts. By 1848 Thomas Antisell, a Young Irelander and physician, reflected that one of the most remarkable features of the age was "the formation of associations, the union of men to carry out a single idea or object [...] By means of it, men of one mind, through a whole country understand one another, and easily act together."[10]

Prominent in this inquisitive culture was the pursuit of antiquarianism, which was well established in Ireland by the 1830s.[11] The main institutional outlet for this interest, the Royal Irish Academy, had been formed in 1785; its findings were published in *Transactions* and, after 1836, in its *Proceedings*, which was cheaper and less academic in tone in order to appeal to a wider readership.[12] The establishment of the *Dublin Penny Journal* in 1832 was also an attempt to broaden access to historical and scientific topics, as it was aimed at the artisan and lower middle classes. It was able to take advantage of reduced costs in print technology and a network of educational institutes and reading rooms to extend its message.[13] Temperance reading rooms and mechanics' institutes had become popular among this demographic from the 1820s, providing spaces in which readership was linked to the promotion of social and moral

---

8   *The Nation*, 5 October 1844.
9   Davis, 24.
10 Antisell, 3.
11 Tilley, 149; see also Quinn, 29–35.
12 Tilley, 465.
13 Ibid., 472–475.

improvement.[14] A survey in 1852 found that half of the members of the mechanics' institutes were shopkeepers and their assistants, and one-fourth were tradesmen: carpenters, masons and workmen.[15] The editor of *The Nation*, Charles Gavan Duffy, would later call these 'reading men' the greatest supporters of the Young Ireland movement. He was a particular advocate of educating working men and saw them as part of the main audience for the group's cultural nationalist output.[16]

3 *The Nation*

Into this mix of political reform, social advancement, and educational and cultural activity was launched the newspaper *The Nation*. Duffy had originally wanted to call it *The National*, in sympathy with the Paris journal of that name. However, he eventually settled on *The Nation* and recalled, "We desired to make Ireland a nation and the name would be a fitting prelude to the attempt."[17] The founders of *The Nation* were all men under thirty and included both Catholics and Protestants. They were given the name 'Young Ireland' by an English journalist who saw similarities with romantic nationalist groups in Europe and used the sobriquet as a form of derision. Eventually the term became widespread and was adopted by members of the group themselves.[18] It also had the advantage of differentiating them from O'Connell and 'Old Ireland.'

For the Young Irelanders the key elements of nation-building were the creation of a body of knowledge about Ireland and a population educated in that knowledge. Ignorance, they argued, had not been Ireland's fault, but its misfortune: "It was in the interests of our ruler to keep us ignorant, that we might be weak."[19] Thomas Davis's essay "Influences of Education" opens with an exhortation to "Educate, that you may be free." Davis argued that the education of the people was the only means for them to become strong enough to gain freedom. He wanted the middle classes to take responsibility for their own learning:

---

14   Ireland's first newsroom opened in Belfast in 1782 and supplied newspapers and periodicals to libraries, commercial libraries, and hotels open to wealthy readers. For a comprehensive survey see Feeney.
15   Leslie, 8; discussed in Legg, 252.
16   Legg, 251.
17   Duffy 1881, 31.
18   Ibid., 291.
19   *The Nation*, 5 October 1844.

> Do our readers understand this? Is what we have said *clear* to *you*, reader!—whether you are a shopkeeper or a lawyer, a farmer or a doctor? [...] you must feel that it is your duty to your family and to yourself, to your country and to God, to *act* upon it, to go and remove some of that ignorance which makes you and your neighbours weak, and therefore makes Ireland a poor province.[20]

The Nation presented serious topics in an accessible way. The Young Irelanders used print in all its forms to spread their message: songs, poems, newsprint, books, and pamphlets. They fully understood the potential of songs in spreading popular nationalist sentiments, and in the first three years of its existence *The Nation* published eight hundred ballads.[21] While most were quickly forgotten, some continued to be sung, and it is for these that the paper is best remembered. A selection of ballads from the newspaper was published in book form in May 1843: *The Spirit of the Nation* cost sixpence and was aimed at a mass audience. Within two months of publication it was claimed that one hundred copies a day were being sold. This success led to the publication of two new editions in January 1844, "one for the drawing room" and the other "for the millions, in the little pocket volume that the farmer can take to the fair, and the labourer to the field with him, and which either can purchase for a trifle."[22] In June the publishers announced a further edition which would be issued in monthly parts for a shilling.[23] *The Voice of the Nation: A Handbook of Nationality* was published in 1844 as a companion to *The Spirit of the Nation*. It contained articles that had appeared in *The Nation* and claimed, with characteristic understatement, that Nationality had never had an organ until *The Nation* was published: "Other political writers advocated it, wished it, helped it, but we devoted ourselves to it [...]"[24]

The Nation was the vital component in the Young Ireland programme. It served a wide and attentive audience and determinedly advertised all the related publications from the Young Ireland stable. It was used to generate excitement and interest in all aspects of the creation of nationhood. For Duffy the purpose of the newspaper was not "to chronicle the small beer of current politics, but to teach opinions."[25] Its popularity meant that *The Nation* was

---

20   Davis, 225.
21   Kenny, 44.
22   *The Nation*, 27 January 1844, in Zimmermann, 80.
23   O'Sullivan, 59–60.
24   Quoted in O'Sullivan, 73.
25   Duffy 1898, 65.

eventually seen as a threat to both the Repeal Association and the British authorities.[26]

4   The Repeal Reading Rooms

Daniel O'Connell had created the template for mobilizing the Irish middle classes on behalf of a political movement. He followed his success on Catholic Emancipation with a campaign for the return of an Irish parliament through the Repeal of the Act of Union. The Loyal National Repeal Association, founded in 1840, utilized a network of local committees and branches, employed mass meetings to raise awareness, and collected funds through the 'Repeal rent,' which was a minimum of a penny a month. The names of subscribers were printed in newspapers, clearly demonstrating that this was not a secret oath-bound political movement but one that was modern and respectable. Repeal reading rooms were part of this organizational infrastructure and were funded out of Repeal Association coffers. O'Connell had little interest in the reading rooms as cultural spaces and viewed them rather as meeting places to spread information about the Repeal movement and and collect funds for it. As a result, the reading rooms received limited funding from the Repeal coffers.[27] For Thomas Davis, Charles Gavan Duffy, and their Young Ireland associates, however, Repeal reading rooms were part of a much broader campaign to cultivate and promote Irish nationality.

The first Repeal reading rooms were instituted in 1842 and formal rules were drawn up in 1844.[28] They appealed to the aspirant middle classes who were generally literate and who sought respectability through political reform. Reading rooms were male spaces throughout the nineteenth century in Ireland;[29] they were to be opened in any district where two thousand enrolled Repealers had subscribed a shilling each within the current year. The subscription gave access to the reading room and its contents. The rooms were to be used for signing petitions, voter registration, and routine Repeal business, after which a reader would be appointed to read aloud from public journals, books, or tracts.[30] The Repeal Association provided an allowance towards the costs of

---

26   The break with O'Connell in 1846 led to the banning of *The Nation* from Repeal reading rooms, a move that was very unpopular among those frequenting the rooms (Barnes, 57).
27   Quinn, 23.
28   For a more detailed account of the Repeal reading rooms, see R. Higgins.
29   Townend, 24–25.
30   Barnes, 51–54.

rent, fire, and light, and an additional £1-6-0 was allowed for newspapers. The rooms replicated the model developed by the Temperance movement, and the allocation of funds was refused to any reading room held in a public house or without the approval of the local clergy.[31] There were eighty-five Repeal reading rooms in Ireland by the end of April 1845. Average attendance was estimated at between fifty and one hundred people, a quarter of whom were described as youths.[32] A report on the rooms from the Repeal Association claimed "peculiar satisfaction [...] as to the effect of the Reading Rooms, in promoting habits of temperance, morality and patriotism, *especially* among the youth."[33]

In 1843 the Association had drawn up instructions for its local representatives, known as Repeal Wardens. Their duties included receiving from the Association a weekly newspaper for every two hundred associates, or a three-day paper for every four hundred enrolled. Moreover, for ten pounds sent to the Association the members of a locality were entitled to a free weekly newspaper.[34] *The Nation* was particularly important, and its lively tone added greatly to its popularity. Three hundred copies were sent weekly to newsrooms and teetotal societies, and eleven hundred went to Repeal Wardens to be read aloud at meetings.[35] As well as *The Nation*, newspapers such as *The Freeman's Journal* and *The Pilot* were supplied by the Repeal Association to reading rooms, along with books on or by Daniel O'Connell, reports from the Repeal Association, and Dr. Robert Kane's *Industrial Resources of Ireland*. Kane's book, first published in 1844, argued that Ireland possessed the natural resources needed to industrialize and modernize; it found support among all political groups, was a popular acquisition in working-men's clubs and private libraries, and reached a wide audience for the price of 7s.[36] As the popularity of Kane's book suggests, for neither Old nor Young Ireland did Irishness mean turning away from modernization. Despite appeals to Ireland's history, they both recognized the importance of industry and science to the cause of independence.

One significant function of the reading rooms was to serve as a repository for formal information. The O'Connellite argument in Ireland was not primarily about the integrity of Irish history and culture, but was premised on an economic and moral case for self-government. Repeal membership cards

---

31 Ibid.; Townend, 20–27.
32 Ray, 333.
33 Ibid.
34 O'Connell, 9–10.
35 Duffy 1881, 387.
36 Adelman, 549–51.

included the dates of significant historical events alongside information on Ireland's land mass, population, revenue, exports, and military population, in order to challenge the fact that it did not have its own Parliament.[37] An appeal to history was contained in the phrase "It was so it will be," which appeared under an image of the Irish Parliament building that was dissolved in 1801. O'Connell understood the emotional power of employing historically significant locations and symbols during his mass meetings, but unlike Young Ireland, his nationalism was pragmatic and political rather than cultural.

For the Young Irelanders, on the other hand, building a case for Repeal was only part of a broader agenda of creating a culture of Irish nationality.[38] Thomas Davis argued that the Repeal Association, having committed itself to the establishment of reading rooms, had "constituted itself the Schoolmaster of the People of Ireland, and must be prepared to carry out this pretention." He contended that "for each separate School—we beg pardon, Reading room—the [Repeal] committee should make separate arrangements."[39] To this end Davis and his fellow Young Irelanders set about not only recommending reading materials for their followers but creating the necessary literature. Davis also suggested that the basic contents of reading rooms should include the Ordnance Index map of Ireland and a townland map of the neighbourhood as well as maps of the five continents. These would supplement the Reports of the Repeal Association that would "soon be a perfect manual of the industrial statistics, topography, history, and county, municipal, and general institutions of Ireland."[40] Among Davis's papers, discovered after his death, was an agenda outlining lists and projects to be undertaken which would map, record, and disseminate all aspects of Irish life, including historical buildings, pictures, busts, statues, a musical circulating library, an Irish biographical dictionary, an illustrated history, and reprints of historical pamphlets.[41]

5 The *Library of Ireland*

In 1845 Davis and Duffy undertook the ambitious *Library of Ireland* series with the clear aim of creating a history for Irish nationality: "To give the country a

---

37 Loyal National Repeal Association membership card, 1845, Burns Library, Boston College.
38 Quinn 1881, 81.
39 Duffy 1845, 243.
40 Ibid., 245.
41 Duffy 1895, 228.

National Library, exact enough for the wisest, high enough for the purest, and cheap enough for all readers."[42] This series published a book every month for two years between 1845 and 1847. In its original form it comprised twenty-two volumes, at one shilling each in paper wrappers.[43] Each title was also issued at several prices and in different binding types in order to reach the widest possible audience. This series was the first large-scale enterprise to be carried out by the publisher James Duffy. He warned that it would require "an immense circulation" to enable its continuation and urged all persons interested in Irish education and nationality to support it.[44] In April 1846 *The Nation* carried a notice stating that due to increasing demand and the inability of the public to procure volumes in towns that had no bookseller, the publisher was "desirous of appointing an active intelligent young man, as agent for the sale of the Library" in sixty towns in Ireland.[45]

This emphasis on the importance of history was, as James Quinn has argued, a new development in Irish nationalism.[46] It was also an ambitious attempt to direct the reading of the lower middle classes. Thomas Davis had bemoaned the fact that the class which was soon to become the rulers of Ireland could generally not afford books and relied instead on "the newspaper, the meeting, and the occasional serial of very modest merits," or, more regrettably, was driven to reading foreign books.[47] Duffy recalled that for the series Davis "ransacked the past [...] to rear a generation whose lives would be strengthened and ennobled by the knowledge that there had been great men of their race, and great actions done on the soil they trod; whose resolution would be fortified by knowing that their ancestors had left their mark for ever on some of the most memorable eras of European history."[48] The *Library of Ireland* covered great orators, politicians and leaders; it produced histories of Irish literature as well as commissioning writers to craft stories which conveyed messages of Irish life and heroism.[49] One hundred years after their publication it was said (in a volume to mark the centenary of Davis's death) of the

---

42 Davis, xiii.
43 O'Hegarty, 110.
44 Benson, 35.
45 *The Nation*, 4 April 1846. It was also requested that "none will apply but those who can be recommended by the Catholic Clergy of their district."
46 Quinn, 60.
47 Davis, 353.
48 Duffy 1895, 113.
49 For a list of the first twenty-two volumes published in the *Library of Ireland* see O'Hegarty, 109–11.

books in the series that "They were the beginning of patriotic literature in Ireland, and their influence has been material and lasting."[50]

History was the bedrock of the series because, in the words of Thomas D'Arcy McGee, it was the "common inheritance."[51] McGee, a Young Irelander and contributor to *The Nation*, wrote a well-respected history of some twenty seventeenth-century Irish writers as part of the series.[52] He reached back to a century which, for him, represented the last remarkable vestige of independence from the English yoke, and therefore offered a romantic touchstone for the nationalist mind.[53] For McGee the earlier century represented one of a shared, if tumultuous, history rather than the embedded divisions of the eighteenth century. The emphasis on Irish history offered Young Irelanders the possibility of creating a nationhood that was rooted neither in religion nor in ancestral blood, both of which were seen to exclude Protestants (and therefore many Young Irelanders). However, the construction of Irishness as springing from environment rather than race ignored the inequalities in Irish life and the consequences of its sectarianism. A version of Irish history that sought to ignore the embedded divisions of class, religion, and gender was therefore always riddled with contradictions.[54]

By 1847 the *Library of Ireland* was discontinued in the midst of the Famine. Nevertheless, the series encouraged the publisher James Duffy to undertake other similar literary publications, and he produced many other little books of a similar size and binding.[55] Moreover, it was an idea Charles Gavan Duffy would revive (with far less success) in 1893 with the *New Irish Library*, which consisted of thirteen volumes. In 1855 Gavan Duffy had emigrated to Australia, where he enjoyed a very successful political career. He returned to Europe two decades later and found his native country experiencing its high point in cultural nationalism, known as the Celtic Revival. Duffy became President of the Irish Literary Society, but his efforts to publish works of Young Ireland literature brought him into conflict with W.B. Yeats over their lack of aesthetic merit. At the inaugural meeting of the Irish Literary Theatre in 1899, Yeats was reported to have said that Thomas Davis "was as fond of literature *qua* literature

---

50 O'Hegarty, 110. Seán T. O'Ceallaigh, the President of Ireland, wrote the Forward for this commemorative volume (see also Andrews).
51 D'Arcy McGee, 247.
52 McGee, 28.
53 Ibid.
54 Boyce, 156–58.
55 O'Hegarty, 113.

as any man, but when he wrote for Ireland, it was not the book he was thinking of but what the book might do."[56]

6 Confederate Clubs

The Young Irelanders split from the Repeal Association in 1846, ostensibly over O'Connell's determination that all members should renounce physical force. They formed the Irish Confederation in January 1847 and were then free to advance their own educational and cultural agendas, though they were deprived of the reach and influence provided by the O'Connell movement. Nevertheless, six months after its founding, the Confederation claimed ten thousand members.[57] The Young Irelanders had been frustrated by the lack of commitment shown by the Repeal Association towards the reading rooms and their contents, and saw in the creation of Confederate Clubs the perfect vehicle for the promotion of reading and knowledge. It was determined that these clubs would "have not only books and papers to read, but lectures, discussions, and business meetings [... and] would breed a race of thinkers that it [would] be impossible for politicians to cajole, or tyrants to keep under."[58] Each club was to be furnished with a list of appropriate books. Duffy was the Chairman of the Committee of Organization for the Confederation and was deeply influential at its inception. He argued that the new organization must "not stop at being a mere physical, but must become a moral and intellectual occupation" and recommended that classes and lectures should be held on Irish history, Irish literature, Irish industrial resources, and industrial studies generally.[59]

However, the Irish Confederation was formed during the worst period of the Irish famine, and this crisis necessarily shaped the nature of the information the Confederation collected and disseminated. *The Nation* and *The Freeman's Journal* published a "Famine Census" in which they listed deaths by parish, and the Confederation Committee passed a motion asking the Secretary to contact members in order to gather statistics on the famine and collateral information which would be communicated on a weekly basis.[60] Duffy continued to endorse the view that power lay in knowledge, but the emphasis was shifting. He wanted the Confederate Clubs to be used to teach the country to strengthen

---

56 Quoted in G. Higgins, 115.
57 Duffy 1847, 3.
58 *The Nation*, July 1847.
59 Duffy 1847, 5 and 11.
60 Royal Irish Academy (hereafter cited as RIA) 23.H.44, [54], Minutes of the Irish Confederation, 18 March 1847.

itself by developing and applying all the resources of the island—by awakening enterprise and by diffusing practical knowledge for each class according to its wants and by "guiding the fervor of the soul, the sincerity of purpose, and all the great moral emotions which were wasted in words, to practical services for the country."[61] The first duty of urban clubs was the encouragement of manufacture, while rural clubs were to work for the full recognition and protection of all those oppressed or imperiled by British legislation.[62]

Confederate Clubs were to be formed in any neighborhood that counted at least twenty members of the Irish Confederation.[63] It was determined that each member should pay whatever sum he could reasonably afford, but not less than one shilling. A further weekly collection of funds was to be undertaken in each club.[64] The Confederation's accounts show that members' subscriptions varied, with many of the original members paying £5 but with the majority of others paying a shilling or 2/6. Income grew throughout the first year of its founding. Subscriptions from 20 October until 10 November 1847 were recorded as £47-15-11, and similar amounts were raised in the previous months. By April 1848 they had raised over £135 in Dublin alone.[65] Some women also paid subscriptions to the Confederation, but these were a small minority; other members chose to remain anonymous, but again, their number was small. Subscribers to the Irish Confederation were drawn primarily from the Catholic middle classes. Lists of members show a large number of priests, merchants, manufacturers, shopkeepers, farmers, doctors, solicitors, and barristers. Booterstown in Dublin was unusual in that its membership consisted of a cork cutter, two builders, a bricklayer, a painter, two gardeners, a servant, and a carpenter.[66]

The geographical spread of subscribers was eventually wide; however, unlike the O'Connellite movement, the initial aim was not to create a mass movement, "an undistinguished mass of supporters" (which this group of intellectuals would have struggled to achieve), but was instead designed to attract "only such Irishmen as thoroughly understand the principles it professes, and heartily desire to work them out."[67] Starting from a Dublin base, it was the intention of the Confederation to grow the clubs out through the suburbs and then into the country. As cosmopolitan meeting places they have been described as

---

61 Duffy 1847, 5.
62 Ibid., 6–7.
63 Ibid., 10.
64 Ibid., 7.
65 RIA 23.4.63, Income book of the Irish Confederation, 23 January 1847 – 23 June 1848.
66 RIA 23.H.40, Address book of the Irish Confederation, 1847–48.
67 Duffy 1847, 9.

"moderate literary groups."[68] However, by March 1848 the records of the Confederation listed thirty-five clubs in Dublin, ninety-one in the rest of the country, and seven in England.[69] Their popularity outside the capital grew throughout the first half of 1848.

Minutes of the Confederation indicate that it subsidized some publications, primarily speeches and pamphlets, which were commissioned by the subcommittee for Public Instruction. In March 1847 the Council of the Confederation voted that Jonathan Swift's *Irish Political Economy*, which had been edited by John Mitchel in a new edition, should be adopted and distributed with its sanction. It was distributed through the four booksellers who had contributed to advertising the book.[70] The dissemination of ideas continued to be vital and the volume was priced at 2d. As Mitchel explained in his Preface, in order "that everybody who can read in all Ireland may have an opportunity of learning what this country's complaint is, and what the infallible remedy, the publication is made in the smallest space and cheapest form."[71]

The Confederation was itself beset with divisions over the issue of physical force, and John Mitchel, an increasingly important and militant member of the group, built up his support among local clubs and set up his own newspaper, *The United Irishman*, in February 1848.[72] The Paris revolution strengthened the position of the militants and galvanized the membership of Confederate Clubs, with many adopting resolutions of delight and admiration of the brave French people. The following month, three prominent Confederates, including Mitchel, were arrested on charges of sedition. The numbers of the Clubs grew exponentially during the summer of 1848, from forty to two hundred twenty-five in just seven weeks.[73] It is estimated that there were over two hundred thirty Clubs in Ireland by the time of Young Ireland's abortive rebellion in 1848, with a membership of forty-five thousand, mostly located outside Dublin.[74] However, the nature of the Clubs had changed entirely, and lectures now covered such topics as "The Pike: Its History and Use" and "The Chemical Properties of Sulphur, Nitrate, and Charcoal, With Their Compounds as Gunpowder &c."[75] Obtaining arms and training in their use became a central feature of the

---

68   Koseki, 6.
69   RIA 23.H.41, Correspondence of the Confederation and Lists of Clubs, May 1847 – March 1848.
70   RIA 23.H.44, [61], Minutes of the Irish Confederation, 24 March 1847.
71   Swift, v.
72   Owens, 55.
73   Koseki, 13.
74   Owens, 56.
75   Ibid., 54.

Confederate Clubs until they were suppressed by the authorities. The Young Ireland rising of 1848 failed to excite widespread rebellion in the country, but it had raised the standard of revolt, and on 26 July 1848 Dublin Castle issued a proclamation making membership of a political club grounds for arrest.[76] The Repeal reading rooms and Confederate Clubs were effectively squashed. *The Nation* was also suppressed, and many Young Ireland leaders were transported as convicts or went into self-imposed exile.[77]

7 Conclusions

The death of Daniel O'Connell in 1847, the ravages of famine, and the suppression of Young Ireland meant that nationalist movements faded in the years immediately following 1848; but reading rooms thrived as civic or religious spaces, and the act of reading retained its politicized nature throughout the rest of the century in Ireland.[78] The Fenians, the revolutionary organization that developed from the 1850s, understood the importance of cultural and sporting networks for political subterfuge. This was well expressed by William O'Brien, who saw in the founding of a Literary Club in Munster in the 1870s "a protection and a recruiting ground for the secret organization," which might, "elevate and broaden our conspirators' conception of patriotic duty."[79] Reading rooms and literary societies remained as central components of all elements of Irish nationalism in the nineteenth century. For some advocates of reading rooms, like the land reformer Michael Davitt in the 1880s, the education of working men was an essential part of the national movement. Other groups, like the Gaelic League in the 1890s, understood the contribution of such rooms to the spread of the Irish language.[80] The historian of reading rooms Paul Townend has argued that the coherence of Irish nationalism in the nineteenth century "was located less in the details of political or social/cultural agendas, and more in the way in which nationalism was experienced, spread, or cultivated."[81] In this sense the 1840s were a vital decade in forging the significance of reading for the national movement. This was a critical juncture when just over half the

---

76 Koseki, 35.
77 *The Nation* was revived by Duffy a few months later. He softened its political tone, but the newspaper never attained its previous popularity and power. Nevertheless, *The Nation* at its height set a standard by which all subsequent Irish newspapers would be judged.
78 Townend, 27 and 29.
79 O'Brien, 30–31.
80 Townend, 35–37.
81 Ibid., 39.

population had become literate, and it was with these readers in mind that cultural nationalists focused their considerable attentions on creating cheap and accessible reading material and on creating communities where men might read.

Bibliography

Adelman, Juliana. "*The Industrial Resources of Ireland* by Robert Kane." In Murphy, ed., 546–52.

Andrews, Ann. *Newspapers and Newsmakers: The Dublin Nationalist Press in the Mid-Nineteenth Century*. Oxford: Oxford University Press, 2015.

Antisell, Thomas. *The Introductory Address to the Irish Polytechnic Institute Read at the First General Meeting, on Wednesday April 12th 1848*. Dublin: Sam Nolan Printer, 1848.

Barnes, Margaret. "Repeal Reading Rooms." *An Leabharlann: Journal of the Library Association of Ireland* 23:2 (1965), 53–57.

Bartlett, Thomas. *Ireland: A History*. Cambridge University Press, 2010.

Benson, Charles. "The Dublin Book Trade." In Murphy, ed., 27–46.

Boyce, George D. *Nationalism in Ireland*. London: Routledge, 1991.

D'Arcy McGee, Thomas. *Irish Writers of the Seventeenth Century*. Dublin: James Duffy, 1846.

Davis, Thomas. *Essays, Literary and Historical*, ed. David James O'Donoghue. Dundalk: W. Tempest, Dundalgan Press, 1914.

Duffy, Charles Gavan, ed. *Thomas Davis: Literary and Historical Essays*. Dublin: James Duffy, 1845.

Duffy, Charles Gavan. *The Irish Confederation, No. 3, Report on Organisation, and Instructions for the Formation and Government of Confederate Clubs*. Dublin: William Holden, 1847.

Duffy, Charles Gavan. *Young Ireland: A Fragment of Irish History, 1840–1850*. New York: D. Appleton, 1881.

Duffy, Charles Gavan. *Short Life of Thomas Davis, 1840–1846*. London: T. Fisher Unwin, 1895.

Duffy, Charles Gavan. *My Life in Two Hemispheres, Volume One*. New York: The Macmillan Co., 1898.

Feeney, Mary. "Print for the People: The Growth of Popular Writings and Reading Facilities in Ireland, 1820–50." Dublin: M.Litt. Thesis, Trinity College Dublin, 1982.

Higgins, Geraldine. *Heroic Revivals: from Carlyle to Yeats*. New York: Palgrave Macmillan, 2012.

Higgins, Roisín. "The *Nation* Reading Rooms." In Murphy, ed., 262–73.

Kenny, Desmond. "The Ballads of the *Nation*: A Study in a Popular Concept," *Cahiers du Centre d'Études Irlandaises* 3 (1978), 31–45.

Koseki, Takashi. *Dublin Confederate Clubs and the Repeal Movement*. Tokyo: Institute of Comparative Economic Studies, Hosei University, 1992.

Legg, Marie-Louise. "Libraries." In Murphy, ed., 243–61.

Leslie, T.E. Cliffe. "An Inquiry into the Progress and Present Condition of Mechanics' Institutions, Part I." *Dublin: Transactions of the Dublin Statistical Society*, Vol. III Session 5, 1851/1852. 1–15.

Murphy, James H., ed. *The Oxford History of the Irish Book, Volume IV: The Irish Book in English 1800–1891*. Oxford: Oxford University Press, 2011.

O'Connell, Daniel. *Instructions for the Appointment of Repeal Wardens and Collectors of the Repeal Fund, Their Duties & c*. Dublin: J. Browne, 1843.

O'Hegarty, Patrick Sarsfield. "The 'Library of Ireland' 1845–1847." In M.J. MacManus, ed., *Thomas Davis and Young Ireland*. Dublin: The Stationery Office, 1945. 109–13.

O'Sullivan, Tadhg. *The Young Irelanders*. Tralee: The Kerryman Ltd., 1944.

Owens, Gary. "Popular mobilization and the rising of 1848: the clubs of the Irish Confederation". In Laurence M. Geary, ed., *Rebellion and Remembrance in Modern Ireland*. Dublin: Four Courts, 2001. 51–63.

Quinn, James. *Young Ireland and the Writing of Irish History*. Dublin: University College Dublin Press, 2015.

Ray, Thomas M. "First Quarterly Report upon Repeal Reading Rooms," *Reports of the Parliamentary Committee of the Loyal National Repeal Association of Ireland, Vol. 2*. Dublin: J. Browne, 1845.

Swift, Jonathan. *Irish Political Economy*, ed. John Mitchel. Dublin: William Holden, printed for the Irish Confederation, 1847.

Tilley, Elizabeth. "Periodicals." In Murphy, ed., 144–72.

Tilley, Elizabeth. "The Royal Irish Academy and Antiquarianism." In Murphy, ed., 463–76.

Townend, Paul. "'Academies of nationality': the reading room and Irish national movements, 1838–1905." In Lawrence W. McBride, ed., *Reading Irish Histories: Texts, Contexts, and Memory in Modern Ireland*. Dublin: Four Courts Press, 2003. 19–39.

Whelan, Kevin. *The Tree of Liberty: Radicalism, Catholicism and the Construction of Irish Identity 1760–1830*. Cork: Cork University Press in association with Field Day, 1996.

Williams, Mark. "History, the Interregnum and the Exiled Irish." In Mark Williams and Stephen Paul Forrest, eds., *Constructing the Past: Writing Irish History, 1600–1800*. Woodbridge: Boydell, 2010. 27–48.

Zimmermann, George Denis. *Songs of Irish Rebellion: Irish Political Street Ballads and Rebel Songs, 1780–1900*. Dublin: Four Courts Press, 2002.

CHAPTER 13

Competing National Movements: School Associations and Cultural Nationalism in the Baltic Region

Jörg Hackmann

Since there were no institutions such as the *matica* or the *macierz szkolna* in the Baltic provinces of the tsarist empire, the framework for a comparative perspective has to be conceived somewhat more broadly, with reference in general to the role of school education in national associations before the First World War. School associations may be regarded as part of historical civil society, and in this context education refers in particular to non-dominant ethnic groups and their striving to develop their own social elites. It is also necessary to consider the transfers and entanglements between national associations in the Habsburg and the tsarist empires, based on the similar premises of the emancipation of small nations and on attempts by the traditional (German) elites to retain their position, not least through educational politics.

1   The Baltic Region

The focus here will be on the Baltic provinces of the tsarist empire, with special emphasis on the Estonian case.[1] The term 'Baltic provinces' (*ostzeiskie gubernii* in Russian) comprises the provinces of Estland,[2] Livonia (Livland) and Courland, which cover most of the territory of today's Estonia and Latvia with the exception of Latgale, the eastern region of Latvia. Before 1917 the administrative divisions between these provinces did not coincide with ethnic boundaries. In particular Livonia, the largest province, was populated by Estonians in the north and Latvians in the south, who also inhabited the province of Courland. The provinces of Estland and Livonia (except the Polish parts

---

1   On the history of the Baltic region see in general: Kasekamp; Plakans 2011; and Kirby. In German there is a very brief presentation by Ralph Tuchtenhagen (2005) and broader descriptions focusing on the German aspects of Baltic history (von Pistohlkors; Wittram; Garleff). On the Estonian and Latvian nations see also Raun 1991; Plakans 1995.
2   The province of Estonia was not identical with today's territory of Estonia.

known as Inflanty) were under Swedish rule from the mid-sixteenth and the early seventeenth centuries, respectively. In 1710 they came under Russian rule during the Great Northern War, which after the Third Partition of Poland in 1795 also included Courland. From 1801 to 1876 these three provinces were administered by a Governor General in Riga, but tsarist politics in particular since the 1880s focused on tightening central control of the region. This tendency went along with strengthening the influence of the Russian language, which had a significant impact on education policies, as will be shown below.[3] The territories of today's Lithuania did not belong to the tsarist Baltic provinces; instead the Lithuanians experienced a specific tsarist cultural and educational politics, in particular after the defeat of the 1863 uprising in Poland and Lithuania.[4]

2   Social Change and Nation Formation

According to the tsarist census of 1897, the Baltic provinces were populated by about 2.4 million people, which consisted, according to their mother tongue, of Latvians (44.8 per cent), Estonians (37.1 per cent), Germans (6.9 per cent), and Russians (4.8 per cent).[5] The issue of nationality requires some clarification. National historiographies often present nations as anachronistic notions, or at least describe their development as a straightforward progress. German historiography focused for a long time on the influence of German pastors and intellectuals in fostering the national movements, thus justifying German cultural hegemony in the region. Against such one-sided national perspectives, Miroslav Hroch's concept of the formation of (small) nations provides a more useful analytical tool.[6] Hroch has analyzed the Estonian case, among others, and his approach has influenced several researchers of Baltic history.[7]

What is important for analyzing the role of schooling in nation-building processes is the fact that until the mid-nineteenth century, the concepts of the Estonian and Latvian nations were based on (external) linguistic assignments, whereas the Estonian-speaking population referred to themselves as

---

3 On Russian politics in the Baltic region see Brüggemann.
4 Staliūnas; Subačius.
5 Raun 1984, based on Troinitskii, vol. 19, 21 and 49.
6 Hroch 1985 (first as Hroch 1968) and in a wider European perspective: Hroch 2005. See also Hroch's comment in *Nationalities Papers* (2010).
7 Raun and Plakans; Wohlfart; Laar 2005. See also Plakans 1974; Hackmann 2010.

maarahvas—'indigenous people'—and started only in the 1860s to define themselves as 'Eesti.'[8] In a similar way, the notion of a group defined by Latvian national identity emerged only from the strivings of an urban middle class in the late 1860s.[9]

The Estonian and Latvian peasant population was widely living in serfdom until the beginning of the nineteenth century, when debates about the abolition of serfdom emerged, comparing the situation to enslaved populations in the European colonies and North America.[10] The first steps toward legal abolition were taken in 1804, followed by laws in 1816 and 1819 granting limited personal freedom to the peasants, but no land. Full emancipation, however, came only with further reforms after 1849, which made it possible for peasants to become the owners of the fields they were cultivating. Another important step was the introduction of municipal self-administration in the villages in 1866, which increased the relevance of literacy. Among the consequences of the peasants' liberation was, as elsewhere, an increased mobility from rural areas into towns. In the Baltic region this led first of all to the growth of Riga, whose population rose from 170,000 in 1881 to over 500,000 in 1913,[11] and to a lesser degree to rising numbers of inhabitants in cities like Tallinn/Reval or Liepāja/Libau. In addition, a class of relatively wealthy and independent Estonian and Latvian peasants emerged, forming the social background of cultural nation-building, which was regarded as a national 'awakening'—an *ärkamisaeg* in Estonian and an *atmoda* in Latvian.[12]

3   Literacy and Schooling before 1800

The tsarist census of 1897 also reveals a rate of literacy in the Baltic provinces that was exceptionally high in the tsarist context: in the province of Estland and most parts of Livonia it was above ninety per cent, and only in eastern Courland was it below eighty per cent.[13] This observation requires a look at the traditions of schooling in the region.

---

8   On nineteenth-century Estonian history see: Raun 1981; Jansen 2007.
9   Hanovs 2012; Plakans 2011.
10 In particular: Merkel; Petri.
11 Hirschhausen, 48.
12 This was the life-long focus of Ea Jansen's research; see in particular: Jansen 2012; Jansen 2007; Jansen and Arukaevu; Jansen 1993.
13 Plakans 2011, 233–34; Karjahärm and Sirk, 150, based on Troinitskii, vol. 49, x–xi; Vahtre, Karjahärm and Rosenberg, 282.

Since the times of Swedish rule (from the mid-sixteenth century until 1710) a widely spread web of primary schools existed following the Church Law of 1686, which required the establishment of native language schools in every parish as a precondition for religious education.[14] The main idea, as textbooks reveal, was primarily to teach the Lutheran catechism and to form loyal subjects of the king. Although the degree of peasant literacy was presumably not very high throughout the eighteenth century, it began to rise significantly at the end of the century, when already at least two-thirds of the Estonian population were able to read and write.[15] Public schooling was supported not only by the institutions of the Protestant church but also by the governor of Livonia, George Browne (in charge 1762–92), and by school laws (*Schulordnungen*) requiring schooling for every boy, whereas the number of primary schools in Courland declined at the end of the eighteenth century after the region became part of the tsarist empire in 1795.[16]

4   The Impact of Estophiles and Lettophiles

The rising level of peasant schooling during the Enlightenment was due first of all to the impact of Lutheran parish priests and the so-called *literati* who migrated from Germany to the Baltic region. In the towns they could preach in German, as Johann Gottfried Herder did in Riga from 1764–69; but in the landed pastorates, either translators or a knowledge of the local languages were required. This explains why a significant number of these pastors showed an interest in collecting information on the region and in publishing Estonian and Latvian grammar and textbooks. One may mention here among many others Alexander Johann and Gotthard Friedrich Stender, August Wilhelm Hupel, Otto Wilhelm Masing, and Johann Heinrich Rosenplänter.[17]

The activities of the Esto- and Lettophiles in the first decades of the nineteenth century were not limited only to individuals, but also led to the formation of voluntary associations, in the form of learned societies that focused on the small languages, such as the *Lettisch-Literärische Gesellschaft* (Latvian Learned Society).[18] This Society finally emerged in 1827 (after an earlier attempt in 1824) and consisted mainly of Lutheran parish priests and sextons, as

---

14   Kasekamp, 51; on the traditions of the Swedish schooling system see Tuchtenhagen 1997.
15   Hasselblatt 2006, 134.
16   Plakans 2011, 164–65.
17   Ibid., 166–67.
18   Ārons; Hehn; Müller.

well as village or parish school teachers. The by-laws focused on the development of the Latvian language, but also included the argument for Latvian nation-building, which may explain why the Society was called in Latvian *Latviešu Draugu Biedrība* (Society of the Friends of the Latvians).[19] With the emergence of a Latvian national movement in Riga in the 1860s, the Society witnessed fierce conflicts between traditional Lettophiles and the politically more radical 'young Latvians.'[20]

As for the Estonian language, the first societies emerged on the island of Saaremaa/Ösel and in Tartu/Dorpat in 1817–18; the latter, however, soon expired. The *Estnische Gesellschaft* (Estonian Society) in Kuressaare/Arensburg was initiated by the Lutheran priest Johann Wilhelm Luce, who designed an elaborate program for developing an Estonian literary language.[21] From 1838 onwards, the most influential of these societies was the *Gelehrte Estnische Gesellschaft* (Learned Estonian Society) in Tartu.[22] The by-laws described the aims of the society: "die Kenntniss der Vorzeit und Gegenwart des ehstnischen Volkes, seiner Sprache und Litteratur, so wie des von ihm bewohnten Landes zu fördern" (to foster knowledge of the history and current state of the Estonian people, their language and literature, as well as of the land inhabited by them).[23] The first major activity referred to the collection and publication of an Estonian epos *Kalevipoeg*, modeled after the Finnish *Kalevala*.[24] Issues of school education and textbooks were discussed periodically by the society until the 1860s, when under the presidency of the historian Carl Schirren a shift in the program away from Estonian culture and towards Baltic regional history was attempted, although without lasting success. Learned societies with a regional or provincial focus, such as the *Estländische Literärische Gesellschaft* (Learned Society of Estland) in Tallinn, also addressed the question of Estonian-language schooling between 1867 and 1874.[25] All in all, until the 1860s issues of Estonian- and Latvian-language school education were promoted not only (and not in the first instance) by ethnic Estonians and Latvians, but to a large degree also by Lutheran clergymen and German-speaking *literati*.

---

19 Manuscript (sine loco, sine anno [1855]) from Latvijas Valsts vēstures arhīvs (Historical State Archive of Latvia), Riga, fonds 7363, apraksts 5, lieta 209.
20 Plakans 1974, 457–59.
21 Põldmäe 1971; Jürjo 2011.
22 For an overview on this society, see Hackmann 2005.
23 *Statut*.
24 Hasselblatt 1998.
25 Jürjo 2012; Robert.

5 The Awakeners

Turning Hroch's model upside down, Mart Laar, a historian from Tartu University and one of the leading politicians of the independence movement of 1987–91 in Soviet Estonia and Prime Minister of Estonia from 1992 to 1994, has suggested focusing on the Estonian protagonists of the *ärkamisaeg*.[26] Although this approach is nationally constricted, it directs the attention towards the inclusion of the emerging group of ethnic Estonian and Latvian intellectuals into school education and towards the conflicts between these new actors with the associations shaped by the traditions of Esto- and Lettophiles.

Teacher seminars were important institutions for forming national elites among the Estonians and Latvians. The teacher seminar in Tartu, established in 1828, was attended mainly by German and Latvian students in the beginning, and the number of Estonians began to rise only from the 1860s onwards.[27] Further seminars were founded by the *Ritterschaften* in Kuuda/Kuda (in Estonia) and Irlava/Irmlau in Courland. A specific focus on the Latvian and Estonian rural population was ascribed to the seminar established in Valmiera/Wolmar in 1837, which was eventually transferred to Valga/Valka/Walk in 1849. It was based on the idea of parish teachers and clerks acting as *Kulturmittler* (cultural mediators).[28] This notion, which meant to keep up the social and religious order in the region, has to be seen against the background of a mass movement of conversion to orthodoxy among the Estonian and Latvian peasants in Livonia. Among the graduates of these seminars were many of the national Latvian and Estonian 'patriots' or 'awakeners': Kārlis Baumanis, the composer of the Latvian national anthem; Indriķis Zīle, a conductor at Latvian song festivals; Carl Robert Jakobson, a newspaper editor and initiator of many Estonian associations; Aleksander Kunileid (Säbelmann), a composer of Estonian national songs; and Ado Grenzstein, an Estonian newspaper editor. Atis Kronvalds, another important Latvian patriot, had studied in Germany and became a docent at the Tartu seminar; while Jānis Cimze, the Valga/Валка seminar director from 1839 to 1881, was very active in promoting folk songs and culture. Both seminars, however, were closed down with the so-called Russification of the school system in 1887 and 1889, respectively.[29] Their place was then taken by Russian-language state seminars, which continued with similar agendas.[30]

---

26 Laar 2005.
27 Karjahärm and Sirk, 67–68.
28 Ibid., 69.
29 Peterson, Bach and Inselberg; *Das erste Dorpatsche Lehrer-Seminar*; Plakans 2011, 228.
30 Vičs, vol. 4, 280–81.

6   Estonian Activities

With the rising social and cultural activities among the Baltic nations in the 1860s, the issue of education in the Estonian and Latvian languages gained relevance. Starting from initiatives in the district of Viljandi/Fellin, where a group of Estonian peasants and parish teachers became quite active, the idea of an Estonian language secondary school emerged.[31] Jakob Hurt,[32] who graduated from Tartu University in theology in 1865 and worked as a teacher in Otepää/Odenpäh afterwards, tried to convince the *Gelehrte Estnische Gesellschaft* to take up this cause as well as publishing an Estonian-language newspaper; but under the presidency of the historian Carl Schirren the Society pursued another policy of spreading German language skills among the Estonians. So it became clear that there was no chance of developing an Estonian language school within this Society.

Instead, the issue of education was taken up and promoted by newly established national associations among the Estonians, among which the Alexander School committees played a prominent role. The idea emerged in 1860 and was pushed forward by a group of Estonian parish teachers and sextons from Tarvastu/Tarwast around Hans Wühner and Jaan Adamson.[33] Tsar Alexander I was chosen as the school patron, in reference to the peasants' liberation decree of 1819. The prime mover was Jakob Hurt, whose understanding of the Estonian nation was based more on culture than on politics. In 1863, the initiators discussed the idea with the *Gelehrte Estnische Gesellschaft* in Tartu, which however (under the presidency of Carl Schirren) was reluctant to support the project.[34] The idea to collect money for the School was announced by Jakob Hurt in his speech at the Estonian song festival in 1869.[35] In 1871 the collection was approved by the tsar, and a central committee was set up. All in all, 146 local committees emerged.[36] In 1874 the committee bought a former manor house near Põltsamaa/Oberpahlen, and the amount of one hundred thousand rubles required for the opening of the School was raised by 1886. When the School was finally opened in 1888, however, it had to become a Russian-speaking middle school due to the general Russification of the education system at that time. A fierce struggle had emerged between Hurt and the more radical wing of Estonian nationalism with Johan Köler and Mihkel Weske, which opened a

---

31   Kasekamp 2010, 79; Jansen 2012.
32   Mohrfeldt; Põldmäe 1988; Laar, Saukas and Tedre; Raun 1991, 64 and 74–76.
33   Kruus 1939b.
34   *Sitzungsberichte*, 29–32.
35   Kruus 1939a, 33–48 and 95–102. See Hasselblatt 2006, 270–71.
36   Kruus 1939b, 48–50.

door for the intervention of the tsarist authorities in 1884, when the local committees were dissolved.[37]

More important than the educational level of the Alexander School was the fact that Estonian should become a language of instruction. The failure of this aim contributed to the public disappointment in the whole undertaking. The School operated only a couple of years until 1906, when it was closed down in the aftermath of the 1905 revolution.[38] As a successor, an agrarian school was opened in 1914 in the manor house of Kõo/Wolmarshof. Only from a later perspective would the relevance of this effort be appreciated, since the frequent committee meetings and the semiannual national assembly in Tartu shaped cohesion among the Estonian population. Furthermore, the aim to educate a group of Estonian teachers was achieved despite the limited possibilities of the School.

The second Estonian association to be mentioned is the *Eesti Kirjameeste Selts* (Society of Learned Estonians), a gathering of intellectuals which emerged from the idea of publishing Estonian textbooks. This is reflected in the first proposed name of the Society: *Vaimuvaranduse ehk Eestikeele õppetuse raamatute laiali laotamise selts* (Spiritual Treasury or Society for the Dissemination of School Books in Estonian). Jakob Hurt was also the head of this initiative; among other leading figures were the aforementioned Harald Wühner and Carl Robert Jakobson. Fifty-four new textbooks were published from 1872 to 1881.[39] Another project of the Society was the introduction of a new Estonian orthography.

Hurt left for St. Petersburg in 1880 to become parish priest of the Estonian congregation, and his rival Jakobson, who was in favor of a more radical stance towards the German elites and of seeking support from tsarist authorities, took over the presidency of *Eesti Kirjameeste Selts* in 1881. In that same year, Tsar Alexander III, following his assassinated father on the throne, began his politics of limiting German political and social influence in the Baltic region. Jakobson organized a delegation of representatives of Estonian voluntary associations to St. Petersburg which demanded, among other issues, taking responsibility for rural schooling away from the German nobility and parish priests and placing it under the tsarist authorities.[40] Jakobson's sudden death

---

37   Ibid., 181.
38   Ibid., 293.
39   Jansen 2012, 232.
40   Jansen 1997, 93–116. The text of this memorandum can be found in the journal *Sakala*, no. 33 (1881).

in 1882 then led the Society of Learned Estonians into a deep crisis and put an end to these national activities.

The decline of the *Eesti Kirjameeste Selts* and the limited educational level of the Alexander School, however, did not mean an end to the national educational efforts of the Estonians. Instead, another school became important for the education of Estonian students: Hugo Treffner's private gymnasium in Tartu, which started in 1883 first with German as the language of instruction and had to shift to Russian some years later.[41]

7 Latvian Activities

A brief look at the Latvian case reveals a similar picture: language issues were the major focus of the Latvian national movement, starting more or less in the same years and at the same place as the Estonian movement. At the University of Tartu Christian Woldemar/Krišjānis Valdemārs and Juris Alunāns organized the first informal gatherings of Latvian students in 1856. Among these 'Young Latvians' were also Krišjānis Barons and Atis Kronvalds, who revived the Latvian evening meetings in 1867. These protagonists of the Latvian national movement were concentrating first of all on Latvian language and culture and on newspaper editions.[42] In distinction to the Estonian movement, the Latvian movement since the 1870s had its main basis among the emerging Latvian bourgeois circles in Riga. This becomes clearly visible when looking at the foundation of the *Rīgas Latviešu Biedrība* (Riga Latvian Society) in 1868: sociability in the native language was a primary goal of the Society.[43] In 1873, *Rīgas Latviešu Biedrība* organized the first Latvian song festival as the first major national manifestation. During the festivities fierce rivalries emerged with the representatives of the older Lettophile associations over the commitment to Latvian nation-building.

The Riga Latvian Society also became active in the field of education. Plans to set up a Latvian Alexander middle school in Riga, closely following the Estonian model, remained without success because the tsarist authorities rejected the Society's request to gather money and to set up a central committee.[44] Instead, the Society opened a Latvian-language Sunday school, and a girls' school in 1884. The main focus, however, was on Latvian teachers at parish and village

---

41   Hasselblatt 2006.
42   Zake. See also Berziņš and Apals.
43   On this society see Wohlfart; Hanovs 2011; Hanovs 2012.
44   Wohlfart, 149–55.

schools. A first teachers' conference was convened at the same time as the first Latvian song festival, and a second one a year later. In addition, the Learned Commission of Riga Latvian Society took care of school textbooks and local school libraries and distributed grants to students.

A further aspect of these Latvian educational initiatives was rather loosely connected to voluntary associations but had a major impact on Latvian nation-building. Krišjānis Valdemārs, after his studies at Tartu, worked first as a clerk in the Ministry of Finance in St. Petersburg and then as a journalist in Moscow in close cooperation with the Slavophile press. Valdemārs's main idea was to establish naval vocational schools, an idea which he had promoted since the years of his studies in Tartu. This idea was eventually supported by Carl Robert Jakobson. Such a naval school for Latvians and Estonians was then erected in Ainaži/Haynasch in northern Livonia in 1864.[45]

As in the Estonian case, private secondary schools played an important role in schooling young Latvians. The most prominent was the girls' progymnasium initiated in Riga in 1900 by Atis Ķeniņš and Anna Rūmane-Ķeniņa. In 1905 they built a new school building for a boys' trade school and a girls' gymnasium designed by the architects Konstantīns Pēkšēns and Eižens Laube as an icon of Latvian national romanticism.

8   New Scope after 1905

During the revolution of 1905, in June the use of languages of instruction other than Russian was readmitted in the Baltic provinces. Together with the announcement in the October Manifesto introducing new procedures for admitting voluntary associations, the way was paved for Estonian, German, and Latvian schooling associations. Actually, the so-called 'temporary rules' of March 1906 regarding voluntary associations did not imply full freedom of association, but introduced a system of registration with only a short period of possible intervention or rejection by the tsarist authorities. Nevertheless, it allowed many new associations to appear and older ones to change and broaden their by-laws and their fields of activity.

However, the Estonian and Latvian schooling activities faced a blowback with tsarist repressions answering the revolutionary events of autumn 1905. Either schools were closed, like the Estonian Alexander School, or school directors such as Atis Ķeniņš had to flee from the Baltic region. Estonian and Latvian

---

45   Woldemar 1878, 149–50; Woldemar 1868; Woldemar 1857. See also Erdmane.

primary-school teachers were active in revolutionary meetings and took part in a teachers' congress in Riga in November 1905, where under the slogan of autonomy a national reorganization of the school system was demanded.[46]

Among the Estonian educational societies, the *Eesti Nooresoo Kasvatuse Selts* (Estonian Society for the Education of Young People) deserves first mention. It opened a girls' gymnasium in Tartu in July 1906.[47] Another important society was the *Eestimaa Rahvahariduse Selts* (Estland Folk Education Society) that was active in the province of Estland with a school in Tallinn. In addition, several local Estonian secondary schools emerged: in Narva and Pärnu/Pernau (a four-year progymnasium for boys and girls in 1906) as well as in other towns.[48] Among the schools addressing Latvian students, the secondary school of Atis Ķeniņš in Riga was transformed into a gymnasium in 1907. In 1908, the *Latviešu Izglītības biedrība* (Latvian Educational Society) was founded, which opened many elementary as well as afternoon schools in Riga. Furthermore, many local societies with schooling agendas emerged in the Latvian regions.[49]

Jewish educational activities, which were promoted by the *Obshchestva dlia rasprostraneniia prosveshcheniia mezhdu evreiami v Rossii* (Society for the Promotion of Enlightenment among the Jews in Russia), broadened in Riga since 1898. Besides supporting Jewish students of public schools, the Society focused on opening a Jewish vocational industrial school, which started in 1906.[50]

9 The Old Elites Strike Back: The *Deutsche Vereine*

The new scope for activities in 1905 was used most forcefully by the so-called German Associations in the Baltic provinces, which first emerged as *Deutsche Schulvereine* and kept this focus on schools until their dissolution in 1914. Formally, these associations were founded shortly after the temporary rules were issued in March 1906, but the first initiatives had already emerged some years earlier in Riga. In 1902, an informal group of German *literati* who called themselves 'Kilimandscharo'—an allusion to the highest mountain in the German Reich at that time in the German colony of Ost-Afrika—discussed the foundation of a school society in order to protect the 'German-Protestant'

---

46 Vičs, vol. 4, 75–85.
47 Kinkar; for a list of associations see 213–18.
48 Ibid.
49 Vičs, vol. 4, 363–68. See also the entries in Kurzemneeks, 133–40.
50 Heinert; Bogojavlenska.

culture of the Baltic region.[51] The main threat was no longer perceived as the Russification of schools and administration, but in a cultural as well as economic competition with the advancing Latvian national movement, as signaled in particular by Ernst Seraphim, a journalist at the *Düna-Zeitung* in Riga.[52] The best counter-strategy in this national rivalry was seen in transforming an already existing social club, the *Euphonie* society from 1797, into a kind of *Schutzverein* that would try to safeguard the economic and cultural interests of the socially disparate German population. New by-laws were approved soon after, and the number of members sprang from sixty to some five hundred. At the same time, the *Euphonie* moved to a cheaper locale, and the sociable expenses of membership fees were constrained. Nevertheless, the society remained limited to the German noble, academic, and economic elites of Riga.

The intention to include all Germans regardless of class or gender as well as all (already existing) German associations under a new umbrella organization was a different paradigm that was then pursued by the *Deutsche Vereine*, which emerged in each of the three Baltic provinces individually but revealed some common features. Firstly, they did not limit their activities to school education but espoused a broader national agenda, so they quickly changed their names from *Deutsche Schul- und Hilfsvereine* to simply 'German associations.' Secondly, they did not abandon the traditional political order in the region, which was organized according to the provincial borders. All of these associations had representatives of the institutions of the (German) nobility as their presidents, whereas vice-presidents were usually recruited from the *literati*. Thirdly, they were by far the largest associations in the region at that time (including the Estonian and Latvian associations): the membership of the *Deutsche Vereine* rose by 1908 to some 37,000 (with a total German-speaking population in the region of about 165,000 according to the census of 1897). These associations were not umbrella organizations, but up to one-fourth of the total Baltic German population were direct members of these unions. In stark contrast to previous associations, women made up the majority of members, although they received little representation on the governing boards apart from the women's section, which in Riga appeared as an independent *Deutscher Frauenbund*. The attempt to create an associational web that would comprise the entire German population did not succeed, although the institutions of German Cultural Autonomy in Estonia after the First World War clearly continued the work of the earlier Baltic German associations.

---

51 Hollander. For more detail, see Hackmann 2012; Henriksson.
52 Seraphim.

Cooperation among the German associations included the publication of a joint calendar (*Kalender*) and maintaining a teachers' seminar in Jelgava/Mitau. The schooling activities included opening their own schools, and thus went beyond focusing solely on the gymnasia maintained by the *Ritterschaften* that had been closed in 1892. Although the German associations welcomed the reopening of the gymnasia in Bērzaine/Birkenruh and Tallinn, their major concern was to found their own new primary and secondary schools in all the major towns of the region. Among these were the Albert-School in Riga and the *Bürgerschule* in Tartu. Some of the newly founded schools received new buildings, as for example in Paide/Weißenstein. The architecture of these new buildings tried to represent the German character of the associations through quotations of a neo-gothic Hanseatic style or by making use of timber-frames. In many cases the school buildings were named *Deutsches Haus*.[53] In 1913, 'iron school funds' were introduced following the Austrian example in order to collect shares for the maintenance of schools independent from school fees. Another aspect was the maintaining of apprentices' dormitories, which was understood as support for German artisans. Such dormitories were erected in Tartu, Riga, and Jelgava.

With regard to political strategies within the *Deutsche Vereine*, however, competing visions prevailed: whereas some of the members were in favor of a strict dissociation from the Estonian and in particular the Latvian national movement, others continued to underline the hegemony of German culture in the Baltic region, which was seen as attractive for the small nations as well. In a similar way, relations with the German Reich were contested in the decade before World War I. Before 1914, loyalty to the tsar was not yet decisively challenged; but this situation changed after the beginning of the war, when the German associations were dissolved by the authorities. After 1917, most of the German-speaking associations tended to stress their loyalty to the Kaiser, based on the advance of the German occupation, which by February 1918 encompassed all three provinces.

Right from their beginnings, the *Deutsche Vereine* sought to establish links with the German *Schutzvereine* like the *Verein für das Deutschtum im Ausland* and with the *Alldeutscher Verband*,[54] whose managing director Artur Geiser frequently visited Riga and organized publicity for the Baltic Germans in Germany. Nevertheless these connections remained limited by the fear that foreign support might serve the Russian authorities as an argument for closing these associations.

---

53 "Im eigenen Heim."
54 See Stackelberg.

Fostering the national cultures of smaller nations was a major driving force behind the formation of voluntary associations in the Baltic region throughout the nineteenth century. These processes were always connected with transcultural transfers. The German *literati* were seeking an orientation towards Germany, but for the issue of supporting indigenous cultures there was hardly a German model apart from the Herderian concept of collecting folk songs. Instead, when protagonists from the small nations began to broaden their activities, the Finnish and Czech cases were cited in particular. When the German secondary schools came under pressure from the tsarist authorities in the period of Russification, German activists started observing developments in the Habsburg Empire more closely and took inspiration from there. Research on the national movements has largely focused on political issues and newspaper debates; but in fact, the backbone of emancipation among the small nations was shaped by cultural and educational aspects, whereas their political initiatives remained rather short-lived. Until the end of the nineteenth century the situation of the German social elites in the region was clearly different from those of the small nations, but the situation began to change around 1900. Against the Latvians' and Estonians' striving for emancipation, the German reaction within the *Deutsche Vereine* intended a 'staying on top'; but strategies for promoting nation-building increasingly made use of similar cultural and educational features. Along with this multi-lateral nationalization of civil society, non-national educational initiatives also survived, as is shown by the example of the 'Luther-Schule', a craftsmen's school of the *Literärisch-praktische Bürgerverbindung* (Learned and Practical Citizens' Association) in Riga, where national differentiation was not a major concern.[55]

From the revolution of 1905 until the First World War this pattern of national schooling initiatives saw several significant changes. Whereas many of the Estonian and Latvian schools were closed during the revolution, the German associations encountered new possibilities. Until 1914, various school initiatives emerged among all the national groups in the Baltic region. After the beginning of the war, the *Deutsche Vereine* were dissolved and did not re-emerge even after the entire Baltic region came under the control of Ober Ost in early 1918. The support of German voluntary associations for the German Reich, however, also proved to be short-term. In contrast, some of the Estonian and Latvian associations and their personnel then became the backbone of the new states from 1919 onwards.

---

55   Busch, 41.

Bibliography

Anonymous. *Das erste Dorpatsche Lehrer-Seminar mit seinen Schülern und Lehrern von seiner Gründung 1828 bis zu seiner Schliessung 1889* [The First Teachers' Seminar in Dorpat with its Students and Teachers from its Foundation in 1828 to its Closure in 1889]. Dorpat: Schnakenburg, 1890.

Anonymous. "Im eigenen Heim. Schul- und Vereinshäuser der Deutschen Vereine in Liv-, Est- und Kurland" [In One's Own Home. School and Association Buildings of the German Associations in Livonia, Estland and Courland], *Kalender der Deutschen Vereine in Liv-, Est- und Kurland* no. 7 (1913), 50–69.

Anonymous. *Kalender der deutschen Vereine in Liv-, Est- und Kurland 1908–1914* [Calendar of the German Associations in Livonia, Estland and Courland]. Riga: Jonck & Poliewsky, 1907–13.

Anonymous. *Sitzungsberichte der Gelehrten Estnischen Gesellschaft* [Proceedings of the Learned Estonian Society]. Dorpat: Karow, Lankmann, Matthiesen, 1861–1938 (1940).

Anonymous. *Statut der gelehrten ehstnischen Gesellschaft zu Dorpat* [By-laws of the Learned Estonian Society]. Dorpat: Lindfors Erben, 1839.

Ārons, Matīss. *Latviešu Literariskā (Latviešu Draugu) Biedrība savā simts gadu darbā. Ainas no vāciešu un latviešu attiecību vēstures* [The Latvian Literary Society (of Friends of the Latvians) in its 100 Years of Activity. Images from the History of the German-Latvian Relations]. Riga: Gulbis, 1929.

Berziņš, Jānis, and Gints Apals. *Latvija 19. gadsimtā. Vēstures apceres* [Latvia in the 19th Century. Historical Reflections]. Riga: Latvijas Vēstures Institūts, 2000.

Bogojavlenska, Svetlana. "Der jüdische Bildungsverein in Riga 1896–1914" [The Jewish Educational Society in Riga, 1896–1914]. In Jörg Hackmann, ed., *Vereinskultur und Zivilgesellschaft in Nordosteuropa. Regionale Spezifik und europäische Zusammenhänge. Associational Culture and Civil Society in North Eastern Europe. Regional Features and the European Context*. Wien/Köln/Weimar: Böhlau, 2012. 237–50.

Brüggemann, Karsten. *Licht und Luft des Imperiums. Legitimations- und Repräsentationsstrategien russischer Herrschaft in den Ostseeprovinzen im 19. und frühen 20. Jahrhundert* [Light and Air of the Empire. Legitimation and Representation Strategies of Russian Rule in Baltic Provinces in the 19th and Early 20th Centuries]. Wiesbaden: Harrassowitz, 2018.

Busch, Nikolaus. *Geschichte der Literärisch-Praktischen Bürgerverbindung in Riga 1802–1902* [History of Literary and Practical Bürgerverbindung in Riga, 1802–1902]. Riga: Häcker, 1902.

Erdmane, Iveta. *Dzelzs vīri, koka kuģi. Veltījums Ainažu Jūrskolai* [Iron Men, Wooden Ships. The Dedication of the Seafaring School in Ainaži]. Ainaži: Ainažu Jūrskolas Muzejs, 2008.

Garleff, Michael. *Die baltischen Länder: Estland, Lettland, Litauen vom Mittelalter bis zur Gegenwart, Ost- und Südosteuropa Geschichte der Länder und Völker* [The Baltic Lands: Estonia, Latvia, Lithuania from the Middle Ages to the Present]. Regensburg: Pustet, 2001.

Hackmann, Jörg. "Von der 'Gelehrten Estnischen Gesellschaft' zu 'Õpetatud Eesti Selts'. Verein und Nation in Estland" [From the 'Gelehrte Estnische Gesellschaft (Learned Estonian Society)' to 'Õpetatud Eesti Selts'. Association and Nation in Estonia]. In Norbert Angermann, Michael Garleff and Wilhelm Lenz, eds., *Ostseeprovinzen, Baltische Staaten und das Nationale. Festschrift für Gert von Pistohlkors zum 70. Geburtstag.* Münster: Lit, 2005. 185–211.

Hackmann, Jörg. "Narrating the Building of a Small Nation: Divergence and Convergence in the Historiography of the Estonian 'National Awakening', 1868–2005." In Stefan Berger and Chris Lorenz, eds., *Nationalizing the Past: Historians as Nation Builders in Modern Europe.* Basingstoke: Palgrave Macmillan, 2010. 170–91.

Hackmann, Jörg. "Nachholende Nationalisierung. Das kurze Leben der Deutschen Vereine in den russländischen Ostseeprovinzen (1905–1914)" [Making up for Nationalisation. The Short Life of the German Associations in the Baltic Provinces of the Russian Empire, 1905–1914]. In Hackmann, ed., *Vereinskultur und Zivilgesellschaft in Nordosteuropa. Regionale Spezifik und europäische Zusammenhänge. Associational Culture and Civil Society in North Eastern Europe. Regional Features and the European Context.* Wien/Köln/Weimar: Böhlau, 2012. 387–418.

Hanovs, Deniss. "Bürgerliche Vereinskultur und die lettische nationale Presse. Der Rigaer Lettische Verein und die Zeitung 'Baltijas Vēstnesis'" [Civic Associational Culture and the Latvian National Press. The Riga Latvian Society and the Newspaper 'Baltijas Vēstnesis']. In Jörg Hackmann and Klaus Roth, eds., *Zivilgesellschaft im östlichen und südöstlichen Europa in Geschichte und Gegenwart.* München: Oldenbourg, 2011. 141–58.

Hanovs, Deniss. "'Verein aller Letten' – ideologische Diskrepanzen und symbolische Praxis des Rigaer Lettischen Vereins 1868–1906" [The 'Society of all Latvians' – Ideological Discrepancies and Symbolical Praxis of the Riga Latvian Society, 1868–1906]. In Jörg Hackmann, ed., *Vereinskultur und Zivilgesellschaft in Nordosteuropa. Regionale Spezifik und europäische Zusammenhänge. Associational Culture and Civil Society in North Eastern Europe. Regional Features and the European Context.* Wien/Köln/Weimar: Böhlau, 2012. 347–86.

Hasselblatt, Cornelius. "Die Bedeutung des Nationalepos 'Kalevipoeg' für das nationale Erwachen der Esten" [The Relevance of the National Epos 'Kalevipoeg' for the National Awakening of the Estonians]. In Jörg Hackmann, ed., *Estland – Partner im Ostseeraum.* Lübeck: Ostsee-Akademie, 1998. 41–56.

Hasselblatt, Cornelius. *Geschichte der estnischen Literatur von den Anfängen bis zur Gegenwart* [History of the Estonian Literature from its Beginings to the Present]. Berlin/New York: De Gruyter, 2006.

Hehn, Jürgen von. *Die lettisch-literärische Gesellschaft und das Lettentum* [The Latvian Literary Society and the Latvian Nation]. Königsberg/Berlin: Ost-Europa-Verlag, 1938.

Heinert, Felix. "Ein jüdisches Bildungsprojekt im lokalen Raum Rigas. Die Institutionalisierung jüdischer Aufklärung in Riga um 1900 und die Zielutopien der Gründer der Rigaer Abteilung des Vereins zur Verbreitung von Bildung unter den Juden in Russland" [A Jewish Project of Bildung in the Urban Space of Riga. The Institutionalization of Jewish Enlightenment in Riga on the Eve of the 20th Century and the Visions of the Founders of the Riga Branch of the Society for the Promotion of Enlightenment among the Jews of Russia], *Zeitschrift für Ostmitteleuropaforschung* 56:1 (2007), 1–49.

Henriksson, Anders. *Vassals and Citizens: The Baltic Germans in Constitutional Russia, 1905–1914*. Marburg: Herder-Institut, 2010.

Hirschhausen, Ulrike von. *Die Grenzen der Gemeinsamkeit: Deutsche, Letten, Russen und Juden in Riga 1860–1914* [The Borders of the Common Ground. Latvians, Russians, Germans and Jews in Riga, 1860–1914]. Göttingen: Vandenhoeck & Ruprecht, 2006.

Hollander, Bernhard. "Erinnerungen an die Jahre 1902–1905. Von der Euphonie, der Vorläuferin des Deutschen Vereins in Livland" [Memories of the Years 1902–1905. On the Euphonie, the Predecessor of the German Association in Livland], *Baltische Blätter für pädagogische und allgemein-kulturelle Fragen* 2 (1924), 111–25.

Hroch, Miroslav. *Die Vorkämpfer der nationalen Bewegung bei den kleinen Völkern Europas. Eine vergleichende Analyse zur gesellschaftlichen Schichtung der patriotischen Gruppen* [The Pioneers of the National Movement among the Small Nations in Europe. A Comparative Analysis of the Social Stratification of Patriotc Groups]. Acta Universitatis Carolinae, Philosophica et Historica. Praha: Univerzita Karlova, 1968.

Hroch, Miroslav. *Social Preconditions of National Revival in Europe. A Comparative Analysis of the Social Composition of Patriotic Groups Among the Smaller European Nations*. Cambridge: Cambridge University Press, 1985.

Hroch, Miroslav. *Das Europa der Nationen. Die moderne Nationsbildung im europäischen Vergleich* [The Europe of Nations. Modern Nation-Building in European Comparison]. Göttingen: Vandenhoeck & Ruprecht, 2005.

Hroch, Miroslav. "Comments," *Nationalities Papers* 38:6 (2010), 881–90. DOI: 10.1080/00905992.2010.515976.

Jansen, Ea. "Voluntary Associations in Estonia. The Model of the 19th Century," *Eesti Teaduste Akadeemia Toimetised. Humanitaar- ja Sotsiaalteadused* 42:2 (1993), 115–25.

Jansen, Ea. "Eesti seltside saadikute audients Vene keisri juures 1881. aastal ja nende märgukiri kui katse osaled 'suures poliitikas'" [The Memorandum of Estonian Societies to the Russian Emperor in 1881 – an Attempt to Participate in 'Real' Politics], *Acta Historica Tallinnensia* 1 (1997), 93–116.

Jansen, Ea. *Eestlane muutuvas ajas. Seisusühiskonnast kodanikuühiskonda* [The Estonian in a Changing Time. From the Estates Society to Civic Society]. Tartu: Eesti Ajalooarhiiv, 2007.

Jansen, Ea. "Eesti Kirjameeste Selts – The Society of Estonian Literati, 1871–1893." In Jörg Hackmann, ed., *Vereinskultur und Zivilgesellschaft in Nordosteuropa. Regionale Spezifik und europäische Zusammenhänge* [*Associational Culture and Civil Society in North Eastern Europe. Regional Features and the European Context*]. Wien/Köln/Weimar: Böhlau, 2012. 225–35.

Jansen, Ea, and Jaanus Arukaevu. *Seltsid ja ühiskonna muutumine. Talupojaühiskonnast rahvusriigini. Artiklite kogumik* [Associations and Changes of Society. From Peasants' Society to the National State. Collected Articles]. Tartu/Tallinn: TA Ajaloo Instituut, 1995.

Jürjo, Indrek. "Johann Wilhelm Ludwig von Luce (1756–1842). Ein Aufklärer auf der Insel Oesel" [Johann Wilhelm Ludwig von Luce (1756–1842). An Enlightener on the Island of Oesel]. In Norbert Angermann, Wilhelm Lenz and Konrad Maier, eds., *Geisteswissenschaften und Publizistik im Baltikum des 19. und frühen 20. Jahrhunderts*. Berlin: LIT, 2011. 15–41.

Jürjo, Indrek. "Die Estländische Literärische Gesellschaft 1842–1918" [The Learned Society of Estland, 1842–1918]. In Jörg Hackmann, *Vereinskultur und Zivilgesellschaft in Nordosteuropa. Regionale Spezifik und europäische Zusammenhänge. Associational Culture and Civil Society in North Eastern Europe. Regional Features and the European Context*. Wien/Köln/Weimar: Böhlau, 2012. 129–78.

Karjahärm, Toomas, and Väino Sirk. *Eesti haritlaskonna kujunemine ja ideed 1850–1917* [The Formation of Estonian Intellectuals and Their Ideas, 1850–1917]. Tallinn: Eesti Entsüklopeediakirjastus, 1997.

Kasekamp, Andres. *A History of the Baltic States*. Basingstoke/New York, NY: Palgrave Macmillan, 2010.

Kinkar, Feliks. *Eesti hariduseltside ajaloost* [On the History of Estonian Educational Associations]. Tartu: Tartu Ülikooli Kirjastus, 1996.

Kirby, David. *The Baltic World 1772–1993: Europe's Northern Periphery in an Age of Change*. London: Longman, 1995.

Kruus, Hans. *Eesti Aleksandrikool* [The Estonian Alexander School]. Tartu: Noor-Eesti Kirjastus, 1939a.

Kruus, Hans. *Jakob Hurda kõned ja avalikud kirjad* [Jakob Hurt's Speeches and Published Writings]. Tartu: Eesti Kirjanduse Selts, 1939b.

Kurzemneeks, G. *Beedribu Kalendars 1913* [Calendar of Associations 1913]. [Jakob Hurt's Speeches and Published Writings]. Jelgava: n.p., 1912.

Laar, Mart. *Äratajad. Rahvuslik ärkamisaeg Eestis 19. sajandil ja selle kandjad* [The Awakeners. National Awakening in Nineteenth-Century Estonia and its Agents]. Tartu: Eesti Ajalooarhiiv, 2005.

Laar, Mart, R. Saukas, and Ü. Tedre. *Jakob Hurt 1839–1907*. Tallinn: Eesti Raamat, 1989.

Merkel, Garlieb Helwig. *Die Letten vorzüglich in Liefland am Ende des philosophischen Jahrhunderts, Beiträge zur baltischen Geschichte* [The Latvians Particularly in Livland at the End of the Philosophical Century]. Wedemark: v. Hirschheydt, 1998.

Mohrfeldt, Aleksander. *Jakob Hurda elu ja töö* [Jakob Hurt's Life and Work]. Tartu: Ilmamaa, 2007.

Müller, Karl. "Die 50 ersten Jahre der lettisch-literärischen Gesellschaft" [The First 50 Years of the Latvian Literary Society], *Baltische Monatsschrift* 23 (1874), 361–81.

Peterson, Carl, Johann Bach and Eduard Inselberg. *Das ritterschaftliche Parochiallehrer-Seminar in Walk, seine Lehrer und Zöglinge 1839–1890* [The Parish Teachers' Seminar of the Ritterschaft in Walk, its Teachers and Pupils, 1839–1890]. Riga: Jonck & Poliewsky, 1898.

Petri, Johann Christoph. *Ehstland und die Ehsten oder historisch-geographisch-statistisches Gemälde von Ehstland. Ein Seitenstück zu Merkel über die Letten* [Estonia and the Estonians or a Historical-Geographical-Statistical Painting of Estonia. A Parallel Piece to Merkel on the Latvians]. 3 vols. Gotha: Ettinger, 1802.

Pistohlkors, Gert von. *Baltische Länder* [The Baltic Lands]. 2 ed., *Deutsche Geschichte im Osten Europas*. Berlin: Siedler, 1994.

Plakans, Andrejs. "Peasants, Intellectuals, and Nationalism in the Russian Baltic Provinces, 1820–90," *Journal of Modern History* 46:3 (1974), 445–75.

Plakans, Andrejs. *The Latvians. A Short History*. Stanford, CA: Hoover Inst. Press, 1995.

Plakans, Andrejs. *A Concise History of the Baltic States*. Cambridge: Cambridge University Press, 2011.

Põldmäe, Rudolf. "Varasem kodu-uurimine ja rahvaluule kogumine Saaremaal" [Early Homeland Research and Folklore Collection on Oesel], *Paar sammukest eesti kirjanduse uurimise teed. Uurimusi ja materjale* 7 (1971), 135–69.

Põldmäe, Rudolf. *Noor Jakob Hurt. Monograafia* [The Young Jakob Hurt. A Monography]. Tallinn: Eesti Raamat, 1988.

Raun, Toivo U. "The Estonians." In Edward C. Thaden, ed., *Russification in the Baltic Provinces and Finland, 1855–1914*. Princeton, NJ: Princeton University Press, 1981. 285–354.

Raun, Toivo U. "The Revolution of 1905 in the Baltic Provinces and Finland," *Slavic Review* 43:3 (1984), 453–67.

Raun, Toivo U. *Estonia and the Estonians*. 2nd ed. Stanford, CA: Hoover Institution Press, 1991.

Raun, Toivo U., and Andrejs Plakans. "The Estonian and Latvian National Movements. An Assessment of Miroslav Hroch's Model," *Journal of Baltic Studies* 21 (1991), 131–44.

Robert, Kyra. "Eesti keel ja kirjandus Eestimaa Kirjanduse Ühingus XIX sajandil" [Estonian Language und Literature in the Learned Society of Estland in the 19th Century], *Keel ja Kirjandus* (1971), 526–34.
Seraphim, Ernst. *Im neuen Jahrhundert. Baltischer Rückblick und Ausblick* [In the New Century. Baltic Look Back and Outlook]. Riga: Jonck & Poliewski, 1902.
Stackelberg, Eduard von. *Nationale Verbände. Ein Vortrag* [National Unions. A Lecture]. Reval/Leipzig: Kluge & Ströhm, 1908.
Staliūnas, Darius. *Making Russians: Meaning and Practice of Russification in Lithuania and Belarus after 1863*. Amsterdam: Rodopi, 2007.
Subačius, Giedrius. "The Letter 'J' and Lithuanian Cyrillic Script: Two Language Planning Strategies in the Late Nineteenth Century," *Journal of Baltic studies* 39:1 (2008), 73–82.
Troinitskii, N.A. *Pervaia vseobshchaia perepis' naseleniia Rossiiskoi Imperii, 1897* [First General Census of the Population of the Russian Empire, 1897]. 89 vols. [St. Petersburg]: Izd. TSentral'nago statisticheskogo komiteta Ministerstva vnutreennikh diel, 1899–1905.
Tuchtenhagen, Ralph. "Bildung als Modernisierung. Schule und sozialer Wandel in Estland und Livland im 19. Jahrhundert" [Education as Modernization. Schools and Social Change in Estland and Livonia in the 19th Century], *Acta Baltica* 35 (1997), 219–30.
Tuchtenhagen, Ralph. *Geschichte der baltischen Länder* [History of the Baltic Countries]. München: C.H. Beck, 2005.
Vahtre, Sulev, Toomas Karjahärm, and Tiit Rosenberg. *Eesti ajalugu V: Pärisorjuse kaotamisest Vabadussõjani* [History of Estonia, vol. V. From the Abolition of Serfdom until the War of Independence]. Tartu: Ilmamaa, 2010.
Vičs, Andrejs. *Latviešu skolu vēsture* [Latvian School History]. 5 vols. Riga: R.L.B. Derīgu grāmatu nodaļas apgāds, 1923–1940.
Wittram, Reinhard. *Baltische Geschichte. Die Ostseelande Livland, Estland, Kurland 1180 – 1918. Grundzüge und Durchblicke, Geschichte der Völker und Staaten* [Baltic History. The Baltic Lands Livonia, Estland, Courland 1180 – 1918. Outlines and Trajectories]. München: Oldenbourg, 1954.
Wohlfart, Kristine. *Der Rigaer Letten Verein und die lettische Nationalbewegung von 1868 bis 1905* [The Riga Latvian Society and the Latvian National Movement, 1868–1905]. Marburg: Herder-Institut, 2006.
Woldemar, C[hristian]. *Über die Heranziehung der Letten und Esten zum Seewesen, nebst Notizen und Aphorismen in Bezug auf die industriellen, intellectuellen und statistischen Verhältnisse der Letten und Esten und der drei baltischen Provinzen überhaupt* [On the Raising of the Latvians and Estonians to Seafaring with Notes and Aphorisms Relating to the Industrial, Intellectual and Statistical Situation of the

Latvians and Estonians and the Three Baltic Provinces altogether]. Dorpat: Laakmann, 1857.

Woldemar, C[hristian]. *Aufruf zu praktischer Thätigkeit zur Hebung unseres Seewesens namentlich im baltischen Meere* [Appeal to Practical Activity for the Improvement of our Seafaring, particularly on the Baltic]. Moskau: Kaiserliche Universitäts-Buchdruckerei, 1868.

Woldemar, C[hristian]. *Meie laewamehed ja laewameeste koolid. Kutse-kiri Eesti rannaäärse rahwale et nad kauge meresõitudest kaubalaewade peal osa wõtma hakkaksiwad* [Our Seafarers and Seafaring Schools. A Letter Inviting the Estonian Littoral People to Begin Participating in Distant Maritime Trading]. Wiliandi: Feldt, 1878.

Zake, Ieva. "Inventing Culture and Nation: Intellectuals and Early Latvian Nationalism," *National Identities* 9:4 (2007), 307–29. DOI: 10.1080/14608940701737359.

CHAPTER 14

The Galician-Ruthenian Matica (1848–1939)

Iryna Orlevych

The eastern part of the Austrian province of Galicia, which was formed at the end of the eighteenth century, consisted of territories that formerly belonged to several pre-modern state formations. Since the late tenth century they were part of Kievan Rus, from the twelfth to fourteenth centuries they formed the core part of the principality of Halych (later referred to as 'Galician' in Latin sources), and from the late fourteenth century they were incorporated into the Polish Kingdom. In the early modern period, cultural and educational societies—brotherhoods founded in the sixteenth to eighteenth centuries—became important centers for the national and cultural development of the Eastern Christian part of the population, the Galician Ukrainians (Ruthenians).[1] In particular, the Stauropegion brotherhood in Lviv, which was an exponent and defender of Ruthenians' national rights for many centuries, achieved outstanding popularity.[2]

As the most economically and culturally backward region of the monarchy, Galicia became an object of the reform measures of the Austrian Empress Maria Theresa and Emperor Joseph II. These reforms created the preconditions for a certain progress in the social, economic, cultural and religious development of the Galician Ruthenians, and also strengthened the social position of the Greek Catholic clergy. Educated priests were the first Ruthenian national 'awakeners' in Galicia and became the leaders of the Ruthenian political movement in 1848.[3] The faithful in Galicia were traditionally called 'Uniates' or United Greeks until 1774, when Austrian Empress Maria Theresa decreed that the Uniates within her realm would henceforth be called Greek Catholics to symbolize their equal status with Roman Catholics.[4]

In the 1780s, in the context of religious reforms aimed at weakening the position of the Catholic Church, the Austrian authorities abolished the brotherhoods. Only the Stauropegion brotherhood managed to survive, and in 1788 it

---

1   The Ukrainian population of Galicia was officially known as 'Ruthenians' until the turn of the twentieth century; to avoid confusion, I use the latter term for the nineteenth-century inhabitants of Austrian Galicia.
2   Isaievych, 205.
3   Himka, 6.
4   Ibid., 5.

was reorganized into an institute.[5] In documents of the Austrian government its representatives were described as "guardians of the Greek Catholic nation" (affirming the recognition of Ruthenians as a separate nation).[6]

The Lviv Stauropegion Institute's activities formed an important part of socio-political, religious, and cultural life of Galicia from the late eighteenth century to the 1860s, and after 1848 it was the only secular institution of the Ukrainian people. The Stauropegion brought together representatives of the Ruthenian intellectual elite, including a patron of the Lviv church of the Assumption and the owner of a Ruthenian bookshop and a school for Ruthenian children that enjoyed considerable respect among Galician society; it also played a noticeable role during the 'Springtime of Nations' in 1848–49.[7] According to its statutes, only a Ruthenian of the Greek Catholic rite with a high status in society could become a member of the Stauropegion Institute. Such requirements characterized the Institute as an élitist organization of the Ruthenian intelligentsia. Among its members were the first historian of Galicia, Denys Zubrytskyi, the city council secretary Stepan Kerechynskyi, the entrepreneur Ivan Tovarnytskyi, and the accounts department advisor Ivan Hurkevych. In the nineteenth century there were between fifty and sixty members.[8] The Stauropegion possessed considerable assets, earning profits from its real estate (the buildings owned by the Institute), donations from Institute members, income from real estate rentals, and profits from its printing house and book sales, loan services, etc.[9] Although the Stauropegion Institute did not manage to achieve the fame of the former brotherhood, it continued to have a great influence among the Galician Ruthenian intelligentsia. It was the only Ruthenian secular establishment at that time which brought together well-known representatives of science, culture, industrial circles, officialdom, and along with the clergy took an active part in the national revival.

Like other Slavic nations within the Austrian Empire in the first half of the nineteenth century, Galician Ruthenians also went through a process of social and spiritual renovation known in the literature as the 'national revival.' In the early stages of the Ruthenian national/cultural activities that later resulted in the Ukrainian national movement, the central role was played by the Greek Catholic clergy. As the stratum closest to people at the social level, clergymen became exponents of their views. Representatives of the clergy undertook

---

5   Orlevych 2001, 16–17.
6   Central State Historical Archives of Ukraine in Lviv (CSHAU in Lviv), fund 129, inventory 2, file 4, sheet 2.
7   See Orlevych 2001, 16–17.
8   Ibid., 22–23; Kyrychuk, 30.
9   Orlevych 2001, 39.

educational and cultural activities, and took action to represent the interests of the Ruthenian people to the Austrian government. In 1816, the Greek Catholic bishop Mykhailo Levytskyi and canon Ivan Mohylnytskyi founded the society of Greek Catholic priests in Przemyśl, which began to focus on education. In 1818, it received permission from the Austrian government to introduce the Ruthenian language into the public schools of Eastern Galicia, opening primary schools with Ruthenian-language instruction, preparing school textbooks, etc.

The priesthood also launched a Galician Ruthenian literary revival. In 1837, three students of the Greek Catholic theological seminary—Markian Shashkevych, Yakiv Holovatskyi, and Ivan Vahylevych—published the literary collection *Rusalka Dnistrova* (The Mermaid of the Dnister) written in the vernacular. This initiated a new national literature in Galicia that was increasingly identified through the second half of the nineteenth century as Ukrainian ('Ruthenian-Ukrainian').

As far back as 1847, in order to publish a Ruthenian periodical, Ivan Hurkevych had suggested founding a Matica society similar to other Slavic Maticas already in existence. The main aim was to found an institute similar to the Czech Matica that would be a defender of Ruthenian literature, publish literary works, collect historical relics, bring Galicians into contact with scholars of all Slavic nations, and would be "a body of pan-Slavic reciprocity."[10]

With the help of the Czech writer František Jáchim, Hurkevych tried to involve Yakiv Holovatskyi and other men of letters in the shaping of the organization and its periodical.[11] Well-known public figures responded to the idea, namely Lev Sosnovskyi, Ivan Tovarnytskyi, Mykhailo Kuzemskyi, the consistory chancellor Mykhailo Malynovskyi, and other ecclesiastical, social, and political figures. Meanwhile, the Stauropegion Institute announced an initiative to publish a periodical; it owned a printing house and had the necessary resources. In the event, the leading members of Ukrainian society actively carried out this project and the foundation of the new society, the Matica, became of secondary importance.

The issue of a national literary language occupied an important place in the social life not only of Galician Ruthenians, but of other Slavs as well. The creation of a shared literary language, together with efforts to expand its functions in society, became a constituent element of the Slavic movements for national self-determination.[12] Therefore, in the 1840s the most burning issue in the cultural life of the Galician Ruthenians was the foundation of a periodical for

---

10 Kril and Steblii, 198 and 201.
11 Ibid., 198.
12 Leshchylovskaia, 10.

the Ruthenian population. The choice of whether to create a literary language on the basis of the vernacular or Church Slavonic, and of whether to use a phonetic or an etymological spelling, had been debated in the intellectual circles of the Galician Ruthenians in the first half of the nineteenth century, and were actively discussed in the Stauropegion Institute. In March 1848, the Institute obtained permission to publish a Ruthenian periodical, with historian Denys Zubrytskyi as its managing editor. Stauropegion members Ivan Hurkevych and Ivan Borysykevych were also invited to join the editorial staff.[13]

The revolutionary events of 1848–49 in the Austrian Empire brought important changes. On 2 May 1848, the Galician Ruthenians founded their first political body: the Supreme Ruthenian Council (SRC). The SRC represented the Ruthenians of Galicia and defended their rights before the Austrian government. Bishop Hryhoriy Yakhymovych became the head of the SRC, with canon Mykhailo Kuzemskyi as his deputy and Ivan Borysykevych, Mykhailo Malynovskyi, Teodor Leontovych, historian Denys Zubrytskyi, and industrialist Ivan Tovarnytskyi among the members of the Council.[14]

The members of the Stauropegion Institute took an active part in this political action along with the clergy. One-third of the SRC founders belonged to the Stauropegion (22 out of 66).[15] The SRC declared the unity of the Galician Ruthenians with the Russian-ruled Ukrainians ('Little Russians').[16] The decision to establish the Galician-Ruthenian Matica (GRM) was made on 17 (29) May 1848 during a meeting of the Supreme Ruthenian Council. Ivan Hurkevych prepared the draft statues of the Matica, which were approved on 16 June 1848.

In 1849, representatives of the Ruthenian elite nurtured plans to launch a number of cultural and educational projects. In the meeting of the Supreme Ruthenian Council in 1849 not only the foundation of a Matica was discussed, but also the construction of a People's Home (a scientific and cultural centre for Galician Ukrainians) or a monument.[17] Due to the liquidation of political societies in the Austrian Empire, on 17 June 1851 the Supreme Ruthenian Council was renamed the Commission for the Construction of the People's Home. This construction was completed in 1864, and in 1901 the Transfiguration Church was built. The society was institutionalized in 1872, with Yosyf Kulchytskyi as its head and Mykhailo Malynovskyi, Teofil Pavlykiv, Vasyl Kovalskyi, Yakiv Shvedzytskyi, and Antin Petrushevych among its leaders. The

---

13 Orlevych, ibid., 107.
14 Ibid., 152.
15 CSHAU in Lviv, fund 180, inventory 1, file 1, sheet 2.
16 Steblii, 155.
17 *Holovna Ruska Rada*, 126.

aim of the society was to educate the Ruthenian people, which they tried to achieve by publishing, maintaining a school for children, and supporting the Transfiguration Church.[18]

The world-view of Ruthenian activists in 1848–49 was characterized by their orientation towards the Austrian Empire (which was seen as a natural defender of the Galician Ruthenians), fidelity to the Greek Catholic Church, and anti-Polishness.[19] The dynamic course of political and cultural events between 1848 and the early 1860s led to the emergence of various factions within the milieu of the Galician Ruthenian patriotic activists: the Austrophiles or 'old Ruthenians,' who were pro-government loyalists; the Russophiles, who supported further integration into the pan-Rus'ian space; and the Ukrainophiles or *narodovtsi*, who advocated cultural-national unity with the Dnieper Ukraine and the national independence of the Ukrainian community (consisting of both Austrain-ruled Ruthenians and Russian-ruled 'Little Russians'). The Austrian government's support for the Poles in the 1860s seriously weakened the Austrophile sentiments of the Ruthenian intelligentsia and turned their attention toward the Russian Empire and Russian Panslavism, resulting in the further spread of Russophilism among the Galician Ruthenians.

Along with the Matica and the People's Home, in 1874 Russophiles founded the Kachkovskyi Society for the dissemination of science, sobriety, and an awareness of industry among the people. Its founder was the priest Ivan Naumovych, and later it was headed by Venedykt Ploshchanskyi, Teofil Pavlykiv, Bohdan Didytskyi, and Filip Svystun, among others. It was an "educational society for peasants,"[20] and many peasants joined the organization; however, it was constantly led by representatives of the Russophile elite. The society earned its income from membership fees, donations, and profits from real estate (it owned two buildings in Brody, an area for development in Sokal, plots of land in Tershiv and Monastyryska, and a building in Valova Street in Lviv). It established a number of branches in the provinces, along with economic societies (the Agricultural Union, the Central Dairy Union), bookshops, and scholarship funds.[21]

The requirements for the members of the societies had a number of common features: a member had to be a Ruthenian of the Greek Catholic rite and hold a certain position in the social hierarchy, which presupposed a certain level of wealth in order to make donations. This gave the societies the character

---

18   Orlevych 2005, 437–38.
19   Sereda, 13.
20   Wendland, 325.
21   Orlevych 2009, 101–03.

of the Ruthenian élitist organizations and led to the fact that the same people were simultaneously members of all the cultural and educational societies and also members of the Russophile party. This was recognized by the Russophiles themselves, and by the members of the Matica in particular. Thus, as far back as 1870, at the general meeting of the Matica, member Yosyf Kulchytskyi remarked that the same people were involved in all the Russophile establishments.[22] The statute provisions of these Russophile institutions ensured the reliability of their financial standing; for example, in the event of the liquidation of the People's Home, its property was to be transferred to the Stauropegion; and if the Galician-Ruthenian Matica ceased to exist, its assets were to be divided between the Stauropegion Institute and the People's Home.[23] The Russophile societies thus became instruments for the Russophiles to achieve their aims.

1   The Organizational Structure of the Matica

According to its founders' conception and the first statutes of the society, the society's aims were to publish and sell at the lowest prices books that would contribute to the strengthening of faith and traditions, and to promote the development of technology, economy, pedagogy, and good education. People of whatever social status and denomination could become founder members, as well as the various societies. However, only those Greek Catholics who were well-educated and faithful citizens of the Austrian monarchy could be elected to the managing board.

The Matica was governed by a board that included the chair, members, a secretary, a cashier, and a controller; the board was elected once a year. Later, in accordance with the 1861 statute, it was elected for five years.[24] The managing board was subordinate to a general meeting of the society, which elected its members. One of the main issues discussed by the board was the recommendation of manuscripts for publication. The Matica's stamp bore an image of the Holy Spirit as a symbol of spirituality. The society's patron was the Galician Metropolitan,[25] taking into consideration the high authority of the clergy in Galicia. The draft of the 1851 statute was discussed by the Matica's leadership and the authorities for a long time.[26] The authorities delayed approval of the

22   *Prohrama*.
23   For further information see: Orlevych 2008; Orlevych 2009.
24   CSHAU in Lviv, fund 148, inventory 1, file 7, sheet 3.
25   Ibid., file 1.
26   Ibid., file 3, sheet 3.

statutes until 1861, making new amendments every time.[27] However, they were finally approved on 23 August 1861 following the constitutional reforms in the Habsburg Monarchy. On 17 September they were also approved by the Greek Catholic Metropolitan Hryhorii Yakhymovych.[28] The statutes were re-approved in 1864 in accordance with the law on societies of 1863. The government's delay in approving the statutes was a sign of its reluctance to sanction the society's activities. The statute regulations envisaged the right of a governmental commissary to inspect the activities of the GRM.[29]

The candidate members chosen for the executive board of the Matica had to be approved by the government.[30] Controversial issues in the society were to be settled by the patron of the society, the Metropolitan.[31] Changes in the statutes reflected the eagerness of the authorities to tighten its control over the society's activities; and regulations on extending the tenure of members of the executive board led to the reduction of democratic principles in the society and to the occupation of leading positions by the same people for long terms.

There were four categories of membership in the society: founding members, regular members, contributors, and honorary members. The founding members could be either individuals (without regard to their nationality) or whole communities and other societies of merit in the fields of art, science, or culture that could serve the Matica's cause of writing works; honorary members were those with achievements in the field of education.

Founding members had the right to receive one copy of all the Matica's editions. Decisions to recommend publication of a book were taken at meetings of the society when at least four participants voted in favor, in addition to the chairperson. They were obliged to ensure that the proposed books were in compliance with regional laws and language norms. Reports on the Matica's activities were considered annually in general meetings, and information on income and expenses as well as the lists of founders and donors were prepared for publication.[32]

New statutes were also drafted in an effort to improve the society's activity. The statute of 1887 (republished in 1895) stated that the primary aim of the Literary Society Galician-Ruthenian Matica was to improve education by publishing books and popular magazines as well as academic journals for the

---

27   "Otchety obshchestva."
28   Ibid., XVIII.
29   CSHAU in Lviv, fund 148, inventory 1, file 6, sheet 7.
30   "Otchety obshchestva," XXVI.
31   Ibid., XXX.
32   Kril Steblii, 200.

spread of generally useful knowledge and morality.[33] The Matica's character became more scholarly in the 1900 statute, which defined its aim as facilitating the development of sciences, philology, the arts, and the education of the Rus people.[34] In comparison with the statutes of the 1850s and 1860s, the spread of popular education was no longer a primary task, giving way to more scholarly interests. This inconsistency in the society's goals can be traced in its title, where the term 'literary' disappears and re-appears. In the draft statute of 1856 the society was named the 'Galician-Ruthenian Matica' and its aim was to facilitate popular education;[35] by 1861 the term 'literary' was introduced, and in 1900 it had become a society of 'sciences, philology, and the arts.'[36] One of the paragraphs in the 1861 statute gives evidence of the lack of clear determination concerning the society's aims: members of the society were free to choose the objects of their literary activity by themselves.[37]

This instability in the aims of the Matica was characteristic of the whole period of its activity, as shown by its unsystematic general meetings and the irregular publication of its periodical (see below). General meetings of the society were held in 1848, 1850, 1864, 1865, 1870, 1887, then again in 1895, 1900, 1907 and 1911.[38] The Matica's activity coincided with the period of preparation for general meetings.

According to the statutes, the Matica's meetings were to begin and conclude with public worship.[39] This tradition to open a general meeting with worship was characteristic of all Russophile societies, and was borrowed from the Stauropegion, which preserved elements of medieval culture.

2   Membership

Among the Matica's members were famous scholars and cultural activists: officials, such as the canon of the Greek Catholic Metropolitan Chapter Myhailo Malynovskyi; the writer Myhailo Ustyianovych; the composer, publicist, and co-editor of *Zoria Halytska* (The Galician Star) Teodor Leontovych; the entrepreneur Ivan Tovarnytskyi; the canon and ambassador to the Diet of Galicia and State Council in Vienna, historian Antin Petrushevych; the historian and

---

33   CSHAU in Lviv, fund 148, inventory 1, file 5, sheet 2.
34   Ibid., file 10.
35   Ibid., file 2, sheet 81.
36   Ibid., file 10, sheet 2.
37   Ibid., inventory 2, file 7, sheet 3.
38   Ibid., file 2, sheet 128, 121, 93.
39   "Otchety obshchestva," XXVI.

professor of history at Lviv University Izydor Sharanevych; the writer, historian, and professor of Ruthenian language and literature at Lviv University Yakiv Holovatskyi; the director of the Ternopil Gymnasium and the Lviv Academic Gymnasium, Father Vasyl Ilnytskyi; the journalist Osyp Monchalovskyi; the writer, journalist, and editor of the Russophile newspaper *Slovo* (Word) Bohdan Didytskyi; the writer, historian, and teacher at the Lviv Franz Joseph Gymnasium Pylyp Svystun; the Doctor of Law Vasyl Lahola; the teacher of mathematics and physics at the gymnasiums of Rzeszów and Lviv Mykola Syvuliak; the lawyers Volodymyr Dudykevych and Semen Bendasiuk; the writers Ivan Sviatytskyi and Mariian Hlushkevych; the journalist Ivan Hrynevetskyi, and others. Most of the society's members were clergymen, which can be explained by their dominant position in Ukrainian social and political life. In the 1850s–1860s the clergy accounted for 60–70% of the membership.[40] In the 1870s, the situation began to change after representatives of the secular intelligentsia entered the political arena, yet the clergy continued to comprise a significant part of the membership.

The number of the Matica's members ranged from one to two hundred persons.[41] In the 1880s–1890s, when the society had a more scholarly character, the number of members was substantially lower, as is evident from records of attendance at general meetings: thirty were present in 1895, thirty-five in 1900.[42] Secular members were dominant in the leadership of the Matica, while the clergy constituted the main body of the membership.[43]

The requirement of high social status for admission to the Russophile societies, such as achievements in science, culture, education, or a corresponding financial position, turned them into elite institutions managed by the same people: outstanding figures in the Russophile movement who created a number of cultural and education societies and were, as a rule, members of all these institutions.[44]

3 Scholarly and Educational Activities and the Issue of National Identity

The Matica was the first Ruthenian cultural and educational organization in Galicia which tried to unite a program of national identity formation with

---

40 CSHAU in Lviv, fund 148, inventory 2, file 7, sheet 102, 105; Kril and Steblii, 206–07.
41 Kril and Steblii, 229.
42 CSHAU in Lviv, fund 148, inventory 2, file 7, sheet 77, 83.
43 Ibid., sheet 102, 105.
44 Orlevych 2001, 97.

academic research and its activities amid the people.⁴⁵ The members of the GRM wanted to engage all the forces of the Ruthenian intelligentsia in their activities. The leadership of the GRM, namely deputy head Ivan Borysykevych, initiated the preparation of the Council of Ruthenian Scholars (CRS). On 2 July 1848, the first meeting of the founder members of the society was held, headed by the Rev. Myhailo Kuzemskyi and his deputies, the lawyers Ivan Borysykevych and Yulian Lavrivskyi. The absence of a unified language concept and unified approaches to orthography, as well as the weakness of the academic research, complicated the Matica's activity. A Council of Ruthenian Scholars was convened in 1848 to define the program of the main philological and historical research. The main aim of this research was the separation of Galician Ruthenians from Polish influences and the shaping of Ruthenian identity in Galicia, which would be based not only on respect for the individual's language and rite (Greek Catholic) but also on serious academic research.⁴⁶ The Council consolidated the approach to the Matica as an academic center for Galician Ruthenians.

The Council of Scholars continued the linguistic debate, which was important for the Ruthenian intelligentsia, and a compromise was found: works intended for public education should be printed in the national language, but scientific works in Church Slavonic.⁴⁷ The decision of the Council reflected the complex outlook of its members, and potentially could stimulate the development of both Russophile and Ukrainophile versions of the national identity of Galician Ruthenians, since even Ukrainophiles did not object to the etymological dictionary used for printing the Matica's editions.⁴⁸

Thereafter, Ukrainophiles and Russophiles found themselves defending two fundamentally different ways to create a literary language. Ukrainophiles advocated the formation of a literary language on the basis of the vernacular, while Russophiles favored the historical principle.⁴⁹ The creation of a literary language on the basis of the vernacular was a courageous undertaking for the Slavic peoples in the nineteenth century, and the results of these efforts were difficult to predict. The establishment of Ukrainian literature on the basis of dialectal sources inevitably limited its generic and stylistic development in the initial stages of its formation and confirmed the doubts of the Russophiles. Moreover, the stylistic development of the literary language on the basis of West Ukrainian models was complicated by Polish and German borrowings.⁵⁰

---

45   Sukhyi, 248.
46   Ibid., 191.
47   Orlevych 2001, 112.
48   Sukhyi, 191.
49   Himka, 55.
50   Masnenko, 133 and 136.

Russophiles believed that it was appropriate to make Church Slavonic the basis for literary language development, arguing that the Russian of that time (or as they called it, the 'Rus' language) had not been influenced externally because Russia had managed to preserve its statehood. Russophiles considered the 'Little Russian' dialect as the first step towards mastering the 'Rus' language because, in their view, the latest developments in pedagogy recognized the important educational role of dialects through which one could successfully influence the hearts and minds of the masses.[51]

The second Council of Ruthenian Scholars was a smaller and less resonant affair. Decisions were made about the publication of religious literature, studying the history of the Ruthenian Church, and establishing a Historical Society. It was necessary to create public schools in all Galician communities and to find ways to disseminate publications through book distributors, some of whom worked as volunteers to make available the magazines of the Matica.[52] Most of these goals were never achieved, but they bear witness to the intention and desire of the intellectuals to develop the national cultural life.

The codification of spelling remained the primary task of general meetings in 1864 as it had been in the 1840s. The question was actively discussed in academic circles, causing disputes due to the lack of a single language strategy. The members of the Matica did not want to settle it and were willing to leave it for the executive board to decide. The participants in the Council turned out to be divided between the advocates of phonetic and etymological spelling. The advocates of phonetic spelling (Klymkovych, Zharskyi, Kachala, and Lavrivskyi are among those who later joined the Ukrainophile camp) tried to bring spelling closer to pronunciation, to emphasize the independence of the Ukrainian language and to introduce into Eastern Galicia the same spelling as in Dnieper Ukraine. The advocates of etymology (Holovatskyi, Didytskyi, Petrushevych, Kovalskyi, Lepkyi, Dobrianskyi, and Zhukovskyi) were in favor of preserving Eastern Slavic language unity. Lavrivskyi suggested accepting an etymological spelling that would take phonetics into account, referring to the existence of similar principles in German literature. In his opinion, pure etymology would be unclear for the people. This standpoint was supported by Holovatskyi and accepted by the general meeting.[53] In the 1850s, when the issue of publishing the society's periodical was discussed, Ilnytskyi was in favour of choosing the vernacular; however, Petrushevych and Holovatskyi supported the etymological approach.

---

51   "Nashy idealy," in *Slovo* 13 (5/17 February 1877).
52   *Zoria Halytska* 29 (29 March/10 April 1850).
53   "Otchety obshchestva," LXXV.

These debates in the Matica about creating a literary language and shaping national identity continued until the 1860s and had the nature of scholarly discussions rather than confrontations. The members of the Matica included representatives of different national orientations, both Russophile and Ukrainophile.

The Matica published historical works by activists whose conceptions differed concerning the issue of the independent existence of the Ukrainian nation. Vasyl Ilnytskyi praised the creative work of Denys Zubrytskyi, Antin Petrushevych, and Izydor Sharanevych, regarding them as authors who had brought fame to the Ukrainian nation. He defined the Ruthenians as one of the existing East Slavic nations with its own language and a long history dating back to Kievan Rus.[54]

In order to spread its scholarly activity, the Matica took the following decisions: in the general meeting of 1864 it decided to establish a history department, headed by Izydor Sharanevych, to promote the publication of popular histories of Galicia.[55] In order to encourage the best intellectual forces to work in the Matica, the society's leadership decided to announce competitions for belletristic and scholarly works.[56] In 1892, the Matica funded archaeological excavations in Halych conducted by Sventsitskyi.[57]

According to the Russophiles, the 'Rus' language was based on the development of three dialects: Little Russian, Great Russian, and Belarusian. As regards the shaping of the 'Rus' language and culture, Russophiles gave preference to the 'Little Russians' on the grounds that in the twentieth century the Russian language was closest to the original 'Rus' because Russia, as an independent state, had managed to preserve it.[58] In the late nineteenth and early twentieth centuries century, Russophiles identified the 'Rus' with 'All-Rus' or Russian.[59] Therefore, the Matica aimed to publish books in the Russian language.[60]

The notion of the Ukrainian ('Little Russian') language as a dialect of the 'Rus' language resulted from historical research about the Ukrainian or 'Little Russian' people as part of the 'Rus' people. The first historian of Galicia was Denys Zubrytskyi, whose historical works served as a theoretical basis for

---

54 See Ilnytskyi.
55 "Otchety obshchestva," LXXI.
56 CSHAU in Lviv, fund 148, inventory 2, file 7, sheet 75.
57 Ibid., sheet 69.
58 "Rech d-ra O. Dudykevycha" [Dr. Dudykevych's speech], *Halichanin* 239 (21 October/3 November 1908).
59 Bendasiuk 1909.
60 Bendasiuk 1930, 98–99.

Galician Russophilism. In his works Zubrytskyi argued for the ethnic unity of the 'Rus people' with Kievan Rus as a state of all Eastern Slavs, which was rooted in Eastern Slavic historical thought as far back as the twelfth century. The idea about one 'Rus' state was established in Russian historiography of the late eighteenth century as well. Other Ukrainian historians in the first decades of the nineteenth century, among them Bantysh-Kamenskyi, Martos, and Markevych, held similar views.[61] Under the influence of Russian historians and historians from Dnieper Ukraine, Zubrytskyi developed this theory in his creative work. He called Kyiv the "mother of Rus cities" and the "center of the Rus world." According to Zubrytskyi, by 'Galicia' one should understand the regions which belonged to the Principality of Halych inhabited by the 'Ruthenian' people.[62]

This conception provided the basis for academic research by the followers of Zubrytskyi: Holovatskyi, Petrushevych, Sharanevych, and other Russophile scholars. Yakiv Holovatskyi explained the differences between the language existing in Galicia and the 'Rus' language as a result of the political and religious alienation of Galicia from Rus, i.e., from all 'Rus people.'[63] According to Antin Petrushevych, until the mid-fourteenth century the 'Rus people' had had close ties unifying the two tribes (Little Russian and Great Russian).[64] Such a search for national identity denied the ethnic differences between Great and Little Russians and Belarusians, encompassing them all in a single ethnic community.[65] Russophiles admitted differences between Little Russians and the Russian people, but only as between the constituents (branches) of a united 'Rus nation.' In the session of the Diet on 11/24 October 1908 Volodymyr Dudykevych, an activist of the Matica and leader of the *novokursnyky* movement, pointed out in his speech that Galicians constitute Little Russians, but at the same time he denied the possibility of the existence of Little Russians as a separate nation along with Great Russians and Belarusians. He emphasized that together they constitute one 'Rus' nation.[66] And there was only one 'Rus' language created not by Great Russians but by "the genius of all Rus people," and mainly by Little Russians; it was brought to its present perfection by men of letters of the whole 'Rus' land involving the most active participation of the

---

61   Doroshenko, 22–23.
62   Zubrytskii, 1–2.
63   Holovatskii, LXXIV.
64   Svintsytskii, 95.
65   Miller, ch. 23.
66   In their documents Russophiles used the term 'Rus' to refer to the unity of the three nations (Ukrainian, Belarusian, and Russian) and did not identify it only with the term 'Russian.'

best writers of Southern Rus—the Little Russians.[67] In the context of creating the 'Rus' language, Russophiles developed Little Russian patriotism and emphasized the prevailing role of Little Russians. The activists of the Matica declared their standpoint during the meeting in 1902, pointing out that the society adhered to the main principle of the Russophile movement: the "tribal and cultural unity of the whole Rus nation."[68]

4 The Matica and Socio-political Life in Galicia

The confrontation between Ukrainophiles and Russophiles, with their differing views on the issues of language and the self-identification of Galician Ukrainians, grew more intense, especially with regard to the right to own Russophile institutions. The Ukrainophiles, dissatisfied with the work of the Matica (the fact that it was not fulfilling what they considered its primary task, the education of Ukrainians in the vernacular), tried to change the situation. They weighed two options: either to join the society in order to change the direction of its activities, or to establish a new society.[69] Russophiles thwarted these attempts. One of the methods of the Russophiles' struggle against Ukrainophiles was the removal of the latter from societies. Thus, in 1865, three Ukrainophiles (K. Klymkovych, P. Horbal, and D. Taniachkevych) were not accepted into the Matica.[70] Such behaviour on the part of the Russophiles prompted the Ukrainophiles to establish their own 'Prosvita' society in 1868.

The political events of 1866 contributed to the strengthening of Russophile sentiment. In 1866, the Polish majority of the Diet sought to ensure its power in the region by introducing an imperial chancellery for Galicia and Krakow. Ruthenian members of the Diet opposed this, fearing the domination of Poles in the region, and argued for the political and administrative division of Galicia. Teofil Pavlykiv made a representation about the political division of Galicia, but it did not receive any support. The Poles took advantage of Austria's defeat in the war with Prussia. In 1866, despite the protests of Ruthenians, the Diet addressed to the Emperor a request to establish a crown chancellery for Galicia. This was a severe blow for the Ruthenian representatives, and consequently on 8 August 1866 the Russophile newspaper *Slovo* featured an article entitled

---

[67] "Rech d-ra V.O. Dudykevycha" [Dr. Dudykevych's speech], *Halichanin* 239 (21 October/3 November 1908).
[68] CSHAU in Lviv, fund 148, inventory 2, file 7, sheet 118.
[69] Belei, 7.
[70] Sedliar 2012, 676–77.

"A Look into the Future" in which the author (Ivan Naumovych) claimed that Galician Ruthenians belong to "the Rus nation, which was distributed geographically beyond the Dnieper River ..."[71] The then editor of *Slovo*, Bohdan Didytskyi, explained that the Ruthenians were forced to do this because the government wanted to reorganize Galicia according to the requirements of the Polish majority of the Diet and give Agenor Gołuchowski authority over Galicia.[72]

The authorities began to accuse the Russophiles of excessive sympathy for Russia. Governor Gołuchowski gave the order to conduct a search in the apartment of Yakiv Holovatskyi in 1866 and 1867. In January 1867, Holovatskyi was removed from teaching at the university, but he was paid half of his salary. Tired of the harassment by the authorities, he moved to Russia. The departure of Yakiv Holovatskyi as a famous scholar and one of the heads of the Matica influenced the decline in its publishing activities.[73]

Other active members of the Matica also withdrew from its management. Its head Mykhailo Kuzemskyi resigned in 1866 and moved to Russia two years later. After Kuzemskyi left for Russia in 1868, Amvrozii Yavorskyi became the head of the society; Mykhailo Malynovskyi, who was in charge of the society from 1877 to 1878, became his deputy. After the death of Yavovskyi in 1884, Malynovskyi became the head again until 1900.

Throughout the 1880s–1890s the activity of the society was marked by the crisis of Russophilism connected with the Russophile orientation of its leadership, the use of etymological spelling and the Russian language in publications, and the struggle against the introduction of the phonetic principle into Ruthenian orthography that was advocated by the Ukrainophiles.

At the same time there was a crisis in the Greek-Catholic Church caused, among other things, by charges of 'apostasy' from the Latin clergy and the Polish elite who assumed absolute power in Galicia in the 1860s; by the indifference of the Austrian government to Ruthenians; and by vacillation between loyalty to Austria and sympathy for Russia. The internal struggles of various national and political movements manifested themselves in the chaotic ritual movement of the 1860s (removing imposed 'Latin' forms from the Greek Catholic rite and returning to old Eastern Christian practices), the mass emigration of priests to the Russian Empire, and the Galician Russophiles' active role in liquidation of the union in Chełm Land (1876).[74] For a number of *obriadovtsi*

---

71   *Slovo* 59 (27 July/8 August 1866).
72   *Slovo* 64 (25 August 1866).
73   Sukhyi.
74   See Turii.

(supporters of Russophilism) the Russian Orthodox Church became an example of "a veritable faith without foreign influences."[75] The Orthodox faith was promulgated by Russophiles under the guise of clearing the Greek Catholic rite of Latinization. In 1882, under the influence of Russophiles, the parishioners of the Galician village of Hnylychky announced their intention to convert to Orthodoxy (the so-called trial of Olha Hrabar). The names of prominent representatives of Russophilism such as Adolf Dobrianskyi, Osyp Markov, Venedykt Ploshchanskyi, Ivan Naumovych, and Mykola Ohonovskyi appear in this trial. They were charged with treason for promulgating Russophilism and Orthodoxy, and for campaigning for the separation of Galicia, Bukovyna, and Transcarpathia from the Austro-Hungarian Empire and joining them with Russia.[76] Although the court did not prove the fact of treason, the investigation and the trial of Olha Hrabar considerably undermined the position of the whole Russophile movement. The Stauropegion printing house soon faced the consequences: the Diet of Galicia stopped giving them annual grants (of two thousand gulden) for the publication of school textbooks and handed the grants instead to the Prosvita Society.[77] In 1883, the Diet refused to provide the Kachkovskyi Society with a subsidy.[78] Similar government measures did not influence the Matica directly, since none of its leaders were among the participants in the trial.

At the beginning of the twentieth century, the activation of the Ukrainian national political movement led a younger generation of the Russophile party to radicalize their activity. In the RNP, which united the Russophile movement, a young generation of activists (*novokursnyky*) supported more radical methods of party struggle, and spoke more clearly about the national identification of Galician Ruthenians with the all-Rus space that united Little Russians (Ukrainians), Great Russians (Russians), and Belarusians, while the leading role belonged to Russia as an independent Slavic state.

The reason for this conflict was the spread of socialist ideas. The social mobilization of the lower classes is one of the constituents of modern nation-shaping, and in the case of Galicia the peasantry formed the societal foundation of the nation and national ideologies had to take their interests into account. This factor explains the relatively great importance of socialist ideas in the Ukrainian national movement.[79] The *novokursnyky*—among them the

---

75   Osadczy, 717.
76   Kyrychuk, 55.
77   Ibid., 59.
78   Orlevych 2009, 104.
79   Kappler, 17–18.

lawyer and journalist Mykhailo Hlushkevych, Dmytro Verhun (1871–1951), Yulian Yavorskyi (1873–1937), Oleksii Herovskyi (1883–1972), Volodymyr Dudykevych, Osyp Monchalovskyi, the writer Ivan Sviatytskyi, the historian Pylyp Svystun, and others—criticized the representatives of the older generation for ignoring the interests of ordinary people, which in their opinion led to the loss of their impact on society. The Ukrainophile parties focused on solving the problems of the peasantry,[80] while the Ruthenians were viewed as too subservient to the authorities, conservative, and authoritarian when managing party organizations as well as cultural and educational societies (like the Stauropegion Institute, the People's Home, the Kachkovskyi Society, or the Galician-Ruthenian Matica).[81] These contradictions led to the foundation of two Russophile parties in 1909: the Galician-Ruthenian Council (*starokursnyky*) and the Ruthenian People's Organization (*novokursnyky*).

Some activists of the *novokursnyky* movement (namely Hrushkevych, Sviatytskyi, Protsyk, and Dudykevych) were also members of the Matica and sought to influence its activities, trying to draw the attention of its leaders to the problems of the peasantry by distributing popular literature in the provinces. Although the older generation of the RNP was aware of the new trends among its younger members, they tried to ignore them. Therefore, in 1900 the Matica member, historian, and writer Ivan Sanotskyi addressed a letter to the Matica's general meeting in which he argued that progress could not be expected of the society because of the conservatism of its activities and its unwillingness to publish works in the Rus language. Positive changes, in his opinion, could be brought about by involving new leaders and members, because both its supporters and its opponents blamed the Matica for being lethargic and inert.[82] His letter remained unanswered.

The need to increase the impact on the peasantry by means of distributing literature in the provinces was discussed at the meeting in 1900, where Volodymyr Dudykevych pointed out that the reason for the Matica's uncompleted tasks as a scholarly society was its poor organization. In his opinion, the Matica should be a leader of literary life in Galicia and have representatives in every area in order to extend its influence.[83] The Matica's statutes were revised for this purpose. At the general meeting in 1907, Ilarion Sventsitskyi and Volodymyr Dudykevych changed the Matica's statutes to reflect its scholarly and

---

80   "Orhanizuimosia!" [Let us organize ourselves!], *Holos naroda* 12 (Lvov, 4/17 December 1909).
81   "Ot redaktsyi" [From the editorial board], *Novaia zhyzn* 1 (1908).
82   CSHAU in Lviv, fund 148, inventory 2, file 93, sheet 14.
83   Ibid., fund 148, inventory 2, file 7, sheet 85.

literary nature to a greater extent.[84] The attempts of the Matica's members to extend its influence into the provinces came into conflict with their eagerness to give it a scholarly character, given that the contents and language of the scholarly and literary works published by the Matica were obscure for the peasantry who made up most of the population of Galicia.

The Russophile societies fulfilled the tasks assigned them by the political bodies of the Russophile movement. At first the Russophile movement was united by the political organization 'Ruska Rada' (the 'Ruthenian Council,' 1870), then by the 'Ruska Narodna Partiia' (RNP: the 'Ruthenian People's Party') founded in 1900. At the RNP convention in 1903 the proposal that the Stauropegion, the People's Home, and the Matica should work on issues concerning the education of the Galician population was discussed.[85]

The RNP deemed that it was necessary to publish literature written in 'Galician dialect' for the peasantry, and in the 'all-Rus language' for the intelligentsia. They reserved the role of a scholarly society for the Matica, and therefore its editions were to be published in a modern Russian literary language. Thus they came forward with the initiative to reestablish the periodical *Sbornyk* (Collection, 1901) and publish it in Russian.

5 Appeals to the Authorities

Despite the statute's principle of non-involvement in political activities, the Matica, like all Russophile societies, was involved in political life and served as a tool for implementing the goals of the Russophiles. Among the main forms of their activities at this time were the struggle to use the 'Rus language' in official documents and for its implementation in higher education (they supported the establishment of departments of Russian language and literature at Lviv and Chernivtsi Universities) along with the fight against phonetic spelling and for the spread of the Orthodox faith. In 1896, the Matica, together with other Russophile institutions, addressed a memorandum to Emperor Franz Joseph with the request to abolish Ukrainian phonetic spelling and use the vernacular in the schools and institutions of Galicia and Bukovyna.[86]

At the Matica meeting in 1907 a decision was taken to send a request to the government to give the 'Rus language' the right to 'citizenship,' and (at the suggestion of Mariian Hlushkevych) to publish popular brochures and practical

---

84   Ibid., sheet 122.
85   Markov, 28–29.
86   CSHAU in Lviv, fund 182, inventory 1, file 14.

courses for learning the 'Rus language.' In 1908, at the suggestion of the society's head, Pylyp Svystun, deputies of the Diet Hlibovytskyi and Dudykevych compiled a memorandum to the senate with a request to establish a 'Rus' Literature Department at Lviv University. The society submitted the same petition to the Diet.[87]

6   Relations with the Greek Catholic Hierarchy

In 1900 Bohdan Didytskyi was elected head of the society; Monchalovskyi, Lahola, Svystun, Yavorskyi, and others became members of the board. At this time the Matica entered into a conflict with the hierarchy of the Greek Catholic Church when the Metropolitan was deprived of the status of patron by a statute adopted in 1901. On 16 November 1904, Metropolitan Andrei Sheptytskyi expressed his protest to the leadership regarding the decision. Bohdan Didytskyi replied with a letter explaining that the decision was taken because the clergy supported the phonetic spelling.[88]

Although over time the relationship between the Russophile societies, including the Matica, and the clergy authorities became aggravated, mainly because of disagreements over issues concerning the national and political life of the Ruthenian Galicians, the Matica still maintained contact with the clergy, and especially with the Metropolitan of the Greek Catholic Church Andrei Sheptytskyi. In the report for 1895–1900 it was stated that with the help of Sheptytskyi when he was Bishop of Stanislaviv, the Matica sent a prayer for Ruthenian children in Brazil,[89] and in 1900 sent him greetings on the occasion of his appointment as Metropolitan of Galicia.[90]

7   Publishing Activities

Publishing was the main activity of the Matica. The works of the SRC were published in a printing house of the Stauropegion Institute as well as in the periodicals *Naukovyi Sbornyk* (Scientific Collection, 1865–68), *Literaturnyi Sbornyk* (Literary Collection, 1869–74, 1885–90, 1896, 1897, 1901, 1902, 1904,

---

87   CSHAU in Lviv, fund 148, inventory 2, file 7, sheet 122, 123.
88   "Mytropolyt Halytskyi," 70–71; Pashaieva, 120–121.
89   CSHAU in Lviv, fund 148, inventory 1, file 93, sheet 13.
90   Ibid., sheet 92.

1905), and *Nauchno-literaturnyi sbornyk* (Scientific and Literary Collection, 1906, 1908, 1930, and 1934).[91]

Three main kinds of literature published by the Matica can be identified: religious literature, textbooks for schools and gymnasiums, and scientific and artistic literature. On 13 March 1850, the Matica sent the government an offer to establish Ruthenian primary schools in Galician villages. For this purpose the society decided to publish school textbooks, which were in short supply. In the early 1850s, the members of Matica translated a few textbooks: Kovalskyi translated a textbook on botany from Serbian, and Malynovskyi "O velikom Bozhem mire" (On the Great World of God, 1852), etc.[92] They published an ABC-book by Dobrianskyi (1849) for schools and one by Hurkevych for colleges (1851), a reading book by Shashkevych (1850), and one by Toronskyi for gymnasiums, *Khrestomatiia ruskoi movy* (A Reader for the Ruthenian Language) by Holovatskyi.[93] In 1861–62 they published eight textbooks on religion for the students of the Greek Catholic gymnasium, seven translated by Tsybyk and the eighth by Poppel.[94] The Matica published approximately thirty thousand copies of textbooks for schools. This increased activity caused dissatisfaction in the government, which in 1853 adopted a resolution that textbooks for Ruthenian primary schools could only be published according to the pattern of existing German ones,[95] while the printing and selling of textbooks were the task of the Matica.[96] Along with textbooks for primary schools, the Matica established a special fund for preparing textbooks for gymnasiums.

Religious books accounted for the largest share of the Matica's publications, and also generated the highest profits from sales since religious literature remained the most popular genre.[97] As for scientific works, the Matica mainly published the works of its activists who did research on linguistic or historic topics, such as Holovatskyi's "An Article about the Southern Ruthenian Language and its Dialects" (1849), Didytskyi's *Mykhail Kachkovskyi and Modern Galician-Ruthenian Literature*, Petrushevych's *Linguistic and Historical Reflections*, and Hushalevych's *The Tale of Ihor Sviatoslavych's Campaign* (1850), along with works of popular science like Levytskyi's *Practical Science of Gardening* (1871).[98]

---

91   Pashaieva and Klimkova, 61–71.
92   "Otchety obshchestva," XXXVIII.
93   Ibid., XXXIV.
94   Sedliar 2008, 86.
95   Kril and Steblii, 210.
96   "Otchety obshchestva," XLI.
97   Kril and Steblii, 211.
98   Holovatskii 1849; Didytskyi, ch. 1; Petrushevych; Hushalevych; Levytskyi.

The Matica also issued a few collections that can be viewed as periodicals due to their structure, among them three issues of the *Halytskyi istoricheskii sbornyk* (Galician Historical Collection; Lviv, 1854, 1856, 1860) in which historical works by Antonii Petrushevych appeared. The first two collections were published in Russian in the modernized Cyrillic alphabet (*grazhdanka*), while under pressure from the authorities the third one was published in traditional Cyrillic. In the first years of its publishing activity the Matica printed books in Cyrillic at the demand of the Austrian authorities in the printing house of Stauropegion and sold them with its help.[99] In 1865, the periodical *Naukovyi sbornyk* (Scientific Collection) began to appear. Until 1868 it came out annually. In 1869, its name was changed to *Literatyrnyi sbornyk* (Literary Collection), which appeared until 1873.

In its publishing projects, the Matica tried to pursue its aim to extend scientific knowledge and to provide ordinary people with education. The collections in which the historical works of Holovatskyi, Petrushevych, Merunovych, and Ploshchanskyi were published were of interest only to a limited readership, so in 1866 the originally planned printing of one thousand copies was revised downwards to three hundred due to its unpopularity. This was also the reason for changing the scientific collection towards more popular and belletristic topics, as evidenced by its name change to *Literaturnyi sbornik* (Literary Collection). In addition, the departure from the editorial board of Yakiv Holovatskyi, who was one of the most famous scholars of that time, affected the publishing activities.

The articles were published in so-called *iazychie* (a language based on Church Slavonic mixed with Russian, with borrowings from Ukrainian and Ukrainian pronunciation), which was one of the reasons for their unpopularity and the suspension of publishing. In 1885, the Matica resumed publishing under the editorship of Bohdan Didytskyi, albeit irregularly and with limited circulation. Historical subject matter connected with the history of Galicia prevailed, and the works of Petrushevych were published most of all; the *Literatyrnyi sbornyk* contained his *Svodnaia Letopis* (Combined Chronicle).

Among the problems of the society was the spread of its publications since the 1850s, because except for the Stauropegion Institute, most of the existing Galician network of bookstores did not belong to Ruthenians. The society appealed to the Greek Catholic hierarchy for help, and as a result in the late 1850s committees to sell the Matica's publications (usually consisting of three

---

99   CSHAU in Lviv, fund 148, inventory 2, file 7, sheet 69.

priests) began to be established in the provinces.[100] The main dealer remained the Stauropegion Institute, as well as other non-Ruthenian bookstores and individuals. In the late nineteenth century the Matica had its own bookstore, which was situated at the People's Home.[101]

The circulation of the Matica's publications ranged from five hundred (scientific papers) to twenty thousand for primers or textbooks, and the circulation of prayers ranged from a few to ten thousand copies. Religious literature was in great demand with the population, while the demand for scientific works, despite their small circulation, remained limited.[102]

The society's activity began to decline after the *Nauchno-literaturnyi sbornyk* ceased publication in 1908. In 1903, Yulian Yavorskyi moved to Russia, and Osyp Monchalovskyi died in 1906, which caused the publications to decline. Non-periodicals almost did not come out at all at that time, except for two grammars by Monchalovskyi and Sventsitskyi. In 1908, Svystun, who was the head of the Matica, made an attempt to resume publication, but only two issues appeared. In *Sbornyk* (1901–06, 1908) the *novokursnyky* Verhun, Hlushkevych, Hlibovytskyi, Lutsyk, Yavorskyi and others published their works, as well as the Russian scholars Budylovych, Lavrov, Speranskiy, Florinskiy, and Frantsev. Monchalovskyi published works about the Ukrainian (Little Russian) language; Svystun and Petrushevych on Galician Ruthenian history; Sventsitskyi on philosophy and manuscripts of the People's Home, or the relations of Carpathian Rus with Russia; Yavorsky on ethnography; Hlushkevych and Verhun mainly lyric poems, etc.

The distinguishing feature of the Russophile movement at this time was the growing political activity of its members, whereas less and less attention was paid to scholarly issues. This badly affected the activity of the Matica, the only Russophile society with a distinctly academic orientation. This period coincided with problems in the activities of the *Ruska Narodna Partiia* (Ruthenian People's Party): splits within the party, persecution by the government, struggles with Ukrainian national democratic forces, etc.[103] As explained by Russophiles, all writers were obliged to take part in political struggle,[104] which, in their opinion, led to a decline in the Matica's activity.

The Matica's withdrawal from cultural and educational activity was one of the reasons for its unpopularity. By 1910 the Kachkovskyi Society managed to

---

100   Sedliar 2010.
101   CSHAU in Lviv, fund 148, inventory 1, file 93.
102   Sukhyi, 205.
103   "Otchety obshchestva," 101.
104   Bendasiuk 1930, 102.

increase its membership to ten thousand, while the Matica's membership numbered only two hundred. It nonetheless organized reading rooms and published popular scientific literature,[105] though it could not compete with the Ukrainophile society 'Prosvita,' which confirmed the unpopularity of Russophile ideas in Galicia. Among the reasons why the Matica's publishing activities were not particularly successful was that it duplicated the tasks and aims of the Russophile societies. At the 1903 convention of the Ruthenian People's Party (founded in 1900) the role of the Stauropegion Institute, the People's Home, and the Matica in educating the Galician population was on the agenda.[106]

The Stauropegion Institute, the People's Home, and the Kachkovskyi Society were also involved in publishing. For instance, the historical work by Vasyl Ilnytskyi *Perehliad Yuzhno-ruskoi istorii vid 1337–1450* (Review of South Ruthenian History from 1337–1450) was published by the Matica and the Stauropegian Institute in the same year.[107]

Along with its publishing activity, the Matica established cultural ties with Russia, sending its representatives to the convention of the Archaeological Society in Moscow, to Pushkin and Gogol jubilee celebrations, and to conventions of Slavic journalists in the West. In Lviv, the Matica organized a celebration on 11 January 1901 to commemorate the eightieth anniversary of the birth of Antonii Petrushevych, and celebrated the fiftieth anniversary of Gogol's death in 1902.

In the matter of book exchanges, the Matica cooperated with the Serbian, Slovenian and Illyro-Croatian Maticas as well as with academic and literary institutions in Russia.[108] The Matica exchanged literature with the Kraków Academy of Sciences, the Museum of the Czech Kingdom in Prague (1900), and the Serbian Matica (1895). The Czech Matica sent a medal made on the occasion of the centenary of the birth of Safarik.[109]

The scientific level of the Matica was highly rated in many Slavic centers, which confirms the contacts of the Galician-Ruthenian Matica with other Slavic Maticas and the fact that it had the potential for development.[110]

---

105   Kril and Steblii, 226.
106   Markov, 28–29.
107   Podolianyn.
108   CSHAU in Lviv, fund 148, inventory 1, file 69, sheet 2, 6.
109   CSHAU in Lviv, fund 148, inventory 2, file 7, sheet 78, 113, 97.
110   Sukhyi, 249.

8 Financial Activities

In order to perform their scientific and educational tasks, the Matica's activists found it necessary first and foremost to accumulate material resources. As the Matica's head Mykhailo Kuzemskyi pointed out, the tasks of the society were to disseminate education among the people by two means: spiritual work and the material resources of the society.[111] The main donors to the society were its own members, namely the Ukrainian entrepreneurs Ivan Tovarnytskyi and Klymentii Merunovych, as well as Metropolitan Mykhailo Levytskyi, who willed one thousand gulden to the Matica.[112] The Matica's fund was formed thanks to donations, membership fees, interests on credit, and money from sales of books. The membership fee for institutional founders was one hundred gulden, and for individual members fifty gulden. They could either pay all at once or in instalments over ten years.[113] Village and town communities and church brotherhoods were institutional members.[114] Often membership fees were not paid. Income from the sale of books, interest on loans, donations, and revenues from printing books constituted the profits of the society.

The financial foundation for the society's activity was made of membership fees, charity donations, and, from 1877, income from real estate. The society's material condition gradually improved from the 1860s to the first half of the 1880s, which made possible the purchase in 1877 of the building at No. 5 Zhovkivska Street, near the St. Mykolai Greek Catholic Church. One characteristic feature of the Matica's activity as well as that of other Russophile societies was a preference for capital accumulation (the purchase of real estate, securities, etc.) to the detriment of their cultural and educational tasks. For example, they postponed action on the foundation of a private 'Rus' gymnasium in the People's Home, which was discussed in the meeting on 28 May 1908.[115] Young Russophiles criticized the construction of the People's Home and the Transfiguration Church (since there were many old temples).[116] The Matica's leaders used to spend less than half of their income on publishing.[117] Aware of the Matica's unsatisfactory publishing activities, they still preferred to increase

---

111   "Otchety obshchestva," XXXIX.
112   "Otchety obshchestva," v.
113   Kril and Steblii, 200.
114   CSHAU in Lviv, fund 148, inventory 1, file 11, sheet 6.
115   *Novaia zhyzn* 1 (1908).
116   Ibid., p. 1.
117   Sedliar 2008, 94.

their accumulation of real estate. In November 1911, they decided to construct a new building instead of the old one, whose condition was considered unsatisfactory. Meanwhile, they complained about the lack of money for publishing.[118] In the 1870s, the Matica refused to publish its financial reports, which made their activity opaque.

The Russophiles were deeply concerned about improving their own financial and economic situation, as was evident from their statute documents. Thus, according to the 1887 statute of the Matica, in the event of its liquidation, their property would be passed to the other two Russophile cultural and educational societies: the Stauropegion Institute and the People's Home.[119] The Matica had lent money for the construction of the People's Home. Until 1863, their expenses for the construction of the People's Home, which began to be repaid in 1863, are indicated in the reports.[120]

9 The Matica during World War I and the Interwar Period

The Russian language of the Matica's editions caused concern among the Austrian authorities, so on the eve of the First World War all Russophile societies, including the Matica, were banned.

One of the main components of the Russophile ideology was loyalty to the authorities. However, given the increasing tension in relations between Russia and Austria-Hungary, the attitude of the authorities to Russophilism deteriorated. In 1912–14, the Austro-Hungarian authorities began to pursue a fierce policy towards the Russophile movement.[121] Ukrainophiles also joined in the campaign against Russophiles. In early May 1914, the Committee of the Ukrainian People's Democratic Party adopted a resolution on the confrontation with the Russophile movement and launched an anti-Russophile propaganda campaign.[122] Before the war, the Austrian authorities had organized three political trials against Russophiles: the trial of the Herovskyi brothers, the Maramures-Sighet trial, and the Lviv trial. The trial of the Herovskyi brothers took place in December 1913; Oleksii and Heorhii Herovskyi had been arrested in Chernivtsi and accused of treason. The Maramures-Sighet trial began on 29 December

---

118   CSHAU in Lviv, fund 148, inventory 1, file 93, sheet 13.
119   Ibid., file 5, sheet 2.
120   Ibid., file 31, sheet 3–4.
121   See Klopova.
122   Wojtowicz-Huber, 217–18.

1913 and ended on 3 March 1914. This trial was directed against Orthodox citizens in Transcarpathia who were accused of treason. On 9 March 1912 the Lviv trial began against a large group of people: Semen Bendasiuk, an active figure of Russophilism; a number of members of Russophile societies, namely the Stauropegion Institute, the People's Home, and the Galician-Ruthenian Matica; two Orthodox priests, Maksym Sandovych and Ihnatii Hudyma; and a student named Vasyl Koldra. They were all accused of attempting to separate Galicia from Austria. This trial ended in June 1914 with the acquittal of all the defendants. Before the Russian offensive began, Austrian authorities arrested the representatives of the Russophile movement and their advocates and sent them to the Talerhof and Terezin concentration camps. Ukrainophiles, Poles, and Jews were also among those arrested. Others who had nothing to do with any political party were arrested as well. The courts handed down death sentences without any compassion for civilians. Military commanders often resorted to frontier justice and executed those suspected of supporting Russophiles. Denunciations by local authorities were one of the reasons for arrests.[123] Semen Bendasiuk was among the prisoners at Talerhof.

The arrests of the Galician Ukrainians in 1914 regardless of their party affiliation forced the representatives of the Ukrainian national movement to demand the release of prisoners and those sent to Talerhof. When the leading Russophile activists Markov, Kurylovych, and Cherliunchakevych were sentenced to death, the representatives of the Ukrainian national movement addressed the Austrian authorities with a request for their pardon.[124] However, the Russophiles considered the Ukrainophiles' attempts to come to their defense to be ineffective. The Russophiles remained offended, and in the interwar period, they created and actively developed the cult of the 'Talerhof tragedy': they organized conventions, published almanacs, etc. In 1936, a Talerhof department was established in the Stauropegion Museum.[125]

When World War I began, Austrian authorities suspended the activities of all the Russophile societies, and the Matica in particular. With the entry of Russian troops into Lviv their activities were resumed; Russophile societies supported the Russian authorities and actively assisted them.[126] During the war, the whole Russophile movement was united under the leadership of Volodymyr Dudykevych. His orders were followed by all the Russophile societies,

---

123 Ibid., 218.
124 Andrusiak, 202.
125 "Talerhofskii otd'l Stavropyhiiskoho Muzeia vo Lvov," *Russkii Holos* 21 (7 June 1936), 755.
126 Orlevych 2011, 245.

including the SRC. In 1918 they issued a statement on the accession of Galicia to Russia.[127]

In 1923 the Russophiles resumed their activities and established the *Ruska Narodna Orhanizatsiia* (RNO, Ruthenian People's Organization).[128] In the same year, the Matica resumed work again, headed by the Rev. Tyt Myshkovskyi, a member of the RNO. Lahola, Yavorskyi, Vavryk, Bendasyuk, and others were members of the board.

In the interwar period the Russophile movement was led by the RNO. In 1928 it changed its name to the *Ruska Selianska Orhanizatsiia* (RSO, Ruthenian Peasant Organization), which, as in previous times, determined the activities of the Russophile cultural and educational societies. It declared its adherence to pre-war Russophilism, mostly of the *novokursnyky* faction. The party defended the theory of the unity of the 'Rus lands,' and saw as its main goal solving the social problems of the Galician peasants. In 1928 and 1936 the RSO, together with all cultural and educational societies, including the Matica, sent a memorandum protesting against attempts by representatives of the Ukrainian national democratic camp to change the name of the 'Ruthenian' people (as they were known in the Polish state) to 'Ukrainians.' The Matica supported these actions financially. In 1936, the RSO addressed the Matica as the institution that signed the memorandum to pay for its printing.[129]

In the interwar period, the members of Matica were mostly secular: journalists, lawyers, historians, linguists and others, with rare exceptions, such as the Matica's head Tyt Myshkovskyi.[130]

A significant figure in the interwar Matica, as well as for the whole Russophile movement, was the journalist, historian, and writer Vasyl Vavryk, who in 1926 published a monograph on Yakiv Holovatskyi and the collection *Halitskaia Rus A.S. Pushkinu* (The Galician Rus up to A[lexandr] S[ergeevich] Pushkin). The Russophiles appreciated his scientific and literary activities, and considered his work on Yakiv Holovatskyi (who in 1837 had published the first collection of poems in Ukrainian and was one of the members of the 'Ruthenian Trinity') as a great success in the recovery of the Matica. In their opinion, this work could unite people around the 'Ruthenian national idea' in the post-war period.[131] Vasyl Vavryk not only determined the scientific and literary

---

127 Ibid., 237.
128 CSHAU in Lviv, fund 130, inventory 1, file 33, sheet 53.
129 CSHAU in Lviv, fund 148, inventory 1, file 101, sheet 4.
130 CSHAU in Lviv, fund 148, inventory 1, file 100, sheet 25.
131 Ibid., file 22, sheet 27.

activities of the Matica, but was also one of its leaders. In 1939, he was elected head of the society.[132]

The society's statutes were ratified in 1937 in accordance with the legislation of the Polish state. The society ceased its activities in 1939 with the arrival of Soviet authorities.

10 Conclusions

The establishment of the Galician-Ruthenian Matica was connected with the wave of political upheavals during the epoch of the 'Springtime of Nations' (1848) and reflected processes that were under way in all the Slavic nations of Central Europe (the Matica was modelled on other Slavic Maticas).

The Activities of the GRM intensified academic research in the fields of national history, ethnography, and philology, among others. The lack of academic resources did not allow them to implement their projects, while the shift to a Russophile standpoint and the introduction of the Russian language in publications made their activity increasingly unpopular.

This unpopularity was a result of the state of Galician society at that time: a narrow circle of intellectuals read these works, but they were confusing for most of the Galician peasantry. The publications were printed in the Russian language, which the Galician peasantry and much of the intelligentsia did not understand. The members of the Matica blamed the lack of popularity of their publishing activities on financial circumstances: insufficient revenue from the People's Home, high membership fees, high costs for the restoration of the People's Home, high taxes, etc. They did not understand that the underlying cause was the loss of popularity and influence of their ideas, which led to the decline of the Russophile movement in Galicia as a whole.

Another reason that made Russophilism unpopular and led to the division of the Russophile movement into *starokursnyky* (advocates of the old course) and *novokursnyky* (advocates of the new course) was the conservative older generation of leaders, their authoritarian methods of management, and their excessive loyalty to the Austrian government. This caused discontent and criticism among the members of the Matica.

The case of the Galician-Ruthenian Matica enables us to survey the social transformations of the Galician Ruthenians, among which a number of major

---

132   Ibid., file 102, sheet 65.

issues can be identified. These include alternative conceptions of national identity. Another is the literary language: the Russophiles advocated etymological spelling and using the Russian language in literary works, or the language most similar to it. If in the early stages of its existence the Matica had acted on behalf of the national interests of all the Galician Ruthenians, in the course of time it became an arena of confrontation between the two most powerful socio-political forces, the Ukrainophiles and the Russophiles, and the latter gained the advantage. Another problem was the radicalization of the Russophile movement, which became apparent in its increasing orientation towards Russia and the printing of the Matica's editions in Russian or in the language closest to Russian. Yet another distinctive feature of the times was an increase in the influence of the secular element over the ecclesiastical one, which was related to general processes of social secularization. All the above-mentioned problems of the Matica's activity are indicators of larger social processes among the Galician Ukrainians.

Bibliography

Andrusiak, Mykola. "Halytske moskofilstvo i Talerhof" [Galician Moscophilism and Talerhof], *Dilo* 4 (1933), 202.

Belei, I. *Dvatsiat i piat lit Istorii Tovarystva "Prosvity"* [Twenty-five Years of the History of the "Prosvita" Society]. Lviv: Vyd-vo Tovarystva 'Prosvita,' 1894.

Bendasiuk, Semen. *Grammatiki russkogo literaturnogo (obshcherusskogo) yazyka dla russkikh v Halychyni, Bukovyni i Uhryi* [A Grammar of standard literary Russian for Russians in Galicia, Bukovyna and Uhry]. Lvov: Typohrafiya Stavrop. Instytuta vo L'vovi, 1909.

Bendasiuk, Semen. "Uczono-literaturnoie obchestvo Halitsko-russkaia Matytsia vo Lvovie (Proshloie i nastoiashcheie)" [The Galician-Ruthenian Matica in Lviv (Past and Present)]. In V.R. Vavryka, ed., *Nauchno-literaturnyi sbornik Halitsko-russkoi Matitsy vo Lvovie*. Lvov: Tipohrafija Stavropihiona pod upr. Macana M., 1930. 85–109.

Didytskyi, Bohdan. *Mykhail Kachkovskyi i sovremennaia halitsko-ruskaia literature* [Mykhail Kachkovskyi and modern Galician-Russian literature]. Lvov: Ocherk byohraf. i ist. liter. Pech. In-ta Stavropihiiskoho, 1867.

Doroshenko, Dmytro. *Narys Istorii Ukrainy* [A Sketch of Ukrainian history]. Lviv: Vyd-vo 'Svit,' 1991.

Himka, Jon Paul. *Religion and Nationality in Western Ukraine: The Greek Catholic Church and Ruthenian National Movement in Galicia, 1867–1900*. Montreal: McGill-Queen's University Press, 1999.

Holovatskii, Yakiv. *Istoricheskiy ocherk osnovaniia Galitsko-Russkoi Matytsi i spravozda i spravozdanie pervoho soboru uchenykh russkykh i liubytelei narodnoho prosvishcheniia* [A historical sketch of the establishment of the Galician-Ruthenian Matica and the report on the first convention of Ruthenian scholars and advocates of public education]. Lvov: Drukarnia Instytuta Stavropyhiiskoho, 1850.

Holovatskii, Yakiv. *Rosprava o yazytsi yuzhnoruskom i yego nerichiiakh* [On the Southern Russian language and its dialects]. Lvov: Instytyt Stavropihijskij, 1849.

Holovna Ruska Rada 1848–1851. Protokoly zasidan i knyha korespondentsii [The Main Ruthenian Council in 1848–1851. Minutes of meetings and correspondence records], eds. O. Turii, U. Kryshtalovych, and I. Svarnyk. Lviv: Instytut Istorii Tserkvy Ukrainskoho Katolytskoho Universytetu, 2002.

Hushalevych, Ioan. *Slovo o polku Ihoria Sviatoslavycha* [The Tale of Ihor's Campaign]. Lvov: Izd. In-ta Stavropig-go, 1850.

Ilnytskyi, Vasyl. *Visty pro zemlu I dii Rysuniv* [On the land and activities of Ruthenians]. Lviv: Instytyt Stavropihijskij, 1870.

Isaievych, Yaroslav. *Bratstva ta yikh rol v rozvytku ukrainskoyi kultury XVI–XVIII st.* [Brotherhoods and their role in the development of Ukrainian culture in the 16th–18th centuries]. Kyiv: Naukova Dumka, 1966.

Kappler, Andreas. "Hromadianska chy etnichna natsiia. Zauvahy z teorii ta istoriohrafii" [Civil or ethnic nation. Comments on theory and historiography]. In *Ukraina. Protsesy natsiotvorennia.* Kyiv: Vydavnyctvo 'K.I.S.,' 2011. 13–28.

Klopova, Marija. "'Russkoe dvizhenie' i ego sudba nakanune Pervoi mirovoi voiny" [The "Russian movement" and its destiny on the eve of World War I]. Electronic resource: http://rys-strategia.ru/publ/1-1-0-1105 (accessed 1 October 2018).

Kril, Myhajlo, and Feodosij Steblii. "Galickaia matica vo Lvovie" [The Galician Matica in Lviv (Part One)]. Moskva: n.p., 1996. 190–233.

Kyrychuk, Oleksandra. *Lvivskyi Stavropihiiskyi instytut u hromadskomu zhytti Halychyny druhoji polovyny XIX–pochatku XX st.* [The Lviv Stauropegion Institute in the public life of Galicia in the second part of the 19th and early 20th centuries]. Lviv: Vydavnyctvo Lvivskoho muzeju istorii relihiji 'Lohos,' 2001.

Leshchylovskaia, Inna. "Vvedenie" [Introduction], *Slavianskie matitsy XIX: Chast pervaia.* Moskva: n.p., 1996.

Levytskyi, Ivan. *Praktychna nauka pro sadovodsto* [Practical gardening]. Lvov: Typ. Stavropyhijskoho Instytuta, 1871.

Markov, Dmytro. *Russkaia i ukrainskaia ideia v Avstrii* [The Rus and the Ukrainian idea in Austria]. Lviv: Sost. A. Hahatko, pech. 'Udilova,' 1911.

Masnenko, Vitalij. "Ukrainska literaturna mova. Istoriia stanovlennia i rozvytku" [The standard Ukrainian language. History of shaping and development]. Electronic resource: http://lib.chdu.edu.ua/pdf/posibnuku/188/48.pdf (accessed 1 October 2018).

Miller, Aleksej. *'Ukrainskii vopros' v politike vlastei i russkom obshchestvennom mnenii (vtoraia polovina XIX veka)* [The 'Ukrainian issue' in government policy and Russian public opinion]. Sankt-Peterburg: n.p., 2000.

"Mytropolyt Halytskyi Andrei Sheptytskyi i Halitsko-russkaia Matytsia" [Galician Metropolitan Andrei Sheptytskyi and the Galician-Ruthenian Matica]. In B. Didyckoho, ed., *Nauchno-literaturnyi sbornik povremennoje izdanie Halitsko-russkoj Matitsy vo Lvovie*. Lvov: Stavropihijskaja tipohrafija, 1905. 66–73.

Orlevych, Iryna. *Stavropihiiskyi instytut u Lvovi (kinets XVIII–60-ti rr. XIX)* [The Stauropegion Institute in Lviv (late 18th c.–1860s)]. Lviv: Vydavnyctvo Lvivskoho muzeju istorii relihiji 'Lohos,' 2001.

Orlevych, Iryna. "Z istorii budivnytstva Preobrazhenskoi tserkvy u Lvovi" [From the history of construction of the Transfiguration Church in Lviv]. In V. Hajuk, J. Daszkevych and L. Muravska, eds., *Istoriia relihii v Ukraini*, Lviv: n.p., (2005).

Orlevych, Iryna. "Tovarystvo 'Narodnyi dim' u Lvovi v 1914–1921 rokakh" [The People's House Society in Lviv in 1914–1921], *Ukraina: kulturna spadshchyna, natsionalna svidomist, derzhavnist* 16 (2008), 275–88.

Orlevych, Iryna. "Lvivskyi Stavropihiiskyi instytut (1914–1925)" [The Lviv Stauropegion Institute (1914–1925)], *Ukraina: kulturna spadshchyna, natsionalna svidomist, derzhavnist* 18 (2009), 153–69.

Orlevych, Iryna. "Tovarystvo imeni Mykhaila Kachkovskoho v natsionalno-politychnomu rusi halytskykh ukraintsiv (1874–1914)" [The Mykhailo Kachkovskyi Society in the national and political movement of Galician Ukrainians (1874–1914)], *Nauka, relihiia, suspilstvo* 4 (2009), 101–09.

Orlevych, Iryna. "Halytske rusofilstvo pid chas Pershoi svitovoi viiny" [Galician Russophilism during World War I], *Visnyk Lvivskoi komerstiinoi akademii, seriia humanitarni nauky* 10 (2011), 235–49.

Osadczy, Wlodzimerz. *Święta Ruś. Rozwój I oddziaływanie idei prawosławia w Galicji* [Holy Rus. The development and influence of the idea of Orthodoxy in Galicia]. Lublin: Wyd. Uniwersytetu M. Curie-Skłodowskie, 2007.

"Otchety obshchestva literaturnogo Galitsko-russkoi maticy" [Reports of the Literary Society of the Galician-Ruthenian Matica]. In *Naykovyj sbornik izdavajemyj literaturnym obszestvom Galicko Rysskoj Maticy*. Lvov: n.p., 1865. I–LXXVII, I–IV.

Pashaieva, Nina, and Lidija Klimkova. "Galitsko-russkaia Matitsa vo Lvove i ei izdatelskaia deiatelnost" [The Galician-Ruthenian Matica in Lviv and its publishing activities], *Kniga. Issledovaniia i materiały* 34 (1977), 61–77. Electronic resource: http://ru-lvov.livejournal.com/6290.html (accessed 1 October 2018).

Pashaieva, Nina. *Ocherki istorii russkogo dvizheniia v Galichine v 19–20 vv.* [Sketches of the history of Russian movement in Galicia in the 19th–20th c.]. Moskva: Klimkova, Lidija, 2001. Electronic resource: http://www.twirpx.com/file/240368/ (accessed 1 October 2018).

Petrushevych, Antin. *Lingvistichesko-istoricheskiie rassuzhdeniia* [Linguistic and historical thoughts]. Lvov: Izd. Galitsko-russkoi Matitsy, 1901.

Podolianyn, Napysav [Vasyl Ilnytskyi]. *Perehliad Yuzhno-ruskoi istorii vid r. 1337–1450* [Reconsideration of South-Russian history from 1337–1450]. Lviv: Nakl. Halytsko Ruskoi Matitsy, 1875.

Prohrama dilanii obloho sobraniia chlenov literaturnoho sedyneniia 'Halytsko-Russkoi Matitsy' vo Lvovi na dniu 27 Avhusta (8 Veresnia) 1870 g. [The program of activities of the general meeting of members of the literary union 'Galician-Russian Matitsa' in Lviv on the 27th of August (September, 8)]. Lvov: n.p., 1870.

Sedliar, Oleksandr. "Halytsko-ruska matytsia: zavdannia, orhanizatsiia, chleny tovarystva (1848–1870)" [The Galician-Ruthenian Matica: mission, organization, members of the society (1848–1870], *Ukraina: kulturna spadshchyna, natsionalna svidomist, derzhavnist* 21 (2012), 668–92.

Sedliar, Oleksandr. "Rozpovsiudzhennia vydan Tovarystva Galytsko-ruska Matytsia (1848–1870)" [The distribution of Galician-Ruthenian Matica editions (1848–1870)], *Visnyk Lvivskoho universytetu, seriia knyhoznavstvo* 5 (2010), 28–51.

Sedliar, Oleksandr. "Vydavnycha diialnist tovarystva 'Halytsko-ruska Matytsia' (1848–1870)" [The publishing activities of the Galician-Ruthenian Matica (1848–1870)], *Visnyk Lvivskoho universytetu, seriia knyhoznavstvo* 3 (2008), 76–115.

Sereda, Ostap. *The Shaping of a National Identity. Early Ukrainophiles in Austrian Eastern Galicia (1860–1873)*. Avtoreferat dysertaciyi na zdobuttya naukovogo stupenya doktora filosofiyi (PhD) zi special'nosti 'Istoriya' [Abstract of Ph.D. diss. in Modern History]. Budapest: Central European University; Ivan Krypiakevych Institute of Ukrainian Studies (L'viv) of the National Academy of Sciences of Ukraine, 2003.

Steblii, Feodosij. "'Vesna narodiv' u Lvovi" [The 'springtime of nations' in Lviv], *Istoriia Lvova* 2 (2007), 148–69.

Sukhyi, Oleksij. *Vid rusofilstva do moskvofilstva (rosiiskyi chynnyk u hromadskii dumtsi ta suspilno- politychnomu zhytti halytskykh ukraintsiv u XIX stolitti)* [From Russophilism to Moscophilism (The Russian factor in the public opinion and socio-political life of Galician Ukrainians in the 19th century)]. Lviv: Lvivskyi natsionalnyi universytet imeni Ivana Franka, 2003.

Svintsytskii, Ilarion. *Obzor snosheniia Karpatskoi Rusi s Rosiiei v pervuiu pol. XIX v.* [An overview of relations between Carpathian Rus and Russia in the first part of the 19th century]. St. Petersburg: Tipohrafija Imp. Akad. Nauk, 1906.

Turii, Oleh. *Hreko-katolytska tserkva ta ukrainska natsionalna identychnist v Halychyni* [The Greek Catholic Church and Ukrainian national identity in Galicia]. Electronic resource: http://tyzhden.ua/History/43211 (accessed 1 October 2018).

Wendland, Anna Veronika. *Rusofily Halychyny, Ukrainski conservatory miz Avstrijejy ta Rosijejy, 1848–1915* [Galician Russophiles, Ukrainian conservatives between Austria and Russia, 1848–1915]. Lviv: Litopys, 2015.

Wojtowicz-Huber, B. *Ojcowie narodu. Duchowienstwo greckokatolickie w ruchu narodowym Rusinow galicyjskich (1867–1918)* [The Fathers of the Nation. The Greek-Catholic clergy in the national movement of Galician Ruthenians (1867–1918)]. Warszawa: Wydawnictwo Uniwersytetu Warszawskiego, 2007.

Zubrytskii, Denys. *Istoriia drevniaho Halychsko-russkoho kniazhestva* [The history of the long-standing Galician-Ruthenian kingdom]. Lvov: Tipom Stavropihianskim, 1852.

CHAPTER 15

Tatar Cultural and Educational Organizations and Charities: Muslim Self-Organization in the Russian Empire

Diliara M. Usmanova

The unique character of Tatar cultural foundations and charities at the beginning of the twentieth century can only be explained within the complex historical context in which they emerged and operated. The early twentieth century is commonly referred to as the Turko-Tatar Renaissance,[1] an era which purportedly saw significant growth in national consciousness along with a rapid upsurge in cultural and social development that characterized the final decades of imperial Russia. Tatar society simultaneously underwent a number of different trends, including the intensification of the process of secularization, the formation of a national (ethnic) consciousness, opposition to this trend from more traditional confessional concepts of identity, and a drive for Muslim unity (so-called pan-Islamism and the concept of a 'Muslim nation'), as well as the intensification of the centrifugal forces within the Islamic *umma*, to name but a few. This melange of frequently opposing tendencies could be seen in full force in the formation and activities of various cultural organizations and charities filling "the gap between the family unit and the government on the one hand [...] balanced against all its social, political and civic implications on the other."[2] Analysis of the activities of such organizations enables us to understand the nature of communication and explore the similarities and differences in the structure of the social, cultural, and ethno-national landscape in post-imperial Russia. More importantly, in light of the population's restricted ability to participate in politics, these types of organizations (foundations, clubs, associations, etc.) took on a kind of substitute role, acting as a space where this push for an active dialogue, for interaction with people of an equivalent level of education and a social, national, and religious status similar to their own, found its voice. The number of these organizations increased dramatically during the time of the first Russian Revolution. However, this trend

---

1 See Validi, who frequently uses this term to denote the state of Tatar society in the decade leading up to the revolution.
2 Zorin *et al.*, 470; Malysheva.

was not limited to the capital cities and regional centers, reaching as far as the hitherto slumbering provincial depths. According to sources dating from the period, approximately 4,800 associations and organizations of this kind were founded in Russia between the years 1906 and 1909.[3]

Despite the fact that the Tatar community considered itself the vanguard of the empire's Muslim population, modern Islamic-Tatar institutes do not appear until later. Up until the beginning of the twentieth century, the Tatars of the Volga-Ural region had no regular press, no professional (or even amateur) theaters, no cultural institutions, and absolutely no political parties. The number of charitable organizations was also relatively small, totaling no more than ten, although charity did represent the most widespread form of societal self-organization through its links with religious tradition (traditional Islamic charity in the form of *zakat*).[4]

What was behind the Muslim population's relatively delayed engagement? It was partially a result of the inaction of the ethnic minority group members themselves, whose low level of public engagement was a product of their traditionally cautious attitude and susceptibility to fear. The typical reaction of Islamic clerics was described in a Tatar newspaper in 1902–03: when the local charitable foundation would hold its meetings in the St. Petersburg apartment of *akhund* (imam) H. Khalitov, the horror-stricken proprietor would shut himself up in his room and say in reference to his brothers in faith meeting next door: "what are these godless heathens up to ..." Either this, or he would try his utmost not to be at home so as to avoid being a party to a dangerous public gathering.[5] Such behavior was rather typical of members of the Islamic priesthood, who were not only wary of violating traditional social principles but also feared persecution at the hands of the police. The Muslim society's lack of action can be explained to a large extent by the opposition it faced from the authorities, who strictly controlled the public lives of the empire's ethnic minority groups and regulated the registration and activities of such organizations meticulously. At any rate, in the eyes of numerous experts (predominantly government officials and Orthodox missionaries), the empire's Muslim population was a slumbering nation whose inaction and indifference with regard to public affairs seemed completely impossible to break. The awakening of this 'slumbering nation' and its incredible surge of activity at the beginning of the twentieth century provoked a response of utterly genuine surprise as

---

3 See: Zorin *et al.*, 480; Mironov.
4 For a general overview of Tatar charitable organizations, see Aynutdinova and Minnullin; Minnullin 2002, 57–58; also Minnullin 2003, 2004, 2007 and 2008.
5 *Qoyash* (20 May 1913), 126.

well as a desire to explain away the unfathomable phenomenon as a product of external influence or the scheming of unspecified pan-Islamist forces.

Virtually anything and everything that the Tatar Muslims could use to demonstrate their honored position as the 'first outpost' of Russia's Muslim world emerged over an exceptionally short space of time during the years of the first Russian Revolution. Before the liberalization of domestic policy in 1905–06, all of these newly-created organizations were established under the guise of charities. This was due in part to the fact that such a model was consistent with the Islamic tradition of alms-giving and charity, and partly because it drew the least opposition from the authorities. A short time afterwards, cultural-educational and other types of community organizations emerged. These can be divided into several categories: general organizations (meaning 'male-only'), 'women-only' and mixed, which, in turn, can be separated into charitable, cultural, economic (mutual-benefit societies), leisure clubs, and so on. However, this classification was merely nominal. In the course of their activities, the organizations did not always adhere strictly to their originally stated framework and went beyond the scope of their official designations.

There is no exact record of the total number of Tatar community organizations. If the charities and cultural-educational organizations operating within the Russian Empire numbered no more than seven or eight at the beginning of the twentieth century, there were already more than a hundred of them by 1917. According to official data from the *Departament Dukhovnykh Del Inostrannyx Ispovedanij* (DDDII, or Department of Religious Affairs of Foreign Confessions—DRAFC), by 1912 there were eighty-seven Muslim organizations in Russia (including Muslim enclaves such as Crimea and the Caucasus region). Five of these were purely religious, forty-eight were charitable, and thirty-four educational.[6] These records are thought to be incomplete. Researchers today calculate that these organizations numbered no fewer than one hundred fifty in 1917, the majority of which were either established or strongly supported by Tatars.[7] The chief focus of this article will be those people referred to as the Volga-Ural Tatars, with regions such as Crimea, the Caucasus, Turkestan, and the Western Krai remaining beyond the scope of our analysis. Furthermore, Tatars also lived in the traditionally 'Muslim' regions of 'inner Russia' (Povolzhye, the Urals)—both disparately and in groups—'pell-mell' with other related Muslim peoples (Bashkirs, Kazakhs, etc.). As a result, any clear demarcation on the basis of ethnicity is impossible. With this in mind, all the Muslim community

---

6 See Rybakov, 763.
7 See Minnulin 2010, 434.

organizations that existed in the Volga-Ural region will be considered in our analysis, along with some from beyond this area.[8]

The first organization of this kind established by Volga-Ural Tatars was the so-called *Muslim Children's Shelter (Yunusov Orphanage)*, which was opened in 1844 in Kazan with funding from the merchants Ibrahim and Ishak Yunusov. Orphans at the shelter received a primary education and were also provided with all the essentials of life up until they reached the legal age of majority. The shelter ran until 1917. Continuing in chronological order, the second to emerge was the *Bekbulatov Foundation for Mutual Charity among Kasimov Tatars* established in 1867 in St. Petersburg. It took its name from its founder, the Kasimov Tatar merchant Husain Bekbulatov. Unlike the Kazan orphanage, the foundation scarcely survived two decades. In addition to its purely charitable work (providing material assistance to those in need), the capital-based foundation established a school for orphans as well as a residential home for the elderly. It was with the activities of these two organizations that the history of organized charity among the Tatars began.

However, in 1898–99 something resembling a system of full-time community organizations, Muslim cultural foundations, and charities emerged, almost like a network. The present discussion will center on the Muslim charities established in St. Petersburg, Troitsk, Orenburg, Kazan, Kasimov, Astrakhan, and Ufa. What characterizes these early Tatar foundations? They were opened almost exclusively in urban centers with a traditionally large number of Muslim (predominantly Tatar) inhabitants. Indeed, the 'advanced level' of the capital's Muslim population in terms of self-organization was totally logical and understandable. Here, by way of their close proximity to the seat of power, Tatar Muslims felt the influence of their Russian surroundings more strongly. Consequently, the capital's Tatar community was always 'at the forefront,' the most active as well as the most exposed to new developments and overriding social trends.

The remaining cities—Kazan, Orenburg, Troitsk, Ufa, and Astrakhan—were either founded specifically as Tatar cities or else had populations where a significant proportion were members of the Tatar merchant class. It was this group that provided the financial backing for the activities of the newly-established foundations. In fact, we know of scores of eminent Tatar mercantile families who assumed a driving role in the creation of these foundations, also providing essential funding for their day-to-day activities. They include the Yunusov, Apanaev, and Kazakov families in Kazan; the Yaushevs in Troitsk; the Agafurovs in Ekaterinburg; and the Husainov and Rameev families in

---

8   On cultural currents among Muslims in Turkestan, see Adeeb, 80–113.

Orenburg. Moreover, the considerable social prestige associated with charity played no small part in motivating merchants and entrepreneurs to participate in the activities of these ethno-national foundations and associations.

Whereas the establishment of charitable and cultural foundations was uncommon prior to the beginning of the twentieth century, during the years of the first Russian Revolution (1905–07)—which saw the country's domestic political climate undergo a course of liberalization and heralded the introduction of freedom of meeting and association (the Proclamation of 17 October 1905)—the situation changed radically. The promulgation of the 'Temporary Regulations on Societies and Unions' (4 March 1906) greatly facilitated the process of establishment and official registration for such organizations. As a result, a campaign to legalize what were in some cases pre-existing structures swept across the Muslim population. By 1912–13, no fewer than eighty had already been opened, and on the eve of the February Revolution there were at least one hundred separate charities and cultural-educational foundations. In less than a decade, their number had increased tenfold.

The pioneers and leaders in this process of self-organization were the Muslim citizens of the Orenburg, Ufa, and Kazan *gubernii*, where there were over twenty structures of this kind—almost a quarter of the total number of equivalent organizations. The Orenburg province, with its traditionally 'Tatar cities' like Orenburg and Troitsk, clearly stands apart from the aforementioned three. Perhaps this was because it was easier for the Tatars to achieve their desired goals in that borderland outpost of the Tatars' native country—with the special status it enjoyed by virtue of the empire's geopolitical interests—than in Povolzhye and its ancestral Tatar capitol of Kazan, where pressure from the administration had always been stronger and government repression relentless. In the period leading up to the First World War, these organizations began to be established outside the traditionally Muslim centers and started to appear in what were thought to be purely Russian cities with small Tatar communities (Arkhangelsk, Vologda, Rostov-on-Don, etc.). Eventually these organizations underwent specialization, focusing more closely on one demographic or another (such as the youth, or women). As a consequence of their delayed and yet simultaneously rapid emergence, all of these associations—which served as a sort of barometer of 'modern civil society'—were characterized by minimal differentiation, an absence of any internal hierarchy, and a structure notably lacking any kind of shape or rigidity.

Any discussion of Tatar community organizations from this period ought to take note of the fact that the name of a given foundation did not always accurately reflect the specifics of its activities. Indeed, more often than not they were liable to mislead. Even if the name referenced charity and charity alone, these kinds of foundations often strayed beyond the narrow bounds of the term, opening schools, founding libraries, holding public functions and staging concerts as well as organizing lectures and settling public disputes. The activities of charitable organizations operating in cities including (but not limited to) Ekaterinburg, Samara, Troitsk, and Kasimov attest to this fact. This leaning towards education was a result of the non-state nature of the entire Muslim educational system, which relied on funding from members of the religious community. The Tatars could not rely on the cooperation (on either a moral or material level) of any governmental institution in the realization of any of their cultural initiatives, which included the establishment of *mektebs* and *madrasa*, the opening of libraries with reading rooms, and the founding of periodical publications. It is for this reason that they made good use of all available fund-raising channels and mobilized their human capital to the best of their abilities. Furthermore, since operating under the banner of a cultural society was complicated and dangerous, since it was viewed as an attempt to unite Muslims behind a single political platform (often designated 'pan-Islamism'), the founders would often try to obscure the true objectives of their organizations.

In addition to the established and traditional charitable foundations, after 1906 unions and associations appeared that were purely cultural in nature, predominantly, and even exclusively, leisure-based. Among these types of organizations were the Kazan-based Oriental Club (*Vostochny Klub / Shäryq Kluby /* the *Muslim Foundation of Kazan*, 1906–15), the *Troitsk Foundation for the Promotion of Theatrical and Dramatic Arts* (Troitsk 1911–17), and the *Orenburg Muslim Foundation for Music and Drama* (1916–23).

One of the most active and successful was the *Muslim Foundation in Orenburg*, which was operational between June 1906 and 1918.[9] As early as January 1899, a group of eminent Tatar businessmen (including the Husainov brothers, the Rameev brothers, and Muhammed-Yusuf Devishev) took the first steps with sponsorship for the creation of an Orenburg Muslim Charity Foundation (*Orenburgskoe Magometanskoe Dukhovnoe Sobranie*). However, their application was rejected. The next opportunity to establish a similar organization

---

9 RGIA (Russian State Historical Archives), f. 821, op. 133, d. 473, l. 72–86: *Ustav Musul'manskogo obschestva v gorode Orenburg* [Regulation of the Muslim Foundation in Orenburg] (Orenburg, 1906); *Otchet Orenburgskogo musul'manskogo obschestva za 1912 god* [Report on the Orenburg Muslim Foundation for 1912] (Orenburg, 1913); *Otchet Orenburgskogo popechenija ob uchaschikhsja musul'manax za 1913 god* [Report on the MFO for 1913] (Orenburg, 1914); D. Denisov, *The Muslim Foundation, Orenburg: Islam in the Urals—an Encyclopaedia* (Moscow and Nizhniy Novgorod, 2009), 254.

arose only after the introduction of freedom of assembly and the simplification of the registration procedure. Its Certificate of Incorporation was registered on 19 July 1906. The Foundation was unusually far-reaching, with an active membership that included top- and mid-level businessmen (the Yaushev, Husainov, Rameev and Tenishev families), clerks, office personnel, intellectuals, religious figures, and members of the secular intelligentsia (journalists, writers, and teachers). In 1907 the Foundation's members numbered 129; in 1908, 296; in 1909, 306; in 1910, 323; in 1911, 267; in 1912, 269; and in 1913, 320. The Foundation's key objective was the provision of material assistance to poor Muslims and working to develop Muslim cultural institutes. In October 1906, the Foundation opened a free Islamic library complete with a reading room, which welcomed over twelve thousand visitors in 1907 alone. By 1914, the library's book collection totalled more than 4,414 volumes. In addition to the library, the Foundation financed three Muslim primary schools operating in the poorest areas of the city, paid the tuition fees of poor schoolchildren and students, and also organized the distribution of hot meals in sixteen of the city's *mektebs*, to name but a few of its initiatives. A special building was also purchased for the use of trainee apprentices, who ran three-month Russian reading and writing courses every summer for children and adults. They organized lectures, popular readings, debates and other public functions at regular intervals throughout the year. Beyond this, they provided those who had fallen on hard times with targeted material assistance and opened free canteens for people suffering as a result of crop failure and hunger. Over the period 1906–12, the Foundation spent more than twenty-five thousand rubles on helping those in need. Some of their planned initiatives included establishing the first ethno-national museum and opening two classroom-skills training courses for teaching staff at the Muslim primary schools. However, the steady progress achieved through the cultural and charitable activities of the Muslim foundations was eventually halted by revolutionary upheaval. By a resolution of the Orenburg provincial Executive Committee dated 30 May 1918, all *Muslim foundation* business was transferred to the Provincial Commissariat for Muslim Affairs.

The history of the founding and nature of the activities of the so-called *Oriental Club*, which existed in Kazan from 1906–15, is an interesting story.[10] The Club was conceived as a place where the city's Muslim population could engage in leisure pursuits. In reality, however, it hovered between two extremes: leisure activities and amusements, but also projects in the 'sublime service' of culture and the nation. Which of these two concerns was closest to the Club? It is difficult to say for certain, since in the context of its tactical plan, the

---

10   For a historical sketch of the founding and activity of the society, see Minnullin 2013.

answer is most likely to be the former; however, in terms of strategy, the latter is more probable. Contemporaries of the Club found its national cultural center the most memorable of all its initiatives: an institution designed to serve the nation and also help mould its cultural image and national identity.

It is difficult to reconstruct the Club's history on the basis of the sources available to us. The Oriental Club's own archive has not survived. It is also unknown whether any personal documents exist that might shed some light on its activities. In the State Archives of the Republic of Tatarstan (GART) there are applications from the club's leaders requesting permission to organize various initiatives along with individual reports from police agents monitoring the club's political activities. However, the archival documents that survive are incredibly scant and one-dimensional. Consequently, newspaper articles[11] and the memoirs of its patrons (mainly describing the theatrical activities of the Club) represent the most significant repository of sources detailing its history. At first glance, all of the procedures for its foundation seem to have been completed relatively quickly: the application signed by twelve members of distinguished Tatar merchant families from Kazan was submitted on 8 November 1906, the Certificate of Incorporation was approved on 30 December 1906, and as early as January 1907, an authorized agent of the public interest group collected the required registration document from the police.[12] The archival documents do not convey how complicated the process of founding an association really was. It was hardly so simple and problem-free; but impersonal archival documents can tell us about the complex preparatory work undertaken by the group initiating it. We can only guess at the numerous obstacles the initiators faced in the 'informal' consultations and negotiations conducted between such a group of 'respected' Muslims and representatives of the official authorities.

The Club came into being in much the same way as other professional clubs (those for intellectuals, officials, etc.); the essential difference was that it was for all intents and purposes a cultural foundation, and thus did not limit its focus to one narrow segment of the population or to specific professional groups. Furthermore, it was established on the basis of ethno-religious principles. Although there was no specific mention of any ethno-religious membership restrictions in the group's charter, it was nonetheless obvious that it served

---

11   Virtually every single Kazan-based periodical (*Volzhskiy Vestnik, Kamsko-Volzhskaya Rech,' Yulduz, Qoyash,* and *An*) regularly featured pieces about the foundation's establishment and activities. The press coverage consisted mostly of advertisements for upcoming lectures and shows, reviews of plays, and opinion pieces on recent benefits and charity events.

12   GART, f. 2, op. 3, d. 3251, l. 1-10b.

as a platform for the city's Muslim and Tatar-speaking population. Like all officially registered associations, the Club had its own Certificate of Incorporation and had to report regularly to the provincial authorities.[13] The founders were said to hold musical and literary events, drama productions, and fêtes and games (with the exception of card games) for the association's members and visitors. They likewise established a library with books and journals, and arranged scientific lectures for the general public. The Club did not discriminate on grounds of class: it targeted all sections of Kazan's Tatar population with the objective of 'providing' an opportunity for its members and their families to spend their holiday time 'comfortably, pleasurably and as beneficially as possible.' In the view of Lutz Hefner, the founding of the Oriental Club (despite the existence of the non-confessional New Club, in which certain Tatar Muslims were also active) is indicative of the propagation of two separate cultures and environments, each segregated from the other.[14]

The history of the Oriental Club goes hand in hand with that of the evolution of Tatar theater insofar as the Club provided a key platform for *Sayar* (meaning 'itinerant' in Arabic), the first professional Tatar theater company. It is even difficult at times to say where the Club ended and the theater company began, so close and intimate was the relationship they shared. We can therefore state with confidence that Tatar professional theater developed simultaneously with the Oriental Club.

22 December 1906 is considered the birth-date of Tatar theater, the date on which the first Tatar-language plays (*The Unlucky Youth* and *For Love*) were performed with official permission before the general public. However, the date itself is not an exact one, but rather provisional. We know that the first amateur theater productions were staged by students (*shakirds*) from the Tatar *madrassahs* as early as 1900–04. Initially they performed at their private residences and then later, quasi-legally, within the walls of the *madrassahs* (e.g. the *Muhammadiya madrassah*) and the Kazan Tatar Teacher Training School. In the spring of 1906, Gabdrauf Niyazbaev (1884–1920), a member of the petty bourgeoisie who later went on to become a renowned Tatar dramatist, submitted a request for permission to stage an amateur Tatar-language play at the New Club.[15] Despite receiving approval, it failed to receive any public exposure. An attempt to organize public theatrical productions in the summer and fall of 1906 was unsuccessful. Its initiator, Rahim-bek Melikov (1886–1936), was

---

13   *Ustav Obschestva musul'man goroda Kazani 'Vostochnyi klub'* [Charter of the Kazan Oriental Club Muslim Foundation] (Kazan, 1907). See also Zorin *et al.*, 457 and 468–526.
14   Zorin *et al.*, 502.
15   GART, f. 1, op. 4, d. 2141, l. 1.

a student at Kazan University and at the same time a member of the *Shimbä* (Saturday) group, which brought together theater aficionados from among young Tatars.[16]

The creative-minded youth that had been the backbone of *Sayar* rallied around the Oriental Club in large numbers, and the vast majority of its performances were staged at venues belonging to the Club.[17] The Club also witnessed other theater companies making their entrances onto the scene (such as the Ufa-based *Nur* company and the Orenburg Tatar Company). In addition to their own Tatar plays, they also staged a series of comedies and other classic works of Russian and foreign plays translated from Russian. While the *Sayar* company's cooperation with the Oriental Club was initially sporadic, it became more consistent after 1910. The Club in itself became a guarantor of regular work for the theater company. After returning to Kazan from its tour of the Ufa and Perm *gubernii*, the *Sayar* company became a regular feature at the Oriental Club. The Club was not just a place where artists performed; they also used it to store their props and costumes and held rehearsals there as well. This all became possible after the renting of a new, more spacious room in 1911.

As we know, every theater company must pay a fixed fee for the venue irrespective of how much a particular show earns at the box office. This fee was approximately 100–150 rubles, which constituted a crippling expense for the humble Tatar theater company. Thus, having at their disposal a venue of their 'own' served to guarantee that the artists' financial position would remain more or less stable. The auditorium was initially designed to hold 150–160 spectators, but following its reconstruction, this figure rose to 300.[18] Stage productions did not always make a profit for the club. On occasion, not infrequently in fact, the company performed at a loss. The Tatar press above all highlighted the moral significance of the Club's activities: through the shows and theater productions it staged, the Club helped to cultivate notions of aesthetic sensibility and public spirit as well as a sense of community and cultural inclusion among the Tatar population. In general, however, Muslim society did not readily take to the theater, as can be seen from an article published in the Kazan-based magazine *An* (meaning 'consciousness') under the title "A Round-up of the 1912–1913 Theatrical/Musical Season at the Oriental Club." Its author, Gabdrakhman Karam—who later went on to become a prominent Tatar theatrical

---

16   GART, f. 1, op. 4, d. 2090, 332–340 and 443–446; d. 2232, 1–12; GART, f. 1, op. 4, d. 2090, 332–340, 443–446; d. 2232, 1–12.
17   Mortazin and Chenekai, 61–63 and 66–67. On the theatrical activity among Tatar youth within the Oriental Club, see also: Goldberg, 67–90.
18   Minnullin 2012, 325.

critic—left no doubt as to the necessity of such initiatives. However much he criticized the poor quality of the plays, he also analysed the list of productions from the point of view of the challenging role they played in the cultural and moral education of the Muslim population. Of particular importance and relevance to the writer were the shifts in the position of Muslims within society and in their perceptions of their own identity. The notion of 'liberating Muslim women'—an expression which gained popularity in the Soviet period—was not viewed by the 'progressive' Muslim intelligentsia of the early twentieth century as a standard stock phrase or a set of empty words. For this reason, the theatrical activities of the Oriental Club were regarded as important steps on the path of progress and religious development for Muslim society.[19]

However, the Oriental Club did not limit itself to just one channel of theatrical activity. In addition to its auditorium and stage, the club-house also contained a full-time public library and reading room, a games room, a canteen, and a lounge/reception area where meetings and public lectures were held. History lectures (in particular a series of lectures given by Gaynetdin Akhmerov in 1909–10 on topics including the history of the Kazan and Siberian khanates and the fate of Süyümbike's Tsaritsyn) and talks by popular personalities on topics of social importance attracted the greatest interest from the general public.[20] For example, a lecture by former deputy of the State Duma Sadri Maksudi on the topic of "The Activities of Muslim Religious Institutions in Russia" (13 January 1914) attracted over five hundred people, whereas the audience for an academic presentation by I.V. Ibrahim entitled "On Galvanism" (March 1909) was extremely small.

A surprisingly large number of people also attended events such as the Muslim New Year celebrations. For instance, on 16 November 1913, Muslims celebrated the year Hijri (the Islamic calendar) 1332 at the Oriental Club. All of the city's Muslim-owned shops were closed for the festival. A concert was organized at the Club and, despite the high ticket price (around 3.5 rubles), it drew a large audience. The concert was composed of *tableaux vivants* symbolizing the transition from the old year to the new. There were kiosks in operation and dances were organized for the youth.[21] This celebration highlighted the unique mixture of purely Muslim customs with typical early twentieth-century leisure activities. In itself, the combination of 'living pictures' with the celebration of the Islamic lunar new year might seem somewhat absurd; yet taken as a whole, the festivities garnered much more interest from the public than did the

---

19 *An* 11 (1913), 194–96.
20 *Kamsko-Volzhskaya Rech'* 98 (4 February 1909); 424 (24 March 1910).
21 *Kamsko-Volzhskaya Rech'* 256 (19 November 1913).

academic lectures. Thus, the Club began to arrange dance events after the shows, which were frequently attended in larger numbers by the youth than were the preceding shows. It is worth noting that the censors and other experts on 'Muslim affairs' often lamented the public's lack of discrimination, their undeveloped taste and the simple-mindedness of the plays performed, which were dominated by music-hall style productions and facile romantic playlets. At the same time, however, any works on relevant issues were carefully filtered out by the censors. Moreover, in the traditional Muslim center of Kazan, the censorship was even more harsh than it was in the provinces.

The Oriental Club's very first meetings were held in the rooms of the Hotel Bulgar. For the first two or three years, the founders hired various rooms at other clubs, including the Merchants' Club, the New Club,[22] and the Clerks' Club. The Oriental Club signed a permanent lease on premises in Apanaev House,[23] which served as its base until 1915. After the outbreak of the First World War the premises had to be vacated and were reassigned for use as a hospital, which meant that the club effectively ceased all its activities (1915).

In-depth analysis of the activities of the biggest and most active societies (Orenburg, Kazan, etc.) indicates that at the beginning of the twentieth century the Muslim population moved beyond the traditional bounds of the family and local community and entered the public space, where they began to explore new forms of cultural leisure pursuits that combined entertainment with education.

Any discussion of the early twentieth-century Tatar cultural organizations' spheres of interest requires one first to identify several focal points of their activity. One of these was institution-based education: establishing schools, co-financing extant ones, and providing academic and other reading materials as well as financial assistance for pupils. Others included general education (organizing lectures for the general public and publishing educational literature) and cultural leisure activities (organizing theater productions and concerts). The aforementioned Oriental Club of Kazan focused its efforts by and large on the latter two goals. Indeed, most of these foundations were engaged predominantly in educational projects, financing various Muslim schools and

---

22 The New Club, which was established as an 'Association for Employees of Government and Public Institutions,' opened its doors in 1900. The Association was based at Kekin's House, but in 1912 it moved to a purpose-built building on the very same street. Today, this building is the K. Tinchurin Tatar Theater. The New Club was one of the most well-subscribed and cultured leisure clubs in pre-revolutionary Kazan.

23 The building was located on the border of the Old Tatar Quarter and the city's Sector 2 area, i.e., the traditionally Tatar parts of the city. Its current address is: ulitsa Tatarstan, dom 8.

opening public libraries and reading rooms in different towns. Examples include the *Troitsk Foundation for the Advancement of Education* (1911); the *St. Petersburg Foundation for the Advancement of Education among Muslims* (1908–17); the *Orenburg Muslim Pupils' Foundation* (1912–18); the *St. Petersburg Foundation for the Advancement of Commercial Education among Muslims* (1914–17); and the *Foundation for the Advancement of Literacy among Muslims* (*Nashir Magarif*, Moscow, 1915).

Not long before the start of the First World War, foundations with a purely academic or educational focus began to appear. For instance, in the spring of 1914 the *Foundation for the Study of the History, Literature, and Ways and Customs of Muslims in Russia* (the Foundation for the Study of Russia's Muslim Peoples) was established in Moscow. It was created on the initiative and with the active participation of the Tatar youth studying at Moscow's institutions of higher education. Members of the foundation in question gave lectures on the history and literature of the Turkic nations; they published their academic research in the Tatar press and in 'weighty' Russian-language journals and even attracted members from various academic societies (such as the Orientalists' Society).[24]

In 1910–12, when the government relaunched its campaign against what it referred to as 'pan-Islamism,' its focus was aimed squarely at the cultural-educational organizations in whose activities the authorities saw a specific and fundamental threat to the policy and unity of the Russian Empire. Therefore, a short time afterwards they began a mass re-registration program for existing organizations that would enable them to shut down any undesirable associations. Beyond this, they ordered searches of the organizations' premises as well as the private residences of their leaders and members. They also seized documents, paying particular attention to any printed publications. A new law was passed "on alterations to the authorization procedure of Certificates of Incorporation for charitable institutions and the rules governing them" (1 June 1911) which made the registration procedure for such organizations more stringent. By 1912, a list had been compiled of twenty-two community organizations (thirteen of which were Muslim) that stood accused of late registration and faced closure. In actual fact, the classified circulars that were disseminated in *gubernii* (provinces) with Muslim populations talked specifically about the threat of pan-Islamism that was allegedly emanating from such cultural-educational associations with their nationalistic aims. Moreover, Tatars were named as the main proponents of pan-Islamism, with their community organizations acting as channels for the promotion of pan-Islamist sentiment.

---

24   RGIA, f. 821, op. 133, d. 473, l. 540–46.

Immediately prior to and during the First World War, these fears and concerns became even stronger among the authorities, especially after Turkey entered the war on the side of Germany. In 1915, Minister of Internal Affairs N.A. Maklakov sent out a special circular to governors and the DDDII recommending that the establishment and registration of all Muslim organizations—except for those exclusively charitable in nature—be halted 'pending clarification regarding Russian Muslims' attitudes to the war events taking place and general Muslim sentiment' (in reality, this meant until the end of the war). Naturally, this measure applied to all cultural-educational organizations, especially those founded by Tatars. In response to the Minister's directive, the head of the Directorate of Religious Affairs replied:

> As experience shows us, the founders and major activists of a wide variety of Muslim organizations typically prove to be Tatars—if not exclusively, then certainly in the majority of cases. In light of the fact that the Tatar minority more or less dominates the aforesaid organizations in localities with a mixed-ethnicity Muslim population, they could easily become instruments for the "Tatarization" of Muslims belonging to other ethnic groups. These things considered, it is most advisable in each individual case for us to gain as accurate a representation of the facts as possible; is it not right, then, that we should apply this principle to each and every newly-established Muslim society, to its founding parties and their general aims? Or rather, in other words, what cause for concern those aims might present us? (September 1915).[25]

A new trend emerged in the authorities' domestic policy, which was characterized by the latest in a series of crackdowns and tightening controls over any and all community structures, and even impacted on the fates of projects initiated by loyalist groups within the Muslim community, including two conservative projects. The first unsuccessful venture was the so-termed *Tsarist People's Muslim Society of the Kazan Province*, which was registered in December 1907 and then dissolved in January 1910. The driving force behind the closure of this society was the opinion of the Office of Public Affairs, whose members believed that organizations like this posed a serious threat to both the peace and state security.[26] The second example was the failure of the project to create the *Sirat al-Mustaqim* ('Straight Path') *Russia-wide Muslim National Union* initiated

---

25   RGIA, f. 821, op. 133, d. 473, l. 529–30. On the functioning of Tatar cultural and educational organizations during the First World War, see Usmanova 2014.
26   GART, f. 1, op. 4, d. 3046, l. 35 and 68; Alekseev.

by a group of conservative Muslim activists in 1913–14.[27] The Union's founders were the merchant Fatih Bayrashev and the *akhund* Safa Bayazitov, who had lived in the capital and had close ties to the government (including within the Department of Legal Affairs and the Directorate of Religious Affairs of Foreign Confessions of the Ministry of Internal Affairs). The Union's charter was based on very much the same wording as was used by the Black Hundred (*Chornaya sotnya*) organizations *Union of Archangel Michael* and *Union of the Russian People*. According to its charter, the aim of the Union was to "unite all Russian Muslims in the study of Islam in both its past and present forms, to educate and make more prosperous all Muslims on the basis of firm rule of law, loyalty to the Crown and the unity and integrity of Russia." It was the founders' vision that the Union would rally the conservative section of Muslim society against the wave of reform taking place within the Muslim *umma*. The Union's activities extended to the European part of the Russian Empire. The concrete operations of the Union covered a wide range of activities. In the religious sphere, it is thought to have organized Hajj pilgrimages and helped to build mosques. In terms of education and learning, it is supposed to have established comprehensive and professional lower and middle schools and governed the national *mekteb*s and *madrassah*s, as well as managing libraries and publishing houses. It is thought to have provided Muslims in need with the widest variety of charity support, including medical care. This nascent organization pursued cultural-educational and charitable objectives more than it did political ones. The liberal press labelled the Union a Black Hundred organization and called on Muslims not to support its founders. Critical articles appeared in major liberal-leaning Tatar publications (*Il,' Bayanelkhaq, Waqt and Yulduz*). The staunchly royalist newspaper *Russkoe Znamya* expressed serious concern about the Muslim party's creation, claiming that "under no circumstances should such an organization ever be allowed to come into being and be afforded legal status." In the end, however, the decisive factor was not so much the negative view held by the Tatar liberal press or the arguments put forth by its conservative Russian counterpart, but rather the fact that the governments of the majority of *gubernii* with what could be considered significant Muslim populations came out against the newly-founded Muslim organization. In their comments they wrote that under no circumstances could they allow the creation of Muslim organizations, even those with conservative leanings, due to the fact that they have invariably shown their potential to fall into the hands of an opposition-minded national intelligentsia and thereby morph into new Muslim centers of activity. Thus, despite increased lobbying efforts and a

---

27   Usmanova 2005.

lengthy bureaucratic exchange, the legalization process of *Sirat al-Mustaqim* was never completed. As a consequence, virtually every single initiative—regardless of whether it was proposed by progressives or staunchly conservative groups—presented a cause for concern for the authorities and was halted in its tracks.

In December 1914, under the initiative of members of the Muslim faction, a conference was held between representatives from Muslim community organizations and charities (around seventy delegates), where they discussed the potential 'redirection' of the community's efforts in response to the ongoing war, i.e., forms and methods of aid provision for wounded soldiers and their families. Despite the fact that a resolution was passed to establish infirmaries for the wounded and traveling ambulance detachments at the front, and to procure funds and material resources for the provision of such charity support, a clear reduction in the level of activity of Muslim volunteers was observed. This coincided with an acute, one might even say theatrical intensification of patriotic ardor from the authorities, which was accompanied by a series of unfriendly actions. Specifically, the government rejected a request for the creation of a unique distinctive badge in the form of a red crescent (modelled on the red star used by similar Christian organizations) for members of the committee and its volunteers, forcing them instead to wear the Christian symbol, which was inappropriate for Muslims. The government simultaneously began to suspect Muslims of excessive sympathy for the enemy—their co-religionists the Ottomans—and began to monitor Muslim sentiment closely, tightening controls on the activities of national organizations and associations, micromanaging them and finding fault in everything they did.[28] The relationship between the organizations and traditional powers could be described as one of profound mutual distrust.[29] This distrust and mutual suspicion could not fail to be reflected in the activities of the Tatar cultural-educational and charitable organizations operating within the Russian Empire.

1   The Major Tatar Charities and Cultural-Educational Organizations, 1867–1917[30]

The Arkhangelsk Muslim Charity and Educational Foundation was created in February 1911. Its founding members included M. Ishmyatov, Z. Fazlulin, and

---

28   Usmanova 2005.
29   On the relations between Muslim society and officials during the First World War, see Usmanova 2014.
30   Information on the creation and activities of these organizations is provided on the basis of the following sources and literature: RGIA, f. 821, op. 133, d. 473, 474 and 475; articles

I. Bikkulov. Among the foundation's masterminds and pioneers was the famous Tatar author Gayaz Iskhaki, who had been exiled to the province not long before. The Foundation's key objectives were working to establish Muslim cultural-educational institutions and providing material assistance to poor Muslims. It ceased its activities during the time of the First World War.

The Astrakhan Muslim Foundation (*Shura-i Islamiyah Jamgiyaty*) was a Muslim cultural-educational foundation and charity operating in Astrakhan between 1905 and 1911.[31] Mustafa Lutfi Izmaylov Shirvanskiy (1873–1926) emerged as one of its founders and leaders. A new-style school for boys and girls was launched in 1906 under the banner of the Foundation. Lessons were taught in Tatar from textbooks and primers brought in from the Ottoman Empire; in the period 1907–09 some of its staff members had even been invited to come from Turkey and teach. A series of Tatar-language periodicals (*Burkhane Tarakki, Khamiyat, Islakh*, and *Tup*) were launched with either full or partial funding from the Foundation. Its members totalled 277 by the beginning of 1910; however later there was an exodus of members and a reduction in the amount of available funds. In August 1910, following accusations of pan-Islamist activities and of having links to such groups in Istanbul, M.L. Izmaylov-Shirvanskiy resigned from his post as chair. The change in leadership did not help; in 1911 the *Shura-i Islamiyah* foundation was closed and its former leader exiled from the city of Astrakhan for anti-governmental and pan-Islamist propaganda.

The Bayraq Society of Progressive Muslims existed between the years 1907 and 1915 in Bayraq, Bugul'ma district, Samara province. The Gubaydullin brothers, both sworn imams, emerged as the cultural-educational foundation's founders after already having been in charge of the local country *madrassah*—*Gabidiyah*—which celebrated its one hundredth anniversary in 1915.

The Bekbulatov Foundation for Mutual Charity operated among St. Petersburg's Kasimov Tatars from 1867 to the early 1880s. This foundation, which was the first officially registered Muslim charity organization, was created within St. Petersburg's Kasimov Tatar community on the initiative of the merchant Khajbully Bekbulatov. Its main objective was the provision of material assistance to those of its members who needed it and the establishment of schools for orphans as well as a residential home for the elderly.

The Charitable Foundation of Moscow Muslim Women was created in March 1913. Its founders were M.P. Asadullaeva, G. Tagieva, M.B. Shirinskaya,

---

taken from encyclopaedias (Islam in St. Petersburg, Islam in the Urals, and Islam in Nizhniy Novgorod, among others), and also Certificates of Incorporation and Memos of charitable organizations published between 1906 and 1916.

31   Imasheva 2015.

and M.H. Shamsutdinova. This Foundation's main objective was providing material assistance for those in need, working to build Muslim women-only educational institutions, and organizing cultural leisure activities for women.

The Village of Imankulova II Charity was a Muslim charity and cultural-educational organization created with the aim of educating the Bashkir people and familiarizing them with political and economic events as well as providing material aid to those in need. The foundation was active between the years 1911 and 1917, with its Certificate of Incorporation receiving approval in March 1913.

A group of conservative Muslim activists attempted to create the conservative socio-political *Sirat al-Mustaqim* ('Straight Path') Russia-wide Muslim National Union in 1913–14. The Union's founders were the merchant Fatih Bayrashev and the capitol-based *akhund* Safa Bayazitov (see above). Failing in his attempt to establish the Sirat al-Mustaqim Union, F. Bayrashev came forward as a founding member of the conservative educational organization Islam and Education.

The Ekaterinburg Muslim Charity Foundation existed between the years 1908 and 1917. Its Certificate of Incorporation was registered on 9 February 1908. A key objective of the Foundation was "providing funds to improve the moral and material situation of the poor Muslims of Ekaterinburg and its surrounding areas, irrespective of gender, age or class." Its members totalled 116 by 1910. The Ekaterinburg businessman and millionaire Zaynetdin Agafurov acted as Chairman of its Management Committee. The Foundation distributed aid to poor Muslims, paid doctors' bills to ensure free medical care, allocated funds for purchasing clothes and shoes for those students of Muslim schools who needed them, and paid maintenance allowances to students of vocational schools. During the First World War, the Foundation also paid maintenance allowances to pupils whose parents had been called to the front. In 1911, the Foundation managed to open the city's first free Tatar-Russian library and reading room, which was located in the Agafurov House building. By 1914 it had subscriptions to sixteen Russian and twenty-six Muslim (Tatar) newspapers and journals and was also buying books in Russian and Oriental languages. Local citizens also donated many of the books it stocked. On 16 January 1913 the organization was required to undergo re-registration since, in addition to the above goals, it also pursued religious objectives. During the war years, the Foundation contributed in a number of ways, providing aid to the wounded and organizing medical ambulance detachments and hospitals for wounded Muslim combatants. Contributions from members and private donations were not the only sources of funding for the foundation's activities; it also generated income through various other means including organizing shows, holding horse races, and leasing cinemas.

Islam and Education (*Islam va Mägärif*) was a Muslim cultural-educational foundation and charity with conservative leanings that was active in Petrograd between the years 1916 and 1918. Its founders were Fatih A. Bayrashev and G.I. Musin. Its major objective was to educate Muslims and raise their culturo-moral and spiritual-religious level. The Foundation provided material assistance to disadvantaged Muslims, established refuges, organized Tatar cultural events, and distributed religious literature. An attempt by Fatih Bayrashev to publish a journal of the same name proved unsuccessful.

The Kasimov Muslim Charity Foundation existed between 1897 and 1917. It evolved out of a splinter-group of the capital-based Bekbulatov Foundation for Mutual Charity among Kasimov Tatars. Gradually, though, it also faded away following the closure of its parent organization. A new charity emerged in 1897 at the initiative of representatives from Kasimov's most prominent Tatar mercantile dynasties: the Akbulatov, Bekbulatov, Baybekov, and Vergazov families. Its objective was "to provide funding for the improvement of the moral and material situation of the poor Muslims living in Kasimov and its surrounding areas." Its Certificate of Incorporation was approved by the Ryazan governor's office on 8 October 1897. In spite of Kasimov's relatively small Tatar community, the organization was well supported financially since many of its representatives were involved in trade and other businesses in Moscow and St. Petersburg as well as other cities in the European part of Russia. Its activities included collecting donations from philanthropists and distributing them according to the specific needs of their intended recipients. The charity also worked actively to establish Muslim cultural-educational institutions. In 1910 the charity funded the construction of a building to house the Tatar library and reading room that had been established in 1906. The library's rich collection consisted of books in Tatar and Russian, and it maintained regular subscriptions to Tatar-language newspapers and journals printed in Kazan, Ufa, Orenburg, Moscow, and other cities in the Empire. It also had a children's section, and the staff organized literary evenings and meet-the-author events. The charity supported the Kasimov Muslim Cemetery and the Khan's Mosque (*Khanskaya Mechet'*) and also built the New Mosque (*Novaya Mechet'*), among other projects.

The Krasnoufimsk Muslim Cultural and Economic Foundation and Charity was operational between the years 1906 and 1913. Its founders were the *petit bourgeois* N.U. Devetyarov, the peasant F.G. Vaisov, and the nobleman A.F. Umitbaev. The Foundation worked to improve the district's cultural landscape and the economic situation of its Muslim population, to provide material assistance to Muslims (especially to *shakirds*), and also to finance a series of *mektebs* and *madrassahs* in the district. In August 1913 it was closed down in accordance with an order from the Ministry of Internal Affairs for the liquidation of twenty-two organizations on the basis of their 'improper registration.' However, this was actually due to concerns about the spread of pan-Islamist propaganda.

The Tatar-Muslim Theater Circle of Kazan was active in 1906–07. Many of its members participated in the first Tatar-language stage productions and also in the activities of *Sayar*, the first professional Tatar theater company.

The Moscow Muslim Charity Foundation existed from 1906 to 1917. Despite having its Certificate of Incorporation approved on 13 May 1906, it did not become active until May 1907. As of 1911 its members numbered 181 and, by 1915, its total number of members was 308. Its honorary members included Mirza Asadullaev and Zakhid Shamil (the son of Imam Shamil). The Chair of its Management Committee (1907–17) was the Moscow businessman Husain Baybekov. Asadullaev House, built in 1913, became the new location for its Management Committee as well as one of the Foundation's schools.

The St. Petersburg Muslim Charity Foundation was founded in 1898 (following an unsuccessful attempt a year earlier). The organization's founding members consisted largely of Azerbaijanis, for the most part entrepreneurs from Baku (including the merchants Zajnabeddin Tagiev and Shamsi Asadullaev), but also included members of the Kazakh aristocracy, who enjoyed elevated social status in Russian society. Its rank and file membership was chiefly composed of Tatars. The foundation's first Certificate of Incorporation was approved on 19 January 1898. The members of its Management Committee were Major General Ali Sheikh-Ali (1898–1904), David Smolskiy (1904–08), General Abdul-Aziz Davletshin (1908–09), State Duma Deputy Oskar Syrtlanov (1910–12) and Zahid Shamil (1913–17). The foundation generated most of its revenue from the interest earned on capital in an untouched fund, members' contributions, one-off donations, and the 'Eastern Evenings' it held each year. According to its charter, its main objective was to provide "mutual aid and charity for the poorest of Muslims in the alms-houses, infirmaries or other charitable institutions" as well as assisting poor Muslim students intending to continue their education in the capitol's institutions of secondary and higher education. The Foundation held both regular annual and special meetings. In the year it was established (1898) it had 125 members, and in 1899 there were 166. Then membership figures began to fall at the beginning of the twentieth century, down to 113 in 1910 and to 77 in 1911. Thanks to the efforts of its trustees, its numbers began to grow once more and the foundation reached its peak in 1913 with 306 members. However, another drop followed in 1915. It is worth noting that attempts in 1903 to introduce addenda to its Certificate of Incorporation that would have widened the foundation's scope of activity (to include building Muslim hospitals, alms-houses and shelters, as well as gathering donations through subscription fees) ended in failure. In an internal memorandum dated 30 April 1903 the DDDII noted that these addenda might have the effect of strengthening the foundation's internal structures and widening the scope of its activities following the formation of the 'united Mohammedan organization' in the capital. Nevertheless, against the new political landscape of the first Russian Revolution and with the liberalization of domestic policy, it succeeded in winning the right to establish shelters in 1904, and in 1906 it was granted the right to found free primary schools. The foundation reached peak activity levels in 1912–13, at the same time as the local Jameh was established and the tercentenary of the House of Romanov was celebrated. During this time, its membership figures grew, as did the total amount of donations and other funding it received. This period also witnessed a number of other developments, including the school's modernization of its teaching methods and related equipment, as well as the introduction of two bursaries named after the national poet Abdullah Tukay (who died in April 1913). Plans were drawn up for the construction of additional hostels and canteens for the homeless and for opening libraries and reading rooms, yet these projects met with opposition from the local authorities. Plans to purchase a special building to be used according to the Foundation's needs likewise came to naught.

The Nizhnii Novgorod Market Muslim Charity Foundation operated between the years 1906 and 1915. Its founders were a group of famous merchants from Kazan and Nizhny Novgorod whose objective was to guarantee material support for fellow Muslims while also undertaking to provide them with moral education.[32] According to its Certificate of Incorporation (approved 21 September 1906), the organization was granted the right to "establish libraries, reading rooms, mektebs, and madrassahs along with various other types of schools; support masjids and associated institutions, support bursars, [...] arrange public lectures, debates, literary evenings and community evenings, assuming it obeyed the general legislation and decrees of the government." The charity was based at the (Makaryev) Market in the territory of Nizhny Novgorod. It was consequently classified as a full-time organization. During seasonal intervals between markets, the charity was managed by a council made up of six members. In terms of financing, it relied on one-time donations, one-time and annual contributions from members, and monies generated from literary evenings and other events, as well as income from properties belonging to the charity.

---

32   Senyutkina and Zagidullin.

The Bushman-Suun-Karakipchak Volost Bashkir Muslim Foundation (Orenburg province, 1907–17) was a Muslim charity and cultural-educational organization created on the initiative of Tatar mullahs from the village of Tlyaumbetova with the aim of educating the rural Bashkir population and familiarizing them with political and economic events, as well as providing material aid to those in need. Its Certificate of Incorporation was approved on 7 July 1907, and in 1910 the Foundation had sixty members. Due to its small membership base, it experienced constant financial problems. It also felt the traditional distrust of the local authorities, and in 1910 there was a series of raids on the homes of its leaders following their denunciation by a conservative imam.

The Iletskaya Zaschita (Sol-Iletsk) Muslim Foundation was a Muslim charity and cultural-educational organization created with the aim of educating the Muslim population and familiarizing them with political and economic events as well as providing material aid to those in need. It spent the majority of its money on support for the city's Tatar educational institutions and on the upkeep of its free Muslim library. Its Certificate of Incorporation was approved on 27 October 1906.

The Seitovskiy Posad Muslim Foundation (Orenburg province) existed from 1908 to 1917. This charity and cultural-educational organization was created with the aim of providing aid to those in need and financing Muslim educational institution in the village of Kargaly. The foundation's Certificate of Incorporation was registered on 27 March 1908, and in the autumn of 1911 it opened a free Muslim library and reading room that stocked 575 volumes in 1914 and had annual subscriptions to six newspapers and three journals printed in Tatar. From 1915 it received an annual grant of three hundred rubles from the district council towards the library's upkeep. In 1915, it founded a vocational school to teach poor Muslim children the art of shoemaking, and established an infirmary for wounded Muslim soldiers, both in conjunction with the local district council. It ceased to exist after 1917.

The Kazan Muslim Foundation (Oriental Club / *Shäryq Cluby*) was active in Kazan between the years 1906 and 1916. It was created with a view towards enabling its members and their families to spend their free time 'comfortably, pleasurably and effectively.' Specifically, the organizational committee proposed holding musical and literary events, drama productions, and fêtes and games (with the exception of card games) for the association's members and visitors. They likewise established a library with books and journals and arranged scientific lectures for the general public. The Club was led by a Council of Elders, one member of which had been a long-serving lecturer at the Kazan Tatar Teacher Training School (1878–1907) and assistant (from 1906) to Kazan University superintendent Ibrahim Teregulov (1852–1921). The 'Elders' concerned themselves with organizational matters and personally maintained order at the evening functions and cultural events. The amount of the annual membership fee (five rubles) aligned the Club with a group of associations that were entirely democratic and in no way élitist. Its members totalled 121 in 1908. The Oriental Club was one of few such organizations that openly declared itself a leisure society, and its history is inseparable from that of the evolution of Tatar theater insofar as the Club provided a key platform for *Sayar*, the first professional Tatar theater company. In addition to theater productions, dances and new year celebrations were extremely popular, as were concerts and lectures on popular topics of historical or societal significance.

The Foundation for the Study of the History, Literature, and Ways and Customs of Muslims in Russia (the Foundation for the Study of Russia's Muslim Peoples, Moscow): its Certificate of Incorporation was approved in 1914 and the organization began operating in the autumn of 1914. Among its founders and active members were the Tatar youth studying at Moscow's institutions of higher learning. Members of its committee included Husain Baybekov, Jemil Aleksandrovich and G. Asanovich. The focus of this association was on the significant role of Polish-Lithuanian Tatars studying in the capital's institutions of higher learning. The composition of the association was varied, both socially (besides students, there were also businessmen) and ethnically (Tatars, Azerbaijanis, Kazakhs, and Uzbeks). At the beginning of 1917 the association had up to sixty members. In light of its complex ethnic composition, and as most of the participants were students enrolled in secular institutions, the reports and debates were in Russian. However, on the whole, the association's sessions were rather infrequent; they did not meet for sessions more than ten times in over two years.[33]

The Kazan Assistance Fund for Poor Muslims was active from 1898 to 1918, having been created on the initiative of Tatar merchants and businessmen working alongside religious and public figures. Its membership grades were classified as follows: honorary, life-time, and full. Some of the Fund's most active members included the local imam Galimdzhan Barudi (G. Galeev), the merchants Sulejman Aitov and Gabdulla Apanaev, and Akhmetzjan Saydashev and his son. By 1911 its members totaled 292. It supported *madrassahs*, *mektebs*, and Muslim cemeteries, provided material assistance to *shakirds* as well as ordinary Muslim residents of Kazan and other cities, and also funded the studies of talented young people wanting to study at institutes of secondary and higher education. The organization operated an orphanage alongside two schools (from 1905), a maternity shelter (from 1914), Russo-Tatar schools for boys and

---

33   For more detail, see Usmanova 2014.

girls (from 1909), a clinic (from 1902), and a Muslim obstetrics center (from 1912). To finance its activities, the Fund relied largely on donations (mostly from Tatar merchants and businessmen), *zakat*, members' contributions, subsidies from the Kazan City Duma (though these were rare), and income generated from entertainment.

The St. Petersburg Foundation for the Advancement of Commercial Education among Muslims operated between the years 1914 and 1917. Its founders included Abdul-Aziz Davletshin, Said-Girej Djantyurin, and Y.A. Muhlio. Its Certificate of Incorporation was approved in December 1914. The Foundation was created in order to promote commercial education among Muslims, and it was placed under the supervision of the Ministry of Trade and Industry. Its planned projects included opening and maintaining commercial educational institutions as well as arranging shows, concerts and public lectures, the proceeds of which were to go towards other initiatives.

The St. Petersburg Foundation for the Education of Muslims (1908–17): its founding members were U.G. Sheikh-Ali, Muhammed-Alim Makustov, and Zahid Shamil, and its Certificate of Incorporation was approved on 20 May 1908. The Foundation's objective was "to raise the cultural level of Muslims through the advancement and improvement of the education system and to develop and streamline extra-curricular education." It opened new schools, improved the standard of teaching in existing ones, and organized courses and public lectures for adults, as well as publishing educational and accessible scientific journals, newspapers, textbooks and pamphlets (both originals and translations). In addition to its educational activities, the foundation also ran cultural-entertainment projects that included shows and concerts as well as dances and public readings. The income generated from these was used to support its educational initiatives. The foundation was not able to realize all of its plans, failing to establish a library and reading room.

The Olekma Muslim Foundation in Yakutiya was founded in January 1914. Its sponsors included the Enikeev brothers of Olekma, who belonged to a well-known Tatar noble family. In addition to I. Enikeev, who taught at the Russo-Tatar school, other sponsors included mullah M. Sadykov, who had moved to Yakutiya a short time before. The Muslims of Yakutiya were predominantly political exiles, their descendants, or Tatar merchants and traders who had moved to the region. The majority of the 825 Muslims living in Olekma in 1914 were Tatars and they, too, helped to establish the Foundation. The local authorities put forth some interesting arguments when assessing its application, with the governor of Yakutiya making some particularly unfavorable comments opposing the Muslims' request. The Irkutsk Governor-General finally agreed to approve the Muslim Foundation on the condition that its activities would be subject to a series of restrictions. Specifically, the municipality would only permit the library to stock books in Russian, because the region did not have the capacity to enforce the censorship of Muslim publications. Although the Muslim Foundation was approved in January 1915, red tape from the local authorities delayed its registration almost until the summer of 1916. Then, having already changed his mind, the Irkutsk Governor-General reported the organization's registration as undesirable to the Ministry of Internal Affairs in August 1916, citing 'the war with Turkey.'

The Orenburg Muslim Women's Foundation (1912–18) was a Muslim charity and cultural-educational foundation established with the objective of educating Muslim women and providing material aid to women and children in need. Its Certificate of Incorporation was registered on 11 May 1912 and its founding members were F.M. Adamova (chair), Z.D. Adamova (secretary), Z.M.Z. Rameeva, F.M. Tenisheva, and M.Y. Husainova (treasurer). The Foundation's members included the wives of merchants and businessmen, teachers at new-style schools, and actresses. The Foundation had 151 members by 1914. By the end of 1912, it had opened a dress-making school, provided free medical care for the pupils of Orenburg's girls' schools, and arranged lectures and readings from books on religion and morality as well as some poetry and literature in translation. The Foundation ceased its activities during the civil war years.

The Orenburg Muslim Foundation for Music and Drama was active between 1916 and 1923. Its Certificate of Incorporation was registered on 21 January 1916. Its founding members were the famous Muslim activists A. Baytursunov, a Kazakh, the Tatar dramatist Kabir Bakirov, and the political writers and brothers, Fatih Karimi and Burkhan Sharaf. The Chair of its Management Committee was I.M. Bikchentaev. The Foundation compiled folk songs and melodies, organized shows and musical evenings, held a Tatar-language theater competition, collected theater costumes, and defended the interests of its Tatar theater company. It also ran a music school and in 1918 released the first Tatar-language book with the purpose of popularizing music as an art form. Though the Foundation ceased its activities in 1919, one of the educational institutions it founded continued operating until 1923 under the name of the Eastern Music School.

The Orenburg Muslim Foundation (Muslim Foundation of Orenburg) brought together top- and mid-level businessmen (from the Yaushev, Husainov, Rameev, and Tenishev families), intellectuals, shop assistants, office personnel, religious figures, and members of the secular intelligentsia (journalists, writers, and teachers). The Foundation's key objective was the provision of material assistance to poor Muslims and working to develop Muslim cultural institutes. It operated from June 1906 to 1918 and was arguably the most active and successful in the Volga-Ural region.

The Orenburg Foundation for the Support of Muslim Students (Orenburg Shakirds' Aid Foundation) was active between the years 1912 and 1918. Its Certificate of Incorporation was registered on 11 May 1912. The Foundation's founding members were predominantly representatives of the secular Muslim intelligentsia, including the Fatih Karimi, Zakir Rameev (Chairman of the Management Committee) and Shakir Rameev, Selim-Girej Dzantyurin, and Singatulla Bikbulatov, as well as various businessman and public figures. The foundation provided financial aid to Muslim pupils studying at institutions of primary, secondary, and higher education across the country. The geographical area in which the Foundation's bursars studied was uncommonly large, including the cities of St. Petersburg, Moscow, Kazan, Orenburg, Perm, Buzuluk, Ufa, and Chelyabinsk. In the autumn of 1913, the Foundation opened a preparatory school in Orenburg for Muslim children between the ages of seven and twelve wishing to study at *gimnazii* (the equivalent of grammar schools) and secondary schools teaching no classics. The period of comprehensive study was four years and included subjects such as Theology, the Russian and Tatar languages, Arithmetic, and Painting. In a relatively short space of time, the Foundation outgrew its narrow regional bounds and became famous throughout the whole of Russia, receiving donations from all parts of the country (from Omsk to Kokand).

The Orsk Muslim Charity Foundation (Orsk Muslim Foundation) operated between the years 1908 and 1917. This charity and cultural-educational foundation was founded in November of 1908 in the city of Orsk (Orenburg province) with the objective of providing material assistance to poor Muslims and working to develop Muslim cultural-educational institutions. Its Certificate of Incorporation was registered on 28 November 1908. The foundation ensured the maintenance of the municipal cemetery, funded the activity of one all-boys' and two all-girls' schools, which included paying the salaries of their teaching staff, maintaining and repairing buildings, along with paying their electricity, heating, and other utility bills. It opened a free Muslim library in 1908 that had 897 volumes by 1918. In the summer of 1911, it organized a set of short-term educational courses for women which were attended by fifteen Muslim women studying subjects including the Fundamentals of Islam, Teaching, and Geography. The Foundation ceased to exist after 1917.

The Perm Muslim Cultural-Economic Foundation and Charity was created in June 1909. Its Certificate of Incorporation was approved in June 1908. Its primary objective was to establish Muslim cultural and religious institutions, which included working to develop and improve the performance of the *madrassahs* and providing material assistance to poor Muslims and students as well as to soldiers and their families. The Foundation initiated bursary programs for poor Muslims in Perm that ran from 1903, and had 166 active members in 1911. The Foundation's most significant projects were the establishment of a trade school in the village of Kosyanovo (1909, where children studied joinery) and the creation of a Muslim section and reading room at the Smylyaev library (Perm, 1908). A search was conducted at the Foundation's headquarters on 29 February 1912, whereupon police officers confiscated receipts and lists of donations in order to check how the funds designated for financing the Muslim school had been spent. As a result, the Foundation's chairman, G.M. Gaynullin, was exiled from Perm, though the Foundation continued to operate for some time afterwards. In the end, having long been under scrutiny by the Ministry of Internal Affairs (since 1910), its application for a Certificate of Incorporation was rejected (1913) citing the precedent of the Vyatka foundation.

The Samara Muslim Charity Foundation existed from 1907 to 1913. Its founding members included imam Muhammed-Fatih Murtazin (Chairman), S. Halfeev, and M. Deberdiev. The Foundation's key objective was the provision of material assistance to poor Muslims and working to develop Muslim cultural institutes. The foundation ran a library and, under the editorship of M.F. Murtazin, it published a journal entitled *Iqtisad* (Economics) during the period 1908–17. The journal stopped being published at the same time as the Foundation itself closed down.

The Union of Polish-Muslim Students was an association of students from among the Polish, Lithuanian, and Belarusian Tatars. The Union functioned semi-legally in St. Petersburg from 1907 to 1910. It included students from St.-Petersburg University: the law students Olgerd and Leon Kryczynski (from Warsaw), Machei Bairashevskii (Vilnius), Edigei Milkamanovich (Grodno), Iakub Shafarevich (Minsk), the students Kalino (Kovno), Tal'kovskii (Vilnius), Ian Krichinskii, Iakub Shinkevich, and others. The Union's purpose was cultural and educational activity, including conducting research on the history of the Polish-Lithuanian Tatars. Meetings were held as discussion clubs. The members of the Union also discussed political issues, as the composition of notes under the title "The view of the Lithuanian Tatars on the situation of the Muslim peoples of Russia" testifies (the document exists in the personal archive of Leon Kryczynski). Additionally, the members of the students' association collaborated with other Muslim organizations in St. Petersburg, joined Muslim cultural, educational, and benevolent organizations, and took part in meetings held under the leadership of Zahid Shamil. Besides that, the Polish-Lithuanian Tatar students in Petersburg corresponded with fellow students from home, studying in other Russian cities (Moscow, Kiev, and others).

The Troitsk Muslim Charity Foundation existed between the years 1898 and 1918. It was the first Muslim charity and cultural-educational foundation to be established in Orenburg province and the entire Ural region. The Foundation's Certificate of Incorporation was registered in 1898 and its Chairmen were Gadbel-Vakhap Yaushev (1901–06) and Mulla-Gali Yaushev (1906–17). In addition to members of the region's richest mercantile dynasty, the Yashuev family, representatives of the Tatar entrepreneurial and merchant class (such as the Shafigullin, Hasanov and Idrisov families) also played a part in the Foundation's activities. Imams and members of the secular intelligentsia (doctors, teachers, and public figures) were also involved in its activities. In 1913 the Foundation had sixty-five members. The Foundation's mission was to "provide funds for the improvement of the material and cultural-moral condition of the Muslims of Troitsk and its surrounding areas." The organization's activities were multifaceted: it provided aid to the hungry in areas suffering from crop failure and targeted support for the poor, financed six Muslim schools, and opened a free library and reading room (named *Nadjat* or 'Salvation,' 1913) and an orphanage, as well as redeveloping the Troitsk Muslim cemetery. The Foundation's activities met with protests from the conservative section of the Muslim *umma* and concern from the authorities, who were worried that it was involved in spreading pan-Islamist propaganda. The Foundation was required to undergo re-registration in 1909 and in 1912 found itself on the verge of closure. However, it continued to exist until the beginning of the Civil War.

The Troitsk Society for the Encouragement of Stage and Theatrical art existed from 1910, and was officially registered on 28 August 1911. The society emerged as a drama circle (1909), which included young people from Troitsk, and participants in literary and musical evenings and gatherings that took place regularly in Troitsk starting at the beginning of the twentieth century. After the 1917 Revolution the first professional Tatar theater in the region was formed on the basis of the Society.

The Chelyabinsk Muslim Charity Foundation was active between the years 1906 and 1917. Its Certificate of Incorporation was registered on 4 February 1906 and its mission was "to provide funds for the improvement of the material and cultural-moral condition of Chelyabinsk's Muslims." The Foundation was closed down in 1912 as part of the audit of Muslim community organizations' activities. The reason given was failure to complete the re-registration procedure. However, as early as February 1913, the imam of the city mosque put forward plans to create a Chelyabinsk Muslim charity foundation to be established in remembrance of the tercentenary of the House of Romanov. By virtue of this ruse, he succeeded in bringing the former organization back to life. Its Certificate of Incorporation was registered on 8 June 1913 and in 1914 the Foundation had 114 members. It provided financial assistance to those in need, gave out bursaries to poor schoolchildren, supported the Muslim library, and paid funeral costs for poor Muslims who had died (most commonly in prison or hospital). It ceased its activities following the 1917 Revolution.

2 Conclusions

The cultural-educational organizations that emerged in the area inhabited by the Volga-Ural Tatars had their own distinctive features and characteristics. The overwhelming majority were created in the decade between the 1905 Revolution and the Russian Revolution of 1917. As a rule, these organizations had a mixed profile; in the smaller cities and localities with less numerous Muslim populations, mixed-type organizations dominated. These groups simultaneously incorporated a variety of functions, including culture and leisure, education, instruction, and charity. This mixed nature of their activities was a result of numerous factors, including a dearth of cultural personnel and the lack of sufficient funds for a clear stratification of efforts. In the larger urban centers (such as Kazan, Ufa, Orenburg, St. Petersburg, and Astrakhan) there was a clear specialization, a division between cultural-educational institutions and charities, and the presence of both female-only and 'male-only' organizations working side by side, although even in such cases, the core group of active members was most often relatively small. Moreover, the various management committees sometimes had the exact same names. The social environment that fostered the creation and activity of such organizations was chiefly that of the merchant class, who provided the financial basis for their establishment and continued existence, and also of the Islamic clergy. Finally, there was also a social group that would become the best-educated and respected as well as the most active in the operations of various ethno-national structures. During the time of the Revolution of 1905–07, this social group mobilized and fortified its position in Tatar society. Along with the secular intelligentsia (teachers, journalists, and public figures), it was most active in the development of various cultural-educational and leisure unions and associations. As a consequence of the disparate nature of the Tatar population in the Russian Empire and the relatively harsh government oppression they experienced, Tatars had no opportunity to create a single cultural or national center. Additionally, every attempt to align these organizations or co-ordinate their efforts and activities was considered as a push for pan-Islamism and pan-Turkism and, as a result, harshly repressed by the authorities. Therefore, under the conditions that prevailed in Russia at the beginning of the twentieth century, the creation of a united network of Tatar-Muslim cultural-educational (and even charitable) organizations was simply inconceivable.

Bibliography

Adeeb, Khalid. *The Politics of Muslim Cultural Reform: Jadidism in Central Asia*. Berkeley: University of California Press, 1998.

Alekseev, Igor. *Pod senju carskogo manifesta: Umerenno-monarkhicheskie organizacii Kazanskoi gubernii v nachale XX veka* [In the Shadow of Royal Proclamation: Early 20th-Century Conservative-Royalist Organizations in the Kazan Guberniya]. Kazan: n.p., 2002.

Aynutdinova, Larisa, and Zavdat S. Minnullin. "Blagotvoritel'nost" [Charity]. *Tatarskaja Enciklopedija*, Vol. 1: A-B. Kazan: Institut Tatarskoj Enciklopedii, 2002. 407–09.

Blagov, Jurij. "K istorii 'Vostochnogo kluba'" [On the History of the Oriental Club], *Tatarstan* 5 (1997), 78–80.

Goldberg, Madina V. *Russian Empire—Tatar Theater: the Politics of Culture in Late Imperial Kazan*. PhD. diss., University of Michigan, 2009.

Häfner, Lutz. *Gesellschaft als lokale Veranstaltung: die Wolgastädte Kazan und Saratov (1870–1914)*. Cologne: Böhlau Verlag, 2004.

Imasheva, M.M. "Dejatel'nost' musul'manskoj nacional'no-konfessional'noi blagotvoritel'noj organizatcii v Astrakhanskoj gubernii v nachale XX veka" [The Activities of the Muslim National-Religious Charitable Organization in Astrakhan Province in the Early 20th Century], *Islamovedenie* 1 (2015), 69–83.

Islam na Nizhegorodchine: enciklopedicheskii slovar' [Islam in Nizhny Novgorod: An Encyclopaedia]. Nizhniy Novgorod: Medina, 2007.

Islam na Urale: enciklopedicheskii slovar' [Islam in the Urals: An Encyclopaedia]. Moscow/Nizhniy Novgorod: Medina, 2009.

Islam v Central'no-Evropeiskoj chasti Rossii: enciklopedicheskii slovar' [Islam in the Central-European Part of Russia: An Encyclopaedia]. Moscow/Nizhniy Novgorod: Medina, 2009.

Islam v Sankt-Petersburge: enciklopedicheskii slovar' [Islam in St. Petersburg: An Encyclopaedia]. Moscow: Medina, 2009.

Khairi, Anvar, ed. *Tatar teatry (1906–1926)* [Tatar Theatre (1906–1926)]. Kazan: Magarif, 2003.

Malysheva, Svetlana. *Prazdnyi den,' dosuzhij vecher: kul'tura dosuga rossijskogo provincial'nogo goroda vtoroi poloviny XIX—nachala XX veka* [Day Off, Leisure Activity: Leisure in the Russian Provincial Town in the Second Half of the 19th Century and the Early 20th Century]. Moscow: Academia, 2011.

Minnullin, Zavdat. "Etapy razvitija i kolichestvennaja kharakteristika musul'manskix blagotvoritel'nyx organizatcij Rossii (XIX—nachalo XX vv.)" [Stages of Development and Collective Characteristics of Russia's Muslim Charity Organizations (19th—Early 20th Centuries)]. *Blagotvoritel'nost' v Rossii. Istoricheskie i social'no-ekonomicheskie issledovanija* [Charity in Russia: Historical and Socio-economic Studies]. St. Petersburg: Liki Rossii, 2007. 105–26.

Minnullin, Zavdat. "O motivacii blagotvoritel'noi dejatel'nosti u tatar (XIX—nachalo XX vekov)" [On the motivations for charitable activities among Tatars (19th century to the early 20th century)]. *Blagotvoritel'nost' v Rossii. Istoricheskie i social'no-ekonomicheskie issledovanija* [Charity in Russia: Historical and Socio-economic Studies]. St. Petersburg: Liki Rossii, 2004. 160–65.

Minnullin, Zavdat. *Shäryq kluby: tarikhi ocherk* [Oriental Club: historical review]. Kazan: Zaman, 2013.

Minnullin, Zavdat. "Tatar Charitable Organizations and Education (to 1917)." *Sluzhebnaya Lestnitsa* 1 (2002), 57–58.

Minnullin, Zavdat. "Tatar Charitable Organizations (Late 19th to Early 20th Centuries)." In D. Ishaqov and S. Ünay, eds., *Tatar History and Civilization*. Istanbul: Research Centre for Islamic History, Art and Culture (IRCICA), 2010. 432–43.

Minnullin, Zavdat. "Tatarskie blagotvoritel'nye obschestva vo vtoroi polovine XIX—nachale XX veka" [Tatar Charity Foundations in the Second Half of the 19th Century to the Early 20th Century]. *Blagotvoritel'nost' v Rossii. Istoricheskie i social'no-ekonomicheskie issledovanija* [Charity in Russia: Historical and Socio-economic Studies]. St. Petersburg: Liki Rossii, 2003. 215–29.

Minnullin, Zavdat. "Vozniknovenie i razvitie musul'manskix blagotvoritel'nyx organizacij Rossii (XIX—nachalo XX vv.)" [The Emergence and Evolution of Russia's Islamic Charitable Organizations (19th Century—Early 20th Century)]. *Uchenye zapiski Kazanskogo gosudarstvennogo Universiteta* [Academic records of Kazan State University]. Serija Humanities, 2008. Vol. 150, Book 8. 198–202.

Minnullin, Zavdat. *Sakhibzhamal Gizzatullina-Volzhskaja: literaturno-khudozhestvennyi, dokumental'nyi, biograficheskij sbornik* [Sakhibzhamal Gizzatullina-Volzhskaja: A Collection of Literary, Documentary and Biographical Works]. Kazan: Jyen, 2012.

Mironov, B.N. "Dobrovol'nye associacii i grazhdanskoe obschestvo v pozdneimperskoj Rossii" [Voluntary Associations and Civil Society in Late Imperial Russia]. *Zhurnal sociologii i socialnoj antropologii* 11:3 (2008), 164–176.

Mortazin, V. and T. Chenekai. *Tatar teatry tarikhynnan* [History of the Tatar Theater]. 2nd ed. Kazan: Magarif, 1996.

Rybakov, S. "Statistika musulman v Rossii" [Muslim Demographics in Russia], *Mir Islama* 2 (1913), 757–763.

Salikhov, Radik. *Uchastie tatarskogo predprinimatel'stva Rossii v obschestvenno-politicheskix protcessax vtoroi poloviny XIX—nachala XX veka: reforma institutov lokal'noi musul'manskoi obschiny* [The Role of Russia's Tatar Entrepreneurial Class in Socio-political Processes from the Second Half of the 19th Century to the Early 20th Century and the Reform of Local Muslim Community Institutes]. Kazan: "Fän" AN RT, 2004.

Senjutkina, Ol'ga, and Il'dus Zagidullin. *Nizhegorodskaja jarmarochnaja mechet'—centr obschenija rossijskix i zarubezhnyx musul'man* [The Nizhny Novgorod Market

Masjid: A Meeting Place for Russian and Foreign Muslims]. Nizhniy Novgorod: Medina, 2006.

Tumanova, Anastasija. *Obschestvennye organizacii i russkaja publika v nachale XX veka* [Community Organizations and the Russian Public in the Early 20th Century]. Moscow: Izdatel'stvo "Novyj khronograf," 2008.

Usmanova, Diliara. "Kontakty volgo-ural'skix i pol'sko-litovskix tatar v pervoi treti XX veka: kul'turno-religioznye i obschestvenno-politicheskie svjazi v musul'manskoi umme Rossii" [The Contacts of Volga-Ural Muslims with Polish-Lithuanian Muslims in the First Third of the 20th Century: Cultural, Religious and Socio-Political Ties in Russia's Muslim Umma], *Lietuvos istorijos studijos* 11 (2014), 81–98, 370–372.

Usmanova, Diliara. "Musul'manskie deputaty Gosudarstvennoi dumy o rossijsko-turetckix vzaimootnoshenijax nakanune i v period Pervoi mirovoi voiny (1907–1916)" [Muslim Deputies in the State Duma on Russo-Turkish Relations immediately before and during the First World War (1907–1916)], *Istoricheskie Zapiski* 8:126 (2005), 253–66.

Usmanova, Diliara. *Musul'manskie predstaviteli v rossijskom parlamente 1906–1916* [Muslim Representatives in the Russian Parliament 1906–1916]. Kazan: "Fän" AN RT, 2005.

Usmanova, Diliara. "Musul'manskoe naselenie Rossijskoj imperii v uslovijax Pervoi mirovoi voiny" [The Muslim Population of the Russian Empire under the First World War]. *Pervaja mirovaja voina i konetc Rossiiskoj imperii* [World War I and the Russian Empire]. v 3-x tomax. Vol. 1. Politicheskaja istorija. St. Petersburg: Liki Rossii, 2014. 575–630.

Usmanova, Diliara. "Sojuz tatar Pol'shi, Litvy, Belorussii i Ukrainy" [Union of Tatars of Poland, Lithuania, Belarus, and Ukraine]. *Islam v Sankt-Peterburge: enciklopedicheskii slovar'*. Moscow: Medina, 2009. 216–17.

Validi, Dzamal. *Ocherki istorii obrazovannosti i literatury tatar do revoljutcii* [Tatar Pre-Revolutionary History, Scholarship and Literature]. Moscow/Petrograd: n.p., 1924.

Yamaeva, Larisa. *Musul'manskij liberalizm nachala XX veka kak obschestvenno-politicheskoe dvijenie (po materialam Ufimskoi i Orenburgskoi gubernii)* [Early 20th Century Muslim Liberalism as a Socio-political Movement: Sources from the Ufa and Orenburg provinces]. Ufa: Kitap, 2002.

Zorin, A.N. et al. *Ocherki gorodskogo byta dorevoluocionnogo Povolzhja* [City Life in Pre-Revolutionary Povolzhye]. Ulyanovsk: Izdatel'stvo Gosudarstvennogo nauchnogo uchrezhdenija "Srednevolzhskij nauchnyj centr," 2000.

Afterword: The Maticas in a World of Empires

Alexei Miller

This project was launched several years ago with a conference exploring the history of institutions called Matica. The first such institution—the Serbian Matica—was established in Pest in 1826, and many more Maticas emerged among the Slavs in the Habsburg Empire in the course of the nineteenth century. Beyond the borders of the Habsburg Empire only two Maticas appeared in the nineteenth century: a Sorbian-Lusatian Matica in Prussia in 1847, and a Silesian Matica in Saxony in 1877. After 1905 and the introduction of freedom of association, Maticas were also created in the Polish lands of the Romanov Empire.

There is a long tradition of discussing the Maticas in the context of Slavic "reciprocity," Austro-Slavism and Pan-Slavism.[1] Joep Leerssen and Miroslav Hroch have considered the Maticas from the broader perspective of nationalism studies. This was one of the initial goals of the project, and papers about more or less similar organizations from other parts of Europe were also presented at the conference and appear in this volume.

In this Afterword I see my task as locating the Maticas in yet another context—namely, the context of imperial studies. We need to see particular Maticas in terms of complex center-periphery relations in order to understand how different agendas were represented in and by various institutions. The very fact that Maticas developed primarily in the Habsburg Empire requires attention and explanation. We also need to look at the imperial context and how it changed during the nineteenth century in order to understand the changes in the roles and tasks of the Maticas.

When the first Matica was created by Serbian merchants in 1826, the Serbian population was divided between the Habsburg and the Ottoman Empires, and both empires were competing for the sympathies and loyalty of the divided ethnic group. It is quite likely that the authorities, when giving their permission to create the new institution, were thinking rather about the possibilities of projecting their influence abroad. At the very same time, the rulers of the

---

[1] See for example Stanley B. Kimball, *The Austro-Slav Revival: A Study of Nineteenth-Century Literary Foundations*, Transactions of the American Philosophical Society Held at Philadelphia for Promoting Useful Knowledge, new series, vol. 63, part 4 (Philadelphia: American Philosophical Society, November, 1973); and Inna I. Leschilovskaia (ed.), *Slavianskie Maticy: 19th vek*. Vols. 1–2, (Moscow, Institut slavianovedenia I balkanistiki RAS, 1996; Славянские матицы: XIX век. Ч. 1–2. М.: Институт славяноведения и балканистики РАН, 1996).

Romanov Empire accorded privileged status to the Armenian Catholicos, whose seat in Echmiadzin was captured by Russia from the Persian empire in 1827, in the hope of extending their own influence over the Armenians under Ottoman rule. The difference was that Saint-Petersburg focused on church structures as a channel of influence, while Vienna was looking for lay agents, since the Serbian Orthodox clergy were far too pro-Russian.

The next Matica was established in Prague in 1831, where Czech nationalist activists were setting an example for "awakeners" of other, less advanced national movements in what Miroslav Hroch has called "small nations," groups whose noble strata had either been exterminated or assimilated by the dominant imperial powers.

It took almost twenty years for the next Maticas to be established, which happened in the context of the revolutionary crisis of the late 1840s. The Ruthenian Matica was created in Galicia in 1848 with considerable help from Vienna, as part of an imperial policy aimed at mobilizing support for previously neglected Ruthenians in order to counterbalance Polish influence in the province. Another task was to limit the pro-Russian sympathies of Ruthenians, who were soon to discover the power of the Orthodox Empire across the border when Russian troops marched through Galicia to suppress the Hungarian uprising. Only much later, in 1882, when the Habsburgs had developed comfortable relations with the Polish elites of Galicia while Poles in Russia and Germany were coming under mounting pressure, were the Poles given an opportunity to create their own Matica. Relations between Vienna and Saint-Petersburg had been rapidly and openly deteriorating since 1881, when the Habsburgs signed an alliance with Germany. At that time Vienna crushed the pro-Russian segment of Ruthenian politicians in Galicia, and saw in the creation of a *Macierz Polska* an instrument for projecting influence towards the Poles in the Romanov Empire. The case of Galicia thus demonstrates how the entanglement of local with inter-imperial factors informed the dynamics of Matica development. The challenge of balancing the interests of various ethnic groups against one another was an important part of the repertoire of imperial elites already in the absolutist period. This factor became even more important later, when the Empire entered the constitutional period of her development. The Poles were the only Slavic group in the region with a strong nobility, and their Maticas differed significantly in terms of the social composition of their activists and their system of funding.

The nineteenth-century Habsburg Empire had inherited a tradition of the significant autonomy of Crownlands, which created strong regional identities. Some nation-building projects involved several Crownlands, and had to overcome regional particularism. This very important dimension of Matica stories can be traced by looking at the Moravian Matice (*Matice Moravská*, 1852) and the Dalmatian Matica (*Matica Dalmatinska*, 1862). They emerged much later than the *Matica Czeska* (1831) and the Illyrian Matica (1842), later renamed the *Matica Hrvatska*. In this volume Daniel Baric describes this situation as follows: "The first maticas were founded in the South Slav area in a time of redefinition of the nation, hence there were competing terms in use. 'Croatian' originally referred to inhabitants of North-West Croatia around Zagreb, whereas other names were given to the populations living in the eastern part of what is nowadays Croatia ('Slavonians') and in Dalmatia, where the term 'Slavo-Dalmatians' differentiated Croats and Serbs from the Italian-speaking population. As elsewhere in Central and Eastern Europe, the cultural patrimony and feeling of belonging to a nation was increasingly shared by a population that was becoming." But Miloš Řezník in his article suggests a more complex interpretation: "both the ambivalence and the engagement between nationality (ethnicity) and territoriality (regionality) can be considered as characteristic of the role of regions as a mediatory 'foil' of nationality and vice versa." In the case of Moravia, and especially of Dalmatia, the extent to which a potential alternative national identity based on Moravian and Dalmatian regionalism was hidden in these initiatives awaits further study. This is also true for the Galician Ruthenians, who felt strongly their differences from Little Russians, as did later Ukrainians from the Romanov Empire. Neither Czech nor Croatian nor Ukrainian historiography can (or wishes to) offer us much help here, as they are not prepared to consider potential alternatives to the implemented scenarios of nation-building.

Local and regional identities rooted in the autonomy of the Habsburg Crownlands could also for some time resist nationalist mobilization. Bömisch (Bohemian) supra-ethnic identity has been well studied, in which nationalist efforts at mass mobilization were not always very successful. It is not by chance that historians of Habsburg Bohemia came up with the concept of *national indifference* to describe the resistance of ordinary people to nationalist agitation and mobilization. Jeremy King has examined the resistance of Budweiser local identity to the corrupting influence of nationalist confrontation, and has used the notion of "national indifference" in this context.[2] Pieter M. Judson has contrasted such "national indifference" with a national activism that sought to turn the heterogeneous borderlands of Habsburg Austria into national property, and has shown how census data pertaining to the "native language" and

---

[2] Jeremy King, *Budweisers into Czechs and Germans: A Local History of Bohemian Politics, 1848–1948* (Princeton: Princeton University Press, 2002), 3–4.

maps drawn on this basis distorted and simplified the real situation.[3] Tara Zahra even included the notion of "national indifference" in the title of her book about nationalists battling for control over children, especially orphans.[4] Her book was soon followed by an article in which she attempted to broaden the concept of "national indifference" by regarding it not only as a characteristic of the late imperial period but as an element of any situation involving nationalist mobilization.[5] The Matica organizations provided important instruments for overcoming such "national indifference."

This task became even more urgent in the 1860s and the subsequent decades, when most of the Matica organizations had been created and the School Matica had become the most popular type of this organization. As a result of their defeat by Prussia in 1866, the Habsburg Monarchy found itself in a dramatically changed situation. First of all, the Habsburgs were expelled from the process of German unification and the creation of the second Reich. Second, the Habsburgs were forced to accept an *Ausgleich* (Compromise) with the Hungarians. This Compromise transformed the state into a dual monarchy, made the Austrian Emperor also the King of Hungary, and divided the former Empire into two parts: Cislethania under Austrian control, and Transleithania in the control of the Hungarian elites. A Constitution was introduced for both parts of the monarchy, but the arrangements and the policies of two sub-empires were very different.

In Transleithania the Magyars, in accord with the dominant tendency of the epoch, launched an active policy of nation-building in the imperial core.[6] The immediate result was pressure on the Serb and Slovak Matitsas in the area, which was considered part of Hungarian national territory and subject to assimilation. In 1874 the Budapest government closed the Slovak secondary schools founded in the 1860s, and by 1875 the Matica Slovenska had also been closed by the authorities. Croatia won its autonomy from Transleithania, partly because of a painful lesson taught to the Hungarians in 1848 by the Croatian Ban Josip Jelacic; it was spared Magyarization, so here the Maticas enjoyed better conditions.

In Cislethania the Fundamental law of 1867 proclaimed that

---

[3] Pieter M. Judson, *Guardians of the Nation: Activists on the Language Frontiers of Imperial Austria*. (Cambridge: Harvard University Press, 2006).

[4] Tara Zahra, *Kidnapped Souls: National Indifference and the Battle for Children in the Bohemian Lands, 1900–1948*. (Ithaca: Cornell University Press, 2008).

[5] Tara Zahra, "Imagined Noncommunities: National Indifference as a Category of Analysis." *Slavic Review* 69:1 (2010), 93–119.

[6] See more in Stefan Berger and Alexei Miller (eds.), *Nationalizing Empires* (Budapest—New York, CEU Press, 2015).

> All national groups within the state are equal, and each one has inviable right to preserve and cultivate its nationality and language [...] In those provinces inhabited by several nationalities, public educational institutions should be set up so that without being forced to learn a second language, those nationalities that are in the minority have adequate opportunity for an education in their own language.[7]

Such an approach was absolutely unique for the European empires of the nineteenth century. It was possible because the imperial elites could no longer promote a German nation-building project. But they also couldn't give the Czechs and/or Poles what had been given to the Hungarians in 1867 without alienating the Germans. The cohesion of the Empire depended on a complex balancing of the interests of recognized ethnic groups, and on various experiments with the cultural, non-territorial autonomy of individuals and groups.[8]

This new approach to nationality issues came together with the introduction of a *Reichsrat* (Parliament) and mass politics. The entanglement of these two factors already in the 1870s created a situation which Pieter M. Judson has described as "culture wars and wars for culture."[9] Judson interprets culture wars as a way to mobilize populations politically in a time of mass politics. But the very legal norms which regulated the cultural and educational sphere tended rather to trigger nationalist mobilization than to promote reconciliation. State funding was guaranteed for schools in local languages which could show at least forty pupils in five consecutive years. But mobilizing a sufficient number of pupils to qualify for funding, and mobilizing enough independent local funding when the minimal forty proved an impossible target, gave the school associations (usually called School Maticas among the Slavs) plenty to do, and they grew like mushrooms. Such efforts were particularly intensive in provinces that were contested by two or more ethnic groups, of which the most vivid example is Cieszyn (Těšín, Teschen) in Silesia, where numerous Polish and Czech School Maticas competed with each other but also with German school associations.

Thus, the Habsburg Monarchy, and after 1867 Cisleithania in particular, provided a unique institutional and political setting for the development of

---

[7] Cited in Pieter M. Judson, *The Habsburg Empire: A New History* (Cambridge: Harvard University Press, 2016), 293.
[8] Boerries Kuzmany, "Habsburg Austria: Experiments in Non-territorial Autonomy," in John Coakley (ed.), *Non-territorial Autonomy in Divided Societies* (London: Routledge, 2017), 43–65.
[9] Judson, ibid.

Matica institutions.[10] In the Russian Empire comparable institutions developed mostly after 1905, especially in those provinces of the Empire and among those ethno-religious groups which were not claimed by the Russian nation-building project as a national territory (see the articles by Diliara Usmanova and Jörg Hackmann).

The Maticas and comparable organizations were part of the history of European peripheral nationalisms, but they were also a part of the history of Empires and were inevitably affected by the imperial nationalisms that developed in imperial core-areas, or indeed by the absence of such nationalism, as was the case in Cislethania after 1867.

---

10   For more, see Andrea Komlosy, "Imperial Cohesion, Nation-Building and Regional Integration in the Habsburg Monarchy, 1804–1918," in Stefan Berger and Alexei Miller (eds.), *Nationalizing Empires* (Budapest—New York: CEU Press, 2015), 369–428.

Index

A Coruña   165–166, 168–172, 174–178
Abergavenny Cymreigyddion Society   240, 245, 246
Acts of Union 1536/1542   233
Aberystwyth   240–242, 245
Alexander School (Estonian)   277–280
Amsterdam   209, 221–222, 226
Anderson, Benedict   1–3, 150
Anglican priests   234, 237, 250
Antwerp   212–213, 221, 226
Austrian Empire (until 1867)   5, 11–27, 35, 38, 59, 98, 125, 181, 205–207, 215, 219–221, 292–293, 295–296, 306, 357

Baltic provinces of Russia   2, 6, 271–273, 280–282
Bardic system   233
Bautzen   5, 79–81, 83, 85–86, 91–93
Bernolák, Anton   24–25, 48n, 50–55
Bible, Welsh   233–234, 247–248
Bilderdijk, Willem   223–224
Bleiweis, Janez   66n, 99, 102, 104–105, 107
Book clubs   4–7
Book history   1–6
Bratislava   13, 49–53, 55, 59
Brno   5, 43, 64, 79, 81, 86, 89, 92–93
Brussels   205, 212–213, 219–222, 225, 227–228
Buda University Press   11–27
Budapest   4, 6, 11–27, 48–49, 51, 54, 56, 59–60, 64, 68n, 112n, 114n
Budweis. *See* České Budějovice
Bulgarian Matica   6

Cambrian Archaeological Association   244–245
Cambrian Register   243
Cambrian societies   237–240
Castro, Rosalía de   163–164
Catalonia   165, 174, 191, 198
Catholicism   12, 24, 31, 48–49, 51–52, 54–57, 78, 81, 83–85, 92, 101–102, 130, 177, 199, 207, 212, 214, 220, 227, 233, 256–257, 292, 296, 306, 310, 315
Čelakovský, František Ladislav   38–39, 44
Celtia   243
Celtic languages   233

Celtic national festivals   242
České Budějovice   76, 359
Chrástek, Michal   61, 62
Chartier, Roger   2
Church Slavonic   11, 19–22, 140, 295, 301–302, 312
Cíger Hronský, Jozef   70
čitalište (Bulgarian)   6
Confederate Clubs   265–268
Conscience, Hendrik   2
Constantinople. *See* Istanbul
Cottbus   79, 83, 85–86, 91–93
Council of Ruthenian Scholars   295, 301–302
Croatian matica   5, 103, 112, 118–119, 123, 125, 127, 130–133, 314
Curros Enríquez, Manoel   163, 166, 168, 171, 173, 175
Cymmrodorion Societies   235–238
Cymreigyddion Societies   237
Cymru Fydd movement   235n, 249
Cyrillic alphabet   11, 13, 16, 127–128, 197, 312
Czech Matica (*Matica Česká*)   5, 30–46, 48, 76, 79–81, 87, 89, 91–93, 97, 102, 125, 134, 294, 314, 359

Dalmatian matica   5–6, 66, 97, 118–134, 359
Davidsfonds   7, 214, 227
Davis, Thomas   255n, 257–258, 260, 262–264
Deutsche (Schul-)Vereine   77, 79, 281–284
Dobriansky, Adolf   62n, 66n, 302, 307, 311
Društvo Srpske Slovesnosti   16, 26
Dubrovnik   120, 125
Duffy, Charles Gavan   255n, 258–260, 262–265, 268n

Edam   209–210
Eisteddfod   236–244, 246, 248–249
Estonia   271, 276, 282
Esztergom   12, 51–52, 55–56
Evro, Naum   142–146, 148, 151n

Famine (Ireland)   8, 255, 264–265, 268
Fándly, Juraj   51–52
Faraldo, Antolín   163–164
Fejes, Jan   53
Félibrige   181–182, 185–196, 198–202

Francisci, Ján 59, 61–62
Franz Joseph I 27, 35–36, 59, 105, 122, 309
French Empire 206–207, 218, 222, 228

Gaganec, Jozef 66
Galicia (Eastern Europe) 5–6, 76–78, 292–297, 300–314, 317–320, 358–359
Galicia (Iberian Peninsula) 8, 162–178
Galician Academy 168–175
Galician Folklore Association 167–168, 174
Galician Language Brotherhoods 165–166, 174–178
Galician-Ruthenian Matica 6, 76, 294–320
German Reich 281, 283–284
Ghent 211–214, 225–227
Glagolitic script 41
Gotčár, Ján 59
Grégoire, Henri 183–184, 192
Gorsedd of the Bards of the Isle of Britain 239, 241–242
Grimm, Jacob 2, 222
Grupche, Kosta 142–146, 148, 151n
Gwyneddigion Society 236–237, 239, 243, 247

Haarlem 209–210
Habsburg Empire (1867–1918) 5, 8, 76–77, 87, 99, 111, 122, 124, 131, 138, 145, 201, 243, 271, 284, 316–317, 357–362
Hamaliar, Martin 53
Habermas, Jürgen 1
Hall, Augusta 240
Hamuljak, Martin 24–26, 54–56
Hattala, Martin 48, 63, 65, 72
Herder, Johann Gottfried 274, 284
Herkel, Jan 25
Holland Institute 222–224, 226, 228
Hollý, Ján 25–26, 52, 54
Holovatskyi, Yakiv 294, 300, 302, 304, 306, 311–312, 318
Hroch, Miroslav 3, 32–33, 75, 87, 182, 199, 272, 276, 357–358
Huizinga, Johan 206
Hurkevych, Ivan 293–295, 311
Hurt, Jakob 277–278

Iași 16
Illyrian Matica 5, 43, 59n, 66n, 76, 103–104, 118–119, 123n, 125–126, 314, 359

Imperial Academy (Brussels) 205, 215, 219–222, 224, 227–228
Islam 8, 140, 325–327, 330–331, 335, 337, 339–344, 350, 352–353
Istanbul 6, 15, 140, 143–145, 341

Jakobson, Carl Robert 276, 278, 280
Jelínek, Václav 51
Jones, Owen 236, 244, 247
Joseph II 49, 51, 207, 292
Jungmann, Josef 31, 34–35, 37–40, 43, 66

Kabina, Franko 68–69
Kachkovskyi Society 296, 307–308, 313–314
Karadžić, Vuk 22
Kazan 328–336, 338, 343–348, 350, 353
Kiev 43, 292, 303–304, 351
Klagenfurt 5, 101
Klaić, Miho 123n, 127
Kollár, Jan 5, 7, 25–26, 48, 50, 53–56, 58, 66n, 69n
Krakow 305, 314
Kraszewski, Józef Ignacy 6, 77
Kuzmány, Karol 48, 58, 62n, 64

Langewiesche, Dieter 3
Latvia 8, 271–284
Learned Estonian Society 275, 277
Leerssen, Joep 357
Leiden 205, 209, 214–218, 222–224, 226, 228
Leipzig 21, 80, 93
Leška, Štefan 53
Letopis (Serbian annual) 4–5, 21–22, 65–66, 108
Levec, Fran 108–109
Levstik, Fran 104–105, 107
Lichard, Daniel 58, 63n
Lithuania 2, 75, 272
Livonia 271, 273–274, 276, 280
Ljubljana 6, 98–99, 102, 104–106, 108–109, 113, 130
Llangollen 240–241, 248
Lom 6
Louvain 219, 221
Loza 151–157
Lusatia. See Sorbian
Lviv 5, 77, 292–293, 296, 300, 309, 314, 317

Maatschappij der Nederlandsche Letterkunde te Leiden. See Society of Dutch Literature (Leiden)
Maatschappij tot Nut van 't Algemeen   204, 208–211, 214, 216, 228–229
Madrid   166, 195, 201
Maior, Petru   16–18
Martin   27, 49, 59, 60n, 62, 63n, 64, 66n, 67, 68n
matica. *See* Bulgarian Matica, Croatian Matica, Czech Matica (*Matica Česká*), Dalmatian Matica, Galician-Ruthenian Matica, Illyrian Matica, Moravian Matica, Serbian Matica (*Matica srpska*), Slovenian Matica (*Matica Slovenska*), Sorbian Matica
Mečiar, Stanislav   70
Micu-Klein, Samuil   16–18
Miletić, Svetozar   62n, 68
Mistral, Frédéric   182, 184–189, 191–194, 196–199, 201–202
Mitchel, John   267
Moravian Matica   5, 79, 81, 87, 89, 91, 93, 134, 359
Moscow   280, 314, 337, 343–344, 347, 350–351
Moyses, Štefan   59, 61n, 62, 66n
Mudroň, Pavol   62n, 69
Murguía, Manuel   162, 164, 168–169
Muslim (islamic) *umma*   8, 325, 339, 352

National Eisteddfod Association   241–242
National Library of Wales   240
Nitra   51, 64
Nonconformist Christian churches   234, 237–238, 249–250
Novi Sad   4–6, 20–21, 25–26, 48

O'Connell, Daniel   256–258, 260–262, 265–266, 268
Obradović, Dositej   21–22
Occitania   190, 198, 200
Ohrid   142, 147, 150
  Archbishopric   140, 142–143
Okáľ, Ján   70
Olomouc   76, 88, 91
Opava   6, 79, 81–82, 87–89, 92–93
Orenburg   328–331, 334, 336–337, 343, 346, 349–350, 352–353
Oriental Club (Kazan)   330–336, 346–347

Orthodoxy   13, 25, 27, 120, 125, 138, 141, 276, 307, 309, 317, 358
Ottmayer, Anton   24, 54
Ottoman Empire   8, 128, 138–142, 144–145, 156–157, 181, 201, 341, 357
Owen, Hugh   236, 241

Palacký, František   5, 31, 34, 36–37, 39–41, 43, 53, 66, 86, 92, 243
Palárik, Ján   58–59
Palkovič, Juraj   50, 52, 53, 55
Pan-Celtic organizations   242–243
Pan-Slavism   5, 7, 25, 27, 66–68, 82, 91, 114, 294, 357
Paris   15, 186, 191–192, 194–195, 207, 219, 221, 258
Paulíny-Tóth, Viliam   59, 64, 68
Pest-Buda   4, 11–27, 48–54, 357
Polakovič, Štefan   70
Pondal, Eduardo   163–164, 169, 175
Popov, Temko   142–143, 146–150
Prague   4, 5, 31, 33, 35–36, 39, 42–44, 64, 66, 73, 76, 78–81, 84, 86, 89–90, 92–93, 122, 243, 314, 358
print (press, technology)   1, 11, 13, 257
Prosvita   6, 305, 307, 314
Protestantism   24, 48–59, 61–62, 78, 83–85, 206, 213, 234, 246–247, 274
public library   3, 30, 53, 61, 67, 78, 86, 124, 168, 210, 213, 262, 331, 333, 335, 342–343, 346, 348, 351
public sphere   1, 7, 125, 166, 178
Pughe, William Owen   244, 247–248

Quinn, James   263

Ratio Educationis   13, 16, 19
Reading room   3, 6–7, 98–99, 103–104, 106, 120, 124, 133, 143, 152, 257, 260–262, 265, 268, 314, 330, 331, 335, 337, 342–343, 345–346, 348, 351–352
Rebellion (Ireland)   267–268
Repeal Association   260–262, 265, 268
Revolution
  of 1848   35–36, 40–41, 44, 56–58, 64, 82, 91, 125, 267, 295, 358
  French Revolution   49, 167, 181–183, 200, 206–207, 234, 236, 256

Russian Revolution of 1905–1907   77, 278, 280, 284, 325, 327, 329, 345, 353
Russian Revolution of 1917   352–353
Ribay, Juraj   53
Riga   272–275, 279–284
Riga Latvian Society   279–280
Royal Institute (Amsterdam). *See* Holland Institute
Rudnay, Alexander   52
Rus (language)   302–305, 308–310, 315, 318
Russian (Romanov) Empire   8, 181, 271, 274, 296, 306, 325–327, 329, 337, 339–340, 343, 353, 357–359, 362

Šafařík, Pavel Josef   5, 25, 37, 41, 48, 92, 114, 314
Santiago de Compostela   163, 165, 170, 173, 175–178
Sasinek, F.V.   66–67
Scott, Walter   2, 4
Secret Macedonian Committee (SMC)   142, 144, 146, 148–150
Serbian Matica (*Matica srpska*)   4–5, 14, 21–23, 26, 30, 48, 112, 127, 314, 357, 360
Shakespeare, William   38, 43
Šibenik   120n, 125, 133
Şincai, Gheorghe   17–18
Shumen   6
Sládkovič, Andrej   65
Slomšek, Bishop Anton Martin   100, 102–103
Slovak Matica   6, 27, 48, 50, 57–73, 76, 80–81, 97, 360
  in America   69
  abroad   70
Slovenian Matica (*Matica Slovenska*)   5, 6, 50, 58, 71, 97–115, 130, 314, 359
Šmidinger, Josef   34
Smoler, Jan Arnošt   5, 80
Society of Dutch Literature (Leiden)   205, 214–218, 222, 224, 228
Society of Learned Estonians   278–279
Society for the Promotion of Enlightenment among the Jews in Russia   281
Society for the Utilization of the Welsh Language   249
Sofia   142–143, 148, 151, 153–155
Sokol clubs   6, 106, 108
Sorbian   5, 79–80, 82–85, 92

Sorbian Matica   5, 76, 79–81, 83–86, 90–93, 357
St. Clair, William   2
St. Cyril   25, 31, 62, 86, 92–93, 103
St. Hermagoras Society   97, 100–101, 103, 105–106, 108, 111
St. Methodius   25, 31, 62, 86, 92–93, 103
St. Petersburg   43, 141n, 150n, 278, 280, 322, 326, 328, 337, 341, 343–344, 348, 350–351, 353, 358
Stauropegion Institute (Lviv)   293–295, 297, 299, 308, 310, 312–314, 316–317
Stephens, Thomas   240, 245–246, 248
Štefko, Matej   58
Strossmayer, Josip Juraj   61, 66
Štúr, Dionýz   65
Štúr, Ľudovít   40, 48–50, 55–57, 63, 65–66, 72
Suchaň, Martin   55
Svishtov   6
Szlávy, József   67

Tablic, Bohuslav   53–54
Tallinn   273, 275, 281, 283
Tartu   275–281, 283
Tatars   8, 325–330, 332–334, 336–344, 346–353
Tatrín (Sons of the Tatras)   51, 56–58
Teschen   77, 88–89, 91–92, 361
The Nation (Dublin)   255, 258–259, 261, 263
Tieftrunk, Karel   44
Toman, Lovro   104–105, 107
Tomek, Václav Vladivoj   36, 38–39, 41–42
Townend, Paul   268
Trieste   6, 115n
Trnava   12, 24, 51–52, 56
Troitsk   328–330, 337, 351–352
Turčiansky Svätý Martin. *See* Martin

Valdemārs, Krišjānis   279–280
Venice   4, 125, 128
Vienna   11, 13, 15–17, 20, 22, 43, 48–49, 58, 64, 77, 83, 89, 104, 106, 118, 120n, 125–126, 129, 155, 206, 219, 299, 358
Viktorin, Jozef   61
Villar Ponte, Antón   173–175
Volga-Ural region   326–328, 349, 353
Vrchovský, Alexander Boleslavín   48
Vyskydenský, Ján   53

Wales   8, 181, 233–250
Warsaw   45, 77, 243, 351

INDEX

Welsh cultural societies   235–238
Welsh history revived   245–247
Welsh language reform   240–241, 247–249
Welsh Manuscripts Society   244–245
Welsh orthography reform   240–241
Welsh university movement   241
Williams, Edward   237, 239, 244
Willemsfonds   7, 204, 211–215, 227, 229
World War One   88, 97, 100n, 101n, 118–119, 123–124, 150, 162, 173–174, 193, 208, 210, 271, 282–284, 316–317, 329, 336–338, 340–341, 349

Yeats, W.B.   264
Young Ireland movement   255, 257–268
Young Macedonian Literary Society (YMLS)   151–153, 155–157

Záborský, Jonáš   58, 65, 67n
Zadar   6, 66n, 118–134
Zagreb   5–6, 59n, 64, 66, 73, 103, 118–123, 125–126, 130–131, 359
Zejler, Handrij   5
Zoch, Ctiboh   57
Zrinski, Subić Nikola   66
Zubrytskyi, Denys   293, 295, 303–304